THE KINGDOM AND
THE GLORY

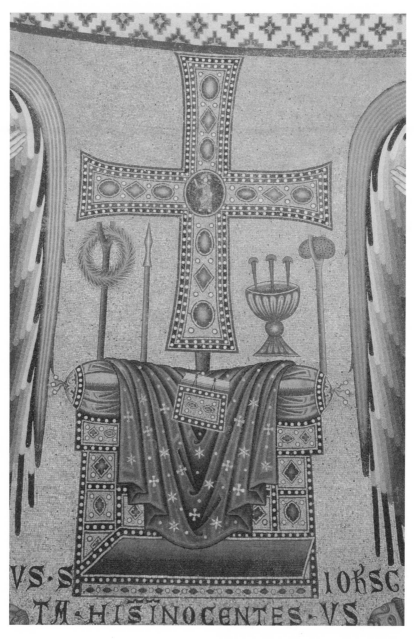

Detail of apse mosaic, Basilica Papale di San Paolo fuori le Mura, Rome. Photograph by Luca Marchi.

MERIDIAN

Crossing Aesthetics

Werner Hamacher

Editor

Translated by Lorenzo Chiesa

(with Matteo Mandarini)

Stanford
University
Press

_____

Stanford
California
2011

THE KINGDOM AND THE GLORY

*For a Theological Genealogy of Economy and Government (*Homo Sacer *II, 2)*

Giorgio Agamben

Stanford University Press
Stanford, California

The Kingdom and the Glory was originally published in Italian
under the title *Il Regno e la Gloria. Per una genealogia teologica
dell'economia e del governo. (*Homo Sacer *II, 2)*
© Giorgio Agamben 2007.

Printed in the United States of America
on acid-free, archival-quality paper

Library of Congress Cataloging-in-Publication Data

Agamben, Giorgio, 1942– author.
[Regno e la gloria. English]
The kingdom and the glory : for a theological genealogy of
economy and government / Giorgio Agamben ; translated by
Lorenzo Chiesa (with Matteo Mandarini).
pages cm. — (Meridian, crossing aesthetics)
"Originally published in Italian under
the title Il Regno e la Gloria."
Includes bibliographical references.
ISBN 978-0-8047-6015-7 (cloth : alk. paper)
ISBN 978-0-8047-6016-4 (pbk : alk. paper)
1. Religion and politics.   2. Power (Philosophy)
3. Political science—Philosophy.   I. Chiesa,
Lorenzo, translator.   II. Mandarini, Matteo,
translator.   III. Title.   IV. Series:
Meridian (Stanford, Calif.)
BL65.P7A3313   2011
201'.72—dc22
2010043992

Contents

Translator's Note   *ix*

Preface   *xi*

§ 1   The Two Paradigms   1
      Threshold   15

§ 2   The Mystery of the Economy   17
      Threshold   50

§ 3   Being and Acting   53
      Threshold   65

§ 4   The Kingdom and the Government   68
      Threshold   106

§ 5   The Providential Machine   109
      Threshold   139

§ 6   Angelology and Bureaucracy   144
      Threshold   165

§ 7   The Power and the Glory   167
      Threshold   194

Contents

§ 8   The Archaeology of Glory   197
        Threshold   253

        Appendix: The Economy of the Moderns   261
            1 The Law and the Miracle   261
            2 The Invisible Hand   277
        Notes   289
        References   291

Translator's Note

Chapters 1 to 5 were translated by Lorenzo Chiesa. Chapters 6 to 8 and the Appendix were drafted by Matteo Mandarini and revised by Lorenzo Chiesa.

In accordance with the author's request, after prior consultation of the original works, all quotations were translated into English in line with his own translation into Italian, with the notable exception of works originally published in English. This also applies to works currently available in English translation, in which case translations were consulted, incorporated, and, where appropriate, modified. Significant phrases and sentences that do not appear in the existing English translations are indicated in braces. I have used the same method to signal the few instances in which the author's personal translation and the English version differ substantially. Page references refer to the English translation or, failing this, to the original.

I wish to thank Giorgio Agamben, Tom Baldwin, Emily-Jane Cohen, Mike Lewis, Frank Ruda, Danka Štefan, and Alberto Toscano for their valuable suggestions and for their help in securing access to sources that proved difficult to obtain.

Oeconomia Dei vocamus illam rerum omnium
administratione vel gubernationem, qua Deus utitur, inde
a conditio mundo usque ad consummationem saeculorum,
in nominis sui Gloriam et hominum salutem.

    —J. H. Maius, *Oeconomia temporum veteris Testamenti*

Chez les cabalistes hébreux, *malcuth* ou le règne, la dernière des
séphiroth, signifiat que Dieu gouverne tout irrésistiblement, mais
doucement et sans violence, en sorte que l'homme croit suivre sa volonté
pendant qu'il exécute celle de Dieu. Ils disaient que le péché d'Adam
avait été *truncatio malcuth a ceteris plantis*, c'est-à-dire qu'Adam avait
rentranché la dernière des *séphires* en se faisant un empire dans l'empire.

    —G. W. Leibniz, *Essais de théodicée*

We must then distinguish between the *Right*, and the *exercise* of supreme
authority, for they can be divided; as for example, when he who hath
the *Right*, either cannot, or will not be present in judging trespasses, or
deliberating of affaires: For Kings sometimes by reason of their age cannot
order their affaires, sometimes also though they can doe it themselves,
yet they judge it fitter, being satisfied in the choyce of their Officers
and Counsellors, to exercise their power by them. Now where the *Right*
and *exercise* are severed, there the government of the Commonweale is
like the ordinary government of the world, in which God, the mover of
all things, produceth natural effects by the means of secondary causes;
but where he, to whom the Right of ruling doth belong, is himselfe
present in all judicatures, consultations, and publique actions, there the
administration is such, as if God beyond the ordinary course of nature,
should immediately apply himself unto all matters.

    —Th. Hobbes, *De Cive*

While the world lasts, Angels will preside over Angels,
demons over demons, and men over men; but in the world
to come every command will be empty.

    —Gloss on 1 Corinthians 15:24

Acher saw the angel Metatron, who was given permission
to sit down and write the merits of Israel. He then said: "It is taught that
on high there will be no sitting, no competition, no back, and no
tiredness. Perhaps, God forbid, there are two powers in heaven."

    —Talmud, Hagiga, 15 a

Sur quoi la fondera-t-il l'économie du Monde qu'il veut gouverner?

    —B. Pascal, *Pensées*

Preface

This study will inquire into the paths by which and the reasons why power in the West has assumed the form of an *oikonomia*, that is, a government of men. It locates itself in the wake of Michel Foucault's investigations into the genealogy of governmentality, but, at the same time, it also aims to understand the internal reasons why they failed to be completed. Indeed, in this study, the shadow that the theoretical interrogation of the present casts onto the past reaches well beyond the chronological limits that Foucault assigned to his genealogy, to the early centuries of Christian theology, which witness the first, tentative elaboration of the Trinitarian doctrine in the form of an *oikonomia*. Locating government in its theological locus in the Trinitarian *oikonomia* does not mean to explain it by means of a hierarchy of causes, as if a more primordial genetic rank would necessarily pertain to theology. We show instead how the apparatus of the Trinitarian *oikonomia* may constitute a privileged laboratory for the observation of the working and articulation—both internal and external—of the governmental machine. For within this apparatus the elements—or the polarities—that articulate the machine appear, as it were, in their paradigmatic form.

In this way, the inquiry into the genealogy—or, as one used to say, the *nature*—of power in the West, which I began more than ten years ago with *Homo Sacer*, reaches a point that is in every sense decisive. The double structure of the governmental machine, which in *State of Exception* (2003) appeared in the correlation between *auctoritas* and *potestas*, here takes the form of the articulation between Kingdom and Government and, ultimately, interrogates the very relation—which initially was not considered—

between *oikonomia* and Glory, between power as government and effective management, and power as ceremonial and liturgical regality, two aspects that have been curiously neglected by both political philosophers and political scientists. Even historical studies of the insignia and liturgies of power, from Peterson to Kantorowicz, Alföldi to Schramm, have failed to question this relation, precisely leaving aside a number of rather obvious questions: Why does power need glory? If it is essentially force and capacity for action and government, why does it assume the rigid, cumbersome, and "glorious" form of ceremonies, acclamations, and protocols? What is the relation between economy and Glory?

Bringing these questions back to their theological dimension—questions that seem to find only trivial answers on the level of political and sociological investigations—has allowed us to catch a glimpse of something like the ultimate structure of the governmental machine of the West in the relation between *oikonomia* and Glory. The analysis of doxologies and liturgical acclamations, of ministries and angelical hymns turned out to be more useful for the understanding of the structures and functioning of power than many pseudo-philosophical analyses of popular sovereignty, the rule of law, or the communicative procedures that regulate the formation of public opinion and political will. Identifying in Glory the central mystery of power and interrogating the indissoluble nexus that links it to government and *oikonomia* will seem an obsolete operation to some. And yet, one of the results of our investigation has been precisely to note that the function of acclamations and Glory, in the modern form of public opinion and consensus, is still at the center of the political apparatuses of contemporary democracies. If the media are so important in modern democracies, this is the case not only because they enable the control and government of public opinion, but also and above all because they manage and dispense Glory, the acclamative and doxological aspect of power that seemed to have disappeared in modernity. The society of the spectacle—if we can call contemporary democracies by this name—is, from this point of view, a society in which power in its "glorious" aspect becomes indiscernible from *oikonomia* and government. To have completely integrated Glory with *oikonomia* in the acclamative form of consensus is, more specifically, the specific task carried out by contemporary democracies and their *government by consent*,[1] whose original paradigm is not written in Thucydides' Greek, but in the dry Latin of medieval and baroque treaties on the divine government of the world.

However, this means that the center of the governmental machine is empty. The empty throne, the *hetoimasia tou thronou* that appears on the arches and apses of the Paleochristian and Byzantine basilicas is perhaps, in this sense, the most significant symbol of power. Here the theme of the investigation touches its limit and, at the same time, its temporary conclusion. If, as has been suggested, there is in every book something like a hidden center, and the book was written to reach—or elude—it, then this center is to be found in the final paragraphs of Chapter 8. In opposition to the ingenuous emphasis on productivity and labor that has long prevented modernity from accessing politics as man's most proper dimension, politics is here returned to its central inoperativity, that is, to that operation that amounts to rendering inoperative all human and divine works. The empty throne, the symbol of Glory, is what we need to profane in order to make room, beyond it, for something that, for now, we can only evoke with the name *zoē aiōnios*, eternal life. It is only when the fourth part of the investigation, dedicated to the form-of-life and use, is completed, that the decisive meaning of inoperativity as a properly human and political praxis will be able to appear in its own light.

§ 1   The Two Paradigms

1.1. Let us begin this investigation with an attempt to reconstruct the genealogy of a paradigm that has exercised a decisive influence on the development and the global arrangement of Western society, although it has rarely been thematized as such outside a strictly theological field. One of the theses that we shall try to demonstrate is that two broadly speaking political paradigms, antinomical but functionally related to one another, derive from Christian theology: political theology, which founds the transcendence of sovereign power on the single God, and economic theology, which replaces this transcendence with the idea of an *oikonomia*, conceived as an immanent ordering—domestic and not political in a strict sense—of both divine and human life. Political philosophy and the modern theory of sovereignty derive from the first paradigm; modern biopolitics up to the current triumph of economy and government over every other aspect of social life derive from the second paradigm.

For reasons that will become clear in the course of the research, the history of economic theology, which developed enormously between the second and fifth centuries AD, has been left in the shadows not only by historians of ideas but also by theologians, to the extent that even the precise meaning of the term has fallen into oblivion. In this way, both its evident genetic proximity to Aristotelian economy and its likely connection with the birth of the *économie animale* and of political economy in the eighteenth century have remained unquestioned. An archaeological study that investigates the reasons for this repression and attempts to go back to the events that produced it is all the more necessary.

א *Although the problem of* oikonomia *is present in countless monographs on individual Church Fathers (Joseph Moingt's book on the* Théologie trinitaire de Tertullien *is in this sense exemplary: it contains a relatively comprehensive treatment of this question between the second and third centuries), until Gerhard Richter's recent work* Oikonomia, *published when the historical part of the present study had already been completed, we lacked a general study of this fundamental theological theme. Marie-José Mondzain's* Image, icône, économie *limits itself to analyzing the implications of this concept for the iconoclastic disputes that took place between the eighth and ninth centuries. Even after Richter's comprehensive study, whose orientation is—in spite of the title—theological and not linguistic-philological, we still lack an adequate lexical analysis that supplements Wilhelm Gass's useful but dated work* "Das patristische Wort oikonomia" (1874) *and Otto Lillge's dissertation* Das patristische Wort "oikonomia." Seine Geschichte und seine Bedeutung *(1955).*

It is probable that, at least in the case of theologians, this peculiar silence is due to their embarrassment in the face of something that could only appear as a kind of pudenda origo *of the Trinitarian dogma (indeed, it is surprising, to say the least, that the first formulation of the fundamental, in all senses, theologumenon of the Christian faith—the Trinity—presents itself initially as an "economic" apparatus). The eclipse of this concept that, as we shall see, is one with its penetration and diffusion in different fields, is testified to by the scanty attention that the Tridentine canons pay to it: just a few lines under the rubric* De dispensatione (dispensatio *is, with* dispositio, *the Latin translation of* oikonomia) et mysterio adventus Christi. *In modern Protestant theology, the problem of* oikonomia *reappeared, but only as an obscure and indeterminate precursor of the theme of* Heilsgeschichte, *while the opposite is true: the theology of the "history of salvation" is a partial and, all in all, reductive resumption of a much broader paradigm. The result of this is that in 1967 it was possible to publish a* Festschrift *commemorating the sixty-fifth anniversary of the publication of Oscar Cullmann's* Oikonomia. Heilsgeschichte als Thema der Theologie *in which the term* oikonomia *appeared in only one of the thirty-six contributions.*

1.2. In 1922, Carl Schmitt encapsulated the theological-political paradigm in a lapidary thesis: "All significant concepts of the modern theory of the state are secularized theological concepts" (Schmitt 2005, p. 36). If our hypothesis about the existence of a double paradigm is correct, this statement should be supplemented in a way that would extend its validity well beyond the boundaries of public law, extending up to the fundamental concepts of the economy and the very idea of the reproductive life of human societies. However, the thesis according to which the economy could be a secularized theological paradigm acts retroactively on theology itself, since it implies that from the beginning theology conceives divine life and the history of humanity as an *oikonomia*, that is, that theology is itself "economic" and did not simply become so at a later time through secularization. From this perspective, the fact that the living being who was created in the image of God in the end reveals himself to be capable only of economy, not politics, or, in other words, that history is ultimately not a political but an "administrative" and "governmental" problem, is nothing but a logical consequence of economic theology. Similarly, it is certainly more than a simple lexical fact that, with a peculiar reversal of the classical hierarchy, a *zoē aiōnios* and not a *bios* lies at the center of the evangelical message. The eternal life to which Christians lay claim ultimately lies in the paradigm of the *oikos*, not in that of the *polis*. According to Taubes's ironic *boutade*, the *theologia vitae* is always in the course of converting itself into a "theozoology" (Taubes, p. 41).

ℵ *A preliminary clarification of the meaning and implications of the term "secularization" becomes all the more urgent. It is perfectly well known that this concept has performed a strategic function in modern culture—that it is, in this sense, a concept of the "politics of ideas," something that "in the realm of ideas has always already found an enemy with whom to fight for dominance" (Lübbe, p. 20). This is equally valid for secularization in a strictly juridical sense—which, recovering the term* (saecularisatio) *that designated the return of the religious man into the world, became in nineteenth-century Europe the rallying cry of the conflict between the State and the Church over the expropriation of ecclesiastic goods—and its metaphoric use in the history of ideas. When Max Weber formulates his famous thesis about the secularization of Puritan asceticism in the capitalist ethics of work, the apparent neutrality of his diagnosis cannot hide its function in the battle he was fighting against fanatics and false prophets for the disenchantment of the world. Similar considerations could be made for Troeltsch. What is the meaning of the Schmittian thesis in this context?*

Schmitt's strategy is, in a certain sense, the opposite of Weber's. While, for Weber, secularization was an aspect of the growing process of disenchantment

*and detheologization of the modern world, for Schmitt it shows on the con-
trary that, in modernity, theology continues to be present and active in an
eminent way. This does not necessarily imply an identity of substance between
theology and modernity, or a perfect identity of meaning between theological
and political concepts; rather, it concerns a particular strategic relation that
marks political concepts and refers them back to their theological origin.*

*In other words, secularization is not a concept but a signature [segna-
tura] in the sense of Foucault and Melandri (Melandri, p. XXXII), that
is, something that in a sign or concept marks and exceeds such a sign or
concept referring it back to a determinate interpretation or field, without
for this reason leaving the semiotic to constitute a new meaning or a new
concept. Signatures move and displace concepts and signs from one field
to another (in this case, from sacred to profane, and vice versa) without
redefining them semantically. Many pseudoconcepts belonging to the philosophical tradition are, in this sense, signatures that, like the "secret indexes"
of which Benjamin speaks, carry out a vital and determinate strategic function, giving a lasting orientation to the interpretation of signs. Insofar as
they connect different times and fields, signatures operate, as it were, as pure
historical elements. Foucault's archaeology and Nietzsche's genealogy (and,
in a different sense, even Derrida's deconstruction and Benjamin's theory of
dialectical images) are sciences of signatures, which run parallel to the history of ideas and concepts, and should not be confused with them. If we are
not able to perceive signatures and follow the displacements and movements
they operate in the tradition of ideas, the mere history of concepts can, at
times, end up being entirely insufficient.*

*In this sense, secularization operates in the conceptual system of modernity
as a signature that refers it back to theology. Just as, according to canon law,
the secularized priest had to wear a sign of the religious order he had once
belonged to, so does the secularized concept exhibit like a signature its past
belonging to the theological sphere. The way in which the reference operated
by the theological signature is understood is decisive at every turn. Thus, secularization can also be understood (as is the case with Gogarten) as a specific
performance of Christian faith that, for the first time, opens the world to man
in its worldliness and historicity. The theological signature operates here as a
sort of trompe l'oeil in which the very secularization of the world becomes the
mark that identifies it as belonging to a divine* oikonomia.

1.3. In the second half of the 1960s, a debate on the problem of secularization involving, to different degrees, Hans Blumenberg, Karl Löwith, Odo Marquard, and Carl Schmitt, took place in Germany. The debate originated from the thesis enunciated by Löwith in his 1953 book *Welt-geschichte und Heilsgeschehen* according to which both German idealism's philosophy of history and the Enlightenment's idea of progress are nothing but the secularization of the theology of history and Christian eschatology. Although Blumenberg, who defended the "legitimacy of modernity," decisively affirmed the illegitimate character of the very category of secularization—as a consequence of which Löwith and Schmitt found themselves against their will on the same side—in point of fact, as has perceptively been noted by commentators (Carchia, p. 20), the dispute was more or less consciously instigated in order to hide what was really at stake, which was not secularization but the philosophy of history and the Christian theology that constituted its premise. All the apparent enemies joined forces against them. The eschatology of salvation, of which Löwith spoke and of which the philosophy of German idealism was a conscious resumption, was nothing but an aspect of a vaster theological paradigm, which is precisely the divine *oikonomia* that we intend to investigate, and the repression of which constituted the foundation of the debate. Hegel was still perfectly aware of this when he stated the equivalence of his thesis on the rational government of the world with the theological doctrine of the providential plan of God, and presented his philosophy of history as a theodicy ("that the history of the world [. . .] is the effective becoming of the spirit [. . .] this is the real theodicy, the justification of God in history"). In even more explicit terms, in the conclusion to his *Philosophy of Revelation*, Schelling summarized his philosophy with the theological figure of an *oikonomia*: "The ancient theologians distinguished between *akratos theologia* and *oikonomia*. The two belong together. It is toward this process of domestic economy (*oikonomia*) that we have wished to point" (Schelling, p. 325). The fact that such an engagement with economic theology has today become so improbable as to make the meaning of Schelling's statements entirely incomprehensible to us is a sign of the decline of philosophical culture. One of the aims of the present study is to make Schelling's statement, which has so far remained a dead letter, comprehensible again.

א *The distinction between* theologia *and* oikonomia, *between the being of God and his activity, to which Schelling alludes is, as we shall see, of fundamental importance in Eastern theology, from Eusebius to the Chalcedonians. Schelling's immediate sources are to be found in the use of the concept of* oikonomia *made in pietistic circles, particularly in authors such as Bengel and Oetinger, whose influence on Schelling is now well documented. However, it is crucial that Schelling thinks his philosophy of revelation as a theory of divine economy, which introduces personality and action into the being of God, and thus renders him "Lord of being" (Schelling, p. 172). From this perspective, he quotes the passage from Paul (Ephesians 3:9) on the "mystery of economy," which lies at the origin of the doctrine of theological* oikonomia:

> Paul speaks of a Plan of God that has not been spoken of for eons but that has now become manifest in Christ: the mystery of God and Christ that has become manifest to the world through Christ's appearance. It is at this point that the ways of a philosophy of revelation become possible. It must not be understood, like mythology, as a necessary process, but in a way that is fully free, as the decision and action of a will that is most free. Through revelation a new, second creation is introduced; it is an entirely free act. (Schelling, p. 253)

In other words, Schelling understands his introduction of an absolute and an-archic freedom in ontology as a resumption and accomplishment of the theological doctrine of oikonomia.

1.4. Between 1935 and 1970, Erich Peterson and Carl Schmitt—two authors who, in different ways, could be defined as "Apocalyptics of the counterrevolution" (Taubes, p. 19)—had a singular dispute. Its singularity was not only due to the fact that the two adversaries, both Catholics, shared common theological presuppositions, but also to the fact that, as shown by the long silence that separates the two dates mentioned above, the jurist's answer was formulated ten years after the death of the theologian who had opened the debate. Moreover, this answer took its cue from the more recent debate on secularization, as shown by the *Nachwort* that concludes it. However, the "Parthian arrow" (Schmitt 2008a, p. 32) cast by Peterson must still have been stuck in Schmitt's flesh if, according to the latter's own words, *Politische Theologie II*, which contained the belated answer, aimed to "rip [it] from the wound" (ibid.). What was at stake in this controversy was political theology, which Peterson put resolutely in question. But it is possible that, as had happened with the secularization debate, this time the explicit stake hid another, exoteric, and more frightful one, which we need to bring to light.

In every theoretical work—and maybe in every human work—there is something like an un-said. There are authors who attempt to approach this un-said and allusively evoke it, while others knowingly leave it unspoken. Both Schmitt and Peterson belong in this second category. In order to understand what is the hidden stake of their debate, we will need to try to expose this un-said. The two adversaries shared a common theological conception that can be defined "Catechontic." As Catholics, they could not fail to profess their eschatological faith in the Second Coming of Jesus. Yet, referring to 2 Thessalonians 2, they both claimed (Schmitt explicitly, Peterson tacitly) that there is something that defers and holds back the *eschaton*, that is, the advent of the Kingdom and the end of the world. For Schmitt, this delaying element is the Empire; for Peterson, it is the Jews' refusal to believe in Christ. According to both the jurist and the theologian, the present history of humanity is therefore an interim founded on the delay of the Kingdom. However, in one case this delay coincides with the sovereign power of the Christian empire ("The belief that a restrainer holds back the end of the world provides the only bridge between the notion of an eschatological paralysis of all human events and a tremendous historical monolith like that of the Christian empire of the Germanic kings" [Schmitt 2003, p. 60]). In the other case, the suspension of the Kingdom due to the Jews' failed conversion founds the historical existence of the Church. Peterson's 1929 work on the *Church* leaves us in no doubt about this: the Church can exist only because "the Jews, as the people elected by God, have not believed in the Lord" (Peterson 1994, p. 247), and, consequently, the end of the world is not imminent. "There can be a Church," Peterson writes, "only on the presupposition that the coming of Christ will not be immediate, in other words, that concrete eschatology is eliminated and we have in its place the doctrine of last things" (ibid., p. 248).

Thus, what is really at stake in the debate is not the admissibility of political theology, but the nature and identity of the *katechon*, the power that defers and eliminates "concrete eschatology." But this implies that what is crucial for both Schmitt and Peterson is ultimately the very neutralization of a philosophy of history oriented toward salvation. At the point where the divine plan of *oikonomia* had reached completion with the coming of Christ, an event (the failed conversion of the Jews, the

Christian empire) that had the power to suspend the *eschaton* took place. The exclusion of concrete eschatology transforms historical time into a suspended time, in which every dialectic is abolished and the Great Inquisitor watches over so that the parousia is not produced in history. Understanding the sense of the debate between Peterson and Schmitt will then also mean understanding the theology of history to which they more or less tacitly refer.

א *The two presuppositions that Peterson relates to the existence of the Church (the failed conversion of the Jews, and the delay of parousia) are intimately connected: this very connection defines the specificity of the particular Catholic anti-Semitism of which Peterson is a representative. The existence of the Church founds itself on the endurance of the Synagogue. However, given that in the end "all Israel will be saved" (Romans 11:26) and the Church must give way to the Kingdom (the essay* Die Kirche *opens with a quotation of Loisy's ironic dictum: "Jésus annonçait le royaume, et c'est l'Église qui est venue"), Israel will also have to disappear. If we do not understand this underlying connection between the two presuppositions, we do not even understand the real meaning of the closure of the "eschatological bureau," about which Troeltsch spoke already in 1925 ("the eschatological bureau is today mainly closed, because the thoughts that constitute its foundations have lost their roots": Troeltsch, p. 36). Inasmuch as it involves the radical putting in question of the connection between the Church and Israel, the reopening of the eschatological bureau is a thorny problem. It is unsurprising that a thinker like Benjamin, who positioned himself at the singular intersection of Christianity and Judaism, did not need to wait for Moltmann and Dodd to carry it out without reservations, yet he preferred to speak of messianism rather than eschatology.*

1.5. Peterson begins his argument by quoting the Homeric verse (*Iliad*, 2, 204) that concludes Book L of *Metaphysics*, "that is, the treatise we are used to calling Aristotle's theology" (Peterson 1994, p. 25): "The world must not be governed badly. 'The rule of many is not good; let there be one {sovereign}.'" According to Peterson, the point at issue in this passage is the critique of Platonic dualism and, in particular, of Speusippus's theory of the plurality of principles, against which Aristotle intends to show that nature is not generated by way of a series of episodes, like a bad tragedy, but has a single principle.

Although the term "monarchy" does not yet appear in Aristotle in this context, we need to emphasize that its meaning is, however, already present precisely in the semantic duplicity according to which, in divine monarchy, the single power (*mia archē*) of the single ultimate *principle* coincides with the power of the single ultimate holder of this power (*archōn*). (Ibid.)

In this way, Peterson is suggesting that the theological paradigm of the Aristotelian unmoved mover is somehow the archetype of the following theological-political justifications of monarchic power in Judaic and Christian circles. The pseudo-Aristotelian treatise *De mundo*, which Peterson analyzes shortly after, in this sense constitutes the bridge between classical politics and the Judaic notion of divine monarchy. While in Aristotle God is the transcendent principle of any movement, who leads the world as a strategist leads his army, in this treatise, the monarch, hidden in the rooms of his palace, moves the world as the puppeteer leads his puppets on strings.

Here the image of divine monarchy is not determined by whether there is one or more principles, but rather by the problem of whether God participates in the powers that act in the cosmos. The author wants to say: God is the presupposition of power [. . .] to act in the cosmos, but precisely for this reason he is not power (*dynamis*). (Ibid., p. 27)

Quoting a motto dear to Schmitt, Peterson summarizes this image of divine monarchy in the formula "Le roi règne, mais il ne gouverne pas" (ibid.).

It is only with Philo that something like a political theology appears clearly for the first time in the form of a theocracy. Analyzing Philo's language, Peterson shows that political theology is clearly a Judaic creation. The theological-political problem is posed for Philo "in the concreteness of his condition of being a Jew" (ibid., p. 30).

Israel is a theocracy, that single people is governed by the *single* divine monarch. *One only* people, *one only* God [. . .] But given that the *single* God is not only the monarch of Israel, but also of the cosmos, for this reason that *single* people—"the people most loved by God"—governed by this cosmic monarch, becomes minister and prophet for all mankind. (Ibid., pp. 28–29)

After Philo, the concept of divine monarchy is taken up by the Christian Apologists, who use it for their defense of Christianity. In a brief survey, Peterson reads from this perspective Justin, Tatian, Theophilus, Irenaeus, Hippolytus, Tertullian, and Origen. But it is only with Eusebius, a court theologian—or, in Overback's venomous witticism, the *friseur* of the theological wig of the Emperor Constantine—that a Christian political theology is comprehensively formulated. Eusebius sees a correspondence between the coming of Christ on earth as savior of all nations and Augustus's establishment of a global imperial power. Before Augustus, man used to live in polyarchy, among a plurality of tyrannies and democracies, but "when the Lord and Savior appeared and, at the same time as his advent, Augustus, first of Romans, became king of the nations, pluralistic polyarchy was dispersed and peace covered all the earth" (Eusebius, *Commentary on the Psalms*, 71, in *PG*, 23). Peterson shows how, according to Eusebius, the process that was begun with Augustus is brought to completion with Constantine. "After Constantine defeated Licinius, political monarchy was restored and, at the same time, divine monarchy was secured [. . .] the *single* king on earth corresponds to the *single* king in Heaven and the *single* sovereign *nomos* and *Logos*" (Peterson 1994, p. 50).

Peterson follows Eusebius's descendants through John Chrysostom, Prudentius, Ambrose, and Jerome up to Orosius, for whom the parallelism between the unity of the global empire and the accomplished revelation of a single God becomes the key to interpret history:

> "In the same year, Caesar—predestined by God for many mysteries—ordered a census of all men in every province of the empire. God made himself seen as a man then, he wanted to be a man then. Christ was born at that time: he was registered shortly after his birth during the Roman census" [. . .] A single God who, in the times when he decided to reveal himself, established this unity of the kingdom is loved and feared by all: the same laws rule everywhere, the laws of those who are subject to the single God. (Ibid., p. 55)

At this point, in an abrupt reversal, Peterson tries to show that, at the time of the disputes on Arianism, the theological-political paradigm of divine monarchy enters into conflict with the development of Trinitarian theology. The proclamation of the dogma of the Trinity marks, from this perspective, the waning of "monotheism as a political problem." In only two pages, political theology—to whose reconstruction the book had been dedicated—is entirely demolished.

The doctrine of divine monarchy had to fail in the face of the Trinitarian dogma just as the interpretation of the *pax augusta* had to fail in the face of Christian eschatology. In this way, not only is monotheism as a political problem abolished theologically and the Christian faith freed from its link with the Roman empire, but a break with any "political theology" is also produced. Something like a "political theology" can exist only in the field of Judaism or Paganism. (Ibid., pp. 58–59)

The note to this passage that concludes the book reads as follows (it is as though the entire treatise were written in view of this note):

To the best of my knowledge, the concept of "political theology" was introduced in the literature by Carl Schmitt's *Politische theologie* (München, 1922). His brief considerations at that time were not laid out systematically. Here we have attempted to demonstrate by means of a concrete example that "political theology" is theologically impossible. (Ibid., p. 81)

א *Eusebius's thesis on the solidarity of the advent of a single global empire, the end of polyarchy, and the triumph of the only true God shows some analogies with Negri and Hardt's thesis according to which the overcoming of nation-states in a single global capitalist empire paves the way for the triumph of communism. However, while the doctrine of Constantine's theological hairdresser had a clear tactical meaning and was the effect not of an antagonism, but of an alliance between Constantine's global power and the Church, the meaning of Negri and Hardt's thesis can certainly not be understood in the same way and thus remains enigmatic to say the least.*

1.6. A passage from a Cappadocian theologian of the fourth century, Gregory of Nazianzus, plays a key strategic role in Peterson's argument. According to the drastic summary provided by Peterson, Gregory conferred upon the Trinitarian dogma its "ultimate theological depth" opposing the "monarchy of the triune God" to the "monarchy of a single person":

Christians [. . .] recognize themselves in God's monarchy; certainly not in the monarchy of a single person in the deity, because this brings with it the germ of internal division [*Zwiespalt*], but in a monarchy of the triune God. This concept of unity cannot be found in human nature. With this development, monotheism as a political problem is eliminated theologically. (Ibid., pp. 57–58)

However, it is strange that, in his belated answer, Schmitt uses the same passage analyzed by Peterson to draw conclusions that are in certain ways the opposite of Peterson's. According to the jurist, Gregory of Nazianzus introduced a sort of theory of civil war ("a genuine politico-theological *stasiology*") into the core of the Trinitarian doctrine (Schmitt 2008a, p. 123) and, in this way, could be said to be still using a theological-political paradigm, one that would refer back to the opposition friend/enemy.

The idea that the elaboration of the Trinitarian theology is in itself sufficient to eliminate any theological-political conception of a divine monarchy is, after all, far from evident. Speaking about Tertullian, Peterson himself evokes the attempts of the Christian Apologists to reconcile the Trinitarian theology with the image of an emperor who exercises the power that is his alone by means of governors and ministers. But even the passage from Gregory of Nazianzus's oration, which Peterson quotes in an offhanded manner, appears to be far from probative when it is brought back to its proper context.

This text is part of a group of five orations that we normally refer to as "theological" because they constitute a veritable treatise on the Trinity. The theology of the Cappadocians, of whom Gregory of Nazianzus was the greatest representative together with Basil of Caesarea and Gregory of Nyssa, was engaged in the elimination of the last Arian and Homoousian resistances and in the elaboration of the doctrine of the single substance in three different hypostases that was finally established at the Council of Constantinople in 381. It was a matter of adapting the Monarchian understanding of the deity, which is implicit in the concept of the *homoousia*, to the assertion of the three hypostases (Father, Son, and Holy Spirit). The difficulty and paradoxical nature of this reconciliation is evident in the text by Gregory that is here in question and whose title is *Peri Yiou*, "About the Son." The passage quoted by Peterson should be understood within this context:

> The three most ancient opinions concerning God are Anarchia, Polyarchia, and Monarchia. The first two are the sport of the children of Hellas, and may they continue to be so. For Anarchy is a thing without order; and Polyarchy is like civil war [*stasiōdes*], and thus anarchical, and thus disorderly. For both of these tend toward the same thing, namely disorder; and this to dissolution, for disorder is the first step to dissolution. But Monarchy is that which we hold in honor. It is, however, a Monarchy that is not limited to one Person,

for it is possible for Unity if [it is] at war with itself [*stasiazon pros heauto*] to come into a condition of plurality; but one which is made of an equality of Nature and a Union of mind, and an identity of motion, and a convergence of its elements to unity—a thing which is impossible to the created nature— so that although numerically distinct there is no severance of Essence. Therefore Unity having from all eternity arrived at Duality by motion, found its rest in Trinity. This is what we mean by Father and Son and Holy Spirit. The Father is the Begetter [*gennētōr*] and the Emitter [*proboleus*]; without passion of course, and without reference to time, and not in a corporeal manner [. . .] (Gregory of Nazianzus, *Select Orations*, XXIX, 2, p. 301)

It is evident that Gregory is here concerned with reconciling the metaphysical terminology of the unity of the divine substance with that— more concrete and almost corporeal—of the Trinity (in particular in relation to the generation of the son in contrast to the nongenerated character of the deity, which had prompted particularly heated debates with the Arians and the Monarchians). For this purpose, Gregory resorts to a metaphorical register that, pace Peterson, can easily be defined as political (or theological-political): indeed, it is a matter of thinking the Trinitarian articulation of the hypostases without introducing a stasis in God, an internecine war. For this reason, using Stoic terminology freely, Gregory does not conceive the three hypostases as substances, but as modes of being or relations (*pros ti, pōs echon*) in a single substance (ibid., 16, p. 307). And yet, he is so well aware of the inadequacy of his attempt and the insufficiency of any linguistic explanation of the mystery, that he concludes his oration with an extraordinary tour de force introducing the Son through a long list of antinomic figures. However, just before this, Gregory provides us with the key to interpreting the whole oration when, following a terminological tradition that was well established by his time, he claims that it can only be understood correctly by those who have learned to distinguish in God between "the discourse of nature and the discourse of economy [*tis men physeōs logos, tis de logos oikonomias*]" (ibid., 18, p. 308). This means that even the passage quoted by Peterson can only be read in the light of this distinction. It is all the more surprising that Peterson remains silent on this.

א *In other words, in Gregory, the* logos *of "economy" is specifically designed to prevent the Trinity from introducing a stasiological, or political, fracture in God. Insofar as even a monarchy can give rise to a civil war, an internal* stasis, *it is only a displacement from a political to an "economic" rationality (in a sense that we shall explain) that can protect us against this danger.*

1.7. An overview of the authors quoted above by Peterson in his genealogy of the theological-political paradigm of the divine monarchy shows that, from both a textual and a conceptual point of view, the "discourse of economy" is so strictly intertwined with that of monarchy that the fact that it is absent in Peterson lets us infer something like a conscious repression. Tertullian is a paradigmatic case in this sense (but, as we shall see, we could say the same about Justin, Tatian, Hippolytus, Irenaeus, etc.). Let us focus on the quotation from the text *Adversus Praxean* with which Peterson opens his analysis of the Apologists' attempt to reconcile the traditional doctrine of divine monarchy with the Trinity:

> "We hold," they say, "to the monarchy": and even Latins so expressively frame the sound, and in so masterly a fashion, that they would think they understood monarchy as well as they pronounce it. (*Tertullian's Treatise Against Praxeas*, 3, 2, pp. 132–133)

The quotation ends here; but Tertullian's text continues as follows:

> But while Latins are intent to shout out "monarchy," even Greeks refuse to understand the economy [*sed monarchiam sonare student Latini, oikonomian intellegere nolunt etiam Graeci*]. (Ibid., p. 133)

Immediately before this, Tertullian contends that

> The simple people, that I say not the thoughtless and ignorant [. . .] not understanding that while they must believe in one only [God] yet they must believe in him along with his *oikonomia* [*unicum quidem (deum) sed cum sua oeconomia*], shy at the economy. They claim that the plurality and ordinance of trinity is a division of unity. (Ibid., 3, 1, p. 132)

The understanding of the Trinitarian dogma on which Peterson's argument is based thus presupposes a preliminary understanding of the "language of economy." We shall be able to identify what is really at stake in the debate between the two friends/enemies about political theology only after we have explored this *logos* in all its articulations.

Threshold

The links between Schmitt and Peterson are more complex and intricate than the two authors are inclined to reveal. In his works, Schmitt refers to Peterson for the first time in the 1927 essay *Volksentscheid und Volksbegehren*; the reference concerns Peterson's doctoral thesis on acclamations in the early centuries of Christian liturgy, which Schmitt considers "fundamental." But, even here, what the two authors share also contains, as we shall see, the seed of their division.

The short and inconspicuous preface to the 1935 book on monotheism fairly summarizes the reasons for the proximity between the two authors as well as the reasons for their disagreement. The reduction of Christian faith to monotheism is presented as the result of the Enlightenment, against which Peterson recalls that "for Christians there is political action only on the presupposition of faith in a triune God," who should be located beyond both Judaism and Paganism, monotheism and polytheism. At this point, the preface announces in a more subdued tone the final thesis of the book on the "theological impossibility" of a Christian political theology: "We shall show here with an historical example the internal problematicity of a political theology that orientates itself on monotheism" (Peterson 1994, p. 24).

More than the critique of the Schmittian paradigm, what is decisive here is the enunciation of the thesis according to which the Trinitarian doctrine is the only possible foundation of a Christian politics. Both authors want to found a politics on Christian faith; but while, for Schmitt, political theology founds politics in a secular sense, the "political action" that is at stake for Peterson is, as we shall see, liturgy (returned to its etymological meaning of "public practice").

The thesis according to which the real Christian politics is liturgy and the Trinitarian doctrine founds politics as participation in the glorious worship of the angels and saints may appear surprising. The fact remains that this is precisely where the watershed that separates Schmitt's "political theology" from Peterson's Christian "political action" lies. For Schmitt, political theology founds a politics in the proper sense as well as the secular power [*potenza*] of the Christian empire that acts as *katechon.* On the other hand, for Peterson, politics as liturgical action rules out any identification with the earthly city (the invocation of the name of Augustine, "who makes himself visible at every spiritual and political turn of the

West," confirms this fact): politics as liturgical action is nothing else than the cultual anticipation of eschatological glory. In this sense, the action of secular powers is, for the theologian, eschatologically irrelevant: what acts as *katechon* is not a political power [*potere*], but only the Jews' refusal to convert. This means that, for Peterson (but his position coincides here with that of a prominent part of the Church), the historical events he witnessed—from the World Wars to totalitarianism, from the technological revolution to the atomic bomb—are theologically insignificant. All but one: the extermination of the Jews.

If the eschatological advent of the Kingdom will become concrete and real only after the Jews have converted, then the destruction of the Jews cannot be unrelated to the destiny of the Church. Peterson was probably in Rome when, on October 16, 1943, the deportation of a thousand Roman Jews to the extermination camps took place with the conniving silence of Pius XII. It is legitimate to ask ourselves whether, at that moment, Peterson became aware of the terrible ambiguity of a theological thesis that tied both the existence and the fulfillment of the Church to the survival or the disappearance of the Jews. This ambiguity will possibly be overcome only if the *katechon*—the power [*potere*] that, postponing the end of history, opens the space of secular politics—is returned to its original relation with the divine *oikonomia* and its Glory.

§ 2   The Mystery of the Economy

2.1. *Oikonomia* means "administration of the house." In the Aristotelian (or pseudo-Aristotelian) treatise on economy, we can thus read that the *technē oikonomikē* differs from politics just as the house (*oikia*) differs from the city (*polis*). This distinction is restated in the *Politics*, in which the politician and the king—who belong to the sphere of the *polis*—are qualitatively opposed to the *oikonomos* and the *despotēs*—who are referred to the sphere of the house and the family. Even in Xenophon (in whose works the opposition between house and city is certainly less pronounced than in Aristotle's), the *ergon* of the economy is said to be the "good administration of the household [*eu oikein ton* (. . .) *oikon*]" (Xenophon, *Oeconomicus*, 1, 2). However, it is important not to forget that the *oikos* is not the modern single-family house or simply the extended family, but a complex organism composed of heterogeneous relations, entwined with each other, which Aristotle (*Politics*, 1253b) divides into three groups: "despotic" relations between masters and slaves (which usually include the management of a farming business of substantial dimensions); "paternal" relations between parent and children; "gamic" relations between husband and wife. These "economic" relations (Aristotle emphasizes their diversity: ibid., 1259a–b) are linked by a paradigm that we could define as "administrative" ["*gestionale*"], and not epistemic: in other words, it is a matter of an activity that is not bound to a system of rules, and does not constitute a science in the proper sense (Aristotle writes that "the term 'head of the family' [*despotēs*] does not refer to a science [*epistēmēn*] but to a certain way of being": ibid., 1255b). This activity rather implies decisions and orders that cope with problems that are each time specific and concern the functional order (*taxis*) of the different parts of the *oikos*. A passage from Xenophon clearly defines this "administrative" nature of *oikonomia*: the latter not only has to do with the need and use of objects, but, first and foremost, with their ordered arrangement (*peri* [. . .] *taxeōs skeuōn*: Xenophon, *Oeconomicus*, 8, 23; the term *skeuos* means "tackle, tool relative to a certain activity"). In this perspective, the house is first compared with an army and then with a ship:

> Once I had an opportunity of looking over a great Phoenician ship [. . .] and I thought I had never seen tackle so excellently and accurately managed. For I never saw so many bits of stuff packed away separately in so small a receptacle [. . .] And I noticed that each kind of thing was so neatly stowed away that there was no confusion, no work for a searcher, nothing out of place, no troublesome untying to cause a delay when anything was wanted for immediate use. I found that the steersman's servant [*diakonon*] [. . .] knows each particular section so exactly, that he can tell even when away where everything is kept and how much there is of it [. . .] I saw this man in his spare time inspecting all the stores that are wanted, as a matter of course, in the ship. (Ibid., 8, 11–15)

Xenophon defines this activity or ordered administration as "control" (*episkepsis*, from which derives *episkopos*, "superintendent," and, later, "bishop"):

> I was surprised to see him looking over them, and asked what he was doing. "Sir," he answered, "I am checking [*episkopō*] to see how the ship's tackle is stored." (Ibid., 8, 15)

Thus Xenophon compares a well-"economized" house to a dance:

> All the utensils seem to give rise to a choir, and the space between them is beautiful to see, for each thing stands aside, just as a choir that dances in a circle is a beautiful spectacle in itself, and even the free space looks beautiful and unencumbered. (Ibid., 8, 21)

Oikonomia is presented here as a functional organization, an administrative activity that is bound only to the rules of the ordered functioning of the house (or of the company in question).

This "administrative" paradigm defines the semantic sphere of the term *oikonomia* (as well as that of the verb *oikonomein* and the noun *oikonomos*) and determines its gradual analogical extension outside its original limits. It is thus already in the *Corpus Hippocraticum* (*Of the Epidemics*, 6, 2, 24) that *hē peri ton noseonta oikonomiē* designates the set of practices and apparatuses that the doctor needs to implement with the patient. In the philosophical field, the Stoics use an "economic" metaphor when they intend to express the idea of a force that regulates and governs the whole from the inside (*tēs tōn holōn oikonomias*: Chrysippus, fragment 937, *Stoicorum veterum fragmenta*, II, 269; *hē physis epi tōn phytōn kai epi tōn zōōn* (. . .) *oikonomei*: Chrysippus, fragment 178, *Stoicorum veterum fragmenta*, III, 43). In this broad sense of "governing, looking after something," the verb *oikonomein* acquires the meaning of "providing for the needs of life, nourishing" (thus, the *Acts of Thomas* paraphrase the expression from the parable in Matthew 6:26 "your heavenly Father feeds them" about the birds of the sky as *ho theos oikonomei auta*, in which the verb has the same meaning as the Italian "governare le bestie" [1]).

It is in a passage from Marcus Aurelius, whose *Meditations* are contemporary with the first Christian Apologists, that the administrative meaning of the term appears with more clarity. Reflecting on the inappropriateness of hastily judging someone else's behavior, he writes:

> It is sometimes a hard matter to be certain whether men do wrong, for their actions are often done with a reference to {an economy} [*kat' oikonomian ginetai*]; and one must be thoroughly informed of a great many things before he can be rightly qualified to give judgment in the case. (*The Meditations of Marcus Aurelius*, 11, 18, 5, pp. 188–189)

Here, following a semantic inflection that will remain inseparable from the term, *oikonomia* designates a practice and a non-epistemic knowledge that should be assessed only in the context of the aims that they pursue, even if, in themselves, they may appear to be inconsistent with the good.

The technical use of the term *oikonomia* in a rhetorical context is particularly interesting: it designates the ordered arrangement of the material of an oration or a treatise ("Hermagoras iudicium partitionem ordinem quaeque sunt elocutionis subicit oeconomiae, quae Graece appellata ex cura rerum domesticarum et hic per abusionem posita nomine Latino caret": Quintilian, *Institutio oratoria*, 3, 3, 9. Cicero translates the term with *dispositio*, that is, "rerum inventarum in ordinem distributio": *De inventione*, 1, 9). Economy is, however, more than a mere arrangement [*disposizione*], since it implies, above and beyond the ordering of the themes (*taxis*), a choice (*diairesis*) and an analysis (*exergasia*) of the topics. In this sense, the term appears in the pseudo-Longinus precisely in opposition to the concept of the "sublime":

> We see skill in invention, and due order and the *oikonomia* of matter, emerging as the hard-won result not of one thing or two, but of the whole texture of the composition, whereas the sublime flashing forth at the right moment scatters everything before it like a thunderbolt. (*Longinus on the Sublime*, 1, 4)

But, as clearly becomes apparent in Quintilian's remark ("oeconomiae, quae Graece appellata ex cura rerum domesticarum et hic per abusionem posita"), in this gradual analogical extension of the semantic sphere of the term, the awareness of the original domestic meaning was never lost. In this sense, there is an instructive passage from Diodorus Siculus in which the same semantic nucleus exhibits, at the same time, both the domestic and the rhetorical acceptation of the term:

> It should be the special care of historians, when they compose their works, to give attention to everything which may be of utility, and especially to the arrangement according to the parts [*tēs kata meros oikonomias*]. This eye to arrangement, for instance, is not only of great help to persons in the disposition of their private affairs [*en tois idiōtikois biois*] if they would preserve and increase their property, but also, when men come to writing history. (Diodorus Siculus, *The Library of History*, V, 1, 1)

It is on this basis that, in the Christian age, the term *oikonomia* is transposed into a theological field, in which, according to a widespread belief, it would acquire the meaning of a "divine plan of salvation" (with particular reference to Christ's incarnation). Given that—as we have seen—a serious lexical investigation is yet to be carried out, the hypothesis of such a theological meaning of the term *oikonomia*, which is usually taken for granted, should first of all be verified.

א *In order to understand the semantic history of the term* oikonomia, *we need to remember that, from the linguistic point of view, what we are dealing with is not really a transformation of the sense (*Sinn*) of the word, but rather a gradual analogical extension of its denotation (*Bedeutung*). Although dictionaries do usually, in such instances, distinguish and list one after the other the various senses of a term, linguists know perfectly well that, in point of fact, the semantic nucleus (the* Sinn*) remains within certain limits and up to a certain point unchanged, and that it is precisely this permanence that allows* *the extension to new and different denotations. What happened to the term* oikonomia *is somehow similar to what has more recently happened to the term "enterprise" ["*impresa*"], which, with the more or less conscious assent of the people concerned, has been extending itself so far as to cover fields, such as the university, which traditionally did not have anything to do with it.*

When, referring to the theological use of the term, scholars (such as Moingt with regard to Hippolytus: Moingt, p. 903; or Markus: Markus 1958, p. 99) speak of an alleged "traditional sense" of oikonomia *in the language of Christianity (which is, precisely that of "divine design"), they end up projecting onto the level of sense what is simply an extension of denotation to the theological field. Even Richter, who in any case denies the existence of a single theological meaning of the term that could be recovered in different contexts (Richter, p. 2), does not seem to distinguish correctly between sense and denotation. In truth, there is no theological "sense" of the term, but first of all a displacement of its denotation onto the theological field, which is progressively misunderstood and perceived as a new meaning.*

In the following pages, we shall abide by the principle according to which the hypothesis of a theological meaning of the term oikonomia *cannot be presupposed, but must be promptly verified each time.*

א *It is well known that, in Plato, the difference between* oikos *and* polis *is not presented, as it is in Aristotle, in terms of an opposition. In this sense, Aristotle is able to criticize the Platonic notion of the* polis *and reproach his master for pushing the unitary nature of the city too far, thus running the risk of transforming it into a household:*

> Is it not obvious that a city may at length attain such a degree of unity as to be no longer a city?—since the nature of a city is to be a plurality, and in tending to greater unity, from being a city, it becomes a household [*oikia*]. (Aristotle, *Politics*, 1261a)

2.2. It is a widespread belief (Gass, p. 469; Moingt, p. 903) that Paul was the first to give a theological meaning to the term *oikonomia*. Yet, a careful analysis of the passages in question does not confirm this hypothesis. Let us take 1 Corinthians 9:16–17:

> If I preach the Gospel [*euangelizōmai*], I have nothing to glory of; for necessity is laid upon me; for woe is unto me, if I preach not the Gospel. For if I do this of mine own will, I have a reward: but if not of mine own will, I have

an *oikonomia* entrusted to me [*oikonomian pepisteumai*, literally: "I have been invested fiduciarily of an *oikonomia*"].

The sense of *oikonomia* is here perspicuous, and the construction with *pisteuō* does not leave any doubt: *oikonomia* is the task (as in Septuagint, Isaiah 22:21) that God has assigned to Paul, who therefore does not act freely, as he would in a *negotiorum gestio*, but according to a bond of trust (*pistis*) as *apostolos* ("envoy") and *oikonomos* ("nominated administrator"). *Oikonomia* is here something that is assigned; it is, therefore, an activity and a task, not a "plan of salvation" that concerns the divine mind or will. One should understand the passage from 1 Timothy 1:3–4 in the same way:

> I urged you to stay on at Ephesus. You were to command certain persons to give up teaching erroneous doctrines and studying those interminable myths and genealogies, which issue in mere speculation and cannot make known the *oikonomia* of God, which works through faith [*oikonomian theou tēn en pistei*, the good activity of administration that God entrusted to me].

But the meaning remains the same even in those passages in which the combination of *oikonomia* with the term *mystērion* has induced interpreters to assume a theological sense that is not necessitated by the text. See, for instance, Colossians 1:24–25:

> Now I rejoice in my suffering for your sake, and in my flesh I complete what is lacking in Christ's afflictions [. . .] according to the *oikonomia* of God, the one which was given to me [*dotheisan*] to make the word of God fully known, the mystery hidden for ages and generations but now made manifest to his saints [. . .]

It has been observed that, although the sense of *oikonomia* is here, as it is in 1 Corinthians 9:17, that of a "fiduciary duty" ("anvertraute Amt"), the apostle seems to imply the further meaning of "divine decision of salvation" (Gass, p. 470). But nothing in the text authorizes us to relate *oikonomia* to a meaning that could perhaps belong only to *mystērion*. Once again, the construction with *didōmi* is perspicuous: Paul has received the task to announce the good news of the coming of the Messiah, and this announcement fulfills God's word, whose promise of salvation had remained hidden and has now been revealed. There is no reason to link *oikonomia* to *mystērion*: the latter term is grammatically an apposition of *logon tou theou*, and not of *oikonomian*.

The interpretation of Ephesians 1:9–10 is more complex:

> [God] has made known to us in all wisdom and insight the mystery of his will, according to his benevolence, which he set forth [*proetheto*] in Christ for the *oikonomia* of the fullness of time, to unite all things in him.

Paul is here speaking about the election and redemption decided by God according to his benevolence (*eudokia*): consistently with this context, he can write that God has assigned to the Messiah the *oikonomia* of the fullness of time, bringing to completion the promise of redemption. Even here *oikonomia* simply refers to an activity ("Sie bezeichnet nur noch ein Tätigsein": Richter, p. 53), and not to a "divine design of salvation" as is wrongly suggested by O. Michel (ibid., p. 67). The fact that Paul is able to present the attainment of the promised redemption in terms of an *oikonomia*—that is, the fulfillment of a task of domestic administration— is far from irrelevant (it is most likely with reference to this passage that the Gnostics will be able to present Jesus as "the man of the *oikonomia*"). We can make similar suggestions regarding Ephesians 3:9:

> To me, though I am the very least of all the saints, this grace was given, to preach to the Gentiles the unsearchable riches of Christ, and to make all men see what is the *oikonomia* of the mystery hidden for ages in God [. . .]

"The *oikonomia* of the mystery" is patently a contraction of the phrase used in Colossians 1:25 ("the *oikonomia* of God, the one that was given to me to make the word of God fully known, the mystery hidden for ages and generations [. . .]"); even here, nothing authorizes us to replace its sense of "realization, administration" with the unattested sense of "plan of salvation."

The use of the term *oikonomos* in 1 Corinthians 4:1 is entirely consistent with these two passages:

> Let a man so account of us, as of servants [*hypēretas*] of Christ, and treasurers [*oikonomous*] of the mysteries of God. Here, moreover, it is required in *oikonomoi*, that a man be found faithful [*pistos*].

The relation between *oikonomia* and mystery is here clear: it is a matter of carrying out faithfully the task of announcing the mystery of redemption hidden in the will of God that has now come to completion.

2.3. If the textual analysis does not allow us to attribute an immediately theological meaning to *oikonomia,* a different point can nevertheless be inferred from the examination of the Pauline lexicon. Paul does not just speak of an *oikonomia* of God, in the sense we have seen, but also refers to himself and the members of the messianic community using exclusively terms that belong to the language of domestic administration: *doulos* ("slave"), *hypēretēs, diakonos* ("servant"), *oikonomos* ("administrator"). Christ himself (even though the name is synonymous with "eschatological king") is always defined with the term that designates the master of the *oikos* (that is, *kyrios,* or *dominus* in Latin) and never with terms that are more openly political, such as *anax* or *archōn.* (The appellation *kyrios* was certainly not neutral: we know from Irenaeus, *Against Heresies,* I, 1, 1, that Gnostics refused to call the Savior *kyrios;* on the other hand, they used the political term "archons" to designate the divine figures of the plerome.) In spite of some very rare and only apparent exceptions (see Philippians 1:27 and 3:20; see also Ephesians 2:19, in which *politeuomai* and *sympolitēs* are, however, used in a decidedly impolitical sense), the lexicon of the Pauline *ekklēsia* is "economic," not political, and Christians are, in this sense, the first fully "economic" men. The lexical choice is all the more significant insofar as, in the *Apocalypse,* Christ—who appears in the guise of an eschatological king—is defined with an unequivocally political term: *archōn* (1:5; *princeps* in the Vulgate).

The strongly domestic tone of the vocabulary of the Christian community is obviously not a Pauline invention; it rather reflects a process of semantic mutation that involves the entire political vocabulary of Paul's times. Starting already with the Hellenistic age and then more explicitly in the Imperial age, the political and economic vocabularies enter a relation of mutual contamination, which tends to render the Aristotelian opposition between *oikos* and *polis* obsolete. The anonymous author of the second book of the pseudo-Aristotelian treatise on *Economy* is thus able to put economy in the strict sense (defined as *idiōtikē,* private) alongside an *oikonomia basilikē* and even an *oikonomia politikē* (a real nonsense from Aristotle's perspective). The contamination of the paradigms is evident in the Alexandrian *koinē* and in the Stoa. In a passage from Philo, whose content Arnim ascribed—possibly in an uncritical way—to Chrysippus, the *oikia* is defined as "a *polis* on a small and contracted scale [*estalmenē kai bracheia*]," and economy as "a contracted [*synēgmenē*] *politeia.*" Conversely, the *polis* is presented as "a large house [*oikos megas*]," and politics as "a {common} economy [*koinē tis oikonomia*]" (Philo, *On Joseph,* p. 438; see also *SVF,* III, 80 = Chrysippus, fragment 323). (The modern metaphor of the political community as a "house"—"the house of Europe" [*la "casa Europa"*]—here finds its archetype.)

Portraying the *ekklēsia* in domestic rather than political terms, Paul was merely following a process that was already taking place; however, he further accelerates this process in a way that involves the entire metaphorological register of the Christian lexicon. Two examples are worthy of note: the use of *oikos* in 1 Timothy 3:15—in which the community is defined as "the house [not 'city'] of God" (*oikos theou*)—and that of *oikodomē* and *oikodomeo*—terms that refer to the construction of a house—in the "edifying" sense of constructing a community (see Ephesians 4:16; Romans 14:19; 1 Corinthians 14:3; 2 Corinthians 12:19). The implications for the history of Western politics of the fact that the messianic community is represented from the beginning in terms of an *oikonomia*—not in terms of a politics—have yet to be appreciated.

‭ *Our textual analysis of the occurrences of the term* oikonomia *will essentially be limited to texts of the second and third century AD, a period during which the concept receives its original form. Later developments in the theology of the Cappadocians and in the late Byzantine theologians will occasionally be treated in Chapter 3.*

2.4. The term *oikonomia* is used three times in Ignatius of Antioch's *Letter to the Ephesians*, in a context where the influence of the Pauline vocabulary is evident.

In 6, 1, the term does not have any theological connotation, even if it refers to a bishop:

> The more anyone observes that a bishop is discreetly silent, the more he should stand in fear of him. Obviously, anyone whom the Master of the household [*oikodespotēs*] puts in charge of His domestic affairs [*eis idian oikonomian*], ought to be received by us in the same spirit as he who has charged him with his duty.

In 18, 2:

> The fact is, our God Jesus Christ was conceived by Mary according to God's *oikonomia* from the seed of David, it is true, but also from the Holy Spirit.

Here, as already noted by Gass, *oikonomia* does not yet mean "incarnation"; but it is also unnecessary to presuppose, as is suggested by Gass, the intricate sense of "a revelatory principle that, in conformity with the highest decision, had to fulfill itself by means of Christ's birth and death" (Gass, pp. 473–474). The syntagma *oikonomia theou* is simply equivalent to "task assigned by God," "activity performed according to God's will" (as in Paul, from whom the syntagma is derived: this passage from Ignatius's letter is full of Pauline quotations). It is important to observe that, in the following passage (19, 1), Ignatius draws a distinction between *oikonomia* and *mystērion*: Mary's virginity, her parturition, and the death of the Lord are "sensational mysteries" (*kraugēs*, as in Paul, Ephesians 4:31), which have happened and been revealed according to an economy. In other words, as in Paul, there is an "economy of the mystery" and not, as will be the case with Hippolytus and Tertullian, a "mystery of the economy."

Even with reference to 20, 1 ("I shall, in the subsequent letter that I intend to write to you, still further explain the *oikonomiai* that I have here only touched upon, regarding the New Man Jesus Christ—the *oikonomiai* founded on faith in Him and Love for Him, on His passion and Resurrection"), the translation "divine plan" is imprecise. If the term *oikonomiai* is not to be understood here in the rhetorical sense of "arrangement of the matter" (which is nevertheless a possibility, given the reference to the composition of a text), the generic meaning "activity ordered for a purpose" is perfectly satisfactory.

2.5. Justin, who is active in Rome around the middle of the second century, uses the term *oikonomia* in the *Dialogue with Trypho*, in which he tries to demonstrate to the Jews that "Jesus is the Lord's Christ" (that is, the Messiah).

In two passages from Chapters 30–31, Justin writes the following:

Even to this day, they [the demons] are overcome by us when we exorcise them in the name of Jesus Christ, who was crucified under Pontius Pilate, the Governor of Judea. Thus, it is clear to all that his Father bestowed upon him such a great power [*dynamin*] that even the demons are submissive both to his name and to the economy of his passion [*tēi tou genomenou pathous oikonomiai*]. (Justin, *Dialogue with Trypho*, p. 46)

If such power [*dynamis*] is shown to have accomplished, and even now accompanies, the economy of his Passion [*tēi tou pathos autou oikonomiai*], just think how great shall be his power at his glorious coming. (Ibid., p. 47)

Here, the syntagma "economy of the passion" designates the passion conceived as the fulfillment of a divine assignment and will, from which a power follows (*dynamis*). This is equally valid for the two passages in which (as in Ignatius, *Letter to the Ephesians*, 18, 2) the *oikonomia* refers to the generation of the savior through the Virgin Mary:

> [Christ] deigned to become Incarnate, and be born of this virgin of the family of David, in order that by this activity [*dia tēs oikonomias tautēs*] he might conquer the serpent [. . .] and the angels who followed his example. (Justin, *Dialogue with Trypho*, p. 69)

> [. . .] the ones from whom Christ was to be born in accordance with the activity that was fulfilled through the Virgin Mary [*kata tēn oikonomian tēn dia tēs parthenou Marias*]. (Ibid., p. 180)

The sense of "assignment" is perspicuous in 67, 6: "I do not admit that he [Christ] submitted to this, as though justification could be acquired by it, but simply to complete the *oikonomia* in accordance with the will of his Father" (ibid., p. 103); and in 103, 3: "[. . .] before Christ fulfilled by his crucifixion the Father's *oikonomia*" (ibid., p. 156). The passage at 134, 2 is closer to Paul's use of the term in the letter to the Ephesians:

> For, as I have said already, in each such action certain *oikonomiai* of the great mysteries were fulfilled [*oikonomiai tines megalōn mystēriōn en hekastēi tini toiautēi praxei apetelounto*]. I will explain what divine *oikonomia* and prophecy were accomplished in the marriages of Jacob. (Ibid., pp. 201–202)

As we can infer from the passage that immediately follows ("The marriages of Jacob were prototypes [*typoi*] of what Christ would do": 134, 3), the "economy of the mystery" refers to Paul's typological doctrine: it is the activity that realizes the mystery that had been announced typologically in the Old Testament. In the last occurrence of the term *oikonomia*, there is no direct theological implication (107, 3):

> Then, when Jonah was vexed because the city had not been destroyed on the third day, as he had announced, a gourd plant sprang up out of the earth thanks to one of God's economies [*dia tēs oikonomias*]. (Ibid., pp. 161–162)

א *The text of the* Apology *of Aristides of Athens, probably written between AD 124 and 140, reached us in a Syriac, an Armenian, and a Greek version—the last is contained in the* Barlaam and Iosaphat *(eleventh century).*

The discordances between these three versions do not allow us to establish whether the Greek text that we quote from here corresponds to the original:

> And having accomplished His wonderful economy [*telesas tēn thaumastēn autou oikonomian*], by a voluntary choice He tasted death on the cross, fulfilling an august economy [*kat' oikonomian megalēn*]. (*The Apology of Aristides the Philosopher*, p. 276)

2.6. Theophilus of Antioch, who was bishop around AD 170, uses the term *oikonomia* four times, without it ever acquiring a directly theological meaning. The first time concerns the task that God assigned to the emperor:

> [The emperor] is not God but a man appointed by God [*hypo theou tetagmenos*], not to be worshipped but to judge justly. For in a certain way he has been entrusted with a duty from God [*para theou oikonomian pepisteuetai*]. (Theophilus, *Ad Autolycum*, I, 11, p. 15)

In two other cases, the sense is in all likelihood the rhetorical acceptation, "arrangement of the matter," with reference to the narration of the Genesis:

> No man can adequately set forth the whole exegesis and all the ordered matter [*tēn exēgēsin kai tēn oikonomian pasan exeipein*], even were he to have ten thousand mouths and ten thousand tongues. (Ibid., 2, 12, p. 45)

> The narrative that concerns them [Cain and Abel] is wider than the arrangement of my exposition [*tēn oikonomian tēs exēgeseōs*]. (Ibid., 2, 29, p. 73)

The generic sense of "ordered arrangement" is also present at 2, 15 (p. 53):

> The disposition of the stars corresponds to the arrangement [*oikonomian*] and order [*taxin*] of the righteous and godly men who keep the law and the commandments of God. For the stars that are clearly visible and radiant exist in imitation of the prophets [. . .]

2.7. Tatian, who was probably a disciple of Justin in Rome, and, according to Irenaeus, the founder of the intransigent sect of the Encratites, seems to develop a theological meaning of the term *oikonomia* in a passage of the *Address to the Greeks* in connection with the relation between the *logos* and the Father. However, a careful examination of the passage shows that he actually transfers into a theological field technical terms from the rhetorical vocabulary.

> The Logos, not having separated [*chōrēsas*] in vain, becomes the first-begotten work of the Father. Him (the Logos) we know to be the principle [*archēn*] of the world. But He came into being by ordered partition, not by a cut [*gegonen de kata merismon, ou kata apokopēn*]; for what is cut off [*apotmēthen*] is separated from the original substance, but that which comes by participation [*meristhen*], having received the distinction of the *oikonomia* [*oikonomias tēn diairesin*], does not render deficient that from which it is taken. (Tatian, *Address of Tatian to the Greeks*, 5, pp. 9–10)

The terminology being used here is that of Stoic rhetoric: *merismos* "is an ordered disposition [*katataxis*] of a kind according to places" (Diogenes, 7, 62, in *SVF*, III, 215); *diairesis* is, along with *taxis* and *exergasia*, one of the divisions of the *oikonomia* (itself a technical term of Hermagoras's rhetoric, as we have seen in Quintilian). The articulation of divine life is here conceived according to the model of the arrangement of the matter in a discourse. This is confirmed by the subsequent passage.

> I myself, for instance, talk, and you hear; yet, certainly, I who converse do not become destitute of *logos* by the transmission of it, but by the utterance of my voice [*proballomenos de tēn phōnēn*, probably a reference to Justin, *Dialogue with Trypho*, 61], I endeavor to reduce to order the unarranged matter in your minds. (Tatian, *Address of Tatian to the Greeks*, 5, p. 10)

An analogous acceptation can be found in Chapter 21:

> Hector also, and Achilles, and Agamemnon, and all the Greeks in general, and the Barbarians with Helen and Paris, being of the same nature, you will of course say are introduced merely for the sake of the disposition of discourse [*charin oikonomias*], not one of these personages having really existed. (Ibid., p. 28)

In the remaining part of the *Address*, the term *oikonomia* refers to the ordered organization of the human body:

> The constitution [*systasis*] of the body is under one management [*mias estin oikonomias*] [. . .] and the eye is one thing, and another the ear, and another the arrangement of the hair and the distribution of the intestines [*entosthiōn oikonomia*], and the compacting together of the marrow and the bones and the tendons; and though one part differs from another, there is yet all the har-

mony of a concert of music in their arrangement [*kat' oikonomian symphōnias estin harmonia*]. (Ibid., 12, p. 17)

or of matter:

> If anyone is healed by matter, through trusting to it, much more will he be healed by having recourse to the power of God [. . .] Why is he who trusts in the ordered arrangement of matter [*hylēs oikonomiai*] not willing to trust in God? (Ibid., 18, p. 24)

Even if there is not yet here a properly theological use of the term, it is interesting to observe that, in order to describe the relation between the Father and his Logos, Tatian resorts to the metaphorical extension of the term *oikonomia* that already existed in a rhetorical context. Just as the ordered arrangement of the matter of a discourse into different parts does not compromise its unity or diminish its power [*potenza*], so the divine Logos receives "the distinction of the *oikonomia*." The first articulation of the Trinitarian procession takes place by means of an economic-rhetorical paradigm.

א *Modern historians of theology have overlooked the importance of the rhetorical meaning of the term* oikonomia *for the constitution of the Trinitarian paradigm. And yet, the fact that the subject of the passage from Tatian is, indeed, the Logos, the word of God, should have hinted at the presence of a rhetorical image. The use of the rhetorical term* diairesis *in Athenagoras (see below, 2.8) proves the correctness of Schwartz's replacement of* hairesis *(present in the manuscript) with* diairesis *in the above quoted passage from Tatian.*

א *In the* Martyrdom of Polycarp, *we find once again the meaning of economy as internal organization of the body. The torn flesh of the martyr allows us to see "the economy of [his] flesh [. . .] even to the lower veins and arteries"* (The Martyrdom of Polycarp *II, 2, p. 315). Even here, the extension of the denotation of the term to physiology does not substantially alter its semantic nucleus.*

2.8. The use of a rhetorical metaphor to express the Trinitarian articulation of the deity can be recovered in Athenagoras, who is a contemporary of Marcus Aurelius and Commodus, and introduces himself as "Christian philosopher" in the seal of his *Embassy for the Christians.* He uses the term *oikonomia* in the common sense of "praxis ordered for a purpose" with reference to the incarnation ("why, even if a god according to a divine *oikonomia* does take flesh upon himself, is he then at once passion's slave?": *Embassy for the Christians*, 21, 4, p. 55). However, in an important passage, he uses another technical term of the rhetorical vocabulary—*diairesis*, strictly linked to *oikonomia*—precisely in order to reconcile the unity with the trinity:

> Who then would not be amazed hearing that those who recognize a God Father and a God Son and one Holy Spirit, and proclaim their power in unity and in order their disposition [*tēn en tēi taxei diairesin*], are called atheists? (Ibid., 10, 5, p. 40)

In the passage that immediately follows, Athenagoras extends economy to the angelic ranks, a singular intuition that Tertullian will remember:

> Nor does our theology stop there, but we assert a multitude [*plēthos*] of angels and assistants [*leitourgōn*] whom God, maker and artificer [*poietēs kai dēmiurgos*] of the universe, set in their places by means of His Word and appointed severally to be in charge of the elements and the heavens and the universe and all it contains and its good order. (Ibid.)

2.9. Irenaeus's treatise *Against Heresies* presents itself as a refutation of Gnostic systems and expounds Catholic faith through an accurate polemical confrontation with them. The strong presence of the term *oikonomia* in his work, which makes of it, if not a proper technical term, at least a *Lieblingswort* (Richter, p. 116) of his thought, should first of all be read in this polemical context. This means, however, that the term *oikonomia* becomes technical in the language and thought of the Fathers of the Church in relation to the use the Gnostics make of it; it is therefore strange that one might try to define its sense, while completely neglecting (as, for example, Richter does) an examination of these authors.

D'Alès, who catalogued the occurrences of *oikonomia* and its Latin equivalents, *dispositio* and *dispensatio*, in the *Adversus haereses*, lists thirty-three instances in which Irenaeus uses it to refer to a properly Gnostic doctrine—for which the term designates the process internal to the plerome and, in particular, "the fusion of the divine aeons from which the person of the Savior results" (D'Alès, p. 6). According to D'Alès, it is against this Gnostic acceptation that Irenaeus, in his use of the term in the profession of the Catholic faith, "forbids himself any allusion to the internal economy of the Trinity, considering the path taken by Tatian

dangerous" (ibid., p. 8). Markus had already observed that such an opposition is not consistent with fact, since in the quoted Gnostic texts,
oikonomia does not really refer to a process internal to the plerome, but
rather, indeed, to the fusion of the aeons that leads to the constitution of
the historical Jesus (Markus 1958, p. 92). We could also add that, even in
the texts that refer to the Catholic faith (in particular, the passage from
Book 4 (33, 7), which D'Alès quotes as a proof), Irenaeus not only speaks
of the "economies" of the Son (significantly enough, in the plural), but
also of the economies of the Father. More generally, the pedantry with
which modern theologians try, at any cost, to keep the economy of incarnation and the economy of the Trinity separate is meaningless at a
time when the term *oikonomia* generically designates divine activity and
government.

What is at stake in the confrontation between Irenaeus and the people
he calls "the disciples of Ptolemaeus of the school of Valentinus" is not so
much the shift of the notion of economy from a process internal to the
plerome to the incarnation of the Son—or from a supratemporal plan to
a plan in the history of salvation (Bengsch, p. 175)—but rather, more generally, an attempt to remove the term *oikonomia* from its Gnostic context
in order to make it the central strategic apparatus of the rising Trinitarian
paradigm. It is only by closely following Irenaeus's polemical confrontation with the Gnosis that it is possible to define his use of the term.

The word appears for the first time with reference to Christ in the guise
of the adjective *oikonomos* at the end of the long exposition of the Gnostic
doctrines of the plerome and the Savior that opens the treatise (Irenaeus,
Against Heresies, I, 7, 2). Following a pattern that is also present in Clement's *Excerpta*, the Savior is composed of a spiritual element, deriving
from Achamoth, a psychic element, and an "economic element of incredible craftsmanship": the Christ who undergoes the passion is not spiritual,
but psychic and "economic." This exposition is followed by a refutation,
in the course of which Irenaeus uses the term "economy" again, this time
in the context of a profession of the faith that the Church received from
the Apostles:

> [. . .] one God, the Father Almighty, Maker of heaven, and earth, and the
> sea, and all things that are in them; [. . .] one Christ Jesus, the Son of God,
> who became incarnate for our salvation; and [. . .] the Holy Spirit, who pro-
> claimed through the prophets the "economies" of God, and the advents, and

the birth from a virgin, and the passion, and the resurrection from the dead
[. . .] (Irenaeus, *Against Heresies*, I, 10, 1, p. 42)

A few lines later, the polemical confrontation is further specified: the different ways in which this single faith is exposed do not imply that one

> should conceive of some other God besides Him who is the Framer, Maker, and Preserver of this universe (as if He were not sufficient for them), or of another Christ, or another Only-begotten. But the fact referred to simply implies this, that one may [more accurately than another] [. . .] explain the operation and the economy of God [*tēn te pragmateian kai oikonomian tou Theou* (. . .) *ekdiēgeisthai*]. (Ibid., I, 10, 3, pp. 43–44)

What is at stake is clearly maintaining the idea of a divine "economy" that causes the incarnation of the Son—which the Gnosis had derived from Paul—while nonetheless avoiding the Gnostic multiplication of divine figures.

A similar preoccupation is evident in Irenaeus's defense of the flesh and its resurrection against those who "despise the entire economy of God, and disallow the salvation of the flesh" (ibid., V, 2, 2, p. 59). Using a remarkable phrase, Irenaeus writes here that, in denying the flesh, the Gnostics "overturn [. . .] the entire economy of God [*tēn pasan oikonomian* (. . .) *anatrepontes*]" (ibid., V, 13, 2, p. 88). The Gnostic radicalization of the dualism (itself of Pauline origin) between the spirit and the flesh subverts the sense of divine activity, which does not admit such an antithesis. And against the Gnostic multiplication of the divine Aeons founded on the number thirty, "image of the superior economy" (ibid., I, 16, 1, p. 69), Irenaeus writes that, in this way, the Gnostics "pull to pieces [*diasyrontes*] [. . .] the economies of God [. . .] by means of Alpha and Beta, and with the aid of numbers" (ibid., I, 16, 3, p. 71). In the same way, the Gnostic proliferation of the gospels "upsets the economy of God" (ibid., III, 11, 9, p. 295). In other words, for Irenaeus, it is, once again, a matter of subtracting economy from its constitutive nexus with the Gnostic multiplication of the hypostases of the divine figures.

The reversal of the Pauline phrase "economy of the plerome" (*oikonomia tou plerōmatos*, Ephesians 1:10) into "accomplishing, fulfilling the economy" (*ten oiokonomian anaplēroun*) should be read in the same way. According to Markus (Markus 1954, p. 213), who was the first to notice such reversal (for instance, in *Against Heresies*, III, 17, 4, and in IV, 33,

10), Irenaeus transforms in this way what was, for the Gnostics, a cosmic-natural process into a historical dispensation (this is a singular conclusion to be drawn by a scholar who has just objected against D'Alès that, for the Gnostics, the endopleromatic process could not be separated from the historical Jesus). Markus seems to forget that, although the Gnostics had somehow appropriated the syntagma "economy of the plerome," the latter is as such, as we have seen, genuinely Pauline. A reading of the first passage shows beyond doubt that Irenaeus is actually trying to withdraw this unclear Pauline phrase from Gnostic interpretations—which make of the "economy of the plerome" the principle of an infinite procession of hypostases—in order strongly to affirm that the economy of which Paul speaks has been accomplished once and for all by Jesus:

> The *Logos* of the Father came in the fullness of time, having become incarnate in man for the sake of man, and fulfilling all the economy of human nature through our Lord Jesus Christ, who is one and the same, as He himself the Lord doth testify, as the apostles confess, and as the prophets announce. (Ibid., III, 17, 4, p. 336)

It has been observed that Irenaeus's strategy removes the concept of "conversion" (*epistrophē*) from the psychomythological context of the passions of Sophia and Achamoth in order to make it the fulcrum of Catholic orthodoxy (Aubin, pp. 104–110) by means of the formula "to convert to the Church of God" (*epistrephein eis tēn ekklēsian tou Theou*). Similarly, the conflict with the Gnosis does not concern the historical character of the figure of the savior (the Gnostics are the first to establish a parallelism between a cosmic-ontological drama and a historical process) or the opposition between an economy limited to the incarnation and an "economy of the Trinity," which could not have been separated in the theological context of the time. Irenaeus's gesture rather amounts to an operation on themes that are common to heretics and "Catholics" in order to return them to what he believes to be the orthodoxy of the apostolic tradition, and redefine them within a clear profession of faith. This means, however, that—inasmuch as a redefinition is never entirely separable from a reception—at least in the case of the concept of *oikonomia* (a notion that the Gnostics were possibly the first to elaborate strategically), the common theme has become the breach through which Gnostic elements have penetrated the orthodox doctrine.

א *The* Excerpta ex Theodoto, *attributed to Clement of Alexandria, have preserved Gnostic doctrines on "economy," which substantially agree with the information given by Irenaeus. In 33, 3, Wisdom, which is also called "Mother," after having delivered the Christ, gives birth to a "ruler of the economy," a figure* (typos) *of the Father who was abandoned by him and is inferior to him (*The Excerpta ex Theodoto, *p. 65). In 58, 1, the Christ, defined as "the great Champion"* (ho megas Agōnistēs), *descends to earth and assumes both the "pneumatic," or spiritual, element that originates from the mother and the "psychic" element that originates from the economy* (to de ek tēs oikonomias to psychikon: *ibid., p. 78). Here, economy seems to designate a salvific activity, which has a typological precursor in an "archon" and finds its realization in Christ.*

The fact that the term oikonomia *belongs to both the Gnostic and the Catholic vocabularies is proved by the divisive discussions among scholars about which passages from the* Excerpta *quote Clement's opinions and which Theodotus's. Such doubt applies especially to the three passages that contain the term* oikonomia *(5, 4; 11, 4; 27, 6), which the editor attributes to Clement but which could easily be attributed to Theodotus.*

א *From a lexical point of view, it is interesting to note that Irenaeus uses* pragmateia *a number of times as a synonym of* oikonomia. *This confirms that* oikonomia *preserves its generic meaning of "praxis, administrative and executive activity."*

2.10. It is a common belief that, with Hippolytus and Tertullian, the term *oikonomia* ceases to be a mere analogical extension of the domestic vocabulary into a religious field, and becomes a technical notion that designates the Trinitarian articulation of divine life. However, even in this case, there is no strategy aimed at clearly defining a new meaning. Rather, the will to transform the *oikonomia* into a *terminus technicus* reveals itself in an indirect way through two unequivocal devices: the metalinguistic reference to the term, which amounts to putting it in quotation marks (thus, in Tertullian, we can read "this dispensation, or *oikonomia*, as it is called": the term is left untranslated in Greek and is transliterated into Latin characters), and the reversal of the Pauline phrase "the economy of the mystery" into "the mystery of the economy," which gives the term a new poignancy without defining it.

Unlike in Irenaeus, the context of this technicization is that of the earliest disputes surrounding the problematic nucleus that will later become the Trinitarian dogma. Both Hippolytus and Tertullian are engaged in a confrontation with adversaries (Noetus and Praxeas) who adhere to a rigorous form of monotheism—and are defined, for this reason, Monarchians—and see the personal distinction between the Father and the Word as in danger of relapsing into polytheism. The concept of *oikonomia* is the strategic operator that, before the elaboration of an appropriate philosophical vocabulary—which will take place only in the course of the fourth and fifth centuries—allows a temporary reconciliation of the trinity with the divine unity. In other words, the first articulation of the Trinitarian problem takes place in "economical," not metaphysico-theological, terms; for this reason, when the Nicene-Constantinopolitan dogmatics achieves its final form, the *oikonomia* will gradually disappear from the Trinitarian vocabulary, and will be preserved only in that of the history of salvation.

Hippolytus's *Contra Noetum* has been defined as "possibly the most important second-century document on Trinitarian theology" (Scarpat, p. xxii). In opposition to Prestige (Prestige, passim), according to whom, in Hippolytus as ultimately in Tertullian, *oikonomia* designates the internal organization of the deity, and not the Incarnation, Nautin—the scholar responsible for the critical edition of the *Contra Noetum*—seems to exclude a theologico-Trinitarian acceptation in a technical sense and restricts the meaning of the term to "divine plan in virtue of which God has a son who is his incarnated Word" (Nautin, p. 140). In the same sense, although this meaning is not attested to until at least a century later, Markus can write that, for Hippolytus, "economy must be the same as incarnation" (Markus 1958, p. 98). Even more surprisingly, Markus adds soon after that Hippolytus—speaking of Christ as the "mystery of the economy"—would be "closely following the Christian tradition," without realizing that Hippolytus is rather literally reversing the canonical Pauline phrase "economy of the mystery" (ibid., p. 99). In spite of being the first to notice that "Hippolytus has simply reversed Paul's phrase from Ephesians 3:9" (Moingt, p. 905), Moingt is so absorbed in demonstrating his thesis according to which the use of *oikonomia* with reference to the procession of the persons in the deity would be Tertullian's invention, that, clearly contradicting himself, he can write that Hippolytus uses the term "according to the meaning established by Paul and the tradition before him" (ibid., p. 907; in other words, the very meaning whose formulation Hippolytus radically reverses).

Here, the debate is compromised by the presupposition that there are two different and incompatible meanings of the term *oikonomia*, the first referring to the incarnation and the revelation of God in time, and the second concerning the procession of the persons within the deity. We have already shown (and Richter's study confirms this conclusion) that this presupposition is generated by a projection of a later theoretical elaboration onto the semantics of a term that, in the second century, simply meant "divine activity of administration and government." The two alleged meanings are nothing but the two aspects of a single activity of "economic" administration of divine life, which extends from the heavenly house to its earthly manifestation.

Let us now turn to Hippolytus's text. From the beginning, the "economic" paradigm has here a precise strategic function. In order to save the divine unity, Noetus affirms that the son is none other than the Father, and consequently denies the reality of the Christ that has been proclaimed in the Scriptures.

> And just because Noetus has no notion, this does not mean that it is the Scriptures that should be thrown out. After all, would not everyone say that there is a single God?—but we shall not deny the economy [*all' ou tēn oikonomian anairēsei*]. (Hippolytus, *Contra Noetum*, p. 48)

Oikonomia does not have here a special meaning, and can simply be translated as "praxis, divine activity aimed at a purpose." Yet, the absolutization of the term (which usually appeared in syntagmatic nexuses such as "economy of God," "economy of the mystery," "economy of the salvation," etc.) in relation to the apparent opposition between unity and trinity certainly confers on it a particular poignancy. The distinction, in God, between a monadic power (*dynamis*) and a threefold *oikonomia* is accountable to the same strategy:

> So even an unwilling person is obliged to confess the Father as God Almighty, and Christ Jesus, the Son of God, as the God who became man [. . .] and the Holy Spirit; and that these really are three. But if he wants to learn how God is shown to be one, he must know that this [God] has a single Power [*dynamis*]; and that as far as the Power is concerned, God is one; but in terms of the *oikonomia*, the display [of it] is triple. (Ibid., p. 64)

This distinction is important since it possibly lies at the origin of both the distinction between *status* and *gradus* in Tertullian (*Treatise Against Praxeas*, 19, 8), and that between theology and economy, which will become common beginning with Eusebius. The fact that this is not a neat opposition, but a distinction that allows one to reconcile the unity with the trinity, becomes evident once we understand that the terminology is here entirely Stoic. In a famous passage, Chrysippus had distinguished in the soul the unity of the *dynamis* from the multiplicity of the modes of being (or, rather, the modes of "having," the "habits," *pōs echon*):

> The power of the soul is one, in a way that, according to its manner of being or behaving [*pōs echousan*], it either thinks, or gets irate, or desires. (Chrysippus, fragment, 823, *SVF*, II, 823; see Pohlenz, vol. 1, p. 91)

The *oikonomia* corresponds to the Stoic doctrine of the modes of being and is, in this sense, a pragmatics.

The key strategic device by means of which Hippolytus confers a new meaning upon *oikonomia* is, however, the reversal of the Pauline syntagma "economy of the mystery" to form "mystery of the economy." This reversal is carried out in two passages, both of which concern the relation between the Father and his *logos*:

> But in whom is God, except in Christ Jesus, the Father's own *logos* and the mystery of the economy [*tōi mystēriōi tēs oikonomias*]? (Hippolytus, *Contra Noetum*, p. 52)

> So the statement "In thee is God" revealed the mystery of the economy—that once the Word had taken flesh and was among men, the Father was in the Son and the Son in the Father, while the Son was living among men. So this, brethren, is what was being pointed out—that the mystery of the economy really was this very *logos* proceeding from the Holy Spirit and the Virgin, which the Son had brought to completion [*apergasamenos*] for the Father. (Ibid., p. 52)

While, in Paul, the economy was an activity carried out to reveal or accomplish the mystery of God's will or word (Colossians 1:24–25; Ephesians 3:9), *now it is this very activity, personified in the figure of the son-word, that becomes a mystery.* Even here, the key meaning of *oikonomia* remains the same, as is evident in the last sentence of the second passage (the Son brings to completion, realizes an economy for the Father). Yet, the sense of "plan hidden in God," which was a possible, though imprecise paraphrase of the term *mystērion*, tends now to be transferred onto the very term *oikonomia*, giving it a new significance. *There is no economy of the mystery, that is, an activity aimed at fulfilling and revealing the divine mystery; it is the very "pragmateia," the very divine praxis, that is mysterious.*

Thus, in the last passage in which it is used—repeating one of Tatian's stylistic features to the letter—*oikonomia* tends persistently to be identified with the harmonic composition of the threefold divine activity in a single "symphony":

> This economy the blessed John, too, passes onto us through the witness of his Gospel, and he maintains that this Word is God, with the words: "In the beginning was the Word, and the Word was with God, and the Word was God" (John 1:1). But then if the Word, who is God, is with God, someone might well say: "What about this statement that there are two gods?" While I will not say that there are two gods—but rather one—I will say there are two persons; and thirdly the economy, the grace of the Holy Spirit. For though the Father is one, there are two persons—because there is the Son as well: and the third, too,—the Holy Spirit. The Father gives orders, the *logos* performs the work, and is revealed as Son, through whom belief is accorded to the Father. By a harmonious economy [*oikonomiai symphōnias*] the result is a single God. (Hippolytus, *Contra Noetum*, p. 74)

With a further development of its—even rhetoric—meaning of "ordered arrangement," economy is now the activity—as such truly mysterious—that articulates the divine being into a trinity and, at the same time, preserves and "harmonizes" it into a unity.

ℵ *The importance that the reversal of the Pauline syntagma "economy of the mystery" into "mystery of the economy" has in the construction of the economic-Trinitarian paradigm is attested by the persistence with which the latter phrase imposes itself as an interpretative canon of Paul's text. Thus, in Theodoretus of Cyrus (first half of the fifth century), we can still find the claim that Paul, in the* Letter to the Romans, *has revealed "{the mystery of the economy and showed the cause of Incarnation}" (Theodoret of Cyrus,* Commentary on the Letters of Saint Paul, *vol. I, p. 72).*

2.11. It is common to identify Tertullian as the first author for whom *oikonomia* is unequivocally referred to the procession of the persons in the deity; yet, we should not expect to find rigor of argument or terminological precision in his works—Gilson defines his way of reasoning as "antiphilosophical," and even "simplistic."

The *oikonomia*—and its Latin equivalents *dispensatio* and *dispositio*—is rather the apparatus with which, in his polemics against the "restless" and "very perverse" Praxeas, Tertullian tries to come to terms with the impossibility of a philosophical formulation of the Trinitarian articulation. He thus begins to make the term more technical—and, at the same time, render it more mysterious—by leaving it in its Greek form:

> We however as always [. . .] *believe* [. . .] in one only *God,* yet subject to this dispensation (which is our word for "*oikonomia*") [*sub hac tamen dispensatione quam "oikonomian" dicimus*], that the one only God has also a Son, his Word who has proceeded from himself [. . .] (*Tertullian's Treatise Against Praxeas,* 2, 1, p. 131)

Shortly afterward, this technicization is reinforced in order to neutralize the "Monarchian" objection of his rival:

> While Latins are intent on shouting out "monarchy," even Greeks refuse to understand the *oikonomia* [*"oikonomian" intellegere nolunt etiam Graeci*]. (Ibid., 3, 2, p. 133)

But, as in Hippolytus, the crucial gesture is the transformation of the Pauline syntagma "economy of the mystery" into *oikonomias sacramentum,* which confers on economy all the semantic richness and ambiguity of a term that means, at the same time, oath, consecration, and mystery:

> As though the one [God] were not all [these things] in this way also, that they are all of the one, namely, by unity of substance, while nonetheless is guarded the mystery of that economy that disposes the unity into trinity [*oikonomias sacramentum quae unitatem in trinitatem disponit*], setting forth Father and Son and Spirit as three, three however not in condition [*statu*] but in degree [*gradu*], not in substance [*substantia*] but in form [*forma*], not in power [*potestate*] but in species [*specie*] [. . .] (Ibid., 2, 4, p. 132)

Kolping has shown that Tertullian does not invent the new Christian meaning of "sacrament," and that he must have found the term in the Latin translations of the New Testament that circulated at his time (in particular, the translation of the *Letter to the Ephesians*: Kolping, p. 97).

The reversal of the perspicuous Pauline syntagma that results in the obscure formula *oikonomiae sacramentum* and the simultaneous attempt to clarify it through a series of oppositions—condition/degree, substance/form, power/species (just as Hippolytus resorted to the opposition *dynamis/oikonomia*)—is all the more significant. Here, the antiphilosophical Tertullian shrewdly draws on the philosophical vocabulary of his time: the doctrine of a single nature that articulates and distinguishes itself into various degrees is Stoic (see Pohlenz, vol. I, p. 438), just as the idea of a distinction that cannot be divided into "parts" but that articulates forces and powers (Tertullian explicitly refers to this distinction in the *De anima*; see Pohlenz, vol. I, p. 439).

The distinction between substantial separation and economic articulation reappears in the *Treatise Against Praxeas*, 19, 8:

> The Father and the Son are two, and this not as a result of separation of substance, but as a result of an economic disposition [*non ex separatione substantiae sed ex dispositione*], while we declare the Son indivisible and inseparable from the Father, another not in condition but in degree [*nec statu sed gradu alium*]. (*Tertullian's Treatise Against Praxeas*, p. 158)

Here, "substance" should be understood in Marcus Aurelius's sense (12, 30, 1): there is a single common *ousia*, which articulates itself in a singular manner into countless individualities, each with its own specific qualitative determinations. In any case, it is essential that, in Tertullian, the economy is not understood as a substantial heterogeneity, but as the articulation—at every turn administrative-managerial or pragmatic-rhetorical—of a single reality. In other words, the heterogeneity does not concern being and ontology, but rather action and praxis. According to a paradigm that will deeply mark Christian theology, the Trinity is not an articulation of the divine being, but of its praxis.

2.12. The strategic meaning of the paradigm of the *oikonomia* is clarified in the long passage from Chapter 3 in which the economy is referred back to its original meaning as "administration of the house." The definition of the juridical-political concept of "administration" has always been problematic for historians of law and politics; they traced its origin back to the canon law of the twelfth–fourteenth century, when the term *administratio* begins to appear together with *iurisdictio* in the terminology of the canonists (Napoli, pp. 145–146). From this perspective, the passage

from Tertullian is interesting since it contains a sort of theological paradigm of administration, which finds its perfect exemplum in the angelical
hierarchies:

> The simple people, that I say not the thoughtless and ignorant (who are al-
> ways the majority of the faithful), since the Rule of Faith itself [*ipsa regula
> fidei*] brings [us] over from the many gods of the world to the one only true
> God, not understanding that while they must believe in one only [God] yet
> they must believe in him along with his *oikonomia*, shy at the economy. They
> claim that the plurality and ordinance [*dispositio*] of trinity is a division of
> unity—although a unity which derives from itself a trinity is not destroyed
> but administered by it [*non destruatur ab illa sed administretur*]. (*Tertullian's
> Treatise Against Praxeas*, 3, 1, p. 132)

At this stage, what is essentially at stake in Tertullian's argument appears
to be the articulation of economy and monarchy in the figure of the administration:

> But while Latins are intent on shouting out "monarchy," even Greeks refuse
> to understand the economy. But if I have gathered any small knowledge of
> both languages, I know that monarchy indicates neither more nor less than a
> single and sole rule [*singulare et unicum imperium*], yet that monarchy because
> it belongs to one man does not for that reason make a standing rule that he
> whose it is may not have a son or must have made himself his own son or may
> not administer his monarchy by the agency of whom he will. Nay more, I say
> that no kingdom is in such a sense one man's own, in such a sense single, in
> such a sense a monarchy, as not to be administered also through those other
> closely related persons whom it has provided for itself as officers [*officiales*]:
> and if moreover he whose the monarchy is has a son, it is not *ipso facto* di-
> vided, does not cease to be a monarchy, if the son also is assumed as partner
> in it, but it continues to belong in the first instance to him by whom it is
> passed on to the son: and so long as it is his, that continues to be a monarchy
> which is jointly held by two who are so closely united. Therefore if also the
> divine monarchy is administered by the agency of so many legions and hosts
> of angels (as it is written, *Ten thousand times ten thousand stood before him
> and thousand thousands ministered unto him*), yet has not therefore ceased to
> belong to one, so as to cease to be a monarchy because it is administered by
> so many thousand virtues, how should God be thought, in the Son and in the
> Holy Spirit occupying second and third place, while they are to such a degree
> conjoint of the Father's substance, to experience a division and a dispersion
> such as he does not experience in the plurality of all those angels, alien as

they are from the Father's substance? Do you account members, and sons, and instruments and the very forces and the whole riches of a monarchy to be the overthrow of it [*membra et pignora et instrumenta et ipsam vim ac totum censum monarchiae eversionem deputas eius*]? (Ibid., 3, 2–5, p. 133)

Let us dwell on this extraordinary passage. First of all, angelology is here mobilized as a theological paradigm of the administration, thus instituting—with a quasi-Kafkian move—a correspondence between angels and officers. Tertullian recovers this image from Athenagoras (without quoting him, as is usual in the former's case); but while in the Athenian apologist and philosopher, the emphasis was on the order and the economy of the cosmos, Tertullian uses the image to demonstrate the necessary compatibility of monarchy and economy. It is equally essential that, affirming the consubstantiality of monarchy and economy, he evokes an Aristotelian motif, without naming Aristotle. As a matter of fact, the treatise on economy attributed to Aristotle opens with the affirmation of the identity of economy and monarchy: "Politics is a poliarchy, economics is a monarchy [*hē oikonomikē de monarchia*]" (Aristotle, *Oeconomica*, I, 1343a). With one of his characteristic gestures, the antiphilosopher Tertullian borrows from the philosophical tradition the nexus that links economy and monarchy, which he develops and reverses: the divine monarchy now constitutively entails an economy, a governmental apparatus, which articulates and, at the same time, reveals its mystery.

The Aristotelian identification of monarchy and economy, which also penetrated Stoicism, is certainly one of the more or less conscious reasons that pushed the Fathers to elaborate the Trinitarian paradigm in economic, and not political, terms. If Tertullian can write that the economy does not imply in any case an *eversio*, this is also possible because, according to the Aristotelian paradigm, the *oikos* remains in any case an essentially "monarchic" structure. However, it is critical that the Trinitarian articulation is here conceived as serving an activity of domestic government, in which it fully resolves itself without implying a division on the level of being. In this perspective, the Holy Spirit can be defined as "the preacher of one monarchy," and, at the same time, "the interpreter of the economy," that is, "the proclaimer of all truth [. . .] according to the mystery of the doctrine of Christ [*oeconomiae interpretatorem* (. . .) *et deductorem omnis veritatis* (. . .) *secundum Christianum sacramentum*]" (*Tertullian's Treatise Against Praxeas*, 30, 5, p. 179). Once again, the "mystery of the economy," interpreted by those very persons who impersonate it and are its actors, is not an ontological, but a practical mystery.

א *If up to this point we have emphasized above all the Christological aspect of the economy, it is because the problem of the divine nature of the third person of the Trinity and its relations with the other two persons is fully thematized only during the fourth century. From this point of view, it is telling that, having consecrated Orations 29 and 30 to the problem of the Son, Gregory of Nazianzus feels the need to add a further oration in order to deal with this divine figure, which had remained almost unmentioned (agraphon) in the Holy Scriptures, and whose treatment is, therefore, particularly "difficult to handle" (dyscheres) (Gregory of Nazianzus, Select Orations, XXXI, 1–2, p. 318). From the point of view of the Trinitarian oikonomia, the problem of the "procession" (ekporeusis) of the third person from the other two is essential, but we cannot treat it here.*

2.13. It has often been noted that time and history assume a particular and decisive meaning in Christianity. It has been said that Christianity is a "historical religion," not only because it founds itself on a historical person (Jesus) and on events that are claimed to have occurred historically (his passion and resurrection), but also because it gives time a soteriological value and meaning. For this—given that it interprets itself from a historical perspective—Christianity brings with it from the very beginning "a philosophy or, better, a theology of history" (Puech, p. 35).

However, it is equally important to add that the Christian notion of history is born and developed under the sign of the economic paradigm, and remains inseparable from it. An understanding of the Christian theology of history cannot therefore be limited, as it usually is, to a generic evocation of the idea of *oikonomia* as a synonym for the providential unfolding of history according to an eschatological design; such an understanding should rather analyze the concrete modalities in which the "mystery of the economy" has literally shaped and determined from top to bottom the experience of history on which we are still largely dependent.

It is in Origen—an author in whose works the term *oikonomia* finds an extensive development—that this essential nexus between *oikonomia* and history can be grasped in a particularly evident way. When something like a notion of history in the modern sense—that is, a process endowed with a sense, albeit hidden—appears for the first time, it is precisely in the guise of a "mysterious economy," which insists on being interpreted and understood as such. In *De principiis*, referring to the enigmatic episodes in the history of the Jews, such as the incest between Lot and his daughters or Jacob's double marriage, Origen writes:

> That there are certain mysterious economies [*oikonomiai tines* (. . .) *mystikai*] made known through the divine scriptures is believed by all, even by the simplest of those who are adherents of the word; but what these economies are, fair-minded and humble men confess that they do not know. If, for instance, an inquirer were to be in difficulty, about the intercourse of Lot with his daughters, or the two wives of Abraham, or the two sisters married to Jacob, or the two hand-maids who bore children by him, they can say nothing except that these things are mysteries not understood by us. (Origen, *On First Principles*, IV, II, 2, p. 272)

The Christian concept of history results from the strategic conjunction of this doctrine of the "mysterious economies" (elsewhere Origen speaks of "a hidden and apocryphal character of the economy [*tēs de oikonomias autou to lelēthos kai apokryphon*]") with the practice of the interpretation of the Scriptures.

In *De principiis*, Origen also writes that "by means of stories [*dia historias*] of wars and the conquerors and the conquered, certain secret mysteries are revealed to those who are capable of examining these narratives" (ibid., IV, II, 8, pp. 284–285). Thus, the duty of the Christian scholar is that of "interpreting history" [*historian allēgorēsai*]" (Origen, *Philocalie*, I, 29, p. 212), so that the contemplation of the events narrated in the Scriptures is not "a cause of error [*planasthai*] for uneducated souls" (ibid., p. 214).

If, unlike what happens in classical historiography, history has for us a meaning and a direction that the historian needs to be able to grasp; if it is not simply a *series temporum* but something in which a purpose and a destiny are at stake, this is first of all due to the fact that our concept of history has been formed according to the theological paradigm of the revelation of a "mystery" that is, at the same time, an "economy," an organization, and a "dispensation" of divine and human life. Reading history amounts to deciphering a mystery that involves us in an essential way; yet, this mystery does not concern anything like pagan fate or stoic necessity, but rather an "economy" that freely arranges creatures and events, leaving to them their contingent character and even their freedom and their inclinations:

We think that God, parent of all things, in providing [*dispensasse*, which translates in all likelihood a form of the verb *oikonomein*] for the salvation of his entire creation through the unspeakable plan of his *logos* and wisdom, has so ordered everything that each spirit or soul, or whatever else rational existences ought to be called, should not be compelled by force against its free choice to any action except that to which the motions of its own mind lead it [. . .] and at the same time that the motions of their wills should work suitably and usefully together to produce the harmony of a single world. (Origen, *On First Principles*, II, I, 2, p. 77)

Christian history affirms itself against pagan fate as a free praxis; and yet, insofar as it corresponds to and realizes a divine design, this freedom is itself a mystery: the "mystery of freedom," which is nothing but the other face of the "mystery of the economy."

ℵ *The link established by Christian theology between* oikonomia *and history is crucial to an understanding of Western philosophy of history. In particular, it is possible to say that the concept of history in German idealism, from Hegel to Schelling and even up to Feuerbach, is nothing besides an attempt to think the "economic" link between the process of divine revelation and history (adopting Schelling's terms, which we have quoted earlier, the "co-belonging" of theology and* oikonomia*). It is curious that when the Hegelian Left breaks with this theological concept, it can do so only on condition that the economy in a modern sense, which is to say, the historical self-production of man, is placed at the center of the historical process. In this sense, the Hegelian Left replaces divine economy with a purely human economy.*

2.14. The treatment of the concept of *oikonomia* that relates it to the theme of providence will have decisive consequences in medieval and modern culture. Such a treatment is to be attributed to Clement of Alexandria, and possibly amounts to his most original contribution to the elaboration of the theological-economic paradigm. As we have seen, in the *Excerpta ex Theodoto*, Clement repeatedly mentions the term *oikonomia* with regard to the Valentinians; but the term appears very often with the whole range of its possible meanings (approximately sixty times in Stählin's index) even in his masterwork, the *Stromata*. Clement is careful to specify that the *oikonomia* does not merely concern the management of the house, but the soul itself (Clement, *The Stromata*, Book I, Chapter VI, p. 307), and that, in addition to the soul, the entire universe also relies on an "economy" (Book III, Chapter IX, p. 392); there is even an "economy of milk" (*oikonomia tou galaktos*), which makes it flow into the breast of the woman who has given birth (Book II, Chapter XVIII, p. 368). But, above all, there is an "economy of the savior" (this combination is typical of Clement: *hē peri ton sōtēra oikonomia*: Book I, Chapter XI; *oikonomia sōteriou*: Book VI, Chapter VI), which was prophesied and has been accomplished with the passion of the Son. And it is precisely from the standpoint of this "economy of the savior" (of the savior, not of salvation: the original meaning of "activity, task" is still present) that Clement binds economy and providence (*pronoia*) tightly together. In the *Protrepticus*, or *Exhortation to the Heathen*, he had defined the histories of the pagans as "vain fables" (*mythoi kenoi*) (Clement, *Exhortation*, 1, 2, 1, p. 171); now, in a decisive move, he writes that "the philosophy that is in accordance with divine tradition establishes and confirms providence, which, being done away with [*(tēs pronoias) anairetheisēs*], the economy of the Savior appears to be a myth [*mythos* (. . .) *phainetai*]" (*The Stromata*, Book I, Chapter XI, p. 312).

Clement is constantly concerned to prevent the "economy of the savior" appearing as a myth or an allegory. He writes that, if somebody says that the Son of God, the Son of the creator of the world, was incarnated in the flesh and was conceived in the womb of a virgin, if he tells how "his material body was formed," how he suffered the passion and was resurrected, all this "appears indeed a parable to those who know not the truth" (ibid., Book VI, Chapter XV, p. 509). Only the idea of providence can make real and consistent what seems to be a myth or a parable: "There being then a Providence, it were impious to think that the whole of prophecy and the economy in reference to a Savior did not take place in accordance with Providence" (ibid., Book V, Chapter I, p. 445).

If we do not understand the very close connection that links *oikonomia* with providence, it is not possible to measure the novelty of Christian theology with regard to pagan mythology and "theology." Christian theology is not a "story about the gods"; it is *immediately* economy and providence, that is, an activity of self-revelation, government, and care of the world. The deity articulates itself into a trinity, but this is not a "theogony" or a "mythology"; rather, it is an *oikonomia*, that is, at the same time, the articulation and administration of divine life, and the government of creatures.

From this the peculiarity of the Christian concept of providence follows. The notion of *pronoia* had been diffused widely in the pagan world thanks to Stoic philosophy; in writing "the economy of creation is good [*ktistheisa* (. . .) *oikonomia*], and all things are well administered: nothing happens without a cause" (ibid., Book IV, Chapter XXIV, p. 437), Clement was repeating ideas that were current in the Alexandrian culture of his time. Yet, insofar as the Stoic and Judaic theme of *pronoia* is linked to the economy of divine life, providence acquires a personal and voluntary character. In opposition to the Stoics and Alexander of Aphrodisias who had claimed that "the essence of the gods lies in providence, just as that of fire lies in heat," Clement eliminates any naturalistic and involuntary character from providence:

> God [is not] involuntarily good, as the fire is warming; but in Him the imparting of good things is voluntary [. . .] God does not do good by necessity, but from His free choice. (Ibid., Book VII, Chapter VII, p. 534)

The debates surrounding the free or fatal, mediate or immediate, general or particular character of providence that, as we shall see, will divide medieval theologians and philosophers from the thirteenth to the seventeenth century find here their archetype.

Connecting economy with providence, not only does Clement embed the temporal economy of salvation in eternity (in "eternal facts and reasons": *The Stromata*, Book VI, Chapter XV, p. 508)—as has been observed (Torrance, p. 227)—but also he initiates the process that will lead to the progressive constitution of the duality of theology and economy, the nature of God and his historical action. Providence means that this fracture, which in Christian theology corresponds to the Gnostic dualism between an idle God and an active demiurge, is—or is claimed to be—actually only apparent. The economic-administrative and the providential paradigms here manifest their fundamental co-belonging.

א *It is precisely this strategic conjunction of economy and providence that clearly shows how, in Clement, the term* oikonomia *still cannot mean, following the common translation that would make the conjunction tautological, "divine plan." It is only from the moment at which Hippolytus and Tertullian reverse the Pauline expression "economy of the mystery" and Clement joins* oikonomia *and* pronoia *together that the meanings of the two terms will start to become indistinguishable.*

A century later, in John Chrysostom, the link between economy and provi-

*dence is solidly established, but this does not diminish its "mysterious" charac-
ter. The economy is now defined as "ineffable," and its link with the "abyss" of
providence is an object of "amazement":*

> Having seen the opening up of an immense sea and, in this part and in this
> point, having wished to probe the abyss of its providence, feeling dizzy before
> the inexpressible nature of this economy and being amazed before what is
> ineffable [. . .] (John Chrysostom, *Sur la providence de dieu*, p. 62)

2.15. The meaning of "exception" acquired by the term *oikonomia* in
the sixth or seventh century, especially in the field of the canon law of the
Byzantine Church, is of particular interest for its semantic history. Here,
the theological meaning of mysterious divine praxis undertaken for the
salvation of humankind coalesces with the concepts of *aequitas* and *epie-
ikeia* originating from Roman law, and comes to signify the dispensation
[*dispensa*] that relieves one from a too rigid application of the canons. In
Photius, the difference and, at the same time, the contiguity of the two
meanings is evident:

> *Oikonomia* means precisely the extraordinary and incomprehensible incarna-
> tion of the *Logos*; in the second place, it means the occasional restriction or
> the suspension of the efficacy of the rigor of the laws and the introduction of
> extenuating circumstances, which "economizes" [*dioikonomountos*] the com-
> mand of law in view of the weakness of those who must receive it. (Photius,
> pp. 13–14)

In this direction, just as an opposition between theology and economy had emerged in theology, so an opposition between "canon" and
"economy" is produced in law, and the exception is defined as a decision that does not apply the law strictly, but "makes use of the economy"
(*ou kanonikos* (. . .) *all' oikonomiai chresamenoi*: Richter, p. 582). In this
sense, in 692, the term enters the legislation of the Church and, with
Leon VI (886–912), the imperial legislation.

The fact that a word designating the salvific activity of the government
of the world acquires the meaning of "exception" shows how complex
the relationships between *oikonomia* and law are. However, even in this
case, the two senses of the term are, in spite of their apparent distance,
perfectly consistent—exactly the same occurs in the Latin Church with
the two meanings of the term *dispensatio*, which initially translates *oikonomia* and later progressively acquires the sense of "dispensation" [*dispensa*].

The paradigm of government and of the state of exception coincide in the idea of an *oikonomia*, an administrative praxis that governs the course of things, adapting at each turn, in its salvific intent, to the nature of the concrete situation against which it has to measure itself.

‫ *The origin of the evolution that leads the term* oikonomia *to assume the meaning of "exception" can be grasped in a letter that the Cappadocian theologian Basil wrote to Amphilochius. Asked about the question of the value of the baptism administered by schismatics, Basil answers that, contrary to the rule that would have wanted it to be invalid, it was initially accepted as valid "for the sake of the economy of the majority"* (oikonomias heneka tōn pollōn: *Basil,* Letter CLXXXVIII, *I, in* Letters and Select Works, *p. 224).*

Threshold

It is now possible to grasp more precisely the decisive meaning of the reversal of the Pauline expression "economy of the mystery" into "mystery of the economy." What is mysterious is not, as with Paul, the divine plan of redemption, a plan that requires an activity of realization and revelation—indeed, an *oikonomia*—that is as such perspicuous. Now, it is the economy itself that is mysterious, the very praxis by means of which God arranges the divine life, articulating it into a Trinity, and the world of creatures, conferring a hidden meaning upon every event. But this hidden sense, following the model of the typological interpretation, is not only an allegoresis and prophecy of other salvific events, which thus arrange themselves to create a history; it rather coincides with the "mysterious economy," with the very dispensation of divine life and its providential government of the world. The mystery of the deity and the mystery of government, the Trinitarian articulation of the divine life and the history and salvation of humanity are, at the same time, divided and inseparable.

In other words, a game that is in all senses decisive is being played out on the field of the *oikonomia*, one in which the very concept of the divine and its relations with all creation that is gradually emerging toward the end of the ancient world is in question. Between the inarticulate unitarism of the Monarchians and Judaism and the Gnostic proliferation of divine hypostases, between the noninvolvement in the world of the Gnostic and Epicurean God and the Stoic idea of a *deus actuosus* that provides for the world, the *oikonomia* makes possible a reconciliation in which a transcendent God, who is both one and triune at the same time, can—while remaining transcendent—take charge of the world and found an immanent praxis of government whose supermundane mystery coincides with the history of humanity.

It is only if all the poignancy of the economic paradigm is restored that it is possible to overcome the exegetic contradictions and the divisions that have prevented modern scholars and theologians from placing it in its real problematic context. As we have seen, at the basis of the polemics that has constantly divided interpreters into two factions lies the alleged caesura between two senses of the term *oikonomia* that are clearly different, the first referring to the articulation of the single divine substance into three persons, the second concerning the historical dispensation of salvation (see Prestige, p. 111; see also Markus in Richter, p. 79). Thus, according to Verhoeven, Evans, and Markus, the economy in Tertullian does not entail anything temporal and refers only to the "internal unfolding of the divine substance in a trinity of persons" (Verhoeven, p. 110). On the other hand, according to Moingt, the economy does not "designate a relation in being" (Moingt, p. 922), but only the historical expression of the deity through the plan of salvation. In other words, the polemics between interpreters relies on the false presupposition that the term *oikonomia* has, like Abel's *Urworte*, two contradictory meanings, and the Fathers who use it would oscillate between these meanings in a more or less conscious way. A more careful analysis shows that we are not dealing with two meanings of the same term, but with the attempt to articulate in a single semantic sphere—that of the term *oikonomia*—a series of levels whose reconciliation appeared problematic: noninvolvement in the world and government of the world; unity in being and plurality of actions; ontology and history.

Not only do the two alleged meanings of the term—that which refers to the internal organization of the divine life, and that which concerns the history of salvation—not contradict themselves, but they are correlated and become fully intelligible only in their functional relation. That is to say, they constitute the two sides of a single divine *oikonomia*, in which ontology and pragmatics, Trinitarian articulation and government of the world refer back to each other for the solution of their aporias. It is in any case essential that the first articulation of what will become the Trinitarian dogma does not initially present itself in ontologico-metaphysical terms, but as an "economic" apparatus and an activity of government, both domestic and mundane, of the divine monarchy ("unitas ex semetipsa derivans trinitatem non destruatur ab illa sed administratur": *Tertullian's Treatise Against Praxeas*, 3, 1). It is only at a later stage, when problems will appear, rightly or wrongly, to have been solved by the post-Nicene dogmatics, that theology and economy will divide and the term will no longer be referred to the organization of the divine life in order to be more specifically attributed to the meaning of history of salvation; but, even at this point, they will not divide completely and will continue to interact as a functional unity.

§ 3 Being and Acting

3.1. The preoccupation that had led the Fathers who first elaborated the doctrine of the *oikonomia* was, by all accounts, to avoid a fracture of monotheism that would have reintroduced a plurality of divine figures, and polytheism with them. It is in order to elude this extreme consequence of the Trinitarian thesis that Hippolytus is careful to repeat that God is one according to the *dynamis* (that is, in the Stoic terminology he uses, according to the *ousia*) and triple only according to the economy. For the same reason, Tertullian firmly objects to Praxeas that the mere "disposition" of the economy does not at all mean the separation of the substance. The divine being is not split, since the triplicity of which the Fathers speak is located on the level of the *oikonomia*, not ontology.

The caesura that had to be averted at all costs on the level of being reemerges, however, as a fracture between God and his action, between ontology and praxis. Indeed, distinguishing the substance or the divine nature from its economy amounts to instituting within God a separation between being and acting, substance and praxis. This is the secret dualism that the doctrine of the *oikonomia* has introduced into Christianity, something like an original Gnostic germ, which does not concern the caesura between two divine figures, but rather that between God and his government of the world.

Let us consider the theology that Aristotle develops at the end of Book L of *Metaphysics*. It would simply be unthinkable to distinguish between being and praxis in the God described here. If the Aristotelian God, as an unmoved mover, moves the celestial spheres, this follows from his nature, and there is no need to presuppose the existence of a special will or a specific activity aimed at the care of the self and of the world. The classical cosmos—its "fate"—is based on the perfect unity of being and praxis.

The doctrine of the *oikonomia* radically revokes this unity. The economy through which God governs the world is, as a matter of fact, entirely different from his being, and cannot be inferred from it. It is possible to analyze the notion of God on the ontological level, listing his attributes or negating, one by one—as in apophatic theology—all his predicates to reach the idea of a pure being whose essence coincides with existence. But this will not rigorously say anything about his relation to the world or the way in which he has decided to govern the course of human history. As Pascal will lucidly realize with regard to profane government many centuries later, the economy has no foundation in ontology and the only way to found it is to hide its origin (Pascal 1962, p. 51). For this, God's free decision to govern the world is now as mysterious as his nature, if not more; the real mystery, which "has been hidden for centuries in God" and which has been revealed to men in Christ, is not that of his being, but that of his salvific praxis: precisely the "mystery of the *oikonomia*," following the decisive strategic reversal of the Pauline syntagma. The mystery that, from this moment on, will not cease to startle theologians and philosophers, and to arouse their attention, is not of an ontological, but of a practical nature.

The economic and ontological paradigms are completely different in their theological genesis: the doctrine of providence and moral reflection will only slowly try to construct a bridge between them, without ever fully succeeding. The fact that Trinitarianism and Christology, before assuming a dogmatic-speculative form, were conceived in "economic" terms is something that will stubbornly continue to mark their subsequent development. Ethics in a modern sense, with its court of insoluble aporias, is born, in this sense, from the fracture between being and praxis that is produced at the end of the ancient world and has its eminent place in Christian theology.

If the notion of free will, which is, all things considered, marginal in classical thought, becomes the central category first of Christian theology and then of the ethics and ontology of modernity, this happens because these find in the above-mentioned fracture their original site and will have to confront it right to the end. If the order of the ancient cosmos "does not amount to the will of gods, but rather to their own nature, which is emotionless and inexorable, which is the bearer of every good and every

evil, inaccessible to prayer [. . .] and dispenses very little mercy" (Santillana, p. 11), the idea of the will of God, which, on the other hand, freely
and shrewdly decides his actions and is even stronger than his omnipotence, is the irrefutable proof of the collapse of the ancient fate and, at the
same time, the desperate attempt to provide a foundation for the anarchic sphere of divine praxis. Desperate, since this will can only entail the
groundlessness of the praxis, that is, the fact that there is no foundation
of acting in being.

ℵ *In Gnosis, the opposition between a god who is foreign to the world and
a demiurge who governs it is more essential than that between a good and an
evil god. Both Irenaeus and Tertullian clearly grasp this "idle" and "Epicurean" character of Marcion's and Cerdo's good God, to whom they oppose a
God who is, at the same time, good and active in all creation. Irenaeus writes
that "they found out the god of Epicurus, who does nothing either for himself
or others" (Irenaeus,* Against Heresies, *3, 24, 2, p. 371). And according to
Tertullian, Marcion would have attributed "the name of Christ [to] a god out
of the school of Epicurus" (Tertullian,* Adversus Marcionem, *I, 25, 3, p. 71).*

The attempt to reconcile the idle god who is foreign to the world with the
actuosus *god who creates and governs it is certainly one of the crucial stakes of
the Trinitarian economy: both the very concept of* oikonomia *and the aporias
that make its definition so arduous depend on it.*

3.2. The problem that makes the image of the world in the classical
tradition explode when it collides with the Christian concept of the world
is that of creation. What is incompatible with the classical concept is here
not so much the idea of a divine operation, but rather the fact that this
praxis does not necessarily depend on being, and nor is it founded on it,
but is the result of a free and gratuitous act of the will. If it is true that
the idea of a divine apraxia finds a solid basis in the Aristotelian tradition,
classical thought, especially starting with the Stoics, does not shrink from
conceiving a divine action, and, in this regard, the Apologists do not fail
to evoke the Platonic demiurge. On the other hand, what is new is the
division between being and the will, nature and action, introduced by
Christian theology. The same authors who elaborate the economic paradigm strongly emphasize the heterogeneity of nature and will in God.
The passage from Origen in which the will marks a real caesura in God
and the creation is, in this sense, exemplary:

{All that exists in heaven and on earth, visible or invisible, insofar as it refers to the nature of God, it is not [*quantum ad naturam Dei pertinet, non sunt*]; insofar as it refers to the will of the creator, it is that which the will of the one who created wanted it to be [*quantum ad voluntatem creatoris, sunt hoc, quod ea esse voluit ille qui fecit*]}. (Origen, *Homily on 1 Kings* 28, I, 11. See also Benz, pp. 330–331)

The pseudo-Justin insists that essence (*ousia*) and will (*boulē*) must be considered to be separate in God. If being and the will were the same thing in God, given that he wants many things, he would be one thing at one time, and another thing at another time, which is impossible. And if he produced by means of his being, given that his being is necessary, he would be obliged to do what he does, and his creation would not be free (Justin, *Opera Iustini subditicia*, pp. 286–291).

As has been suggested (Coccia, p. 46), the very motif of creation ex nihilo emphasizes the autonomy and freedom of divine praxis. God has not created the world due to a necessity of his nature or his being, but because he wanted it. To the question "why did God make heaven and earth?" Augustine answers: "quia voluit," "because he wished to" (Augustine, *A Refutation of the Manichees*, I, 2, 4). Centuries later, in the heyday of Scholasticism, Thomas Aquinas clearly restates *contra Gentiles* the impossibility of founding creation in being: "God acts, not *per necessitatem naturae*, but *per arbitrium voluntatis*" (*Contra Gentiles*, Book 2, Chapter 23, n. 1). In other words, the will is the apparatus needed to join together being and action, which were separated in God. The primacy of the will, which, according to Heidegger, rules over the history of Western metaphysics and reaches its completion with Schelling and Nietzsche, has its roots in the fracture between being and acting in God and is, therefore, from the beginning in agreement with the theological *oikonomia*.

א *The reconstruction of the theological apparatus founded on the notion of the will is at the center of Benz's book* Marius Victorinus und die Entwicklung der abendländischen Willenmetaphysik, *which should be regarded as the starting point for any genealogical investigation into the primacy of the will in modern philosophy. Benz shows how both Neoplatonic motifs (the concept of the will in Plotinus as identical with power [*potenza*] and as a good that "wills itself") and Gnostic themes (the will in Valentinus and in Marcus as* autobouletos boulē, *a will that wills itself) come together in the construction of a "metaphysics of the will" in Western philosophy. Through Victorinus,*

*these Neoplatonic and late ancient motifs enter Augustine's thought and deter-
mine his concept of the Trinity.*

*When Thomas Aquinas identifies in God essence and will ("Est igitur vol-
untas Dei ipsa eius essentia": Contra Gentiles, Book 1, Chapter 73, n. 2), he
is actually only radicalizing this primacy of the will. Given that what God's
will wants is his very essence ("principale divinae voluntatis volitum est eius
essentia": ibid., Book 1, Chapter 74, n. 1), this implies that God's will always
wants itself; it is always will to will.*

*In the wake of his teacher Ignace Meyerson, Jean Pierre Vernant restated
in an important study (Vernant, passim) that the modern notion of the will
is a concept that is essentially alien to the tradition of Greek thought, and
was formed through a slow process that coincides with the one that led to the
creation of the Ego.*

3.3. It is only from the standpoint of this fracture between being and
praxis that the sense of the controversy over Arianism, which deeply divided the Church between the fourth and the sixth centuries, becomes
fully intelligible. The dispute often seems to revolve around differences
that are so subtle and minimal that it is not easy for modern readers to
appreciate what was really at stake in a conflict whose fierceness involved,
together with the emperor, almost the entirety of Eastern Christianity.
It is well known that the problem concerned the *archē* of the Son; but
archē here does not have a merely chronological meaning; it does not
simply stand for a "beginning." As a matter of fact, both Arius and his
adversaries agree in saying that the Son was generated by the Father, and
that this generation took place "before eternal times" (*pro chronōn aiōniōn*
in Arius, *Letter to Alexander*, in Athanasius, p. 458; *pro pantōn tōn aiōnōn*
in Eusebius of Caesarea, *Letter of Eusebius*, in Athanasius, p. 75). Arius
is even careful to specify that the Son was generated *achronos*, outside
of temporality. In other words, what is in question here is not really a
chronological precedence (time does not exist yet), or just a problem of
rank (many anti-Arians share the opinion that the Father is "greater" than
the Son); it is rather a matter of deciding whether the Son—which is to
say, the word and praxis of God—is founded in the Father or whether he
is, like him, without principle, *anarchos*, that is, ungrounded.

A textual analysis of Arius's letters and the writings of his adversaries
shows, indeed, that the decisive term in the controversy is precisely *anarchos* (without *archē*, in the double sense that the term has in Greek: foun-

dation and principle). In his *Letter to Alexander* (p. 458), Arius writes that
"We acknowledge One God, alone Ingenerate, alone Everlasting, alone
anarchos." The Son, who was generated by the father before and outside
of time, nevertheless has his *archē*, his principle-foundation, in the father,
and receives his being from him:

> Thus there are Three Hypostases. And God, being the cause of all things, is
> anarchic and altogether Sole [*anarchos monōtatos*], but the Son being begot-
> ten apart from time by the Father, and being created [but Arius had specified
> shortly before, "not like all other creatures"] and founded [*themeliōtheis*, from
> *themelios*, which refers to the foundations also in an architectural sense] before
> ages [. . .] who derived only being from the Father. (Ibid.)

It is in the same sense that Eunomius affirms that only God the Father is
"beginningless, everlasting, unending [*anarchōs, aidiōs, ateleutētōs*]" (*Expositio Fidei*, 2, p. 151); the Son is, rather, "existing 'in the beginning,' so
not without beginning [*en archēi onta, ouk' anarchon*]" (ibid., 3, p. 153).

Against this thesis, which gives the Logos a solid foundation in the
Father, the bishops assembled at Serdica by Emperor Constantius in 343
clearly affirm that the disagreement does not revolve around the generated or ungenerated character of the Son ("none of us denies that the Son
is generated, but generated before all things"), but only around his *archē*:
"He could not have existed absolutely [*pantote*], if he had had an *archē*,
since the *logos* that exists absolutely does not have an *archē*" (ibid., p. 134).
The Son "reigns together with the Father absolutely, anarchically, and infinitely [*pantote, anarchōs kai ateleutētōs*]" (ibid., p. 136).

The Nicene thesis, which was ultimately victorious, here shows its
coherence with the doctrine of the *oikonomia*. Just as the latter is not
founded on the nature and being of God, but in itself constitutes a "mystery," so the Son—that is, the one who has assumed the economy of salvation—is unfounded in the Father, and is, like him, *anarchos*, without
foundation or principle. *Oikonomia* and Christology are in agreement
and inseparable, not only historically, but also genetically: as was the case
with praxis in the economy, so in Christology the *Logos*, the word of God,
is eradicated from being and made anarchic (from this derive the constant reservations of many supporters of the anti-Arian orthodoxy against
the term *homousios*, imposed by Constantine). If we do not understand
this original "anarchic" vocation of Christology, it is not even possible to
understand the subsequent historical development of Christian theology,

with its latent atheological tendency, or the history of Western philosophy, with its ethical caesura between ontology and praxis. The fact that Christ is "anarchic" means that, in the last instance, language and praxis do not have a foundation in being. The "gigantomachy" around being is also, first and foremost, a conflict between being and acting, ontology and economy, between a being that is in itself unable to act and an action without being: what is at stake between these two is the idea of freedom.

א *The attempt to think in God the problem of a foundation that is absolutely unfounded is evident in a passage from Gregory of Nazianzus.*

The *anarchon* [the unfounded], the *archē* and that which is with the *archē* are one God. For the nature of that which is anarchical does not consist in being anarchical, but being unbegotten. For the nature of anything lies, not in what it is not but in what it is. It is the positing [*thesis*] of what is, not the withdrawal [*anairesis*] of what is not. And the *archē* is not, because it is an *archē*, separated from that which is anarchical: the *archē* is its nature, just as the anarchical is not the nature of this. For these things regard nature, but are not nature itself. That again which is with what is anarchical, and with the *archē*, is not anything else than what they are. Now, the name of that which is anarchical is Father, and the name of the *archē* is Son, and of that which is with the *archē*, the Holy Spirit. (Gregory of Nazianzus, *Select Orations*, XLII, XV, p. 390)

The Hegelian dialectic finds in this passage its theological paradigm: in order to obtain the Hegelian position of foundation it is sufficient to place at the center of this triadic movement the force of the negative ("that which is not").

The paradox of the Trinitarian economy, which needs to hold together what it divided, clearly appears in another Cappadocian theologian, Gregory of Nyssa. In a passage from his Great Catechism *(or* Catechetical Oration*), he affirms that both Greeks and Jews can accept that there is one* logos *and one* pneuma *in God; and yet, what "both parties would perhaps equally reject, as being incredible and unfitting to be told of God" is precisely "the economy according to man of the Word of God [*tēn de kata anthrōpon oikonomian tou theou logou]."* Soon after Gregory adds that the latter indeed implies that what is in question is not simply a faculty (*exis*), like the word or the knowledge of God, but "a power essentially and substantially existing [*kat' ousian (. . .) yphestōsa dynamis]" (Gregory of Nyssa,* Great Catechism, *p. 478). In other words, the function of the Trinitarian economy is to hypostasize, to give real existence to the* logos *and to the praxis of God, and, at the same* *time, to affirm that this hypostatization does not divide the unity, but "econo-mizes" it (the Cappadocians are the first to use strategically the Neoplatonic term* hypostasis *in this sense, in this case in its verbal form* hyphistamai*).*

In Marcellus of Ancyra, an author of the fourth century whose "economic theology" in particular has caught the attention of modern scholars, we can clearly see how the relation between economy and substance is conceived as an opposition between operation (energeia*) and nature* (physis*). If the divine nature remains monadic and undivided, this is because the* logos *separates only in the operation* (energeia monē*). For this, the economy according to the flesh (or second economy, as Marcellus has it) is, so to speak, temporary: it will finish with the parousia, when Christ (following 1 Corinthians 15:25) will have subjected his enemies and stepped on them. In the same sense, Marcellus can thus write that the* logos *has become, through the incarnation, the son of Adam* kat'oikonomian, *while we are his sons* kata physin *(Seibt, p. 316).*

ℵ *The theological division between being and praxis is still at the center of the disputes that, in the Byzantine theology of the fourteenth century, opposed Greg-ory Palamas to Barlaam and Prochorus. The profession of faith of the Athonites thus begins with a neat opposition between God's being* (ousia*) and his opera-tion* (energeia*): "We anathematize those who say that the divine essence and the operation are indistinct and one and the same. Furthermore, I believe that this operation and the essence of God are uncreated [*aktiston*]" (Rigo, p. 144).*

3.4. The fracture between being and praxis is marked in the language of the Fathers by the terminological opposition between theology and *oikonomia*. This opposition, which is not yet present as such in Hippoly-tus, Tertullian, and Clement of Alexandria, is, however, as we have seen, foreshadowed in them by the distinction between *dynamis* and *oikonomia* (thus, in Clement's *Excerpta* each angel "has his own *dynamis* and his own *oikonomia*": I, 11, 4, p. 51). In Eusebius of Caesarea, the antithesis is already fully articulated, even though it is not a real opposition, so much so that he can open his *Ecclesiastical History* precisely with the enunciation of the two *topoi* from which a single discourse follows:

And my *logos* will begin, as I said, with the economy and theology of Christ, which are higher and greater than those based on man. For he who would commit to writing the history that contains the Church's narrative, must be-gin from the first with the beginning of the *oikonomia* of Christ Himself (since we have been deemed worthy to derive even our name from Him), an *oikonomia* more divine than most men imagine. (Eusebius, *Ecclesiastical History*, I, 1, 7–8, p. 4)

The terminological distinction corresponds, in Eusebius, to the distinction between the divinity and the humanity of Christ, which he compares with the difference between head (*kephalē*) and feet:

> Now since in Him there are two modes of being, and the one may be likened to the head of the body, in that He is conceived of as God, and the other may be compared to the feet, in that for our salvation He assumed human nature of like passions with us. (Ibid., I, 2, 1, p. 4)

Starting with the Cappadocians, in particular with Gregory of Nazianzus, the opposition theology/*oikonomia* becomes technical: not only does it indicate two different fields (the nature and essence of God, on the one hand, his salvific action, on the other; being and praxis), but also two different discourses and rationalities, each having its own conceptuality and its specific characters. In other words, there are, with regard to Christ, two *logoi*, one that concerns his divinity, and one that relates to the economy of the incarnation and salvation. Each discourse, each rationality, has its own terminology, which should not be confused with the other if we want to interpret it correctly:

> To give you the explanation in one sentence, you are to apply lofty names to the divinity, and to that nature in Him which is superior to passions and incorporeal; but all humble names to the composite condition of Him who for your sakes emptied Himself and was Incarnate—and, avoiding to say worse things, was made Man—and afterward was also exalted, so that, abandoning what is carnal and earthly in your doctrines, you may learn to ascend with the divinity, and you will not remain permanently among visible things, but will rise up with Him into the world of thought, and come to know which *logos* is of nature, and which of the economy. (Gregory of Nazianzus, *Select Orations*, XXIX, XVII, pp. 307–308)

The distinction between these two rationalities is restated in the oration consecrated to the feast of nativity, in which, having evoked the infinity and unknowability of God, Gregory writes:

> This, however, is all I must now say about God; for the present is not a suitable time, as my present subject is not theology, but economy. (Ibid., XXXVIII, VIII, p. 347)

Approximately fifty years later, Theodoret of Cyrus shows himself to be perfectly aware of the distinction between these two rationalities and, at the same time, of their reciprocal articulation. He writes that "it is therefore necessary for us to realize that some names are appropriate to theology, some to the economy" (*Commentary on the Letters of Saint Paul*, vol. 2, *The Letters to the Hebrews*, 4, 14; see also Gass, p. 490). If we confuse the two *logoi*, even the integrity of the economy of the incarnation is threatened, and we run the risk of falling into the Monophysite heresy. If, on the one hand, any undue transfer of the categories of one rationality to the other must be avoided (John of Damascus will write that "it is not right to transfer to the economy what has reference to matters of theology": *Exposition of the Orthodox Faith*, III, XV, p. 62), the two rationalities remain nevertheless linked, and the clear distinction between the discourses should not be turned into a substantial caesura. The care with which the Fathers avoid both confusing and separating the two *logoi* shows that they are aware of the risks implicit in their heterogeneity. Arguing against a hypothetical representative of Monophysitism in the *Eranistēs*, Theodoret thus affirms that the Fathers' "object was to give us at one and the same time instruction on the theology and the economy, lest there should be supposed to be any distinction between the Person of the Godhead and the Person of the Manhood" (Theodoret, *Dialogues*, p. 233).

The Patristic distinction between theology and economy is so tenacious that it can be recovered in modern theologians in the guise of the opposition between immanent and economic Trinity. The first refers to God as he is in himself and is for this reason also called the "Trinity of substance"; the second refers to God in his salvific action, by means of which he reveals himself to mankind (for this reason, it is also called the "Trinity of revelation"). The articulation between these two Trinities, different and inseparable at the same time, is the aporetic task that the Trinitarian *oikonomia* bequeaths to Christian theology—in particular to the doctrine of the providential government of the world—which therefore presents itself as a bipolar machine, whose unity always runs the risk of collapsing and must be acquired again at each turn.

3.5. The radical gap, and at the same time the necessary solidarity between theology and economy, possibly shows itself most clearly in the controversies about monotheletism that divide the Fathers in the seventh century. We do have a text, Maximus the Confessor's *Dispute with Pyr-*

rhus, in which the strategic sense of this difficult articulation becomes fully comprehensible. According to the Monotheletists, whose manifesto is Heraclius's *Ekthesis* (638) and who are represented in the dialogue by Pyrrhus, there are two natures in Christ, but only one will (*thelēsis*) and one activity (*energeia*), "which performs both divine and human works" (Simonetti, p. 516). Dyophysitism, brought to the extreme, may end up introducing a division even in the economy—that is, in the divine praxis—identifying in Christ "two wills that oppose one another, almost as if God's *logos* intends to realize the salvific passion while what is human in him obstructs and contrasts with his will" (ibid., p. 518). Monotheletists wish to avoid this division. Responding to Maximus, who affirms that two wills and two different operations must necessarily correspond to the two natures of Christ, Pyrrhus thus claims that "that has been said by the Fathers with regard to theology, and not economy. It is not worthy of a thought that loves truth to transfer to economy that which has been affirmed with regard to theology, putting together such an absurdity" (*PG*, 91, 348).

Maximus's answer is categorical and shows that the articulation of the two discourses coincides with a problem that is decisive in all senses. He writes that if what the Fathers say about theology were not also valid for the economy, "then, after the incarnation, the Son is not theologized together [*syntheologeitai*] with the Father. And if he is not, then he cannot be enumerated together with him in the invocation of baptism, and faith and predication will be vain" (ibid.). In another work, emphasizing the inseparability of theology and economy, Maximus can thus write: "The incarnated *logos* of God [that is, the representative of economy] teaches theology" (*PG*, 90, 876).

It is not surprising that a radical "economism"—which, distinguishing two wills in the Son, threatens the very identity of the Christological subject—needs to affirm the unity of theology and economy, while a "theologism"—which attempts to protect at all costs that unity—does not hesitate to strongly oppose the two discourses. The difference between the two rationalities continuously intersects with the level of theological disputes and, just as Trinitarian and Christological dogmatics were formed together and cannot be divided in any way, so theology and economy cannot be separated. Just as the two natures coexist in Christ, following a stereotypical formulation, "without division or confusion" (*adiairetos kai asynchytos*), so the two discourses must coincide without confusing themselves, and differentiate themselves without dividing. What is at stake in their relation is not only the caesura between the humanity and the divinity of the Son, but, more generally, that between being and praxis. Economic and theological rationality must operate, as it were, "in divergent agreement," so that the economy of the son is not negated and a substantial division is not introduced in God.

However, the economic rationality, by means of which Christology came to know its first, uncertain formulation, will not cease to cast its shadow on theology. When the vocabulary of the *homoousia* and of the *homoiousia*, of the hypostasis and of nature, have almost completely covered over the first formulation of the Trinity, the economic rationality—with its pragmatic-managerial, and not ontologic-epistemic, paradigm—will continue to operate underground as a force that tends to undermine and break the unity of ontology and praxis, divinity and humanity.

‏ *The fracture between being and praxis, and the anarchic character of the divine* oikonomia *constitute the logical place in which the fundamental nexus that, in our culture, unites government and anarchy becomes comprehensible. Not only is something like a providential government of the world possible just because praxis does not have any foundation in being, but also this government—which, as we shall see, has its paradigm in the Son and his* oikonomia—*is itself intimately anarchic. Anarchy is what government must presuppose and assume as the origin from which it derives and, at the same time, as the destination toward which it is traveling. (Benjamin was in this sense right when he wrote that there is nothing as anarchic as the bourgeois order. Similarly, the remark of one of the Fascist dignitaries in Pasolini's film* Salò *according to which "the only real anarchy is that of power" is perfectly serious.)*

From this follows the insufficiency of Reiner Schürmann's attempt—in his nonetheless wonderful book on the Principe d'anarchie—*to think an "anarchic economy"—that is, an unfounded economy—from the perspective of the overcoming of metaphysics and the history of being. Among post-Heideggerian philosophers, Schürmann is the only one to have understood the nexus that links the theological notion of* oikonomia *(which he, however, leaves unquestioned) to the problem of ontology and, in particular, to Heidegger's reading of the ontological difference and of the "epochal" structure of the history of being. It is in this perspective that Schürmann tries to think praxis and history without any foundation in being (that is, in a completely an-archic way). But ontotheology always already thinks the divine praxis as lacking a foundation in being, and, as a matter of fact, intends to find an articulation between that which it has always already divided. In other words, the* oikonomia *is always already anarchic, without foundation, and a rethinking of the problem of anarchy in our political tradition becomes possible only if we begin with an awareness of the secret theological nexus that links it to government and providence. The governmental paradigm, of which we are here reconstructing the genealogy, is actually always already "anarchic-governmental."*

This does not mean that, beyond government and anarchy, it is not possible to think an Ungovernable [un Ingovernabile*], that is, something that could never assume the form of an* oikonomia.

Threshold

At the end of classical civilization, when the unity of the ancient cosmos is broken, and being and acting, ontology and praxis, seem to part ways irreversibly, we see a complex doctrine developing in Christian theology, one in which Judaic and pagan elements merge. Such a doctrine attempts to interpret—and, at the same, recompose—this fracture through a managerial and non-epistemic paradigm: the *oikonomia*. According to this paradigm, the divine praxis, from creation to redemption, does not have a foundation in God's being, and differs from it to the extent that it realizes itself in a separate person, the *Logos*, or Son. However, this anarchic and unfounded praxis must be reconciled with the unity of the substance. Through the idea of a free and voluntary action—which associates creation with redemption—this paradigm had to overcome both the Gnostic antithesis between a God foreign to the world and a demiurge who is creator and Lord of the world, and the pagan identity of being and acting, which made the very idea of creation unconvincing. The challenge that Christian theology thus presents to Gnosis is to succeed in reconciling God's transcendence with the creation of the world, as well as his noninvolvement in it with the Stoic and Judaic idea of a God who takes care of the world and governs it providentially. In the face of this aporetic task, the *oikonomia*—given its managerial and administrative root—offered a ductile tool, which presented itself, at the same time, as a *logos*, a rationality removed from any external constraint, and a praxis unanchored to any ontological necessity or preestablished norm. Being both a discourse and a reality, a non-epistemic knowledge and an anarchic praxis, the *oikonomia* allowed theologians to define the novelty of Christian faith for centuries and, at the same time, make the outcome of late classical, Stoic, and neo-Pythagorean thought that had already oriented itself in an "economic" sense merge with it. It is in the context of this paradigm that the original kernels of the Trinitarian dogmatics and of Christology were formed: they have never fully dissociated themselves from this genesis, remaining tributary to both its aporias and successes.

We can then understand in what sense it is possible to say that Christian theology is, from its beginning, economic-managerial, and not politico-statal [*politico-statuale*]—this was our original thesis contra Schmitt. The fact that Christian theology entails an economy and not just a politics does not mean, however, that it is irrelevant for the history of Western political ideas and practices. On the contrary, the theological-economic paradigm obliges us to think this history once more and from a new perspective, keeping track of the decisive junctures between political tradition in the strict sense and the "economic-governmental" tradition—which, what is more, will acquire a precise form, as we shall see, in the medieval treatises *de gubernatione mundi*. The two paradigms live together and intersect with one another to the point of constituting a bipolar system, whose understanding preliminarily conditions any interpretation of the political history of the West.

In his great monograph on Tertullian, Moingt rightly suggests at a certain point that the most correct translation of the phrase *unicus deus cum sua oikonomia*—the only one able to hold together the various meanings of the term "economy"—would probably be "a single God with his government, in the sense in which 'government' designates the king's ministers, whose power is an emanation of the royal power and is not counted along with it, but is necessary to its exercise"; understood in this way, "the economy means the mode of administration by means of a plurality of the divine power" (Moingt, p. 923). In this genuinely "governmental" meaning, the impolitical paradigm of the economy also shows its political implications. The fracture between theology and *oikonomia*, being and action, insofar as it makes the praxis free and "anarchic," opens in fact, at the same time, the possibility and necessity of its government.

In a historical moment that witnesses a radical crisis of classical conceptuality, both ontological and political, the harmony between the transcendent and eternal principle and the immanent order of the cosmos is broken, and the problem of the "government" of the world and of its legitimization becomes the political problem that is in every sense decisive.

§ 4   The Kingdom and the Government

4.1. One of the most memorable figures of the prose cycle of the Grail Legend is that of the *roi mehaignié*, the wounded or mutilated king (the word *mehaignié* corresponds to the Italian *magagnato* [in poor shape; shabby]) who reigns over a *terre gaste*, a devastated land, "where crops do not grow and trees do not bear fruits." According to Chrétien de Troyes, the king was wounded in battle between his thighs and mutilated in such a way that he cannot stand or ride. For this reason, when he wants to enjoy himself, he asks to be put in a boat and goes fishing (the nickname "Fisher King" originated here), while his falconers, archers, and hunters scour his forests. This must be, however, a rather strange kind of fishing, given that Chrétien specifies shortly after that it has been fifteen years since the king last left his room, where he is kept alive with communion bread that is served to him in the holy Grail. According to another and less authoritative source—which recalls Kafka's story about the hunter Gracchus—the king lost his hounds and his hunters while hunting in the forest. Once he reached the seashore, he found a glimmering sword on a boat, and when he attempted to pull the sword from its sheath, he was magically wounded between the thighs by a spear.

In any case, the mutilated king will be healed only when, at the end of his *quête*, Galahad will smear his wound with the blood left on the tip of the spear that inflicted the wound on Christ's side.

This figure of a mutilated and impotent king has been given the most various interpretations. In a book that has exercised a considerable influence not only on Arthurian studies but also on twentieth-century poetry, Jesse Weston has juxtaposed the figure of the Fisher King with the "divine principle of life and fertility," that "Spirit of Vegetation" that, following the studies of Frazer and the Anglo-Saxon folklorists, the author recovers—with a good dose of eclecticism—in rituals and mythological figures that belong to the most divergent cultures, from the Babylonian Tammuz to the Greek-Phoenician Adonis.

These interpretations overlook the fact that the legend undoubtedly also contains a genuinely political mythologem, which can be read, without forcing things, as the paradigm of a divided and impotent sovereignty. Even if he does not lose any of his legitimacy and sacredness, the king has in fact for some reason been separated from his powers and activities, and reduced to impotence. Not only can he not hunt and ride (here these activities seem to symbolize secular power), but he must also stay in his room while his ministers (the falconers, archers, and hunters) govern in his name and place. In this sense, the splitting of sovereignty dramatized in the figure of the Fisher King seems to evoke the duality that Benveniste identifies in Indo-European regality between a mostly magic-religious and a more properly political function. But, in the Grail legends, the emphasis is rather put on the inoperative and separated character of the mutilated king, who will be excluded from any concrete activity of government at least until he is healed by the touch of the magic spear. The *roi mehaigné* thus contains a kind of anticipation of the modern sovereign who "reigns but does not govern"; in this sense, the legend could have a meaning that concerns us more closely.

4.2. At the beginning of his book on *Monotheism as a Political Problem*, just before tackling the problem of divine monarchy, Peterson briefly analyzes the pseudo-Aristotelian treatise *On the World*, which represents for him something like a bridge between Aristotelian politics and the Judaic idea of divine monarchy. While, in Aristotle, God is the transcendent principle of every movement, who leads the world like a strategist leads his army, in *On the World*—Peterson observes—God is compared with a puppeteer who, remaining invisible, moves the threads of his puppet, or with the Great King of the Persians who lives hidden in his palace and governs the world by means of the innumerable crowd of ministers and officials.

> Here, the crucial question for the image of divine monarchy is not whether there is one or more powers [*Gewalten*], but whether God participates in the powers [*Mächten*] that act in the cosmos. The author wants to say: God is

the precondition for powers to act in the cosmos (he uses the term *dynamis*, adopting a Stoic terminology, but he means rather the Aristotelian *kynesis*), yet, precisely for this reason, he himself is not power: *le roi règne, mais il ne gouverne pas.* (Peterson 1994, p. 27)

According to Peterson, in the pseudo-Aristotelian treatise, metaphysico-theological and political paradigms are strictly entwined. The ultimate formulation of a metaphysical image of the world—Peterson writes, repeating almost literally a Schmittian thesis—is always determined by a political decision. In this sense, "the difference between *Macht* (*potestas*, *dynamis*) and *Gewalt* (*archē*), which the author of the treatise posits with regard to God, is a metaphysico-political problem," which can assume different forms and meanings and can be developed in the direction of the distinction between *auctoritas* and *potestas* as much as in that of the Gnostic opposition between god and the demiurge.

Before analyzing the strategic reasons for this peculiar *excursus* on the theological meaning of the opposition between kingdom and government, it is a good idea to examine more closely the text from which it takes its marks in order to check if it is well founded. The unknown author—who according to the majority of scholars could belong to the same circle of Hellenistic Stoic Judaism from which Philo and Aristobulus came—does not really distinguish between *archē* and *dynamis* in God, but rather, with a gesture that brings him close to the Fathers who elaborate the Christian paradigm of the *oikonomia*, between essence (*ousia*) and power (*dynamis*). The ancient philosophers—he writes—who have claimed that the entirety of the perceptible world is full of gods formulated an argument that does not apply to the being of God, but to his power (Aristotle, *De mundo*, 397b). While God actually dwells in the highest region of heaven, his power, "extend[s] through the whole universe, [. . .] and [is] the cause of permanence [*sōtērias*, 'salvation'] to all that is on this earth" (ibid., 398b). He is, at the same time, savior (*sōtēr*) and generator (*genetōr*) of all that occurs in the cosmos. Yet, he "endures not all the weariness of a being that administers and labors on one's own [*autourgou*], but exerts a power that never wearies; whereby he prevails even over things that seem far distant from him" (ibid., 397b). The power of God, which almost seems to become autonomous from his essence, can thus—in a clear reference to Chapter X of Book L of Aristotle's *Metaphysics*—be compared with the head of an army in a battle ("all is hurry and movement in obedience to one word of command, to carry out the orders of the leader who is supreme over all": *De mundo*, 399b) or—in an image that is almost identical to that used by Tertullian for the *oikonomia* of the Father—with the imposing administrative apparatus of the king of the Persians:

> The king himself, so the story goes, established himself at Susa or Ecbatana, invisible to all, dwelling in a wondrous palace [*basileion oikon*] within a fence gleaming with gold and amber and ivory. And it had many gateways one after another, and porches many furlongs apart from one another, secured by bronze doors and mighty walls. Outside these the chief and most distinguished men had their appointed place, some being the king's personal servants, his bodyguard and attendants, others the guardians of each of the enclosing walls, the so-called janitors and "listeners," that the king himself, who was called their master and deity, might thus see and hear all things. Besides these, others were appointed as stewards of his revenues and leaders in war and hunting, and receivers of gifts, and others charged with all the other necessary functions [. . .] and there were couriers and watchmen and messengers [*aggeliaforoi*] and superintendents of signal-fires. So effective was the organization, in particular the system of signal-fires, which formed a chain of beacons from the furthest bounds of the empire to Susa and Ecbatana, that the king received the same day the news of all that was happening in Asia. Now we must suppose that the majesty of the Great King falls as far short of that of the God who possesses the universe, as that of the feeblest and weakest creature is inferior to the king of Persia. Wherefore, if it was beneath the dignity of Xerxes to appear himself to administer all things and to carry out his own wishes and superintend the government of his kingdom, such function would be still less becoming for a god. (Ibid., 398a–398b)

In a characteristic move, the administrative apparatus through which the sovereigns of the earth preserve their kingdom becomes the paradigm of the divine government of the world. At this stage, the author of the treatise is, however, concerned to specify that the analogy between the power of God and the bureaucratic apparatus should not be pushed to the point of completely dividing God from his power (just as, according to the Fathers, the *oikonomia* should not entail a division of the divine substance). Unlike worldly sovereigns, God in fact does not need "many hands" (*polycheirias*), but "by simple movement of that which is nearest to [him], imparts [his] power to that which next succeeds, and thence further and further until it extends to all things" (ibid., 398b). If it is true that the king reigns but does not govern, his government—his power—cannot be separated completely from him. The fact that there is in this sense an almost perfect correspondence between this Judaic-Stoic idea of the divine government of the world and the Christian idea of a providential economy is proved by a long passage from Chapter Six that describes such a government precisely in terms of a providential organization of the cosmos:

> The single harmony produced by all the heavenly bodies singing and dancing together springs from one source and ends by achieving one purpose, and has rightly bestowed the name not of "disordered" but of "ordered universe" upon the whole. And just as in a chorus, when the leader gives the signal to begin, the whole chorus of men, or it may be of women, joins in the song, mingling a single studied harmony among different voices, some high and some low; so too is it with the God that rules the whole world. For at the signal given from on high by him who may well be called their chorus-leader, the stars and the whole heaven always move, and the sun that illuminates all things travels forth on his double course, whereby he both divides day and night by his rising and his setting, and also brings the four seasons of the earth, as he moves forward toward the north and backward toward the south. And in their own due season the rain, the winds, and the dews, and all the other phenomena that occur in the region that surrounds the earth, are produced by the first, primeval cause [. . .] (Ibid., 399a)

The analogy between the images of the *De mundo* and those used by the theorists of the *oikonomia* is such that we should not be surprised to find the term *oikonomeō* with regard to the divine government of the world, when it is compared to the action of the law in a city ("the law of a city, fixed and immutable [. . .] governs all the life of the state [*panta oikonomei*]," ibid., 400b). It is all the more peculiar that, even in this occasion, Peterson refrains from making the slightest remark about economic theology—which would clearly allow us to relate this text to Judaic-Christian political theology.

4.3. In his late and resentful reply to Peterson, Carl Schmitt analyzes with particular care the use of the "notorious formula" *le roi règne, mais il ne gouverne pas* made by the theologian in his 1935 treatise. "I think," Schmitt writes not without irony, "it is exactly this interpolation, in this context, which is the most intriguing contribution that Peterson—maybe unconsciously—attributed to political theology" (Schmitt 2008a, p. 67).

Schmitt traces the formula back to Adolphe Thiers, who uses it as a key-word for parliamentarian monarchy, and even earlier, in its Latin version (*rex regnat, sed non gubernat*), to the seventeenth-century polemic against Sigismund III, king of Poland. For Schmitt, the resolute gesture with which Peterson moves the formula back in time and transfers it to the dawn of Christian theology is all the more astounding. "[This] shows how much reflection and thought can be invested in a useful politico-theological or politico-metaphysical formulation" (ibid., p. 68). The real contribution of Peterson to political theology would thus not amount to having been able to demonstrate the impossibility of a Christian political theology, but to having grasped the analogy between the liberal political paradigm that separates kingdom from government and the theological paradigm that distinguishes between *archē* and *dynamis* in God.

However, even here, the apparent disagreement between Peterson and Schmitt hides a more essential solidarity. Both authors are, as a matter of fact, earnest enemies of the formula: for Peterson, it defines the Hellenistic-Judaic theological model that lies at the basis of the political theology he intends to criticize; for Schmitt, it provides a symbol and a keyword to the liberal democracy against which he wages his battle. Even in this context, it is crucial to examine not only what it says but also what it omits to say in order to grasp the strategic implications of Peterson's argument. It should be evident by now that the difference between kingdom and government does not, in fact, have a theological paradigm only in Hellenistic Judaism—as Peterson seems to be taking for granted—but also and especially in the Christian theologians who, between the third and the fifth centuries, elaborated the distinction between being and *oikonomia*, theological rationality and economic rationality. In other words, the reasons why Peterson is interested in keeping the Kingdom/Government paradigm within the limits of Judaic and pagan political theology are exactly the same as those that caused him to remain silent about the original "economic" formulation of the Trinitarian doctrine. After eliminating, against Schmitt, the theological-political paradigm, it was a matter of avoiding at all costs—this time in agreement with Schmitt—its replacement by the theological-economic paradigm. A new and more detailed genealogical investigation of the theological presuppositions and implications of the difference Kingdom/Government then becomes all the more urgent.

א *According to Peterson, an "economic" paradigm in the strict sense is an inherent part of the Judaic legacy of modernity, in which banks tend to take the place of the temple. Only the sacrifice of Christ at the Golgotha marks the end of the sacrifices in the Jewish temple. In fact, according to Peterson, the driving away of the merchants from the temple shows that behind the sacrifice at the Golgotha lies "the dialectic of money and sacrifice." After the destruction of the temple, the Jews have attempted to replace sacrifice with alms.*

> But the money that is offered to God and accumulated in the temple transforms the temple into a bank [. . .] The Jews, who had renounced the political order, when they declared that they had no king [. . .] condemning Christ because of his words against the temple, intended to save the economic order. (Peterson 1995, p. 145)

It is precisely this substitution of economy for politics that is rendered impossible by the sacrifice of Christ.

> Our banks have been transformed into temples, but they themselves make evident in the so-called economic order the superiority of the bloody sacrifice at the Golgotha and demonstrate the impossibility of saving what is historical [. . .] Just as the secular kingdoms of the people of earth can no longer be "saved" in the political order after the eschatological sacrifice, so even the "economical order" of the Jews cannot be preserved in the guise of a connection between the temple and money. (Ibid.)

In this way, both political and economic theology are excluded from Christianity as a purely Judaic legacy.

4.4. Schmitt's aversion toward any attempt to divide Kingdom from Government and, in particular, his reservations concerning the liberal-democratic doctrine of the separation of powers—which is strictly linked to such a division—emerges many times in his work. Already in the 1927 *Verfassungslehre*, he quotes the formula *le roi règne, mais il ne gouverne pas* in relation to the "Belgian-style parliamentarian monarchy," in which the direction of affairs is in the hands of the ministers, while the king represents a kind of "neutral power." The only positive meaning that Schmitt seems to acknowledge in the separation of Kingdom from Government is that it is possible to refer it back to the distinction between *auctoritas* and *potestas*.

The question posed by a great teacher of German public law, Max von Seydel, what then remains of "régner" if one removes "gouverner?," is answerable in reference to the fact that one distinguishes between potestas and auctoritas and that the distinctive meaning of authority is made evident in regard to political power. (Schmitt 2008b, p. 315)

Schmitt clearly states what this meaning is in his 1933 essay *State, Movement, People*, in which, in an attempt to outline the new constitution of the national-socialist *Reich*, he re-elaborates from a new perspective the distinction between Kingdom and Government. Although during the radical political-social conflicts of the Weimar Republic, he energetically defended the extension of powers to the president of the *Reich* as the "warden of the constitution," Schmitt now affirms that the president "has gone back to a kind of 'constitutional' position of authoritarian head of State *qui règne et ne gouverne pas*" (Schmitt 1933, p. 10). Facing this sovereign who does not govern, there now is, in the person of the chancellor Adolf Hitler, not only a function of government (*Regierung*), but a new figure of political power that Schmitt names *Führung*, and that indeed is to be distinguished from traditional government. It is in this context that Schmitt delineates a genealogy of the "government of men" that seems to anticipate, with a vertiginous glimpse, the genealogy that, in the second half of the 1970s, will occupy Michel Foucault in his courses at the Collège de France. Like Foucault, Schmitt sees in the pastorate of the Catholic Church the paradigm of the modern concept of government:

Leading [*führen*] is not commanding [. . .] For its power of dominion over believers, the Roman Catholic Church has transformed and completed the image of the shepherd and the flock in a theological-dogmatic idea. (Ibid., p. 41)

Similarly, in a well-known passage of *The Statesman*, Plato

considers the various comparisons that one can make about a statesman in relation to a doctor, a shepherd, and a pilot, and privileges the image of the pilot. The latter has reached all the languages influenced by Latin through the word *gubernator* and has become the term for government [*Regierung*], like in *gouvernement, governo, government*, or like in the *gubernium* of the ancient Habsburg monarchy. The history of this *gubernator* contains a nice example of how an imaginary comparison can become a juridico-technical concept. (Ibid., pp. 41–42)

א *Against this governmental background Schmitt tries to outline the "fundamentally German meaning" (ibid., p. 42) of the national-socialist concept of* Führung, *which "does not derive from baroque allegories or representations [an allusion to the theory of sovereignty that Benjamin develops in his* Ursprung*] or from a Cartesian* idée générale," *but is "a concept of the immediate present and of an effective presence" (ibid.). This distinction is however not so simple, since there is not a "fundamentally German" meaning of the term, and the word* Führung, *just like the verb* führen *and the noun* Führer—*unlike the Italian* duce, *which had already known a specialization in a political-military sense, for instance, in the Venetian* doge—*refers back to an extremely broad semantic field, which includes all the cases in which somebody guides and orients the movement of a living being, a vehicle, or an object (obviously including the case of the* gubernator, *that is, the sea pilot). After all, earlier in his essay, analyzing the triple articulation of the new material national-socialist constitution into "State," "movement," and "people," Schmitt had defined the people as the "impolitical side [*unpolitische Seite*] that develops under the protection and in the shadow of political decisions" (ibid., p. 12), thus attributing to the party and the* Führer *an unmistakable pastoral and governmental function. Yet, according to Schmitt, what distinguishes the* Führung *from the pastoral-governmental paradigm is that while in the latter "the shepherd remains absolutely* transcendent *with regard to the flock" (ibid., p. 41), the former is rather defined "by an absolute equality of species [*Artgleichheit*] between the* Führer *and his followers" (ibid., p. 42). The concept of* Führung *appears here as a secularization of the pastoral paradigm, one that eliminates its transcendent character. However, in order to subtract the* Führung *from the governmental model, Schmitt is obliged to give a constitutional status to the concept of race, by means of which the impolitical element—the people—is politicized. For Schmitt there is only one possible way to achieve this politicization, that is, by turning the equality of lineage into the criterion that, in separating what is foreign from what is equal, decides at each turn who is a friend and who an enemy. Not without analogies with the analysis that Foucault will develop in* Il faut défendre la société, *racism thus becomes the apparatus through which sovereign power (which, for Foucault, coincides with the power over life and death while, for Schmitt, it corresponds with the decision over the exception) is reinserted into biopower. In this way, the governmental-economic paradigm is brought back to a genuinely political sphere, in which the separation of powers loses its meaning and* *the act of government (Regierungakt) gives way to the single activity "by means of which the* Führer *affirms his supreme* Führertum. "

4.5. A theological paradigm of the division between Kingdom and Government can be found in Numenius. This Platonic philosopher, who was active around the second half of the second century AD and exercised a considerable influence over Eusebius of Caesarea and, through him, on Christian theology, distinguishes in fact between two gods. The first, defined as a king, is foreign to the world, transcendent, and completely inoperative; while the second is active and deals with the government of the world.

The entirety of fragment 12, preserved by Eusebius (*Preparation for the Gospel*, 11, 18, 8), revolves around the problem of the operativeness or inoperativeness of the first god:

> For it is not at all becoming that the First God should be the Creator [*dēmiourgein*]; also the First God must be regarded as the father of the God who is Creator of the world. If then we were inquiring about the creative principle, and asserting that He who was pre-existent would thereby be preeminently fit for the work, this would have been a suitable commencement of our argument. But if we are not discussing the creative principle, but inquiring about the First Cause, I renounce what I said, and wish that to be withdrawn [. . .] the First God is inoperative [*argon*] with regard to all kinds of work and reigns as king [*basilea*], but the Creative God [*dēmiourgikon*] governs [*hēgemonein*], and travels through the heaven. (Ibid., p. 536)

Peterson had already observed that what is crucial here is not so much whether there is one or more gods, but rather whether the supreme divinity is or is not participating in the forces that govern the world: "From the principle according to which God reigns but does not govern, one draws the Gnostic consequence that God's kingdom is good, but the government of the demiurge—the demiurgic forces, which can also be considered under the category of functionaries—is evil, or, in other words, that the government is always wrong" (Peterson 1994, pp. 27–28). In this sense, a Gnostic political conception is not simply one that opposes a good god to an evil demiurge, but one that distinguishes also and especially between a god who is idle and without relation to the world from a god who actively intervenes in it in order to govern it. That is, the opposition between Kingdom and Government is part of the Gnostic legacy in modern politics.

What is the meaning of this distinction? And why is the first God defined as a "king"? In an instructive study, Heinrich Dörrie has reconstructed the Platonic origin of this regal metaphor of divinity (more precisely, it originated in the circle of the Ancient Academy). It goes back to the exoteric excursus of the second Platonic (or pseudo-Platonic) Letter, which distinguishes a "King of All" [*pantōn basilea*], who is the cause and the end of all things, from a second and a third god, around whom revolve second and third things (Plato, *Letters*, II, 312e). Dörrie follows the history of this image through Apuleius, Numenius, Origen, Clement of Alexandria, up to Plotinus, in whose *Enneads* the image appears four times. In the strategy of the *Enneads*, the metaphor of the god-king, with its equation between heavenly and earthly powers, would allow us "to clarify Plotinus's theology against the Gnostics" (Dörrie, p. 233):

> Plotinus appropriates it because he sees in it a fundamental point of his theology. On the other hand, we must refer here to the representation of God that had been predominant for some time, which does not distinguish between earthly and heavenly powers: God must be surrounded by a court that is ordered hierarchically just like the earthly sovereign. (Ibid., p. 232)

Numenius's theology thus develops a paradigm that is not only Gnostic, but that circulated in early and middle Platonism and that, by presupposing two (or three) divine figures that are at the same time different and coordinated, certainly aroused the interest of the theorists of the Christian *oikonomia*. However, the specific function of Numenius's theology is that it links the figures of the god-king and the demiurge to the opposition between operativeness and inoperativeness, transcendence and immanence. That is, it represents the borderline case of a tendency that radically divides Kingdom and Government, separating a monarch who is basically foreign to the cosmos from the immanent government of earthly things. In this perspective, it is interesting to note that, in fragment 12, *basileus* (referred to the first god) is terminologically opposed to *hēgemonein* (referred to the demiurge), which indicates a specific and active function of guidance and command: *hēgemōn* (like the Latin *dux*) can be, in turn, the animal that leads a flock, the driver of a cart, the military commander, and, technically, the governor of a province. However, if the distinction between Kingdom and Government is certainly clear, even in Numenius the two terms cannot be unrelated, and the second god somehow represents a necessary complement of the first. In this sense, the demiurge is compared with the pilot of a boat: just as the latter scans the sky to orientate himself, so the former "gazes at the highest god, not at the sky" in order to orientate himself in his governmental function (fragment 18). Another fragment compares the relationship between the first god and the demiurge with that of the seeder and the farmer: the earthly god transplants, takes care, and distributes the seeds that the first god spread in the souls (fragment 13). In point of fact, the god that governs needs the inoperative god and presupposes him, just as this requires the activity of the demiurge. In other words, everything seems to suggest that the kingdom of the first god forms a functional system with the government of the demiurge, just as, in the Christian *oikonomia*, the god who carries out the work of salvation acts according to the will of the father, even if he is an anarchic hypostasis.

א *In the history of the early Church, Marcion is the most radical supporter of the Gnostic antinomy between a god who is foreign to the world and an earthly demiurge ("Gott ist der Fremde" is the motto with which Harnack summarizes Marcion's gospel: Harnack, p. 4). From this perspective, the Christian* oikonomia *can be seen as an attempt to overcome Marcionism, in that it inserts the Gnostic antinomy within the divinity and, in this way, reconciles the divinity's noninvolvement with the world with its government. The god who has created the world now faces a nature that has been corrupted by sin and has become foreign to him; the savior god, to whom was entrusted the government of the world, needs to redeem it for a kingdom that is not, however, of this world.*

א *In Apuleius's Apologia, we find a peculiar figure of* deus otiosus *who is, however, also a creator. Here, the* summus genitor *and the* assiduus mundi sui opifex *are defined as "sine opera opifex," builder without work, and "sine propagatione genitor," father without begetting (Apologia, 64).*

4.6. The philosophical paradigm of the distinction between Kingdom and Government is contained in the final chapter of Book L of Aristotle's *Metaphysics*, the same text from which Peterson extracts the quotation that opens his treatise against political theology. Aristotle has just expounded what goes by the name of his "theology," in which God appears as the first immovable mover who moves the celestial spheres and whose form of life (*diagōgē*) is, in essence, thought of thought. The chapter that follows, the Tenth, is dedicated—apparently without any logical consistency—to the problem of the relation between the good and the world (or the way "in which the nature of the universe contains the good"), and is traditionally interpreted as a theory of the superiority of the paradigm of transcendence over that of immanence. In his commentary to Book XII of the *Metaphysics*, Thomas Aquinas thus writes that "the separate good of the universe, which is the first mover, is a greater good than the good of order which is found in the universe" (Thomas Aquinas, *Commentary on the Metaphysics of Aristotle*, Book XII, Lesson XII, n. 2631). The author of the most recent critical edition of the *Metaphysics*, William D. Ross, similarly affirms that "the doctrine here stated is that goodness exists not only immanently in the world but transcendently in God, and even more fundamentally in Him, since He is the source of the good in the world" (Ross, p. 401).

The passage in question is actually one of the most complex and fraught with implications for the entire treatise: it cannot in any way be simplified in these terms. In it, transcendence and immanence are not simply distinguished as superior and inferior, but rather articulated together so as almost to form a single system, in which the separated good and the immanent order constitute a machine that is, at the same time, cosmological and political (or economic-political). And this is all the more relevant insofar as, as we shall see, Chapter X of the *Metaphysics* was always interpreted by medieval commentators as a theory of the divine government (*gubernatio*) of the world.

But let us turn to the passage that interests us. Aristotle begins by expounding the problem in the guise of a dichotomic alternative:

> We must now consider also in which of two ways the nature of the universe contains the good or the highest good, whether as something separate [*kechōrismenon*] and by itself [*kath'hauto*], or as the order [*taxin*] of the parts. (Aristotle, *Metaphysics*, 10, 1075a)

If transcendence is here defined by means of the traditional terms of separation and autonomy, it is instructive to note that the figure of immanence is, on the other hand, that of order, that is, the relation of every thing with other things. The immanence of the good means *taxis*, order. This model is, however, soon complicated and, through a comparison taken from military science (which is almost certainly at the origin of the analogous image we encountered in *De mundo*), the alternative is turned into a compromise:

> Probably in both ways, as an army [*strateuma*] does. For the good is found both in the order and in the leader [*stratēgos*], and more in the latter; for he does not depend on the order but it depends on him. (Ibid.)

The passage that follows clarifies in what sense we have to understand the notion of an immanent order if it is to be reconciled with the transcendence of the good. To this end, Aristotle abandons the military metaphor and resorts to paradigms taken from the natural world and, above all, the administration of the house:

> All things are ordered together [*syntetaktai*] somehow, but not all alike—both fishes and fowls and plants; and the world is not such that one thing has nothing to do with another, but there is something [that connects them in an orderly manner]. For all are ordered together to one end. (But it is as in a house [*en oikiai*], where the freemen are least at liberty to act at random, but all things or most things are already ordained for them, while the slaves and the beasts do little for the common good, and for the most part live at random; for this is the sort of principle [*arkē*] that constitutes the nature of each.) I mean, for instance, that all must at least come to be dissolved into their elements, and there are other functions similarly in which all share for the good of the whole. (Ibid.)

It is odd that the reconciliation between transcendence and immanence through the idea of a reciprocal order of things is entrusted to an image of an "economic" nature. The unity of the world is compared with the order of the house (and not that of a city), and yet, this very economic paradigm—which, for Aristotle, is as such necessarily monarchical—allows in the end the reintroduction of an image of a political nature: "But entities do not want to have a bad political constitution [*politeuesthai kakōs*]. 'The rule of many is not good; let there be one {soveriegn}'" (ibid., 1076a). As a matter of fact, in the administration of a house, the unitary principle that governs it manifests itself in different modes and degrees, in accordance with the different nature of the individual beings that make up its parts (with a formulation that will have a long theological and political legacy, Aristotle links together the sovereign principle and nature, *archē* and *physis*). Free men, as rational creatures, are in an immediate and conscious relation with the unitary principle, and do not act at random, while slaves and domestic animals cannot but follow their nature, which however contains, albeit to different extents, a reflection of the unitary order, which makes it possible for them to act in agreement toward a common goal. Eventually, this means that the immovable mover as transcendent *archē* and the immanent order (as *physis*) form a single bipolar system, and that, in spite of the variety and difference of natures, the house-world is governed by a single principle. Power—every power, both human and divine—must hold these two poles together, that is, it must be, at the same time, kingdom and government, transcendent norm and immanent order.

4.7. Any interpretation of *Metaphysics*, L, X should begin with an analysis of the concept of *taxis*, "order," which is not defined thematically in the text, but only exemplified by means of the two paradigms of the army and the house. After all, the term appears several times in Aristotle's work, but is never the object of a real definition. In *Metaphysics*, 985b, for instance, it is mentioned together with *schēma* and *thesis* with regard to the differences that, according to the Atomists, determine the multiplicity of entities: *taxis* refers to the *diathigē*, the reciprocal relation, which is exemplified by the difference between AN and NA. Analogously, in *Metaphysics*, 1022b, the disposition [*disposizione*] (*diathesis*) is defined as "the arrangement of that which has parts, in respect either of place or of potency or of kind." And, in the *Politics* (1298a), the constitution (*politeia*) is defined as *taxis* (reciprocal order) of the powers (*archai*), and "there are as many forms of constitution as there are possible *taxeis* between the parts." It is therefore precisely in the passage that interests us here that this generic meaning of the term "order" is replaced by its strategic displacement at the junction between ontology and politics, which makes of it a fundamental *terminus technicus* of Western politics and metaphysics, even if it has rarely been investigated as such.

As we have seen, Aristotle begins by opposing the concept of order to what is separated (*kechōrismenos*) and for itself (*kath'hauto*). That is to say, order structurally implies the idea of an immanent and reciprocal relation: "All things are ordered together [. . .] and the world is not such that one thing has nothing to do with another" (*Metaphysics*, 1075a). The phrase used by Aristotle (*thaterōi pros thateron mēden*) decidedly inscribes the concept of order in the sphere of the category of relation (*pros ti*): order is thus a relation and not a substance. But we can understand the meaning of this concept only if we become aware of its location at the end of Book L of the *Metaphysics*.

Book L is, in fact, entirely dedicated to the problem of ontology. Those who have some familiarity with Aristotle's philosophy know that one of the fundamental exegetical problems that still divides interpreters is that of the double determination of the object of metaphysics: separate being and being as being. Heidegger wrote that "this dual characterization of *prōtē philosophia* does not contain two radically different trains of thought, nor should one be weakened or rejected outright in favor of the other. Furthermore, we should not be over-hasty in reconciling this apparent duality" (Heidegger 1962, p. 12). As a matter of fact, Book L contains Aristotle's so-called theology, that is, the doctrine of the separate substance and of the immovable motor, which, despite being separated from them, moves the celestial spheres. At this point, Aristotle introduces the concept of order as a way to tackle the splitting of the object of metaphysics. Order is the theoretical apparatus that allows us to think the relation between the two objects, which immediately presents itself, in the passage we quoted above, as the problem of the way in which the nature of the universe contains the good: "We must now consider also in which of two ways the nature of the universe contains the good or the highest good, whether as something separate and by itself, or as the order of the parts" (*Metaphysics*, 1075a). Transcendence, immanence, and their reciprocal coordination correspond here to the splitting of the object of metaphysics, and to the attempt to keep together the two figures of being. Yet the aporia lies in the fact that order (that is, a figure of relation) becomes the way in which the separate substance is present and acts in the world. The eminent place of ontology is in this way displaced from the category of substance to that of relation, of an eminently practical relation. The problem of the relation between the transcendence and immanence of the good thus becomes that of the relation between ontology and praxis, between the being of God and his action. That this shift encounters some fundamental difficulties is evident from the fact that Aristotle does not tackle the problem directly, but simply relies on two paradigms, a military one and a genuinely economic one. Just as, in an army, the ordered deployment of soldiers must be in relation with the command of the strategist and, in a house, the different beings who inhabit it—each following its own nature—actually conform to a single principle, so the separate being maintains a relation to the immanent order of the cosmos (and vice versa). In any case, *taxis*, order, is the apparatus that makes possible the articulation of the separate substance with being, of God with the world. *Taxis* names their aporetic relation.

Although there is absolutely no notion of providence in Aristotle, and he could not in any case have conceived the relation between the immovable mover and the cosmos in terms of *pronoia*, it is easy to understand how later philosophers, beginning already with Alexander of Aphrodisias, found in this passage from the *Metaphysics* the foundation for a theory of divine providence. In other words, without this being one of his aims, Aristotle transmitted to Western politics the paradigm of the divine regime of the world as a double system, formed, on the one hand, by a transcendent *archē*, and, on the other, by an immanent concurrence of secondary actions and causes.

א *Will Durant was one of the first scholars to put the Aristotelian god in relation to the paradigm Kingdom/Government: "Aristotle's God [. . .] is a* roi fainéant, *a do-nothing king; 'the king reigns, but he does not rule'" (Durant, p. 80).*

א *In his commentary on Book L of the* Metaphysics, *Averroes poignantly observes that one can infer the radical outcome of Gnostic ditheism from the Aristotelian doctrine of the two modes in which the good exists in the universe, "in virtue of order and in virtue of that thanks to which order exists":*

> There are people who say that there is nothing for which God does not care, because they claim that the Sage must not leave anything without providence and must not do evil [. . .] Other people refuted this theory through the fact that many things happen that are evil, and the Sage should not produce them [. . .] Some people carried on their reflection on this to the point that they said that there are two gods, a god who created evil and a god who created good. (Ibn Rushd, *Metaphysics*, p. 201)

According to Averroes, Gnostic ditheism would find its paradigm in the fracture between transcendence and immanence that Aristotelian theology bequeathed to the modern age.

4.8. The turning of the concept of order into a fundamental paradigm, both metaphysical and political, is one of the achievements of medieval thought. Insofar as Christian theology had adopted the canon of transcendent being from Aristotelianism, the problem of the relation between

God and the world could only become, in any sense, the most decisive question. However, the relation between God and the world necessarily entails an ontological problem, since it is not a relation between two entities, but one that concerns the preeminent form of being itself. In this perspective, the passage from Book L provided a valuable and, at the same time, aporetic model. It thus became the constant point of reference that oriented the incredibly numerous treatises *De bono* and *De gubernatione mundi*.

If, in order to analyze this paradigm, we choose here the work of Thomas Aquinas (rather than that of Boethius, Augustine, or Albert the Great—who are, along with Aristotle, Thomas's principal sources with regard to this problem), it is not only because the concept of order becomes with him "a central principle" (Silva Tarouca, p. 342) and almost "the current that pervades the entirety of his thought" (Krings 1941, p. 13), but also because the dissymmetries and conflicts that it implies are here particularly evident. Following an intention that deeply marked the medieval vision of the world, Thomas tried to make of order the fundamental ontological concept, which determines and conditions the very idea of being; and yet, precisely for this reason, the Aristotelian aporia reaches with him its most radical formulation.

The scholars who studied the idea of order in Thomas's thought noted the twofold character that defines it (order, like being, can be said in many ways). *Ordo* expresses, on the one hand, the relation of creatures with God (*ordo ad unum principium*) and, on the other, the relation of creatures with themselves (*ordo ad invicem*). Thomas often explicitly asserts this structural duplicity of order: "Est autem duplex ordo considerandus in rebus. Unus, quo aliquid creatum ordinatur ad alium creatum [. . .] Alius ordo, quo omnia creata ordinantur in Deum" (*Summa Theologiae*, I, q. 21, a. 1, ad 3; see also Krings 1941, p. 10). "Quaecumque autem sunt a Deo, ordinem habent ad invicem et ad ipsum Deum" (*Summa Theologiae*, I, q. 47, a. 3). That this duplicity is strictly linked to the Aristotelian aporia is proved by the fact that Thomas resorts to the paradigm of the army ("sicut in exercitu apparet": *Contra Gentiles*, Book III, Chapter 64, n. 1) and quotes repeatedly and in an explicit way the passage from Book L of the *Metaphysics* we discussed earlier ("Finis quidem universi est aliquod bonum in ipso existens, scilicet ordo ipsius universi, hoc autem bonum non est ultimus finis, sed ordinatur ad bonum extrinsecum ut ad ultimum fine; sicut etiam ordo exercitus ordinatur ad ducem, ut dicitur in XII

Metaphys.": *Summa Theologiae*, I, q. 103, a. 2, ad 3). But it is in Thomas's commentary on the *Metaphysics* that the splitting of the two aspects of order is referred back, without reservations, to the twofold paradigm of the good (and of being) in Aristotle. Here, not only does the *duplex ordo* correspond to the *duplex bonum* of Aristotle's text, but the problem is soon specified as that of the relation between the two orders (or between the two figures of the good). Thomas notes that Aristotle

> says, first, that the universe has both the separate good and the good of order [*bonum ordinis*]. For there is a separate good, which is the first mover, on which the heavens and the whole of nature depend as their end or desirable good [. . .] And since all things having one end must agree in their ordination to that end, some order must be found in the parts of the universe; and so the universe has both a separate good and a good of order. We see this, for example, in the case of an army [. . .] (Thomas Aquinas, *Commentary on the Metaphysics of Aristotle*, Book XII, Lesson XII, 2629–2630)

Although the two goods and the two orders are strictly linked, they are not yet symmetrical: "The separate good of the universe, which is the first mover, is a greater good [*melius bonum*] than the good of order which is found in the universe" (ibid., 2631). This imbalance between the two orders manifests itself in the difference between the relation of every creature to God and its relations with other creatures, which Aristotle expresses through the economic paradigm of the government of the house. Every creature—Thomas remarks—is in relation to God through its own particular nature, exactly as in the case of a house:

> In an ordered household or family different ranks of members are found. For example, under the head of the family there is a first rank, namely, that of the sons, and a second rank, which is that of the slaves, and a third rank, which is that of the domestic animals, as dogs and the like. For ranks of this kind have a different relation to the order of the household, which is imposed by the head of the family, who governs the household [. . .] And just as the order of the family is imposed by the law and precept of the head of the family, who is the principle of each of the things which are ordered in the household, with a view to carrying out the activities which pertain to the order of the household, in a similar fashion the nature of physical things is the principle by which each of them carries out the activity proper to it in the order of the universe. For just as any member of the household is disposed to act through the precept of the

head of the family, in a similar fashion any natural being is disposed by its own nature. (Ibid., 2633–2634)

The aporia that marks like a thin crack the wonderful order of the medieval cosmos now begins to become more visible. Things are ordered insofar as they have a specific relation among themselves, but this relation is nothing other than the expression of their relation to the divine end. And, vice versa, things are ordered insofar as they have a certain relation to God, but this relation expresses itself only by means of the reciprocal relation of things. The only content of the transcendent order is the immanent order, but the meaning of the immanent order is nothing other than the relation to the transcendent end. *"Ordo ad finem" and "ordo ad invicem" refer back to one another and found themselves on one another.* The perfect theocentric edifice of medieval ontology is based on this circle, and does not have any consistency outside of it. The Christian God is this circle, in which the two orders continuously penetrate one another. Since that which the order must keep united is in point of fact irremediably divided, not only is *ordo*—like Aristotle's being—*dicitur multipliciter* (this is the title of Kurt Flasch's dissertation on Thomas), but *ordo* also reproduces in its own structure the ambiguity that it must face. From this follows the contradiction, noticed by scholars, according to which Thomas at times founds the order of the world in the unity of God, and at times the unity of God in the immanent order of creatures (see Silva Tarouca, p. 350). This apparent contradiction is nothing other than the expression of the ontological fracture between transcendence and immanence, which Christian theology inherits and develops from Aristotelianism. If we push to the limit the paradigm of the separate substance, we have the Gnosis, with its God foreign to the world and creation; if we follow to the end the paradigm of immanence, we have pantheism. Between these two extremes, the idea of order tries to think a difficult balance, which Christian theology is always in the process of losing and which it must at each turn regain.

א *Order is an empty concept, or, more precisely, it is not a concept, but a signature [segnatura], that is, as we have seen, something that, in a sign or a concept, exceeds it to refer it back to a specific interpretation or move it to another context, yet without exiting the field of the semiotic to construct a new meaning.*

The concepts that order has the function of signing are genuinely ontologi-
cal. That is, the signature "order" produces a displacement of the privileged
place of ontology from the category of substance to the categories of relation
and praxis; this displacement is perhaps medieval thought's most important
contribution to ontology. For this reason, when in his study on ontology in
the Middle Ages, Krings reminds us that, "being is ordo *and the* ordo *is be-*
ing; the ordo *does not presuppose any being, but being has the* ordo *as its*
condition of possibility" (Krings 1940, p. 233), this does not mean that being
receives a new definition through the predicate of order, but that, thanks to
the signature "order," substance and relation, ontology and praxis enter into
a constellation that represents the specific legacy that medieval theology leaves
to modern philosophy.

4.9. Before Thomas, the text in which the aporetic character of order
appears most strongly is Augustine's *De genesi ad litteram*. Here, while
discussing the six days of creation and the meaning of the number 6,
Augustine suddenly quotes *Wisdom*, 11: 21: "Omnia mensura et numero et
pondere disposuisti," that is, one of the texts upon which the theological
tradition agrees to found the idea of an order of creation (Albert, Thomas's teacher, uses these terms as synonymous with *ordo*: "creata [. . .] per
pondus sive ordinem": *Summa Theologiae*, q. 3, 3, a. 4, I). The quotation
gives rise to a philosophical digression on the relation between God and
order, and on the very place of order, which is certainly one of the pin-
nacles of Augustine's theology. Augustine begins by asking the question of
whether "these three, measure, number, weight, in which, as it is written,
God has arranged all things, were somewhere or other before the whole
natural cosmos was created, or whether they too were created; and if they
existed beforehand, where were they?" (Augustine, *The Literal Meaning of
Genesis*, 4, 3, 7, p. 246). The question regarding the place of order is immediately turned into a question on the relation between God and order:

> After all, before creation there was nothing except the creator. Therefore they
> were in him. But how? I mean, we read that these other things that have been
> created are also in him; so are these three identical with him, or rather are in
> him by whom they are governed and directed [*a quo reguntur et gubernantur*]?
> And how are these identical with him? God, after all, is neither measure nor
> number nor weight, nor all of them together. Or, rather, as we ordinarily
> understand measure in the things we measure, and number in the things we
> number or count, and weight in the things we weigh, no, God is not these

things; but insofar as measure sets a limit [*modum praefigit*] to everything, and number gives everything its specific form [*speciem praebet*], and weight draws [*trahit*] everything to rest and stability, he is the original, true and unique measure which defines for all things their bounds, the number which forms all things, the weight which guides all things; so are we to understand that by the words *You have arranged all things in measure and number and weight* nothing else was being said but "You have arranged all things in yourself"? It is a great thing, a concession granted to few, to soar beyond everything that can be measured and see measure without measure, to soar beyond everything that can be numbered and see number without number, to soar beyond everything that can be weighed and see weight without weight. (Ibid., 4, 3, 7–8, p. 246)

It is important to dwell on this extraordinary passage, in which the paradoxical relation between God and order finds its most radical formulation and, at the same time, displays its connection with the problem of *oikonomia*. Measure, number, and weight, that is, the order by means of which God has arranged creatures, cannot themselves be created things. Therefore, although they are certainly also present in things, insofar as God "so arranged all things that they would have measure and number and weight" (ibid., 4, 5, 11, p. 248), they are outside of things; they are in God or coincide with him. God is, in his own being, *ordo*, order. And yet he cannot be measure, number, and order in the sense in which these terms define the order of created things. God is, in himself, *extra ordinem*, or rather, he is order only in the sense of an *ordering* and *arranging*, that is, not in the sense of a substance, but in that of an activity. "He is not measure, number, and weight in an absolute way, but *ille ista est* in a completely new way [. . .] in the sense that *ordo* is no longer given as *mensura, numerus, pondus*, but as *praefigere, praebere, trahere*, as *finishing, forming, ordering*" (Krings 1940, p. 245). The being of God, as order, is structurally *ordinatio*, that is, praxis of government and activity that arranges [*dispone*] according to measure, number, and weight. It is in this sense that the *dispositio* (which we should not forget is the Latin translation of *oikonomia*) of things in the order means nothing else but the *dispositio* of things in God himself. Immanent and transcendent order once again refer back to each other in a paradoxical coincidence, which can nevertheless be understood only as a perpetual *oikonomia*, as a continuous activity of government of the world, one that implies a fracture between being and praxis and, at the same time, tries to heal it.

Augustine clearly claims this in the paragraphs that immediately follow, in which he interprets the verse of Genesis, "He rested on the seventh day from all His work which He had done" (2, 2). According to Augustine, this verse should not be understood in the sense that, at a certain point, God ceased to operate.

> It is not, you see, like a mason building houses; when he has finished he goes away, and his work goes on standing when he has stopped working on it and gone away. No, the world will not be able to go on standing for a single moment, if God withdraws from it his government [*si ei Deus regimen sui subtraxerit*]. (Augustine, *The Literal Meaning of Genesis*, 4, 12, 22, p. 253)

On the contrary, all creatures are not in God as part of his being, but only as the result of his incessant operation:

> We are not in him, I mean to say, like his substance [*tamquam substantia eius*] [. . .] but evidently, since we are something different from him, we are only in him because he is working at this, and this is his work by which his Wisdom *reaches end to end mightily and governs* [*disponit*] *all things sweetly*, and it is by this arrangement that "in him we live and move and are." From this the conclusion follows that if he withdraws this work from things, we will neither live nor move nor be. It is clear therefore that not for one single day did God cease from the work of government [*ab opera regendi*]. (Ibid., 4, 12, 23, p. 254)

The transformation of classical ontology that is implicit in Christian theology is perhaps nowhere clearer than in these passages from Augustine. Not only is the substance of creatures nothing other than the activity of the divine *dispositio*, such that the being of creatures utterly depends on a praxis of government—it is, in its essence, praxis and government—but the very being of God—insofar as it is, in a special sense, measure, number, and weight, that is, order—is no longer only substance or thought, but also and in the same measure *dispositio*, praxis. *Ordo* names the incessant activity of government that presupposes and, at the same time, continually heals the fracture between transcendence and immanence, God and the world.

The promiscuity, if not the short-circuit, between being and *dispositio*, substance and *oikonomia* that Augustine introduces in God is explicitly theorized by Scholasticism, in particular by Albert and Thomas, especially with regard to the problem of order in God (*ordo in divinis*). These authors distinguish to this end between local and temporal orders, which cannot take place in God, and *ordo originis* or *ordo naturae,* which correspond to the Trinitarian procession of the divine persons (see Krings 1941, pp. 65–67). The continuity between the problem of the *ordo* and that of the *oikonomia* is here apparent. God is not order just insofar as he arranges [*dispone*] and orders the created world, but also and especially insofar as this *dispositio* has its archetype in the procession of the Son from the Father, and of the Spirit from both. Divine *oikonomia* and government of the world perfectly correspond to one another. "The order of nature in the reciprocal flux of the divine persons," Albert writes, "is the cause of the flux of creatures from the first and universal acting intellect" (*Summa Theologiae*, I, 46). For his part, Thomas writes,

> The order of nature is that through which someone is from other [*quo aliquis est ex alio*]; and in this way a difference of origins is posed, and not one of temporal priority, and the difference of kind is excluded. For this reason we cannot admit that there is in God a simple order, but only an order of nature. (Thomas Aquinas, *Commentary on Sentences*, Book 1, d. 20, q. 1, a. 3, qc. 1)

Trinitarian *oikonomia, ordo,* and *gubernatio* constitute an inseparable triad, whose terms interpenetrate, insofar as they name the new figure of ontology that Christian theology bequeaths to modernity.

א *When Marx, starting with the 1844* Economic and Philosophical Manuscripts, *thinks the being of man as praxis, and praxis as the self-production of man, he is after all secularizing the theological idea of the being of creatures as divine operation. After having conceived of being as praxis, if we take God away and put man in his place, we will consequently obtain the result that the essence of man is nothing other than the praxis through which he incessantly produces himself.*

א *In* De ordine, *I, 5, 14, Augustine expounds this all-pervasive character of the concept of order, including in it even the most negligible and contingent events. The fact that the noise of a mouse woke up Licentius, one of the protagonists of the dialogue, during the night, and that in this way Augustine came to talk to him, belongs to the same order as the letters that will constitute the book that will follow one day from their conversation (the book Augustine is actually writing). Both orders are in turn contained in the very order of the divine government of the world:*

Who will deny, great God, that you administer all things with order? [. . .] The little mouse has come out in order for me to wake up [. . .] And if one day what we told each other were transcribed into letters and became known to people [. . .] certainly the fluttering of leaves in the fields and the movement of the unworthy little animals in the houses would be as necessary as those letters in the order of things.

4.10. The theological paradigm of the distinction between Kingdom and Government is present in the double articulation of divine action as creation (*creatio*) and conservation (*conservatio*). In his commentary on the *Liber de causis*, Thomas writes that "we should keep in mind that the action of the first cause is twofold: one inasmuch as it establishes things, which is called creation; another inasmuch as it governs things already established [*res iam institutas regit*]" (Thomas Aquinas, *Commentary on the Book of Causes*, p. 137). The two operations of the first cause are correlated, in the sense that, through creation, God is the cause of the being of creatures and not only of their becoming, and, for this reason, they need the divine government in order to preserve themselves in being. Resuming the Augustinian theme of the incessant government of the world, Thomas writes that "the *esse* of all creaturely beings so depends upon God that they could not continue to exist even for a moment, but would fall away into nothingness unless they were sustained in existence by the operation of the divine virtue" (Thomas Aquinas, *Summa Theologiae*, 1, q. 104, a. 1). This twofold structure of the divine works constitutes the model for the activity of secular regality:

Looking at the world as a whole, there are two works of God to be considered: the first is creation; the second, God's government of the things created. These two works are, in like manner, performed by the soul in the body since, first, by the virtue of the soul the body is formed, and then the latter is governed and moved by the soul. Of these works, the second more properly pertains to the office of kingship. Therefore government [*gubernatio*] belongs to all kings (the very name king is derived from the fact that they direct the government) [*a gubernationis regimine regis nomen accipitur*], while the first work does not fall to all kings, for not all kings establish the kingdom or city in which they rule but bestow their regal care upon a kingdom or city already established. We must remember, however, that if there were no one to establish the city or kingdom, there would be no question of governing the kingdom [*gubernatio regni*]. The very notion of kingly office, then, comprises the establishment of a city and kingdom, and some kings have indeed established cities in which to rule; for example, Ninus founded Nineveh, and Romulus, Rome. It pertains also to the governing office to preserve the things governed, and to use them for the purpose for which they were established. If, therefore, one does not know how a kingdom is established, one cannot fully understand the task of its government. Now, from the example of the creation of the world one may learn how a kingdom is established. In creation we may consider, first, the production of things; secondly, the orderly distinction of the parts of the world. (Thomas Aquinas, *On Kingship*, Book Two, Chapter II, pp. 55–56)

Kingdom and government, creation and conservation, *ordo ad deum* and *ordo ad invicem* are functionally correlated, in the sense that the first operation implies and determines the second, which, on the other hand, distinguishes itself from the former and, at least in the case of secular government, can be separated from it.

ℵ *In* Nomos of the Earth *(p. 82), Schmitt refers the distinction between constituent and constituted power, which in the 1928* Verfassungslehre *he juxtaposed with the Spinozan distinction between* natura naturans *and* natura naturata, *to the distinction between* ordo ordinans *and* ordo ordinatus. *As a matter of fact, Thomas, who rather speaks of* ordinatio *and* ordinis executio, *understands creation as a process of "ordering" ("sic patet quod Deus res in esse produxit eas ordinando":* Contra Gentiles, *Book 2, Chapter 24, n. 4), in which the two figures of order are articulated together ("ordo enim aliquorum ad invicem est propter ordinem eorum ad finem": ibid.). It would be interesting to investigate from this perspective the possible theological sources of the distinction between* pouvoir constituent *and* pouvoir constitué *in Sieyès, for whom the people take the place of God as a constituent subject.*

4.11. The Latin treatise known as *Liber de causis* or *Liber Aristotelis de expositione bonitatis purae* had a strategic function in the construction of the Kingdom-Government paradigm. We cannot understand the rank and decisive importance that this obscure Arabic summary of Proclus, translated into Latin in the twelfth century, had for theology between the twelfth and fourteenth centuries, if we do not understand at the same time that it contains something like the ontological model for the providential machine of the divine government of the world. The first epistemological obstacle that this machine met with concerned the way in which a transcendent principle could exercise its influence on the created world and make its "regime" effective—which was precisely the problem that Chapter X of Book L of the *Metaphysics* had bequeathed to medieval culture. It is precisely this question that the pseudo-epigraphic treatise tackles in the guise of a Neoplatonic hierarchy of the causes. That is, the Aristotelian problem of the relation between the transcendent good and the immanent order—which was decisive for medieval theology—was solved by means of a doctrine of the causes: the *Liber Aristotelis de expositione bonitatis purae* is actually a *Liber de causis*.

Let us follow, through Thomas's commentary, the strategy that is implicit in the theological reception of this book. From the beginning, it is a matter of constructing a hierarchy, as the anonymous compiler had done on a Neoplatonic basis, and, at the same time, an articulation of the first and second causes. The treatise opens with the following words: "Every primary cause infuses its effect more powerfully [*plus est influens super suum causatum*] than does a universal second cause" (1, 1). But while in the division of the causes operated by the text the emphasis is placed at each turn on the sublimity and separateness of the first cause, which not only precedes and dominates the second causes, but also carries out all that they operate "per modum alium et altiorem et sublimiorem," the constant preoccupation of Thomas's commentary is to stress the coordination and articulation between the two levels. He interprets the claim according to which "the first cause aids the second cause in its activity, because the first cause also effects every activity that the second cause effects" (Thomas Aquinas, *Commentary on the Book of Causes*, p. 6) in a purely functional sense, which shows that the two causes integrate with each other in order to make their action effective:

> The activity by which the second cause causes an effect is caused by the first cause, for the first cause aids the second cause, making it act. Therefore, the first cause is more a cause than the second cause of that activity in virtue of which an effect is produced by the second cause [. . .] The second cause is the cause of the effect through its potency, or power. Therefore, that the second cause is the cause of its effect is due to the first cause. To be the cause of the effect, therefore, lies primarily in the first cause and only secondarily in the second cause. (Ibid., pp. 8–9)

What is also new in Thomas's commentary is the specification of second causes as particular causes, which contains an implicit strategic reference to the distinction between general providence and special providence (which, as we shall see, defines the structure of the divine government of the world):

> For it is clear that the extent to which some efficient cause is prior, to that extent does its power extend itself to more things [. . .] But the proper effect of the second cause is found in fewer things. So it is more particular [*unde et particularior est*]. (Ibid., p. 10)

Thomas's interest in the functional articulation between the two orders of causes is evident in the attention with which he describes the linking together of the causes in the production of a (substantial or accidental) effect:

> The order is *per se* when the intention of the first cause respects the ultimate effect through all the mediating causes, as when a craftsman's art moves the hand, and the hand the hammer that pounds out the iron, to which the intention of the art reaches. The order is *per accidens*, however, when the intention of the cause proceeds only to the proximate effect. But that something else is in turn brought about by that effect lies outside the intention [*praeter intentionem*] of the first agent, as, when someone lights a candle, it is outside its intention that the lighted candle in turn light another, and that one another. (Ibid., p. 11)

But it is in the commentary on the Propositions 20–24 that the strategic nexus between the hierarchy of causes in the treatise and the paradigm of the providential government of the world becomes more evident. What is in question here is the way in which the first cause governs (*regit*) created things while remaining transcendent with regard to them ("praeter quod commisceatur cum eis"). Proposition 20 thus specifies that the fact that the first cause governs the world does not jeopardize its unity or transcendence ("regimen non debilitat unitatem eius exaltatam super omnem rem"), and does not even hinder the efficacy of its government ("neque prohibet eam essentia unitatis seiuncta a rebus quin regat eas"). That is, we are presented with a kind of Neoplatonic solution to the Aristotelian aporia concerning the transcendent good. On the other hand, the fact that Thomas's commentary orients the reading of the text toward a theory of providence is proved by the immediate connection that he establishes between the formulations of the text and the economic-providential paradigm of the divine government of the world. Not only does a quotation from Proclus explicitly introduce this theme ("every divine thing [. . .]

provides for secondary things": ibid., p. 122), but the passage from the anonymous author is used against the traditional arguments of those who deny providence:

> We should note that in human government we see it happen that the one who has a charge of ruling a number of things must be drawn from his own government to many things. But he who is free from the charge of governing others is more able to preserve uniformity in himself. Hence the Epicurean philosophers asserted that in order to conserve divine quiet and uniformity the gods could have charge of no government. Instead, they are entirely at leisure, caring about nothing, so that in this way they are seen to be happy. And so, against this [the author] begins in this proposition by saying that these two things are not contrary in the first cause and that the universal government of things and the supreme unity [. . .] do not impede one another. (Ibid., pp. 121–122)

In the same sense, Proposition 23, which distinguishes and coordinates science and government, is interpreted as a thesis "de regimine secundae causae," that is, on the twofold way in which the second cause carries out its action in the government of the world, at one time according to its nature (this is the model of the *ordo ad invicem*), and at another time according to its participation in the first cause (*ordo ad deum*). The action of the second cause is thus compared with a heated knife that, according to its nature, cuts, but according to its participation in fire, burns ("sicut cultellus ignitus, secundum propria formam incidit, in quantum vero est ignitus urit"). Once again, the Aristotelian aporia concerning the transcendent good is solved by means of the articulation between transcendence and immanence:

> Thus, each of the highest intelligences that is called "divine" has a double action: one insofar as it abundantly participates in the divine goodness, and another according to its proper nature. (Ibid., p. 132)

But this also means, following the division between what is general and what is particular according to which providential action is articulated, that the government of the world redoubles itself into a *regimen Dei* or *causae primae*, which is extended to all created things, and a *regimen intelligentiae* or *causae secundae*, which concerns only some of them:

> And so it is that the government of the first cause, which is according to the

essence of goodness, extends to all things [. . .] But the rule of an intelligence, which is proper to it, does not extend to all things. (Ibid., p. 133)

If we now turn to the treatise *De gubernatione mundi* (*Summa Theologiae*, I, qq. 103–113), we see that it is precisely the hierarchical connection of first and second causes that provides us with a model of the articulation between general and special providence through which the divine government of the world is carried out.

God governs the world as a first cause ("ad modum primi agentis": ibid., I, q. 105, a. 5, ad 1), bestowing on created things their form and proper nature, and preserving them in being. But this does not prevent his operation from entailing also the operation of the second causes ("nihil prohibet quin una et eadem actio procedat a primo et secundo agente": ibid., I, q. 105, a. 5, ad 2). The government of the world thus results from the articulation of a hierarchy of causes and orders, of the Kingdom and particular governments:

> From every cause there results some sort of order in its effects, since a cause has the meaning of being a principle. In consequence there are as many orders as there are causes, with one order contained under another, even as one cause is subordinated to another in such a way that the higher cause is not subject to the lower, but the other way round. There is a clear example in human affairs: the domestic order [*ordo domus*] depends on the father of the family; that order in turn is subordinated to the municipal order [*sub ordine civitatis*] deriving from the city's ruler; the municipal order comes under the regimen of the king, who is the source of order in the whole realm. (Ibid., I, q. 105, a. 6)

Insofar as it is considered in its connection with the first cause, the order of the world is unchangeable and coincides with divine prescience and goodness. On the other hand, insofar as it entails an articulation of second causes, it makes room for a divine intervention "praeter ordinem rerum."

The *Liber de causis* is so important for medieval theology because by distinguishing first causes from second causes it discovered the articulation between transcendence and immanence, general and particular, upon which the machine of the divine government of the world could be founded.

4.12. The discussions that led to the canonists' elaboration of the "political type" of the *rex inutilis* between the twelfth and thirteenth centuries is the place in which the distinction between the Kingdom and the Government finds for the first time its technical formulation in the juridical field. What lies at the basis of these discussions was the doctrine of the pontiff's power to depose the temporal sovereign, which had been formulated in a letter from Gregory VII to Hermann of Metz. Gregory refers here to Pope Zachary's deposition for inadequacy of the last Merovingian king, Childeric III, and his replacement with Pippin, Charles the Great's father. This text is important, since it was included by Gratian in his *Decretum* and thus served as a reference for the elaborations of later canonists. Asserting the primacy of the *sacerdotium* over the *imperium*, Gregory writes, "another Roman pontiff deposed a king of the Franks, not so much because of his evil deeds as because he was not equal to so great an office [*tantae potestati non erat utilis*], and set in his place Pippin, father of Charles the Great, releasing all the Franks from the oath of fealty which they had sworn to (the king)" (*Decretum,* c. 15, q. 6, c. 3; see Peters, p. 281). The chroniclers of the twelfth century had already turned Childeric into the prototype of the *rex ignavus et inutilis,* who embodies the gap between nominal regality and its real exercise ("Stabat enim in rege sola nominis umbra; in Pippino vero potestas et dignitas efficaciter apparebat. Erat tunc Hildericus rex ignavus et inutilis [. . .]": Geoffrey of Viterbo, *Pantheon,* in *PL,* 198, 924d–925a). But it was thanks to the canonists, especially Hugh of Pisa, that the *rex inutilis* was turned into the paradigm of the distinction between *dignitas* and *administratio,* the office and the activity in which it expresses itself. According to this doctrine, the illness, old age, madness, or sloth of a prince or prelate should not necessarily lead to his deposition, but rather to the separation between the *dignitas,* which remains attached to his person, and the practice, which is entrusted to a *coadiutor* or *curator.* The fact that what was at stake was not only something practical but also involved an actual doctrine of the separability of sovereign power is proved by the precision with which the *Glossa ordinaria* to the passage of the *Decretum* that reported the case of two Roman emperors who reigned simultaneously assigns the *dignitas* to one, and the *administratio* to the other, thus ratifying at one and the same time the unity and divisibility of power ("Dic quod erant duae personae, sed tamen erant loco unius [. . .] Sed forte unus habuit dignitatem, alter administrationem": quoted in Peters, p. 295).

It is on the basis of these canonistic elaborations that, in 1245, at the demand of the Portuguese clergy and nobility, Innocent IV issued the decretal *Grandi*, with which he assigned to Afonso of Boulogne, brother of King Sancho II—who had been shown to be unable to govern—the *cura et administratio generalis et libera* of the kingdom, yet leaving the regal *dignitas* to the sovereign.

In other words, the radical case of the *rex inutilis* lays bare the twofold structure that defines the governmental machine of the West. Sovereign power is structurally articulated according to two different levels, aspects, or polarities: it is, at the same time, *dignitas* and *administratio*, Kingdom and Government. The sovereign is structurally *mehaignié*, in the sense that his dignity is measured against the possibility of its uselessness and inefficacy, in a correlation in which the *rex inutilis* legitimates the actual administration that he has always already cut off from himself and that, however, formally continues to belong to him.

Thus, the answer to Von Seydel's question "what is left of reigning if we take governing away from it?" is that the Kingdom is the remainder that poses itself as the whole that infinitely subtracts itself from itself. Just as, in the divine *gubernatio* of the world, transcendence and immanence, *ordo ad deum* and *ordo ad invicem*, must be unceasingly distinguished for providential action to unceasingly rejoin them, so the Kingdom and the Government constitute a double machine, which is the place of a continuous separation and articulation. The *potestas* is *plena* only to the extent that it can be divided.

א *Not without noticeable hesitations, medieval jurists developed the distinction between* merum imperium *and* mistum imperium. *Following one of Irnerius's glosses, they called* imperium *that without which there cannot be a jurisdiction* (sine quo nulla esset iurisdictio), *but then distinguished as "pure" the* imperium *considered as such and, on the other hand, called "mixed" the* imperium *that involves an actual* iurisdictio (Costa, pp. 112–113). *In Stephen of Tournai's* Summa *this distinction is developed into the idea of a clear separation between* iurisdictio *and* administratio, *between a* potestas *and its practice:*

> If the emperor grants somebody the jurisdiction and the power to judge [*potestas iudicandi*], but does not allot him a province or a people to be judged, he will then have the title, that is the name, but not the practice [*habet quidem titulum, idest nomen, sed non administrationem*]. (Stefan von Doornick, p. 222)

4.13. An analysis of the canonistic notion of *plenitudo potestatis* can give rise to some instructive considerations. According to the theory of the primacy of the pontiff's spiritual power over the temporal power of the sovereign, which found in Boniface VIII's bull *Unam sanctam* its polemical expression and in Giles of Rome's *De ecclesiastica potestate* its doctrinal layout, the plenitude of power lies with the Supreme Pontiff, to whom belong both of the swords discussed in Luke 22:38 ("Domine, ecce duo gladii hic. At ille dixit eis: Satis est"), interpreted as the symbols of spiritual and material power. The debate about the primacy of one power over the other was so fierce, and the struggles between the partisans of the empire and those of ecclesiastic power so violent and persistent, that historians and scholars ended up overlooking what should have been a preliminary question: Why is power originally divided? Why does it present itself as always already articulated into two swords? As a matter of fact, even the supporters of the pontifical *plenitudo potestatis* admit that power is structurally divided and that the government of men (*gubernacio hominum* is the technical term that Giles uses recurrently) is necessarily articulated into two (and only two) authorities [*potestà*] or swords:

> In the government of men and in the rule of the human race or in the rule of the faithful, there are only two powers and two swords [*due potestates et duo gladii*]: the priestly and the royal or imperial power—that is, a spiritual and a material sword. (Giles of Rome, *On Ecclesiastical Power*, p. 108)

In his treatise, Giles cannot help asking the question as to "why there are two swords in the Church and neither more nor fewer" (ibid., p. 107). If the spiritual power is higher than any other and naturally extends its government to material things just as the soul governs the body, "what need was there, then, to institute another power and another sword [*aliam potestatem et alium gladium*]?" (ibid., p. 108). The co-substantiality and co-originarity of the split between the two powers in the Church is proved by Giles's interpretation of Luke 22:38.

> And if due consideration be given to the words of the Gospel, the way in which the Church possesses both swords is perfectly illustrated by the two swords [there mentioned]. For, as Bede says, one of those swords was drawn and the other remained in its sheath. And so, although there were two swords, we read that only one sword was drawn, with which Peter struck the servant of the High Priest and cut off his right ear. What, therefore, does this mean— that while there were two swords, the one was drawn and the other remained

in its sheath—if not that the Church possesses two swords: the spiritual as user [*quantum ad usum*], which is represented by the drawn sword, and the material, not as user, but as commander [*quantum ad nutum*]. (Ibid., pp. 51–52)

In addition, the two swords,

> exist now, under the Law of Grace; they existed under the Written Law; and they existed under the law of nature [. . .] These two swords, then, always were and are different things. (Ibid., pp. 20–21)

If the division of power is structural to such an extent, what is the reason for this? The large number of answers given by Giles is a function of their often evident insufficiency, and it is possible that the decisive answer is to be read, as it were, between the lines of those adduced. An initial reason for the duality lies in the "great excellence and the very great perfection [*nimia excellencia et nimia perfectio*] of spiritual things" (ibid., p. 108). Spiritual things are, in fact, so noble that, in order to avoid the possibility of deficiencies and negligences with regard to them, it was necessary to establish a second power, which specifically takes care of corporeal things, so that the spiritual power may be entirely devoted to spiritual things. But the reason for their distinction is, at the same time, the foundation of their strict articulation:

> But, as has been noted, when the two powers are such that the one is general and extended [*generalis et extensa*] and the other particular and limited [*particularis et contracta*], it must be that the one is under the other, is instituted through the other, and may act only by commission of the other. (Ibid., p. 109)

Giles compares the relation between the two with the connection that, according to the medieval doctrine of generation, exists between celestial virtue (as a first cause) and the seed that is in the animal when it mates (as a second cause). "There would be no power in the seed of a horse to produce a horse unless it had this from the power of heaven" (ibid.). But it is precisely here that that the aporetic character of the relation between the two powers comes to light. The two swords are clearly divided, and yet, the second, the material one, is included in the first. The *plenitudo potestatis* that rests with the pontiff is, in fact, defined by Giles as "that fullness of power [that] resides in some agent when that agent can do without a secondary cause whatever it can do with a secondary cause" (ibid., p. 187). For this reason, that is, insofar as the pontiff has a power in which every power is contained ("posse in quo reservatur omne posse": ibid.), his *potestas* is said to be full.

> And, so that we may pass to the government of men by way of those natural phenomena which we see in the government of the world, we shall say that fullness of power does not reside in the heaven or in any secondary agent whatsoever; for the heaven cannot do without a secondary cause what it can do with a secondary cause. For example, although the heaven and a lion bring about the generation of a lion, the heaven could not produce a lion without a lion, nor could it produce a horse without a horse. (Ibid., pp. 187–188)

On the other hand, the spiritual power can produce its effect without the aid of second causes, and yet, it needs to separate itself from the material sword. There is something lacking in spiritual power, in spite of its perfection, and that something is the effectiveness of the execution. Turning to the doctrine of the distinction between the titularity of an office and its execution, Giles argues that

> by reason of her power and lordship, the Church as such has a superior and primary lordship in temporal things, but she does not have an immediate jurisdiction and [right of] execution [. . .] Caesar and the temporal lord, however, do have such a jurisdiction and [right of] execution; and so we see that there are distinct powers, we see that there are distinct rights, we see that there are distinct swords. But this distinction does not mean that the one power is not under the other, the one right under the other, and the one sword under the other. (Ibid., pp. 199–200)

The actual reason for the distinction between primary and secondary power, titularity and execution, is that it is a necessary condition for the proper functioning of the governmental machine:

> But if there were only one sword in the Church, namely the spiritual, then those tasks which must be performed in the government of men would not be as well done; for the spiritual sword would then neglect many tasks which should be performed in the spiritual sphere, because it would itself be obliged to attend to material affairs [. . .] Therefore, the fact that a second sword was instituted is not due to a lack of power on the part of the spiritual: rather, it is for the sake of good order and decency [*ex bona ordinacione et ex decencia*] [. . .] It is not due to a lack of power on the part of the spiritual sword that a second sword, which is called material, has been instituted. Rather, this is

in order to secure the correct implementation of the execution [*propter benefi-cium execucionis*]. For the spiritual sword could not execute spiritual tasks or devote itself to spiritual matters so well or so beneficially if it did not have the aid of the material sword [. . .] (Ibid., pp. 110–111)

Beyond the dispute about the primacy of one sword over the other, to which scholars have exclusively devoted their attention, it turns out that what is primarily at stake in the division between the two powers is guar-anteeing the possibility of the government of men. This possibility re-quires the supposition of a *plenitudo potestatis* that, however, must imme-diately distinguish itself from its actual exercise (its *executio*), which then constitutes the secular sword. From a theoretical point of view, the de-bate is not so much between the supporters of the primacy of priesthood or the empire, but between the "governmentalists" ["*governamentalisti*"] (who conceive power as always already articulated according to a double structure: authority [*potestà*] and execution; Kingdom and Government) and the promoters of a sovereignty in which it is not possible to separate power from act, *ordinatio* from *executio*. Gelasius I's well-known dictum according to which "duo quippe sunt [. . .] quibus principaliter mundus hic regitur: auctoritas sacra pontificum, et regalis potestas" (*Epistolae et decreta*, 8, in *PL*, 59, 42a)—which he addressed to the emperor Anastasius in 494, that is, well before the beginning of the conflict between the two swords—must be translated—after all, in an absolutely literal way—as: the world is governed through the coordination of two principles, the *auctoritas* (that is, a power without actual execution) and the *potestas* (that is, a power that can be exercised); the Kingdom and the Government.

א *In this perspective, it is possible to clarify the position of those who, like John Quidort, refuse to accept the theory of the pontiff's* plenitudo potestatis, *since it implies an unnatural separation of power* [potenza] *from act, and power* [potere] *from execution. Referring most likely to Giles of Rome, John writes in his* De potestate regia et papali *that*

some claim that the secular power belongs to the pope immediately and ac-cording to his primary authority, but that the pope does not have the imme-diate execution of it, which he delegates to the prince [. . .] It can certainly happen that somebody has the power to do something, but not the act, be-cause of some hindrance, like, for example, if one has the power to build, but not the act, since he lacks the matter, or because of a corporal defect, as in the case of a dumb person who cannot speak. These are hindrances that befall the conferring of power. But only a foolish person would bestow the priesthood upon somebody if he knew that he was hindered in this way. Therefore, it is meaningless to say that the pope receives immediately from God the power of the secular sword, whose exercise, however, is not usually his responsibility. If this were the case, God would act against nature, as the latter never gives to anybody a virtue separated from the act, since those who have the power also have the act [*cuius potentia, eius est actus*]. (Quidort, p. 120)

Here, the conflict does not concern only and especially the primacy of one power [potere] over the other, but the separation of titularity from exercise, of the Kingdom from the Government.

ℵ *Peters followed the progeny of the figure of the medieval* rex inutilis *in the notion of* roi fainéant *between the sixteenth and seventeenth centuries. The term appears in the fourteenth century in the* Grandes chroniques de France *to translate the* rex nihil faciens *of medieval chronicles, and is later applied, according to its double meaning of sluggish ("qui fit nule chose") and dissolute ("adonné à la paillardise, oisiveté et vices"), to the last of the Carolingian monarchs. In his 1643* Histoire de France, *Mezeray contemptuously applies it to the last of the Merovingian kings, "tous fainéants, hébetez, et plongés dans les ordures du vice" (Peters, p. 543). We can then find it applied to Louis VI, Charles VI, and Henry III of France, as well as, among other English kings, to Henry III, Henry VI, and even the figure of King Arthur in some courtly novels (Peters, p. 547).*

4.14. The theological model of the separation of power from its exercise is found in the distinction between absolute and ordered power [*potenza*] in God—that is, in the doctrine of divine impotence, of what God, in spite of his omnipotence, cannot do (or cannot not do). According to this doctrinal complex (which was founded on a passage from *De natura et gratia*—1, 7, 8—in which Augustine answers the question as to whether Christ could have prevented Judas's betrayal by saying that he certainly could have done it, but he had not wanted it: "Potuit ergo, sed noluit"), God, with regard to his power considered as such (*de potentia absoluta*), could do anything that did not entail a contradiction (for instance, embodying himself as a woman, instead of as Jesus, to save men; or damning Peter and saving Judas; or even just destroying all of his creation). But *de potentia ordinata*, that is, with regard to his will and wisdom, he can only do what he has decided to do. In other words, the will constitutes the apparatus that, dividing power into absolute and ordered power, allows to contain the unacceptable consequences of divine omnipotence (and, more generally, of any doctrine of power), but without negating it as such. Thomas writes that

> nothing can be within divine power which is not held in the wisdom and justice of his mind and will. All the same, since his will is not bound of necessity to this or that particular objective [. . .] there is no reason why something should not be within divine power which God does not will, and which is no part of the present order he has established. We conceive of understanding and wisdom as directing, will as commanding, and power as executing; as for what lies within power as such, God is said to be able to do it by his absolute power [. . .] As for what lies within his power as carrying out the command of his just will, he is said to be able to do it by his ordinate power. Accordingly, we should state that by absolute power God can do things other than those he foresaw that he would do and pre-ordained to do. Nevertheless nothing can come to pass that he has not foreseen and pre-ordained. (Thomas Aquinas, *Summa Theologiae*, 1, q. 25, a. 5, ad 1)

What is interesting about this theological apparatus is that, contrary to those who rejected any distinction between absolute and ordered power, it made it possible to reconcile God's omnipotence with the idea of an ordered, nonarbitrary, and nonchaotic government of the world. But this de facto amounted to making the distinction in God between his absolute power and its effective exercise, between a formal sovereignty and its execution. Limiting absolute power, ordered power constitutes it as the foundation of the divine government of the world. The nexus between this theological problem and the juridical-political problem of the separation between sovereignty and its exercise is evident, and was soon noticed by canonists. With regard to a decretal by Innocent IV that denied an abbot the power to suspend a monk's vow of poverty, the distinction between absolute and ordered power was thus applied by Hostiensis and other canonists to the problem of the papal *plenitudo potestatis*, to show that, *de potentia ordinata*, the pontiff must abide by the law, although *de potentia absoluta* he is not bound by it (Courtenay, pp. 107–108).

Once again, the *plenitudo potestatis* is shown to have an inner articulation that structurally divides it, and the doctrine of what God cannot do becomes the paradigm of the distinction between power [*potere*] and its exercise, the Kingdom and the Government.

In Matthew of Acquasparta's questions on providence, God's impotence clearly displays its governmental meaning. Giving a negative answer to the question of whether God could have created a rational creature who could not sin, Matthew explains that this is impossible not because of an impotence on the part of God, but because it would have made the providential government of the world pointless. As a matter of fact, creating a rational creature completely unable to sin would mean, on the one hand, denying him free will and, on the other, making the grace by means of which God preserves and governs creatures useless.

> Every rational creature, insofar as it is a creature, must be preserved by God and needs the creator's continuous maintenance [*manutenentia*], for if he ceased to govern the things that he had created, these things would go to ruin [. . .] The general influence of divine maintenance is not sufficient for the preservation of the moral good of creatures: the latter also needs that of grace. For this, just as God cannot make it so that a creature preserves itself, so he cannot make it so that by nature and by itself it cannot sin. (Matthew of Acquasparta, p. 292)

God's impotence functions to make possible a righteous government of the world.

Threshold

We can now better understand the Arthurian mythologeme of the *roi mehaignié*. It is the reflection in the literary field of a transformation and splitting of the concept of sovereignty that must have troubled deeply contemporary minds. Although, as we have seen, it had some precedents in the Gnostic doctrine of the idle god and some parallelisms in the tradition of Roman law, this transformation is essentially carried out, from a technical point of view, in a canonistic field. The theological model of this separation is the doctrine of divine impotence, that is, the distinction between *potentia absoluta* and *potentia ordinata*. Hugh of Pisa and the *Grandi* decretal—with which Innocent IV, in the case of the *rex inutilis* Sancho II, separated regality from its exercise—gave to this distinction a juridical form of whose general meaning and political implications they were perhaps not fully aware. However, it is certain that, as has been observed, "*Grandi*, indeed, contained the results of the most articulate legal tradition which Europe had seen since the age of Justinian, but few territorial monarchies were capable, in 1245, of profiting fully from that tradition" (Peters, p. 304). The conflict that was here in question is not, however, so much between "legal authority" (which, due to the decretal, rested with the Earl of Boulogne) and "personal loyalty" (which was still owed to the sovereign Sancho II), as between a sovereignty inseparable from its exercise and a regality that is structurally divided and separable from government (or, in Foucault's terms, between territorial sovereignty and governmental power).

It is in this perspective that we can interpret the debate that, in the first few decades of the fourteenth century, opposes John XXII to Ockham. According to John, the laws that God has established are identical with his essence and, consequently, are eternal and unchangeable. Therefore, he cannot act otherwise than how he has chosen to act. Absolute and ordered powers are the same thing, and their distinction is purely nominal.

> It is impossible for God to save according to absolute power a man devoid of the sacrament of baptism, because this was decided from eternity according to ordered power, which is to be identified with God and cannot be changed [. . .] Some claim that God can do many things according to the absolute power which he cannot do according to the ordered power, but this is false and wrong, for the absolute power and the ordered power in God are the same thing and can be distinguished only by name, like Simon and Peter, which name the same person. Just as it is impossible that somebody hits Simon without hitting Peter, or that Peter does something that Simon does not, insofar as they are the same man, so it is impossible for God to do according to the absolute power things that are different from those he does according to ordered power, for they are the same thing and differ and can be distinguished only by name. (Quoted in Courtenay, p. 162)

What Ockham proposes against this thesis is the irreducibility of absolute power to ordered power: these are not two powers, but two different ways in which we say that God can or cannot do something, or two internal articulations of a single divine power in respect to the act.

> If one looks closely at this issue, saying that God can do things according to the absolute power which he cannot do according to the ordered power means nothing else than God can do things that he had not decided to do [*quae tamen minime ordinaret se facturum*]. But if he were to do these things,

he would do them according to the ordered power, for if he did them, he would have decided to do them. (Quoted in Courtenay, p. 164)

For Ockham, as a more modern thinker, it is essential to preserve the contingency of decision against an understanding of acting, professed by Muslims and "old women" (*vetulae*), that reduces it to pure necessity ("from this would follow that no creature could do anything that he does not actually do, so that all would happen according to necessity and nothing in a contingent way, like the infidels claim, and the ancient heretics, and also the occult heretics, the lays and the old women": quoted in ibid.).

What is at stake in this conflict is, in the final analysis, the functioning of the governmental apparatus. While, for the pontiff, the difference between the two levels or moments of the apparatus is purely nominal, so that the act of real government always already determines the power, and the Kingdom is fully identified with the Government, for Ockham, the Kingdom (absolute power) exceeds and always in some way precedes the Government (the ordered power), which reaches and determines it only at the moment of the *executio*, yet without ever exhausting it completely. In other words, two different conceptions of the government of men confront each other: the first is still dominated by the old model of territorial sovereignty, which reduces the double articulation of the governmental machine to a purely formal moment; the second is closer to the new economico-providential paradigm, in which the two elements maintain their identity, in spite of their correlation, and the contingency of the acts of government corresponds to the freedom of the sovereign decision. And yet, because of a peculiar inversion, this very paradigm that is, so to speak, more "democratic" is also close to the position of those canonists and theologians (like Duns Scotus) who, in the same years, elaborate the doctrine of the *potentia absoluta* as a model for exceptional powers [*poteri eccezionali*]. Insofar as it structurally exceeds ordered power [*potenza ordinata*], absolute power [*potenza assoluta*] is—not only in God, but in every agent (and, in particular, in the pontiff)—that which allows one to act legitimately "beyond the law and against it":

> Potest agere conformiter illi legi rectae, et tunc secundum potentiam ordinatam (ordinata enim est in quantum est principium exsequendi aliqua conformiter legi rectae) et potest agere praeter illam legem vel contra eam, et in hoc est potentia absoluta, excedens potentiam ordinatam. (Duns Scotus, quoted in Courtenay, p. 112)

§ 5   The Providential Machine

5.1. Michel Foucault's 1977–1978 course at the Collège de France, entitled *Sécurité, territoire, population,* is devoted to a genealogy of modern "governmentality." Foucault begins by distinguishing three different modalities in the history of power relations: the legal system that corresponds to the institutional model of the territorial State of sovereignty and that defines itself through a normative code that opposes what is allowed to what is prohibited, and consequently establishes a system of punishments; the disciplinary devices that correspond to the modern societies of discipline and put into practice, alongside the law, a series of police, medical, and penitentiary techniques to order, correct, and modulate the bodies of subjects; finally, the apparatuses of security that correspond to the contemporary state of population and the new practice that defines it, which Foucault names "the government of men." Foucault is careful to specify that these three modalities do not succeed one another chronologically or mutually exclude each other, but co-exist and are articulated with one another in such a way that, nevertheless, one of them constitutes at each turn the dominant political technology. The birth of the state of population and the primacy of the apparatuses of security thus coincide with the relative decline of the sovereign function and with the coming to light of a governmentality that defines the essential political problem of our time, and for the characterization of which Foucault uses the formula that we have already encountered in Schmitt and Peterson:

> While I have been speaking about population a word has constantly recurred [. . .] and this is the world "government." The more I have spoken about

population, the more I have stopped saying "sovereign." I was led to designate or aim at something that again I think is relatively new, not in the word, and not at a certain level of reality, but as a technique. Or rather, the modern political problem, the privilege that government begins to exercise in relation to rules, to the extent that, to limit the king's power, it will be possible one day to say, "the king reigns, but he does not govern," this inversion of government and the reign or rule and the fact that government is basically much more than sovereignty, much more than reigning or ruling, much more than the *imperium*, is, I think, absolutely linked to the population. (Foucault, p. 76)

Foucault identifies the origins of governmental techniques in the Christian pastorate, that "government of souls" (*regimen animarum*) that, as a "technique of techniques," defines the activity of the Church until the eighteenth century, when it becomes the "model" and "matrix" (ibid., p. 147) of political government. One of the essential characters of the pastorate is that it refers to both individuals and the entirety of mankind; it looks after men *omnes et singulatim*; it is this double articulation that is transmitted to the activity of government in the modern State, which is, for this reason, both an individualizing and a totalizing activity. Another essential trait shared by the pastorate and the government of men is, according to Foucault, the idea of an "economy," that is, an administration of individuals, things, and wealth ordered according to the model of the family. If the pastorate presents itself as an *oikonomia psychōn*, an "economy of the souls," "the essential issue of government will be the introduction of economy into political practice" (ibid., p. 95). Government is actually nothing other than "the art of exercising power in the form [. . .] of economy" (ibid., p. 95), and the ecclesiastic pastorate and political government are both located within an essentially economical paradigm.

Although, in his "economic" definition of the pastorate, Foucault quotes Gregory of Nazianzus (ibid., p. 192)—an author who, as we have seen, plays an important role in the elaboration of the Trinitarian economy—he seems to ignore completely the theological implications of the term *oikonomia*, to which our research is devoted. But the fact that, in this perspective, the Foucauldian genealogy of governmentality can be extended and moved back in time, right up to the point at which we are able to identify in God himself, through the elaboration of the Trinitarian paradigm, the origin of the notion of an economical government of men and the world, does not discredit his hypotheses, but rather confirms their theoretical core to the very extent to which it details and corrects their historico-chronological exposition. Thus, the lesson of March 8, 1978, is devoted, among other things, to an analysis of Thomas Aquinas's *De regno* and aims to show that, in medieval thought, and especially in Scholasticism, there is still a substantial continuity between sovereignty and government: "If the sovereign can and must govern in the extension and uninterrupted continuity of exercise of his sovereignty, it is insofar as he is part of this great continuum extending from God to the father of the family by way of nature and pastors [. . .] This great continuum from sovereignty to government is nothing else but the translation of the continuum from God to men in the—in inverted commas—'political' order" (ibid., p. 234). According to Foucault, this continuity is broken for the first time in the sixteenth century, when a series of new paradigms, from Copernicus's and Kepler's astronomy to Galileo's physics, from John Ray's natural history to the Grammar of Port-Royal, show that God "only rules the world through general, immutable, universal, simple, and intelligible laws," which is to say that God "does not govern it in the pastoral sense [but] reigns over the world in a sovereign manner through principles" (ibid., p. 235).

On the contrary, we have shown that the first seed of the division between the Kingdom and the Government is to be found in the Trinitarian *oikonomia*, which introduces a fracture between being and praxis in the deity himself. The notion of *ordo* in medieval thought—and especially in Thomas Aquinas—is only able to suture this division by reproducing it inside itself as a fracture between a transcendent and an immanent order (and between *ordinatio* and *executio*). But it is even more surprising that, in his genealogy of governmentality, Foucault mentions Thomas's booklet *De regno* while leaving aside the treatise *De gubernatione mundi*, in which he could have found the basic elements of a theory of the government as distinct from the kingdom. Besides, the term *gubernatio*—beginning from a certain moment in time and certainly already in Salvian's book *De gubernatione Dei*—is synonymous with providence, and the treatises on the divine government of the world are nothing else but treatises on the way in which God articulates and carries out his providential action. *Providence is the name of the "oikonomia," insofar as the latter presents itself as the government of the world.* If the doctrine of *oikonomia*—and that of providence that depends on it—can be seen, in this sense, as machines that found and explain the government of the world, and become fully intelligible only in this way, it is equally the case that, conversely, the birth of the governmental paradigm becomes comprehensible only if it is set against the "economic-theological" background of providence with which it is in agreement.

It is all the more surprising that, in the 1977–1978 course, the notion of providence is never referred to. And yet the theories of Kepler, Galileo, Ray, and the Port-Royal circle that Foucault refers to do nothing other than to radicalize, as we shall see, the distinction between general and special providence into which the theologians had transposed, in their own way, the opposition between the Kingdom and the Government. The passage from ecclesiastical pastorate to political government, which Foucault tries to explain—in all truth, in not terribly convincing a way—by means of the emergence of a whole series of counterpractices that resist the pastorate, is far more comprehensible if it is seen as a secularization of the detailed phenomenology of first and second, proximate and distant, occasional and efficient causes, general and particular wills, mediated and immediate concourses, *ordinatio* and *executio*, by means of which the theoreticians of providence had tried to make the divine government of the world intelligible.

א *When we undertake an archaeological research it is necessary to take into account that the genealogy of a political concept or institution may be found in a field that is different from the one in which we initially assumed we would find it (for instance, it may be found in theology and not in political science). If we limit our analysis to strictly speaking "political" medieval treatises, such as Thomas's* De regno *or John of Viterbo's* De regimine civitatum, *we are faced with what, to the modern eye, appears to be an inconsistency, and with a terminological confusion that, at times, makes it impossible to establish a convincing connection between modern political categories and medieval concepts. However, if we take into consideration the hypothesis, which we have followed, that the genealogy of modern political concepts is to be sought in the treatises* De gubernatione Dei *and in the writings on providence, then the above-mentioned connection becomes clear. Once again, archaeology is a science of signatures [*segnature*], and we need to be able to follow the signatures that displace the concepts and orient their interpretation toward different fields.*

It is the failure to attend to this methodological warning that not only prevented Foucault from articulating his genealogy of governmentality all the

way to the end and in a convincing way, but also compromised Michel Senel-
lart's valuable researches on the Arts de gouverner. Du "regimen" médiéval
au concept de gouvernement. *The modern concept of government does not*
continue the history of the medieval regimen, *which represents a kind of dead*
end, so to speak, of Western medieval thought, but that, far wider and more
articulated, of the treatises on providence, which, in turn, originates from the
Trinitarian oikonomia.

5.2. An exhaustive reconstruction of the immense debate on providence
that, in pagan, Christian, and Judaic cultures, began with the Stoics and
reached almost without interruption the threshold of modernity is out of
the question. Rather, this debate interests us only to the extent to which
it constitutes the place in which the theologico-economical paradigm and
the fracture between being and praxis that it entails take the form of a
government of the world and, vice versa, the government presents itself
as an activity that can be thought only if ontology and praxis are divided
and coordinated "economically." In this sense, we can say that the doctrine of providence is the privileged theoretical field in which the classical
vision of the world, with its primacy of being over praxis, begins to crack,
and the *deus otiosus* gives way to a *deus actuosus.* Here, we need to analyze
the meaning and the implications of this divine activity of government.

It has often been noted that one of the crucial points of the dispute
on providence concerned, from the very beginning, the distinction between general and particular (or special) providence. At its base lies
the stoic distinction between that which can be found in a primary
way (*proēgoumenōs*) in the plans of providence and that which is rather
produced as a concomitant or secondary effect (*kat' epakolouthēsin* or
parakolouthēsin) of it.

The history of the concept of providence coincides with the long and
fierce debate between those who claimed that God provides for the world
only by means of general or universal principles (*providentia generalis*)
and those who argued that the divine providence extends to particular
things—according to the image in Matthew 10:29, down to the lowli-
est sparrow (*providentia specialis* and *specialissima*). If we accept general
providence and reject, entirely or in part, particular providence, we have
the position of Aristotelian and late classical philosophy, and, in the end,
deism (which, in Wolff's words, "concedes that God exists, but denies
that he takes care of human things": Wolff, 11, 2, p. 191). If, on the other

hand, we accept at the same time the two forms of providence, we have the position of the Stoics, theism, and the dominant trend of Christian theology, for which the problem of how to reconcile special providence with man's free will arises.

However, what is really at stake in the debate is not man's freedom (which the proponents of the second thesis attempt to preserve through the distinction between remote and proximate causes), but the possibility of a divine government of the world. If the Kingdom and the Government are separated in God by a clear opposition, then no government of the world is actually possible: we would have, on the one hand, an impotent sovereignty and, on the other, the infinite and chaotic series of particular (and violent) acts of providence. The government is possible only if the Kingdom and the Government are correlated in a bipolar machine: the government is precisely what results from the coordination and articulation of special and general providence—or, in Foucault's words, of the *omnes* and the *singulatim*.

5.3. The providential machine appears for the first time in a passage from Chrysippus's *Peri pronoias* (*On Providence*) (*SVF*, II, 336), where it already displays the essential character that will define its functioning up to the thresholds of modernity, that is, the strategic conjunction of two apparently different problems: that of the origin and justification of evil, and that of the government of the world. The link Chrysippus establishes between these two problems is so strong that it can still be recovered at the heart of the hair-splitting postmortem debate with Bayle that Leibniz stages in his *Theodicy*. In order to prove his theory that the existing world is *la meilleure des républiques*, Leibniz claims that the evil that can be found in it does not follow from an immediate will of God, but is the unavoidable consequence that is concomitant with the choice that God made of the best possible world:

> It follows that the evil that is in rational creatures happens only by concomitance, not by antecedent will but by a consequent will, as being involved in the best possible plan; and the metaphysical good which includes everything makes it necessary sometimes to admit physical evil and moral evil, as I have already explained more than once. It so happens that the ancient Stoics were not far removed from this system. (Leibniz, p. 258)

At this stage, in order to both substantiate his theory and reduce his opponent to contradiction, Leibniz retrieves the—as a matter of fact, quite faithful—paraphrase that Bayle had made of the passage from Chrysippus:

"Chrysippus," he says, "in his work on Providence examined among other questions this one: *ei ai tōn anthrōpōn nosoi kata physin gignontai* [whether diseases happen according to nature]. Did the nature of things, or the providence that made the world and the human kind, make also the diseases to which men are subject? He answers that the chief design of Nature was not to make them sickly, that would not be in keeping with the cause of all good; but Nature, in preparing and producing many great things excellently ordered and of great usefulness, found that some drawbacks came as a result, and thus these were not in conformity with the original design and purpose; they came about as a sequel to the work, they existed only as consequences which were somehow necessary, and which Chrysippus defined as *kata parakolouthēsin* [according to concomitance]. For the formation of the human body, Chrysippus said, the finest idea as well as the very utility of the work demanded that the head should be composed of a tissue of thin, fine bones; but because of that it was bound to have the disadvantage of not being able to resist blows. Nature made health, and at the same time it was necessary by a kind of concomitance that the source of diseases should open up." (Ibid.)

It is this connection, which is not to be taken for granted, between the problems of evil and of providence that Chrysippus bequeaths to Christian philosophy and theology.

5.4. The treatise and questions on providence attributed to Alexander of Aphrodisias—a commentator of Aristotle active around the second century AD—constitute a perfect example of how, precisely in this problematic context, the different philosophical schools tend to converge with and differentiate themselves from each other according to certain constant orientations. Alexander was facing opponents—the Stoics—who argued that "nothing of what happens in the world happens without the intervention of providence" and that the gods—in this similar to scrupulous masters who control all that happens in their house—look after both the world in general and particular things (Alexander of Aphrodisias, *La provvidenza*, pp. 102–103). Against this idea of providence, Alexander does not cease to repeat that a god who was constantly engaged in paying attention to every single individual and every particular thing would show itself thereby to be of a lower rank than the things he provides for. He thus opposes the paradigm of the kingdom to that of the pastorate (that is, once again, the Kingdom to the Government): while the pastor is inferior to the beings he takes care of, since his perfection is bound to their well-being,

> the providence exercised by a king over the things he governs does not proceed in this way: he does not take care of everything, universal and particular things, continuously or in a way that none of the things that are subjected to him—and to which he would dedicate all his life—would slip his mind. The mind of the king prefers to exercise his providence in a universal and general way: his duties are indeed too noble and dignified for him to take care of these trivialities. (Ibid., p. 117)

Certainly God is the first source of all providence, but this does not mean that he observes and knows every inferior being:

> Not even a man can provide for all that is in his house, to the point of taking care of mice, ants, and all the other things that are in it. Therefore, we need to say that the fact that a noble man puts in order in their place all the things that are in his house and administers them according to what is convenient is not the most beautiful of his acts nor is it worthy of him. He rather needs to take into consideration the most important things, while these kinds of actions and preoccupations should remain irrelevant for him. If thus this behavior is not worthy of a sensible man, it is all the more unworthy of God: indeed, he is too high for us to say of him that he looks after men, mice, and ants [. . .] and that his providence includes all the earthly things. (Ibid., p. 119)

We see here that the double articulation of providence is already constituted, an articulation that, later in Christian theology, will take the name of *providentia generalis* and *providentia specialis*; here, it is presented as providence for itself (*kat' hauto*) and accidental (*kata symbebēkos*) providence. But what is decisive in Alexander is the way in which he tries to think a third intermediate model, which neutralizes these oppositions and seems to constitute for him the true paradigm of providential action.

Alexander writes that the providence of the gods for the things that are in the sublunar world cannot be a primary activity, intentionally carried out in view of these things, because in that case, since all that is in view of something is inferior to it, God would be inferior to the entities of the sublunar world (ibid., p. 143). But it would equally be absurd to state that providence is produced in a purely accidental way, because this would amount to the claim that God is in no way aware of it, while he cannot but be the wisest of beings. Here, Alexander outlines the paradigm of a divine action that avoids both the model of voluntary activity and that of the unwitting accident, a paradigm that presents itself, so to speak, in the paradoxical guise of a conscious accident or of a consciousness without aim. Alexander calls "nature" that which corresponds to this providential canon and consistently defines this nature as a "divine technique" (ibid., p. 149):

> The divine power which we also call "nature" makes subsist the things in which it is found and gives them a form according to a certain ordered connection, but this does not happen in virtue of some decision. Nature does not exercise decision and rational reflection with regard to all the things that it does, since nature is an irrational power. (Ibid., p. 151)

Precisely for this reason, Alexander is able to assimilate natural movements to those produced by mechanical automata, which "seem to dance, fight and move with movements endowed with order and rhythm, because their creator has arranged them in this way" (ibid.). But while in the case of art products artisans set themselves a given purpose, nature as a divine technique comes to completion in an involuntary way—which is however not accidental—"only thanks to a continuous succession of generated beings" (ibid., p. 153).

5.5. How should we understand this particular intermediate nature of providential action—involuntary, yet not accidental? Alexander specifies and refines his model in Question 2, 21. He writes that if it were possible to find an intermediate term between the "for itself" and the "by accident," then the alternative that makes providential action unintelligible would disappear. The latter neither takes as the aim of its activity the fact that it is useful to the being it provides for (providence for itself), nor is it simply accidental.

> We say that somebody provides for something when he sets as his aim to benefit the object in question, and in view of this benefit he acts and carries out actions by means of which he considers himself to be able to achieve the aim that he has set, taking as the objective of his activity the benefit of the being he provides for.
>
> We say that a being provides for another by accident [*kata symbebēkos*], when

the one that is said to be providing for does not do anything to benefit the one which he provides for, but it happens that the latter takes some benefit from the things the other does. Yet the one that provides for is in this way completely unaware of this accidental consequence. Indeed it seems that somebody finds a treasure accidentally if he initially was digging for some other purpose and did not anticipate finding it. And somebody was killed accidentally by lightning, since the lightning did not fall for that purpose, nor was there any awareness on the part of the demiurge that created the lightning. (Alexander of Aphrodisias, *La provvidenza*, p. 236)

According to Alexander, the nature of the providential action—and here lies its particular importance—is neither the "for itself," nor the "by accident," neither what is primary, nor what is collateral, but what could be defined as a "collateral effect that is calculated."

The knowledge of some of the consequences of what happens for some other purpose eliminates their accidental character, since something is accidental when it seems to happen against expectations, while a forecast seems to be the indication of a rational connections of facts [. . .] The being that does not act in view of something, but knows that it benefits it and wants it, can be said to provide for it, but neither for itself nor by accident. (Ibid., pp. 236–240)

In Alexander, the theory of providence—in accordance with the Aristotelian theology from which he begins—is not intended to found a Government of the world, but the latter—that is, the correlation between what is general and what is particular—results, in a contingent but knowing way, from the universal providence. The god that reigns, yet does not govern, thus makes possible the government. In other words, the government is an epiphenomenon of providence (or of the kingdom).

Defining in this way the nature of the providential act, Alexander transmitted to Christian theology the possible canon of a divine *gubernatio* of the world. Whether providence manifests itself only in the universal principles or descends to earth to look after the lowest particular things, it will in any case need to pass through the very nature of things and follow their immanent "economy." The government of the world occurs neither by means of the tyrannical imposition of an external general will, nor by accident, but through the knowing anticipation of the collateral effects that arise from the very nature of things and remain absolutely contingent in their singularity. Thus, what appeared to be a marginal phenomenon or a secondary effect becomes the very paradigm of the act of government.

It is therefore not surprising that an Arabic author of the ninth century, Jabir ibn Hayyan, could interpret Alexander's thought on providence in a way that turns it into a kind of original paradigm of liberalism, as if the master, providing for his own interests and those of his house, could also be useful—it does not matter how knowingly—to the little animals that hide in it:

> Alexander of Aphrodisias's book is characterized by the fact that, according to him, the ninth sphere does not deliberately exercise its providence over this world: there is nothing in this world that escapes its providence, but only accidentally. To demonstrate this, he gives the following example: the master of a household or of a palace does not look after the feeding of the mice, the lizards, the cockroaches and the ants that live in it, or provide for their subsistence, as he does for him and his family. However, providing for his household, he accidentally also provides for these little animals. (Ibid., p. 167)

ℵ *The theory, of Stoic origin, of the negative collateral effect of providence is fully articulated by Philo. The irreducibly harmful and "malevolent" elements of creation (from lightning to hail, from poisonous snakes to scorpions) are conceived as concomitant effects, or blurrings [*bavures*] of the providential structure of the cosmos:*

> And hail and snow-storms, and other things of that kind, are {collateral effects} [*epakolouthei*] of the cooling of the air. And, again, lightnings and thunders arise from the collision and repercussions of the clouds [. . .] And earthquakes, and pestilences, and the fall of thunderbolts, and things of that kind [. . .] {are not primary works of nature, but follow necessary things as concomitant effects} [. . .] As for reptiles, those which are venomous have not been called into existence by an immediate providence, but by {collateral effects}, as I said before; for they are brought into life when the moisture which is in them changes to a more violent heat. (Philo, *On Providence [Fragment II]*, pp. 753–754)

Modern governmental reason reproduces precisely the double structure of providence. Every act of government aims at a primary target, yet, precisely for this reason, it can lead to "collateral damages,"[1] which can be expected or unexpected in their specifics, but are in any case taken for granted. The computation of collateral effects, which can even be considerable (in the case of war, they entail the death of human beings and the destruction of cities), is, in this sense, an inherent part of the logic of government.

א *The idea that special providence, brought to an extreme, leads to absurd consequences, can also be found in Christian theologians. The following passage from Jerome is significant* (Commentarium in Abacuc Prophetam, *I, I; PL, 25, 1286 a–b):*

> It is absurd to extend the majesty of God to the point of making him aware of how many mosquitoes are born and die at any moment, of the number of fleas and the immense multitude of flies, or of how many fish are born in the sea and similar issues. We should not be fatuous adulators of God who reduce providence to the level of these issues.

5.6. In Stoic thought, where the concept originated, providence is strictly entwined with the problem of fate. Plutarch's treatise *On Fate* offers, in this sense, an instructive example of how a pagan philosopher active between the first and second centuries of the Christian era could contribute, without the least intention, to the elaboration of the governmental paradigm.

Plutarch begins by defining the concept of fate (*heimarmenē*): following a Stoic model that clearly shows how ontology had by then redoubled itself into a pragmatics [*prammatica*], he distinguishes between fate as a substance (*ousia*) and fate as an activity (*energeia*, "effectiveness"). As a substance, fate amounts to the soul of the world that is divided spatially into three parts: the heaven of the fixed stars, the part containing the "errant" planets, and the part located beneath the heavens in the terrestrial region. As an activity—and this is the aspect that seems to interest Plutarch the most—fate is assimilated to a law (*nomos*) "determining the course of everything that comes to pass" (Plutarch, *On Fate*, 568d, p. 313).

However, what is decisive is the way in which Plutarch uses the paradigm of the law to articulate the connection between fate in general and fate in particular (*kata meros* or *kath' ekastha*: ibid., 569d, p. 321). Just as civil law (*politikos nomos*: ibid.) does not address this or that individual, but arranges according to a universal condition (*hypothesis*, "presupposition") all that happens in the city, so fate establishes the general conditions according to which connections between particular facts will then take place (ibid., pp. 321–323). In other words, from the perspective of fate, all that happens is considered as the effect of an antecedent. Plutarch thus identifies what pertains to destiny with what is effectual or conditional (*to ex hypotheseōs*):

> Let us next determine the character of what is "consequent of an hypothesis," and show that fate is of that character. We meant by "consequent of an hypothesis" that which is not laid down independently, but in some fashion is really "subjoined" to something else, wherever there is an expression implying that if one is true, another follows. (Ibid., 570a, p. 323)

The principle according to which "everything conforms to destiny [*panta kath' heimarmenēn*]" (ibid., 570c, p. 325) has a meaning only if we specify that the phrase "conforms to destiny" does not refer to the antecedents, but exclusively to the order of the effects and consequences. "And we must call 'destined' and 'in conformity with destiny' only the things that are effects of what has been established primarily [*proēgēsamenois*] in the divine appointment of things" (ibid., 570e, p. 327). That is, destiny divides what is real into two different levels: that of the general antecedents (*proēgoumena*) and that of the particular effects. The former are somehow *in* destiny, but do not occur *according to* destiny, and destiny is that which results effectually from the correlation between the two levels.

It is at this stage that Plutarch introduces his doctrine of providence, which is nothing but a more rigorous formulation of his theory of fate. Like the fate-substance, providence also has a triple figure, which reflects the schema of the three divine orders of the second pseudo-Platonic Letter. The first and supreme providence is the intellection or the will of the primary god, "beneficent to all things," in accordance with which every being has been ordered "as is best and most excellent" (ibid., 572f, p. 343). It "has begotten destiny, and includes it in a sense" (ibid., 574b, p. 351). The second providence, which was created together with destiny and is, like it, included in the first providence, is that of the secondary gods that walk through heaven; mortal things are arranged and preserved in conformity with it. The third providence, which was created "after destiny" and is contained within it, rests with the demons who are commissioned to oversee and order the individual actions of men. According to Plutarch, only the first providence is worthy of its name. It is the "eldest of all beings," and as such superior to destiny, since "all that conforms to destiny conforms to providence" but not vice versa (ibid., 573b, pp. 343–345).

While destiny was compared with a law, the first providence is similar to a "political legislation appropriate to the souls of men" (ibid., 573d, p. 347).

For Plutarch, providence and fate are, at the same time, different and strictly intertwined. If the first providence corresponds to the level of what is primary and of the universal, fate, which is contained by providence and partly identical with it, corresponds to the level of particular effects that derive from it. But nothing is more ambiguous than the relation of "collaterality" or of "effectuality" (*akolouthia*). It is necessary to measure the novelty that this concept introduces into classical ontology. Overturning the Aristotelian definition of the final cause and its primacy, it transforms what appeared in Aristotle as the aim into an "effect." Plutarch seems to be aware of it when he observes that "perhaps a stickler for precision in such matters might insist that on the contrary it is the particulars that have priority, and that the universal exists for their sake—the end being prior to what serves it" (ibid., 569f, pp. 322–323). In other words, what is specific to the providence-fate machine is its functioning as a bipolar system that ends up producing a kind of zone of indifference between what is primary and what is secondary, the general and the particular, the final cause and the effects. And although Plutarch, like Alexander, was not in the least aiming at a governmental paradigm, the "effectual" ontology that results from his work in a way contains the condition of possibility for government, understood as an activity that, in the last instance, is not targeting the general or the particular, the primary or the consequent, the end or the means, but their functional correlation.

א *Modern science's image of the world has often been opposed to the theological concept of a providential government of the world. However, in their conceptual structure they are more similar than we customarily think. First of all, the model of general providence is based on eternal laws that are entirely analogous to those of modern science. But it is in particular the relation between the first and second causes that presents evident analogies to modern science's image of the world. Didier Deleule has shown that, in modern thought, from Hume to Adam Smith, a concept arises that, in a perfect analogy with the theory of providence, breaks with the primacy of final causes and replaces them with an order produced by the contingent game of immanent effects. The order of the world does not refer back to an initial plan, but results from the continuous series of the proximate causes; therefore, it works not like a*

brain, but like a womb (Deleule, pp. 259–267). As a matter of fact, in spite of
the idea of a divine ordinatio, *the twofold structure of the providential order*
can be perfectly reconciled with the contingency of the second causes and their
effects. The government of the world does not result from the imposition of a
general and indefectible law, but from the correlation between the general law
and the contingent level of the second causes.

5.7. It should not therefore surprise us that, in his treatise on destiny, Alexander decidedly takes sides against the Stoic providence-fate apparatus.

He begins by showing that, given the Aristotelian classification of the four causes (efficient, material, formal, final), fate cannot find a place in any of these without contradictions, or include in itself the totality of events. Following this argument, he is led to attend to an order of events, of tics and meaningless gestures, that ancient man seemed to ignore, like "the touching and pulling out of hairs, and as many actions as resemble this" (Alexander of Aphrodisias, *On Destiny*, p. 21), or to those remnants, refuse, and anomalies that cannot be inscribed in any finalism or in any destinal connection.

> Of what will they say the superfluities that grow in certain parts of the body are the causes, or of what the monstrosities and creatures unnatural, who even at the start are incapable of life? [. . .] Nay, let someone tell us of what result are the decayed and withered fruits the cause? And of what is the doubling of certain leaves the cause? [. . .] No[t] every generated thing [is] from the moment it exists, a cause of something to be. (Ibid., p. 101)

Alexander is perfectly aware of the fact that his opponents claim to reconcile fate with man's capacity for action, and to found through fate the very possibility of a government of the world. He quotes the passage from a treatise in which the nexus fate-government is affirmed explicitly: "So then all things do not take place according to destiny, and the government [*dioikesis*, the administration] of the universe is not free from prevention or interference! Well then [. . .] there is no ordered world [*kosmos*]; and as there is no cosmos, there are no gods" (ibid., p. 155). Another proponent of fate claims that if we introduced into the world a movement without cause, "the universe would be scattered, would be rent asunder [. . .] and would no longer remain one and eternal, or governed according to one order and one *oikonomia*" (ibid., p. 97). Against these ideas, Alexander resolutely asserts the contingent character (that is, open to the possibility of not producing itself) of human actions. In the conclusion of the treatise we thus read "of those things alone is any man the master, namely, such as it is equally in his own power not to do" (ibid., p. 163) ("power" [*potere*] is the correct term for "*exousian*," not "freedom," as most current translations render it). And yet, just as in the treatise on providence the intention to contain providence within the field of what is general led Alexander to elaborate an ontology of collateral effects that is no longer Aristotelian, but seems to anticipate modern governmental theories, so here the rejection of fate leads him to support in all fields a theory of contingency that can be perfectly reconciled with modern techniques of government. In fact, for the latter, what is essential is not really the idea of a predetermined order, so much as the possibility of managing the disorder; not the binding necessity of fate, but the constancy and computability of a disorder; not the uninterrupted chain of causal connections, but the conditions of the maintenance and orientation of effects that are in themselves purely contingent.

5.8. In the *Questions on Providence*, a text preserved in a medieval Latin translation and attributed to Proclus, the problem of the government of the world does not seem to be posed. Providence is a straightforwardly ontologico-gnoseological problem that coincides with that of the nature and object of divine knowledge; Proclus's precise task consists in firmly establishing *pronoia* in the one and in being. The first Question thus asks whether the object of divine knowledge is universal realities or, rather, individual entities. The answer is that providence, as the highest rank of divine knowledge, grasps—according to a paradigm that should by now be familiar to us—both the whole and individuals, *omnes et singulatim*. But the problem remains essentially a problem of knowledge, and not one of praxis and government. In the same sense, the second Question examines the problem of the way in which providence knows contingent things. Although these are, in themselves, undetermined and manifold, providence knows them as if they were necessary. In fact, the nature of knowledge is determined by the nature of the one who knows, and not by the known object; therefore providence is not "distributed into parts together with things which are the objects of its knowledge, nor moved about them [. . .] but *the one* of Providence abiding in *the one*, is at the same time immutable and indivisible, and knows all things in a way which is eternally the same" (Proclus, *Two Treaties*, p. 8).

The third Question investigates the problem of the essential relation that binds providence, whose nature is identical to that of the one, to contingent things; it is in this context that the problem of government begins to take shape. As a matter of fact, if there were not any kind of connection (*colligatio*) between earthly contingent things and the superior reality, there could be neither a unity nor a government according to the intelligence (*gubernatio secundum intelligentiam*). Proclus entrusts this connection to the demons and the gods.

> And the Gods, indeed, will possess this knowledge exemptly, extending to all things their providential attention: but daemons, distributing into parts the superessential illuminations which they receive from them, are allotted a different prefecture over different herds of animals, as far as to the last partition, as Plato says; so that some of them preside over men, others over lions, and others over other animals, or have dominion over plants. And, still more partially, some are the inspective guardians of the eye, others of the liver, and others of the heart. But all things are full of Gods [. . .] (Ibid., pp. 23–24)

But here, as in the following Question—which deals with the way in which the gods participate in the world—providence remains an essentially ontological category, which refers back to a kind of gradual and constant effusion of divine being, in which individual beings participate in different degrees according to the specific power of their nature.

Let us now turn to the Letter to Theodore, which was passed on to us along with the Questions, in which Proclus examines the problem of fate and its relation with providence. Theodore, who was a "mechanicus," that is, a sort of engineer, conceives of the world as an immense mechanism ruled by an ineluctable necessity, where each sphere is contained by another through gears that, starting from a single moving principle, determine the movement of all living and nonliving beings. The principle that, according to Theodore, moves and unites this machine-world (*mundiale opus*) as a kind of superengineer (*mechanicus quidam*) is fate or providence.

Against this unitary model of the machine-world, which rules out any freedom (in it, the *autexusion, id est liberi arbitrii*—as the Latin translator paraphrases—would become an empty name [Proclus, *Tria Opuscula*, p. 334]) and any possibility of a divine government of the world, Proclus states that providence and fate rather constitute a system that is hierarchically articulated into two levels. The latter does not rule out freedom and entails a substantial distinction between the two elements or levels. At any point in the universe the primary efficient causes are distinguished from the effects ("ubique autem factivae causae ab effectibus distinctae sunt": ibid., p. 344), and the acting principle cannot be located on the same level as its effects ("faciens non est tale, quale factum": ibid., p. 346). In other words, this doctrine presupposes a binary ontology that splits reality into two levels, a transcendent and an immanent one: providence corresponds to the order of transcendent primary causes, while fate corresponds to that of the effects or immanent secondary causes. Providence, that is, the primary cause, is the source of the good, while fate, as a secondary cause, produces the immanent connection of the effects ("providentiam quidem causam esse bonorum hiis quibus providetur, fatum autem causam quidem esse et ipsum, sed connexionis cuiusdam et consequentiae hiis quae generantur": ibid., p. 342). Together, they work like a two-stroke machine, in which the destinal connection of the effects (fate as *causa connexionis*) carries out and realizes the providential effusion of the transcendent good.

Although the idea of a divine *gubernatio* of the world is not yet enunciated as such, the splitting of being into two different and coordinated levels is the precondition that will allow Christian theology to construct its governmental machine.

א *This is not the place to pose the problem of the attribution to Proclus of the leaflets translated by William of Moerbeke. Such attribution relies only on the partial agreement between the Latin text and that of three treatises written by the Byzantine scholar Isaac Sebastocrator in the eleventh century, which are supposed to plagiarize the original text by Proclus. It is, however, certain that the ontology that is described in these leaflets is not Neoplatonic, but rather Stoic or Christian. The idea of a creator of the world is repeatedly advanced. It is possible that the author of the leaflets was not Proclus, but a representative of that Judaic-Christian view of the world (at any rate, not a classical one) that we have already encountered a number of times.*

5.9. The text that has handed down the apparatus providence-fate to Christian theology is Boethius's *De consolatione philosophiae*. The entire conversation between the disconsolate Boethius and Lady Philosophy, who has chased away as "{theatrical prostitutes}" the muses of poetry, revolves around the way in which the world is governed by God ("quibus [. . .] gubernaculis regatur": 1, 6) and the reasons for the apparent triumph of evil over good and of fortune over justice. The only authentic remedy for the state of confusion and oblivion in which Boethius has fallen is the "{true doctrine about the world's government [veram de mundi gubernatione sententia]}" (ibid., p. 19). For this reason, after having dispelled Boethius's initial doubts, the sweet and strict teacher who had once taught him how to "transfer to public administration what I had learned from you in the course of our private leisure" (1, 4, p. 10) now smilingly consents to explain to him the difficult doctrine of providence and fate, whose aporias she herself compares with the Hydra's heads: once one has been removed, countless others spring up in its place (4, 6).

Providence and fate, transcendence and immanence, which already in Plutarch and Proclus formed a double-faced system, are now clearly articulated with each other to constitute a perfect machine for governing the world. Philosophy explains to her pupil that the generation and movement of the universe receive causes, order, and form from the mind of God. But the latter has established a twofold manner of governing things ("rebus gerendis": ibid.):

> When this manner is thought of as in the purity of God's understanding, it is called Providence, and when it is thought of with reference to all things, whose motion and order it controls, it is called by the name the ancients gave it, Fate. If anyone will examine their power, it will soon be clear to him that these two aspects are different. Providence is the divine reason itself. It is set at the head of all things and disposes of things. Fate, on the other hand, is the planned order [*dispositio*: this is part of a Latin vocabulary which presupposes that of the *oikonomia*] inherent in things subject to change through which Providence binds everything in its own allotted place. Providence includes all things at the same time, however diverse and infinite, while Fate controls the motion of different individual things in different places and at different times. So this unfolding of the plan in time when brought together as a unified whole in the foresight of God's mind is Providence; and the same unified whole when dissolved and unfolded in the course of time is Fate. They are different, but the one depends on the other. The order of Fate is derived from the simplicity of Providence. (Ibid., p. 104)

The twofold character of the government of the world—and, at the same time, the unitary nexus that binds together its two aspects—has possibly never been affirmed with more peremptory clarity than it is in this passage. The power that runs the world results from the interaction between a transcendent principle, which is simple and eternal, and an immanent ("inhaerens rebus") *oikonomia*, which is articulated in time ("explicata temporibus") and space ("locis [. . .] distributa"). The two principles are heterogeneous, yet interdependent ("alterum [. . .] pendet ex altero"), not only because fate follows from providence, but also because, as is explained in the ode that concludes the chapter, if fate did not constrain things in their movement, "those things which stable order now protects, / Divorced from their true source would fall apart."

Lady Philosophy says explicitly that this is a full-blown paradigm of government in the following passage, in which the economy of the universe is described with images and a vocabulary that evoke the complex administration of a kingdom or of an empire:

> God in his Providence constructs a single fixed plan of all that is to happen, while it is by means of Fate that all that He has planned is administered [*amministrat*] in its many individual details in the course of time. So, whether the work of Fate is done with the help of divine spirits of Providence, or whether the chain of Fate [*fatalis series*] is woven by the soul of the universe, or by the obedience of all nature, by the celestial motions of the stars, or by the power of the angels, by the various skills of other spirits, or by some of these, or by all of them, one thing is certainly clear: the simple and unchanging form of things to be managed [*gerendarum* (. . .) *rerum*] is Providence, and Fate is the ever-changing web, the disposition in and through time of all the events which God in His simplicity has entrusted to manage. Everything, therefore, which comes under Fate, is also subject to Providence, to which Fate itself is subject, but certain things which come under Providence are above the chain of Fate. These are the things which rise above the order of change ruled over by Fate in virtue of the stability of their position close to the supreme Godhead. (Ibid., p. 105)

Here, providence and fate appear as two powers that are hierarchically co-ordinated, in which a sovereign decision determines the general principles of the organization of the cosmos, and then entrusts its administration and execution to a subordinated, yet autonomous, power (*gestio* is the juridical term that indicates the discretionary character of the acts carried out by one subject on behalf of another). The fact that there are issues that are directly decided by sovereign providence, and thus remain alien to destiny's management, does not refute the division of power on which the system relies. The *magistra* explains to her bewildered disciple that the government of the world is all the better ("res optime reguntur": ibid.) if simplicity, remaining in the divine mind, lets the destinal connection of the causes take its course, that is, if sovereign providence (the Kingdom—Boethius speaks explicitly of a "regnum providentiae": ibid.) lets fate (the Government) administer and constrain the actions of men ("fate holds sway over the acts and fortunes of men": ibid.).

From this follows the fated and miraculous character that seems to cover the actions of government. Since the transcendent sovereign knows and decides what fate later constrains in the immanent connection of the causes, to the one who is taken by these, fate—that is, government—appears as a majestic and impenetrable miracle ("Hic iam fit illud fatalis ordinis insigne miraculum, cum ab sciente geritur quod stupeant ignorantes": ibid.). And although things may appear to be unjust and confused, and evil people seem to triumph while the good suffer, everything that happens is nevertheless promptly inscribed in the providential order. As a matter of fact, even evil people actually desire the good, but they are perverted in their desire by error: nothing takes place as a consequence of evil, and the providential government can never change its course ("Nihil est quod mali causa ne ab ipsis quidem improbis fiat; quos [. . .] bonum quaerentes pravus error avertit, nedum ordo de summi boni cardine proficiens a suo quoquam deflectat exordio": ibid.).

Let us now try to analyze the curious relation that links providence to fate in the governmental machine. Although they are clearly different, they are nevertheless merely two aspects of a single divine action, the *duplex modus* of a single activity of the government of the world that, with a knowing terminological ambiguity, presents itself now as providence and now as fate, now as intelligence and now as *dispositio*, now as transcendent and now as immanent, now as contracted in the divine mind and now as unfolded in time and space. The activity of government is, at the same time, providence, which thinks and orders the good of everybody, and destiny, which distributes the good to individuals, constraining them to the chain of causes and effects. In this way, what on one level—that of fate and individuals—appears as incomprehensible and unjust, receives on another level its intelligibility and justification. In other words, the governmental machine functions like an incessant theodicy, in which the Kingdom of providence legitimates and founds the Government of fate, and the latter guarantees the order that the former has established and renders it operative.

א *Salvian, bishop of Marseille in the fifth century, begins his treatise* De gubernatione Dei *by evoking in passing the pagan sources of a doctrine of providence. First of all Pythagoras, then Plato "and all the Platonic Schools," who "acknowledge God as the governor of all creation," the Stoics, who "bear witness that He remains, taking the place of the governor [*gubernatoris vice*]*, within that which He directs"; last, Virgil and Cicero, whom he quotes—like the previous authors—from secondary sources (Salvian, 1, 1, p. 27). In fact, Salvian knows the classical authors only through the citations of the Apologists; the formation of his doctrine of providence is entirely independent of the governmental paradigm that we have so far reconstructed in late classical philosophy (in particular, it lacks any reference to the bipartition general/special providence). His examples are almost exclusively limited to the Bible, where the divine providence expresses itself most especially in the guise of judgment and punishment.*

However, it is significant that even in this context the providential paradigm tends to constitute itself in the guise of government. The metaphor of the gubernator *remains closely linked to its naval origin, but is also broadened to include what for Salvian are the three aspects of every activity of government:*

> What could they have felt more proper and more reverent regarding the concern and watchfulness of God than to have likened Him to a helmsman [*gubernatori*]? By this they understood that as the helmsman in charge of a ship never lifts his hand from the tiller [*gubernaculo*], so does God never remove His inmost attention from the world. Just as the helmsman steers, completely dedicated in mind and body to his task, taking advantage of the wind, avoiding the rocks and watching the stars, in like manner our God never puts aside the function [*munus*] of His most loving watch over the universe. Neither does He take away the guidance [*regimen*] of His providence, nor does He remove the tenderness [*indulgentiam*] of His mercy. (Ibid., p. 28)

*The second book of the treatise is devoted to the definition, through Biblical examples (*per testimonia sacra*), of the three figures of providence, which Salvian defines as* praesentia, gubernatio, *and* iudicium, *and which constitute an extraordinary anticipation of the modern tripartition of powers; here, however, these are reunited in a single holder. Presence, which corresponds to sovereignty, is symbolized by the eye that invigilates and sees; government is symbolized by a hand that leads and corrects; judgment (judiciary power) is symbolized by the word that judges and condemns. Yet, the three powers are strictly entwined and imply one another:*

His presence should first be proved, because He who will rule or judge must doubtless be present in order to rule or judge. The divine Word, speaking through the Holy Scripture, says: "The eyes of the Lord, in every place, behold good and evil." Behold here God is present, looking upon us, watching us through His vision wherever we are [. . .] The good are watched over for the sake of preserving them; the evil, that they may be destroyed [. . .] Let us now see whether He who watches governs us, although the very reason for His watchfulness [*ratio aspiciendi*] has within itself the cause of His governance [*causam (. . .) gubernandi*]. He does not watch us with this end in view: that, having beheld, He may neglect us. The very fact that He deigns to watch is to be understood as non-neglect, especially since, as Scripture has already testified, the wicked are observed for their destruction, the good for their salvation. By this very fact the economy of the divine government [*dispensatio divini gubernaculi*] is shown, for it is the function of just government to govern and deal with men individually, according to their respective merits. (Ibid., pp. 55–57)

5.10. The theological paradigm of government is contained in Thomas Aquinas's treatise *De gubernatione mundi* (*Summa Theologiae*, 1, qq. 103–113). Here, government is not defined thematically, but through the articulation of a series of *quaestiones*, which progressively determine its specific characters. First of all, government is opposed to chance, just as order is opposed to what happens fortuitously:

> Some of the earliest philosophers, in maintaining that everything happens by chance, excluded any sort of government from the world. But this opinion is proved impossible on two counts. The first is the evidence present in the world itself. For we observe among beings of nature that what is best comes to pass either always or most of the time. This would not be the case were there not some providence guiding such beings to an end, the good. Such guidance is what government means. Therefore this regular pattern in things clearly points to the world's being governed. An example from Cicero, quoting Aristotle: if you were to go into a well-laid-out home, from its arrangement you would get a good idea of the arranger's plan. (Ibid., 1, q. 103, a. 1)

The second reason seems to come closer to a definition of government and concerns the appropriateness that the things created by God reach their end: "The highest perfection of any being consists in the attaining of its end. Hence it is appropriate to God's goodness that, as he has brought things into being, he also guides them toward their end. This is what governing them means" (ibid.). The generic meaning of governing is thus "guiding creatures toward their end." Thomas specifies that created things need to be governed since, if they were not preserved by the *manus gubernatoris,* they would fall back into the nothingness from which they originated. But in what way is the divine government of the world carried out? It is by no means a matter of a force that, following a common representation, intervenes from the outside and directs the creatures, like the shepherd's hand leads his sheep. What defines divine government is (in a resumption of the Aristotelian identity between *archē* and *physis*) the fact that it fully coincides with the very nature of the things that it directs. Following a paradox that perfectly corresponds to the structure of the order, the divine government of creatures has no other content than the natural necessity inherent in things:

> The natural necessity inherent in things that are fixed on one set course is itself an imprint, as it were, from God's guidance of them to their end, even as the trueness of the arrow's flight toward the target is an impetus from the archer and not from the arrow itself. Note this difference, however, that what creatures receive from God constitutes their nature; what a man imposes artificially on the beings of nature is a coercion. The comparison then is this: a necessity of propulsion in the arrow's flight is a sign of the archer's aiming it; a necessity of nature in creatures is a sign of the provident God's governing them. (Ibid., q. 103, a. 1, ad 3)

Therefore, government defines itself as a very particular form of activity, which is necessarily not violent (in the sense of "against nature," which this term assumes in medieval thought—as opposed to *spontaneus, qui sponte fit*) and articulates itself by means of the very nature of governed things. Divine government and the self-government of the creature coincide; governing can only mean—according to a paradigm that the physiocrats and the theoreticians of the "science de l'ordre," from Le Trosne to Mercier de la Rivière, would rediscover five centuries later—knowing the nature of things and letting it act.

If, however, this identity between natural order and government were both absolute and undifferentiated, government would then be a worthless activity, which, given the original imprint of nature at the moment of creation, would simply coincide with passivity and laissez-faire. But this is not the case. It is in the answer given to the questions "whether God is active in every agent cause" and "whether God has the power to do anything outside of the order inherent in creation" that the concept of government receives its specific determinations. Thomas was facing (or rhetorically pretended to be facing) two opposed theses: that of "Islamic fate," according to which God acts immediately in every natural action with a continuous miracle ("solus Deus immediate omnia operatur": ibid., 1, q. 105, a. 5) and, on the other hand, that according to which the intervention of God is limited to the original gift of nature and of the *virtus operandi* at the moment of creation.

Thomas argues that the Islamic thesis is impossible because it amounts to eliminating the order of causes and effects in creation. As a matter of fact, if fire did not warm us because of the disposition of its own nature, but because God intervened to produce heat each time that we light a fire, then all creation, deprived of its operative virtue, would become useless: "If all creatures are utterly devoid of any activity of their own, then they themselves would seem to have a pointless [*frustra*] existence, since everything exists for the sake of its operation" (ibid.). On the other hand, the opposite thesis that intends to safeguard the freedom of creatures drastically separates them from God and threatens to make them fall back into the nothingness from which they originated. How can we then reconcile divine government with the self-government of creatures? How can government coincide with the nature of things and yet intervene with it?

As we have seen, the solution of this aporia passes through the strategic distinction between first and second causes, *primum agens* and *secundi agentes*. If we consider the world and the order of things as dependent on the first cause, then God cannot intervene in the world or do anything outside of or against it, "because then he would be doing something contrary to his foreknowledge, his will or his goodness" (ibid., 1, q. 105, a. 6). The proper space of an action of government of the world is not, therefore, the necessary space of the *ordo ad Deum* and of first causes, but the contingent one of the *ordo ad invicem* and of second causes.

> If we take the order in things as it depends on any of the secondary causes, then God can act apart [*praeter*] from it; he is not subject to that order but rather it is subject to him, as issuing from him not out of a necessity of nature, but by decision of his will. He could in fact have established another sort of pattern in the world; hence when he so wills, he can act apart from the given order [*praeter hunc ordinem institutum*], producing, for example, the effects of secondary causes without them or some effects that surpass the powers of these causes. (Ibid.)

In its preeminent form, the sphere of divine action *praeter ordinem rerum* is the miracle ("Unde illa quae a Deo fiunt prater causas nobis notas, miracula dicuntur": ibid., 1, q. 105, a. 7).

This action of government is, however, only possible (as we have already seen in Augustine) insofar as God, as first cause, gives to creatures their form and preserves them in being ("dat formam creaturis agentibus, et eas tenet in esse": ibid., 1, q. 105, a. 5). He therefore acts intimately within things ("ipse Deus est proprie causa ipsius esse universalis in rebus omnibus, quod inter omnia est magis intimum rebus; sequitur quod Deus in omnibus intime operetur": ibid.).

At this point, the meaning of the structural splitting of the *ordo* and its nexus with the bipartite system Kingdom/Government, ontology/*oikonomia*, begins to become evident. The Kingdom concerns the *ordo ad deum*, the relation of creatures to the first cause. In this sphere, God is impotent or, rather, can act only to the extent that his action always already coincides with the nature of things. On the other hand, the Government concerns the *ordo ad invicem*, the contingent relation of things between themselves. In this sphere, God can intervene, suspending, substituting, or extending the action of the second causes. Yet, the two orders are functionally linked, in the sense that it is God's ontological relation with creatures—in which he is, at the same time, absolutely intimate with them and absolutely impotent—that founds and legitimates the practical relation of government over them; within this relation (that is, in the field of the second causes) his powers are unlimited. The splitting between being and praxis that the *oikonomia* introduces in God actually functions like a machine of government.

5.11. From this fundamental bipolar articulation of God's power over the world also derives the other essential character of the divine activity of government, that is, its being split between a power of rational deliberation and an executive power, which necessarily entails a plurality of mediators and "ministers." Answering the question "whether all things are governed by God immediately," Thomas begins by stating that "with respect to government two elements are to be taken into account: the plan for governing [*ratio gubernationis*], that is, providence, and the carrying out [*executio*] of this plan. As to the first, God governs all things immediately; as to the second, he governs some things through the mediation of others" (ibid. 1, q. 103, a. 6). Governmental rationality is, as a matter of fact, a "knowledge having a practical aim, that consists in a knowledge of particulars, the sphere of actions" (ibid.), and as such it certainly rests with God. But since "that form of governing will be better which communicates a higher perfection to the governed [. . .] God governs things in such a way that he establishes some beings as causes over the governing of others" (ibid.), that is, as the executors of his *ratio gubernationis*. The strict analogical correlation between the divine government of the world and the secular government of the cities of the earth is proved by the fact that Thomas illustrates his hypothesis by means of a genuinely political paradigm: just as the power of a *rex terrenus* who uses ministers for his government is not for this reason diminished in his dignity, but is rather made more illustrious by it ("ex ordine ministrorum potestas regia praeclarior redditur": ibid., 1, q. 103, 1. 6, ad 3), so God, leaving to others the execution of his governmental *ratio*, makes his government more perfect.

In the *Summa contra Gentiles* (Book 3, Chapter 77), the distinction between the two aspects of the divine government of the world is strongly restated. The correlation between *ratio gubernandi* and *executio* corresponds to the correlation between *ordinatio* and *ordinis executio*; the first is carried out by means of a *virtus cognoscitiva*, and the second through a *virtus operativa*. But while, on the theoretical level, it is necessary to extend the *ordinatio* down to the smallest details, on the level of the executive practice, the divine government needs to make use of subordinate agents (*agentes inferiores*), who are the executors of divine providence. "It belongs to the dignity of a ruler to have many ministers and a variety of executors of his rule, for, the more subjects he has, on different levels, the higher and greater is his dominion shown to be. But no ruler's dignity is comparable to the dignity of the divine rule. So, it is appropriate that the execution of divine providence be carried out by diverse levels of agents" (ibid., n. 4).

‎א *The conceptual distinction between a power of general ordering (*ratio gubernandi, ordinatio*) and an executive power appears in the field of theology before it does in politics. The modern doctrine of the division of powers has its paradigm in this articulation of the providential machine. But even the modern distinction between legitimacy and legality, which appears in the monarchic France of the age of Restoration, has its archetype in the double structure of providence. What Schmitt calls the "legislative State," that is, the modern rule of law in which every activity of government presents itself as an* *application and execution of a law enforced impersonally, is, in this perspective, the extreme outcome of the providential paradigm, in which Kingdom and Government, legitimacy and legality coincide.*

5.12. In Question 116 of the treatise on the government of the world, Thomas analyzes the providence-fate machine in terms that are almost identical to Boethius's description. To the question "is there fate in created things?" Thomas answers that the divine providence brings to completion its effects using intermediate causes ("per causas medias suos effectus exequitur": *Summa Theologiae*, 1, q. 116, a. 2). According to the double structure of providence that is by now familiar to us,

> we can therefore look at this ordering [*ordinatio*] of effects in two ways. First, with respect to God himself, and from this point of view the ordering of effects is called Providence. Second, with respect to the intermediate causes ordered by God to bring about certain effects, and from this point of view it has the character of fate [*rationem fati*]. (Ibid.)

In this sense, fate depends on God, and is nothing else but "the economy [*dispositio*] itself, or the series, that is, the order of the secondary causes" (ibid., 1, q. 116 a. 2, ad 1). *Dispositio*, Thomas specifies, does not here mean something like a quality or a property of an entity, but should be understood in the "economic" sense of order, which does not concern the substance, but the relation ("secundum quod dispositio designat ordinem, qui non est substantia, sed relatio": ibid., 1, q. 116, a. 2, ad 3). If it is considered in relation to its divine principle, this order is single and unchangeable, while it is manifold and changeable in the second causes. And yet not all creatures are submitted to the government of fate to the same extent. Here the problem of providence shows its essential connection with that of grace.

Thomas writes that providence does not arrange rational creatures in the same way as the other creatures (*Contra Gentiles*, Book 3, Chapter 147). Rational creatures are in fact assigned the intellect and reason, which make them capable of seeking the truth. Furthermore, through language, they can communicate among themselves and form a society. However, the ultimate aim of rational creatures exceeds their natural faculty and thus demands a kind of government that is different ("diversus gubernationis modus": ibid.) from that of inferior creatures. This special and higher way of governing ("altior gubernationis modus": ibid.) is grace. "If man is ordered to an end which exceeds his natural capacity, some help must be divinely provided for him, in a supernatural way, by which he may tend toward his end" (ibid., n. 3).

The divine government of men has therefore two eminent modes: nature and grace. For this, starting from the end of the sixteenth century, the problem of the government of the world will overlap more and more with that of the modes and the efficacy of grace: the treatises and debates on providence will take the shape of analyses and definitions of the figures of grace as preventative grace, concomitant grace, gratuitous grace, habitual grace, sufficient grace, efficient grace, and so on. And not only do the forms of government immediately correspond to the figures of grace, but the necessity for the gratuitous help of God, without which man cannot achieve his aim, corresponds to the necessity of government, without which nature would not be preserved in its being. In any case, just as in the case of nature, grace subscribes to the principle according to which the providential government cannot in any way constrain the free will of men. For this, grace as a figure of government cannot be seen as a "divine compulsion to the good" ("coactio homini [. . .] ad bene agendum:" ibid., Chapter 148).

> That divine help is provided to man so that he may act well is to be understood in this way: it performs our works in us, as the primary cause performs the operations of secondary causes, and as a principal agent performs the action of an instrument. Hence, it is said in Isaiah (26:12–13): "Thou hast wrought all our works for us, O Lord." Now the first cause causes the operation of the secondary cause according to the measure of the latter. So, God also causes our works in us in accord with our measure, which means that we act voluntarily and not as forced. Therefore, no one is forced to right action by the divine help. (Ibid., n. 3)

The government of the world is the place of a concurrence between grace and our freedom, such that, as Suárez will reassert against the "Lutheran error," "the necessity of grace is combined with the real use of liberty and the use of liberty [. . .] cannot be separated from the operation and cooperation of grace" (Suárez, p. 384). The providential paradigm of the government of men is not tyrannical, but democratic.

5.13. We cannot understand the functioning of the governmental machine if we do not realize that the relation between its two poles—the

Kingdom and the Government—is essentially vicarious. Both the emperor and the pope define themselves as *vicarius Christi* or *vicarius Dei*, and it is known that the exclusive claim to this title gave rise to a long series of conflicts between spiritual and secular powers. Maccarone and Kantorowicz have reconstructed the history of these claims through which what was originally, especially in the East, the exclusive title of the emperor became, from the fifth century onward, at least in the West, the title par excellence of the bishop of Rome. But, in the perspective of the Trinitarian economy, the vicariousness of power—of any power—appears in a particular light, which, so to speak, makes of it the essential structure of supreme power, the intimate vicissitudinary articulation of the *archē*.

The vicariousness of pontifical power with regard to Christ was theologically founded on the delay of the *parousia*.

> Given that Christ had to subtract his carnal presence from the Church [*praesentiam suam carnalem erat Ecclesiae subtracturus*], it was necessary to institute ministers who would administer sacraments to men. These are called priests [. . .] And after the subtraction of Christ's corporeal presence, given that questions concerning faith were going to occur, which would have divided the Church, whose unity requires the unity of faith [. . .] the one who has this power is Peter, and his successors. (Quidort, p. 111)

Yet, according to a principle that has its paradigm in Paul, the power of Christ is in turn vicarious with respect to that of the Father. In 1 Corinthians 24:28, Paul in fact clearly affirms that, by the time the end comes, after having subjected to himself every power (with the exception of that of the Father, from which his power derives), Christ will return the Kingdom to God, who had subjected everything to Christ. In other words, the power of Christ is, in its relation to the Father, an essentially vicarious power, in which he acts and governs, so to speak, in the name of the Father. And, more generally, the intra-Trinitarian relation between the Father and the Son can be considered to be the theological paradigm of every *potestas vicaria*, in which every act of the vicar is considered to be a manifestation of the will of the one who is represented by him. And yet, as we have seen, the an-archic character of the Son, who is not founded ontologically in the Father, is essential to the Trinitarian economy. *That is, the Trinitarian economy is the expression of an anarchic power and being that circulates among the three persons according to an essentially vicarious paradigm.*

It is not surprising that the same vicarious structure can be found in secular power. In *On the Government of Rulers* (Book 3, Chapter 13), Thomas writes that Augustus wielded a vicarious power with respect to Christ, who was the real monarch and lord of the world ("verus erat mundi Dominus et Monarcha, cuius vices gerebat Augustus"). The entire duration of Augustus's principality is thus presented as if it were a "deputizing for [*fare le veci*] Christ's monarchy" ("quas quidem vices monarchiae post Christi veri domini nativitatem gessit Augusto": ibid.). The Norman Anonymous writes in the same sense that "the king is God and Christ, but according to grace [. . .] Even the one who is by nature God and Christ acts by means of his vicar; the latter acts in his stead [*per quem vices suas exequitur*]." But also Christ, who is God by nature, somehow acts by grace, "since according to his human nature he is deified and sanctified by the Father" (Kantorowicz 2005, pp. 101–102). And in the fourth century, the Ambrosiaster had already claimed that the king owns the *imperium* of God as a vicar, since he bears its image (ibid., p. 114).

In other words, power has the structure of a *gerere vices*; it is in its very essence *vices*, vicariousness. That is, the term *vices* names the original vicariousness of sovereign power, or, if you like it, its absolutely insubstantial and "economical" character. The twofold (or threefold) structure of the governmental machine (Kingdom and Government, *auctoritas* and *potestas*, *ordinatio* and *executio*, but also the distinction of powers in modern democracies) acquires in this perspective its proper sense. The Government certainly acts vicariously with regard to the Kingdom; but this has a meaning only within "an economy of the in lieu of [*un'economia delle veci*]," in which the two powers depend on each other.

In other words, vicariousness entails an ontology—or better, the replacement of classical ontology with an "economic" paradigm—in which no figure of being is, as such, in the position of the *archē*, while what is original is the very Trinitarian relation, whereby each figure *gerit vices*, deputizes for the other [*fa le veci dell'altra*]. The mystery of being and of the deity coincides entirely with its "economical" mystery. There is no substance of power, but only an "economy," only a "government."

Threshold

We can now attempt to list in the guise of theses the essential characteristics that have been brought to light by our analysis of the providential paradigm. These characteristics define a kind of *ontology of the acts of government.*

1. Providence (the government) is that through which theology and philosophy try to come to terms with the splitting of classical ontology into two separate realities: being and praxis, transcendent and immanent good, theology and *oikonomia.* Providence presents itself as a machine aimed at joining back together the two fragments in the *gubernatio dei,* the divine government of the world.

2. Providence represents, in the same sense and to the same extent, an attempt to reconcile the Gnostic splitting between a God who is foreign to the world and a God that governs, which Christian theology had inherited through the "economical" articulation of the Father and the Son. In the Christian *oikonomia,* God as creator faces a corrupted and extraneous nature, which God as savior—who was entrusted with the government of the world—needs to redeem and save for a kingdom that is not, however, "of this world." The price to be paid by the Trinitarian overcoming of the Gnostic splitting between two deities is the fundamental extraneousness of the world. The Christian government of the world consequently assumes the paradoxical figure of the immanent government of a world that is and needs to remain extraneous.

ℵ *This "gnostic" structure, which the theological* oikonomia *has transmitted to modern governmentality, reaches its apex in the paradigm of the government of the world that the great Western powers (in particular the United States) try today to put into practice on both a local and a global scale. Independently of whether what is at stake is the breakup of preexisting constitutional forms or the imposition, through military occupation, of so-called democratic constitutional models upon peoples for whom these models turn out to be unworkable, the basic point is that a country—and even the entire world—is being governed by remaining completely extraneous to it.*

The tourist, which is the radical reincarnation of the Christian peregrinus in terra, *is the planetary figure of this irreducible extraneousness with regard to the world. In this sense, he is a figure whose "political" meaning is consubstantial with the prevailing governmental paradigm, just as the* peregrinus *was the figure that corresponded to the providential paradigm. In other words, the pilgrim and the tourist are the collateral effects of the same "economy" (in its theological and secularized versions).*

3. Although the providential machine is unitary, it articulates itself, for this very reason, into two different planes or levels: transcendence/immanence, general providence / special providence (or fate), first causes / second causes, eternity/temporality, intellectual knowledge/praxis. The two levels are strictly entwined, so that the first founds, legitimates, and makes possible the second, while the second concretely puts into practice in the chain of causes and effects the general decisions of the divine mind. The government of the world is what results from this functional correlation.

4. In its pure form, the paradigm of the act of government is, consequently, the collateral effect. Insofar as it is not aimed at a particular purpose, but derives, as a concomitant effect, from a general law and economy, the act of government represents an area of undecidability between what is general and what is particular, between what is calculated and what is not-wanted. This is its "economy."

5. In the providential machine transcendence is never given by itself and separated from the world, as in Gnosis, but is always in relation to immanence. On the other hand, the latter is never really such, since it is always thought as an image or a reflection of the transcendent order. Accordingly, the second level presents itself as an execution (*executio*) of what has been arranged and ordered on the first (*ordinatio*). The division of powers is consubstantial with the machine.

6. The ontology of the acts of government is a vicarious ontology, in the sense that, within the economical paradigm, every power has a vicarious character, deputizes for another [*fa le veci di un altro*]. This means that there is not a "substance" of power but only an "economy" of it.

7. The very distinction and correlation between the two levels, between the first and second causes, between the general and the particular economy, guarantees that the government is not a despotic power that does violence to the freedom of creatures. On the contrary, it presupposes the freedom of those who are governed, which manifests itself through the works of the second causes.

It should be clear by now in what sense we can say that the providential apparatus (which is itself nothing but a reformulation and development of the theological *oikonomia*) contains a kind of epistemological paradigm of modern government. It is known that, in the history of law, a doctrine of government and of public administration emerges late (not to mention administration law, which, as such, is purely a modern creation). But well before jurists began to formulate its first elements, philosophers and theologians had already elaborated its canon in the doctrine of the providential *gubernatio* of the world. Providence and fate, with the procession of notions and concepts in which they articulate themselves (*ordinatio/executio*; Kingdom and Government; immediate and mediated government; *primi agentes/agentes inferiores*; primary act/collateral effect, etc.), are not only, in this sense, theological-philosophical concepts, but categories of law and politics.

As a matter of fact, the modern State inherits both aspects of the theological machine of the government of the world, and it presents itself as both providence-State and destiny-State. Through the distinction between legislative or sovereign power and executive or governmental power, the modern State acquires the double structure of the governmental machine. At each turn, it wears the regal clothes of providence, which legislates in a transcendent and universal way, but lets the creatures it looks after be free, and the sinister and ministerial clothes of fate, which carries out in detail the providential dictates and confines the reluctant individuals within the implacable connection between the immanent causes and between the effects that their very nature has contributed to determining. The providential-economical paradigm is, in this sense, the paradigm of democratic power, just as the theological-political is the paradigm of absolutism.

In this sense, it is not surprising that the collateral effect presents itself more often as consubstantial with every act of government. What the government aims at can be obtained, due to its very nature, only as a collateral effect, in an area in which general and particular, positive and negative, calculation and unexpected events tend to overlap. Governing means allowing the particular concomitant effects of a general "economy" to arise, an economy that would remain in itself wholly ineffective, but without which no government is possible. It is not so much that the effects (the Government) depend on being (the Kingdom), but rather that being consists of its effects: such is the vicarious and effectual ontology that defines the acts of government. And when the providential paradigm begins to wane—at least in its transcendent aspect—the providence-State and the destiny-State increasingly tend to identify themselves with the figure of the modern rule of law, in which the law regulates the administration and the administrative apparatus applies and implements the law. But even in this case, the decisive element remains the one to which, from the beginning, the machine as a whole was destined: the *oikonomia*, that is, the government of men and things. The economic-governmental vocation of contemporary democracies is not something that has happened accidentally, but is a constitutive part of the theological legacy of which they are the depositaries.

§ 6 Angelology and Bureaucracy

6.1. In 1935, the same year when he resolutely denies the possibility of a Christian political theology in his monograph, *Monotheism as a Political Problem*, Peterson also affirms the "political" and "public" character of the celestial city and—through its liturgical participation in it—of the Church. He does so, unexpectedly, in the form of a short treatise on angels (*Das Buch von den Engeln. Stellung und Bedeutung der heiligen Engel im Kultus*, 1935), which, although it went unnoticed in the theologian's bibliography, should be read alongside the better-known work that, in a way, it brings to completion.

"The development of the Church," writes Peterson, "leads from the earthly to the celestial Jerusalem, from the city of the Jews to that of the angels and saints" (Peterson 1994, p. 197). In this perspective, the Church is constantly described in the treatise using "political" images: in the same way as profane political assemblies, even the Christian *ekklēsia* can be defined as "the assembly of citizens of the celestial city with full rights [*Vollbürger*], that gather together to carry out acts of worship" (ibid., p. 198). Even the Pauline text is read, by way of a somewhat violent interpretation, politically: the term *politeuma* in Philippians 3:20, that the Vulgate renders as *conversatio* (way of life, conduct), is translated as "citizenship," and a note suggests, albeit hesitantly, that the verb *apographesthai* in Hebrews 12:23 (which in all probability has the eschatological meaning of "being written in the book of life"), actually means "inscription in the register of the citizens of the celestial city" (ibid., p. 231). In any case, Peterson's thesis is that, precisely insofar as it keeps to its path toward its celestial goal, the Church "necessarily comes, through worship, into relation with the inhabitants of the celestial city," that is, with angels, "citizens of heaven," and with the blessed (ibid.). In other words, it is a case of demonstrating that all of the cultual expressions of the Church should be understood "either as a participation of the angels in earthly worship or, vice versa, [. . .] as participation in the worship that the angels offer to God in heaven" (ibid., p. 199).

The strategic meaning of the cultual link that is thus established between the Church and the celestial city is clarified a few pages later. Analyzing the so-called liturgical "intervals" of the Book of Revelation, which according to Peterson reveal acclamations stemming from the ceremonies of imperial worship, he announces the, at first glance, surprising thesis that "the cult of the celestial Church and, therefore, also the liturgy of the earthly Church that is bound to the celestial, have an originary relation [*ursprüngliche Beziehung*] with the world of politics" (ibid., p. 202).

The old Augustinian theme according to which the celestial city will be constituted by the angels and the blessed, who will take the place of the fallen angels so as to restore the perfect number of the Kingdom, assumes in Peterson a strongly political flavor. The images that Augustine borrows from the political vocabulary of his time so as to describe the celestial Jerusalem ("[. . .] adiunctis etiam legionibus et exercitibus angelorum, ut fiat illa una civitas sub uno rege, et una quaedam provincia sub uno imperatore, felix in perpetua pace et salute [. . .]": Augustine, *Expositions on the Book of Psalms*, 36, 3–4) are interpreted literally by Peterson as the foundation of the "politico-religious [*religiös-politische*]" character of the celestial city and, therefore, of the Church that, through worship, communicates with it: "It is a case of the politico-religious concept or, in other words, of the concept of order [*Ordnungsbegriff*] of a celestial hierarchy that the worship of the Church issues in. This is a further confirmation of our thesis that Christian worship has an originary relation to the political sphere" (Peterson 1994, p. 214).

While in the book on *Monotheism as a Political Problem* Peterson resolutely denies, in contrast to Schmitt, the legitimacy of a political-theological interpretation of Christian faith, he nonetheless affirms at the same time with equal determination the politico-religious character of the Church. For this reason it is all the more striking that he continues to make comparisons with the profane political sphere: "In the same way that the emperor, in being accompanied by his bodyguards, expresses the publicity [*Öffentlichkeit*] of his political dominion, so Christ appearing at mass with angels as his bodyguards, expresses the publicity of his politico-religious lordship" (ibid., p. 223). But this "public" character has not "been conferred on the Church by the State; it belongs to it from its origin, inasmuch as it has a Lord that, in the same way as he has a celestial kingdom, also possesses a celestial publicity" (ibid.). The political nature of which Peterson speaks consists, in other words, entirely in the relation that worship establishes, by way of the participation of angels, with this "celestial publicity": "The relation between the *Ekklēsia* and the celestial *polis* is [. . .] a political relation, and for this reason the angels must always enter into the acts of worship of the Church" (ibid.).

The reason for the exclusion of political-theology begins to be revealed here: if politics, from the Christian standpoint, is solely an angelological-cultual relation between the Church and the celestial kingdom, all extrapolation of this "politico-religious" character from the worldly sphere is illegitimate.

In Christian eschatology, every possible theological meaning of worldly politics has been exhausted once and for all: "That celestial worship has an originary relation with the political world in the Book of Revelation is explained by the fact that the apostles have abandoned the earthly Jerusalem, as the center of politics and worship, to turn to the celestial Jerusalem, as a city and regal court, but also as a temple and place of worship. Another fact is linked to this, that is, that the anthem of the Church transcends all national anthems, in the same way that the language of the Church transcends all others. To conclude, it should be noted that such an eschatological transcendence has as a final consequence that the entire universe is borne along by the song of praise" (ibid., p. 206).

6.2. The thesis that summarizes the theological strategy of the treatise is that the angels are the guarantors of the originary relation between the Church and the political sphere, of the "public" and "politico-religious" character of worship that is celebrated both in the *ekklēsia* and in the celestial city. But if we now ask what this "politicality" consists in, we will be surprised to see that the "publicity," which finds both its heraldic emblem and its originary reality in the angels, is defined solely through the song of praise. Christian worship has a genuine relation to the political sphere only to the extent that it tends "to transform Church worship into a service similar to the cult of angels; but this is possible only by bringing into worship a song of praise [*Lobgesang*] that is similar in its essence to the song of praise of the angels" (ibid., p. 214). For this reason, according to Peterson, liturgy culminates in the *Sanctus* [*trisagio*], in the hymn that glorifies God through the triple acclamation *Sanctus, sanctus, sanctus*; and as it is said of the angels that "they sing with untiring lips and ceaseless praise the *Sanctus*, we can for this very reason participate continuously in the angelical liturgy in the form of a daily and nightly service" (ibid., p. 215).

That the song of praise and glory is not merely one characteristic of the angels among others, but defines their essence and therefore their "politicality," is affirmed without reservation by Peterson in the conclusion of his treatise.

> In this exuding and flowing [*Verströmen und Ausströmen*] in words and song, in this phenomenon consists the essence of these angels [. . .] It is not a case of angels being, to begin with and abstractly, "angels in general," that sing in addition, but rather of angels that are such inasmuch as they spread, in the way we have described, in the glorification of the *Holy, holy, holy*. It is this cry [*Ruf*] that properly constitutes their essence; in this exuding they are what they are, that is, Cherubims and Seraphims. (Ibid., p. 226)

If the politicality and truth of the *ekklēsia* is defined by its participation in the angels, then men can also reach their full celestial citizenship only by imitating the angels and participating with them in the song of praise and glorification. The political vocation of man is an angelic vocation, and the angelic vocation is a vocation to the song of glory. The circle is closed:

> The celestial songs correspond to the songs of the Church, and the intimate life of the Church is articulated according to the participation in the celestial song. The angels are the expression of the public character of worship that the Church offers to God: and since the angels are in relation with the politico-religious world in heaven, it follows that, through them, even the worship of the Church is necessarily related to the political sphere. Finally, if through their song the angels distinguish in the Church the "angel-intimating" [*Engel-Ähnliche*] and the "people" [*Volk*], they are also those that awaken the mystical life of the Church, which achieves completion when man, incorporated into the angelic choruses, begins to praise God from the depths of his creaturely being. For this reason we also sing in the *Te Deum*:

Te deum laudamus, te Dominum confitemur,
Te aeternum Patrem omnis terra veneratur,
Tibi omnes Angeli, tibi caeli et universae Potestates
Tibi Cherubim et Seraphim incessabili voce proclamant:
Sanctus, sanctus, sanctus Dominus deus Sabaoth,
Pleni sunt caeli et terra majestatis gloriae tuae. (Ibid., p. 230)

The brief note to the text of the *Te Deum*, which closes the treatise as if to seal it, underlines for the last time the politicality that is in question in worship:

It should be noted that the *Te Deum* defines God as *Pater immensae majestatis* and the Son as *Rex gloriae*. Even the *Te Deum* confirms the politico-religious character of the language of Christian worship. (Ibid., p. 243)

6.3. Of course, Peterson could not be unaware that the attribute of the song of praise through which he defines the angels constitutes, in the Christian tradition of angelology, only one aspect of their being. Gregory the Great—whose *Homelia in Evangelium,* one of the incunabula of Christian angelology Peterson refers us to on more than one occasion—clearly expresses the dual function of the angels. Commenting on the verse from Daniel (7:10) "Millia millium ministrabant ei et decies millies centena millia assistebant ei," he writes "administering [*ministrare*] differs from assisting [*assistere* meaning 'standing before, in the presence of someone'], because the angels that serve as God's ministers emerge to bring to us the announcements, whereas those angels that assist bask in his intimate contemplation and are thus not sent to work outside" (*Homelia in Evangelium,* II, 34, 11–12, in *PL,* 76, 1254c). And since those who administer are more numerous than those who mainly assist, the number of assistants is defined, whereas that of those who minister remains undefined (*millia millium* was perceived to express a generic number). Alexander of Hales and Philip the Chancellor define this dual character of the angelic condition as a duality of "virtues" ("The spirits, which we call angels, have two virtues: the virtue of administering [*virtus administrandi*] and that of assisting God [*virtus assitendi Deo*], that is, of contemplating": Alexander of Hales, *Glossa in quatuor libros sententiarum Petri Lombardi,* II, d. 10, p. 98) or "forces" ("The angels have two forces [*duplicem vim*], the contemplative, which assists God, and the administrative, which is concerned with us: the contemplative force, or assistive, is more noble than the one concerned with us," Philip the Chancellor, *Summa de bono*, vol. 1, Chapter "De bono gratie," § "De bono gratie in angelis," q. 2, p. 384). And Bonaventure summarizes the fundamental division in the nature of angels with the image of Jacob's ladder:

> Angelic operations can be reduced to two: the contemplative operation and the administrative [. . .] And it is through these two that the angelic spirits and their operations can be distinguished. The contemplative consists in an ascent to the highest things; the administrative in the descent to human ones. The two encounter one another on the ladder on which the angels climb and descend [. . .] (*De div. II, De sanctis angelis I,* coll. 2)

In *The Banquet* (Book II, Chapter 4, p. 49), Dante distinguishes in the same way between two "blessednesses" in the nature of angels, the contemplative blessedness with which the angels see and glorify the face of God, and the "blessedness" of "governing the world," which corresponds in men to "active (that is, civil) life."

Of the two functions it is the second—the administrative, where the angels collaborate in the divine government of the world (for this reason Bonaventure calls it *opus gubernationis*)—which attracts most of the medieval theologians' attention. It defines the vocation of angels to such an extent that Ambrose was able to write that, whereas men are created "in the image" (of God), the angels are created "*ad ministerium*" (*Explanatio super Psalmos*, 17, 13).

Following these premises, beginning with the *quaestio* 106, Aquinas's treatise *De gubernatione mundi* becomes a treatise on angelology, which takes up more than half of the entire book and constitutes the broadest treatment that the "Angelic Doctor" has dedicated to this theme. Having answered in the affirmative to the questions of whether the world in general is governed, and if it is governed by God, Aquinas confronts the problem, decisive from the point of view of the ministerial function of angels, "Whether all things are governed by God immediately" (*Summa Theologiae*, I, q. 103, a. 6, ad 3, p. 25). Against those who claim that God can govern everything alone, without the need of intermediaries, and that it is not possible that he has need of ministers, as a *rex terrenus*, Aquinas maintains instead that a government is all the more perfect if it makes use of intermediaries for its execution.

Since the carrying out of government is for the sake of bringing the governed to their perfection, the form of governing will be better which communicates a higher perfection to the governed. Now there is more excellence in a thing's being both good in itself and a cause of good in others, than in its simply being good in itself. Consequently, God governs things in such a way that he establishes some beings as causes over the governing of others [. . .] That a king have ministers of his reign is not an indication only of limitation but also of majesty, since the panoply of ministers displays the king's power. (Ibid., p. 27)

Bonaventure is even more explicit in this regard: if God, like all sovereigns, could do alone what he makes the angels do, he, in truth, needs the angels "so that in the ministry and in the operations a congruous and fitting order is conserved [*ut salvetur in ministerio et actionibus decens et congruus ordo*]" (*In quatuor libros sententiarum*, Book 2, Commentarius 10, art. 1, q. 1, ad. 1).

Having thus established the necessity and ministerial character of angels, in the subsequent seven Questions Aquinas painstakingly analyzes and describes the modes of their reciprocal illumination, their complex hierarchical relations, the nature of their language, the order and hierarchies of the fallen angels, the dominion of angels over corporeal beings and the modes of their action with regard to man, the ministry and missions of angels and, finally, the nature of the custodian angels.

Central to all these analyses are the concepts of hierarchy, ministry, and order. Even before confronting them thematically in a close reading of *The Celestial Hierarchy* by Dionysius the Aeropagite, Aquinas discusses them indirectly and allows them to emerge in each Question, showing a veritable hierarchical obsession that concerns both the angelic and human ministries. Thus, with regard to illumination, he excludes the possibility that a lesser angel might be able to illuminate one higher in the hierarchy (whereas, in an exception to the usual parallelism that Aquinas establishes between the celestial and earthly hierarchies, in the case of the ecclesiastical hierarchy it is possible that those beneath can teach their superiors). In the section on the language of angels (*Summa Theologiae*, I, q. 107, a. 2, pp. 111–113), Aquinas treats the problem of whether a lesser angel can speak to one who is higher in the hierarchy with extreme seriousness (the answer is positive but not without reservations). In discussing the government of corporeal creatures by angels, the hierarchical principle of the offices and ministries of the angels is raised to a universal law that also includes civil hierarchies:

> It is commonly found in human affairs, as well as in nature, that a particular power is controlled and governed by a universal one as, for example, the bailiff's power is controlled by the power of the king. Among the angels also, as stated before, the higher angels [. . .] are above the lower ones [. . .] (Ibid., I, q. 110, a. 1, p. 5)

The general division of angels into two great classes or categories is reaffirmed by Aquinas when he compares paradise to a royal court, which appears to be somewhat similar to a Kafkaesque castle, in which the functionaries are ordered by rank in accordance to the greater or lesser distance between them and the sovereign:

> Angels are represented as being present and as administering by analogy with those who attend [*famulantur*] upon a king. Some remain always present to the king and hear his commands directly. And there are others (for example, those in charge of the provincial administration) to whom the royal commands are announced by those present to the king. These latter are said to be ministers but not to be present. (Ibid., I, q. 112, a. 3, p. 43)

The caesura between assistants and administrators (that is, between contemplation and government) cuts through each angel, which is divided between the two poles that are constitutive of the angelic function, which is at once administrative and mysteric:

> We must therefore note that all angels see the divine essence directly, and in this respect all those who minister are also said to be "*present to God.*" Thus Gregory says, *those sent on an external ministry for the sake of our salvation can be present to God always and see the face of the Father.* Nevertheless, not all the angels are capable of apprehending the hidden secrets of the divine mysteries in the same clear light of the divine essence, but only the higher angels through whom these secrets are made known to the lower ones. (Ibid.)

א *The problem of whether the administering angels are more or less numerous than the assisting ones and, more generally, the problem of the number of angels was a subject upon which opinion differed. Aquinas summarizes this as follows:*

Gregory says that there are more angels ministering than remain present because he understands the text, *Thousands of thousands ministered to him,* not in a multiplicative sense but in the partitive sense as though it meant thousands *out of* thousands. Thus the number of ministering angels is indefinite and this signifies that it goes beyond any finite number. The number of those present, however, is finite since it is added, *and ten thousand times a hundred thousand were present to him* [. . .] This view accounts for the number of angelic orders, since six minister and three remain present. However, Dionysius declares that the angelic population exceeds every population of material things, so that, just as the higher bodies immeasurably transcend the lower bodies in greatness, the higher beings of non-material nature transcend all the things of material nature [. . .] But since it is written [by Dionysius] *ten thousand times a hundred thousand,* those present are said to be many more than those on ministry [. . .] {Such figures should not however be taken literally, as though the angels were so many but no more; their number is much greater inasmuch as it exceeds every material multitude.} (Ibid., I, q. 112, a. 4, ad 2, pp. 45–47)

The prevalence of the glorious-contemplative aspect over the administrative (or vice versa) is translated here immediately into a numerical excess. In any case, it is interesting to note that the first time that we see the idea of a multitudo *or of an infinite mass of rational living beings, it does not refer to men but to citizens of the celestial city; and yet, it is not a case of a formless mass but of a multitude that is perfectly and hierarchically ordered.*

6.4. The introduction of the theme of hierarchy into angelology—and even the invention of the very term "hierarchy"—is the work of an apocryphal author whose gesture is one of the most tenacious mystifications in the history of Christian literature, and it is still waiting to be uncovered. The ambiguity that has marked its reception, especially in the Latin West since the ninth century, has led to the confusion of what is in truth a sacralization of ecclesiastical hierarchy (and, perhaps, every hierarchy) with a mystical theology. And yet a reading that has freed itself from the screen of the tralatitious interpretation leaves us in no doubt as to the strategy of the apocryphal author, who wrote a *Celestial Hierarchy* soon after his *Ecclesiastical Hierarchy:* it is a case, on the one hand, of placing the angels in a hierarchy, arranging their ranks according to a rigidly bureaucratic order and, on the other hand, of angelifying the ecclesiastical hierarchies, by distributing them according to an essentially sacred gradation. In other words, it is a case of transforming the *mysterium* into a *ministerium* and the *ministerium* into a *mysterium,* following a contiguity whose meaning in medieval Christian culture Kantorowicz had already made the object of study (Kantorowicz 2005, p. 195).

The very invention of the term "hierarchia" (which is a specific contribution of the apocryphal author, whose vocabulary is otherwise heavily dependent upon Proclus) is clear-sighted. As Aquinas rightly notes, it does not mean "sacred order" but "sacred power" ("sacer principatus, qui dicitur hierarchia": *Summa Theologiae*, I, q. 108, a. 1, 3, p. 121). In fact, the central idea that runs throughout the Dionysian corpus is that what is sacred and divine is hierarchically ordered, and its barely disguised strategy aims—through the obsessive repetition of a triadic schema that descends from the Trinity, via the angelic triarchies, to the earthly hierarchy—at the sacralization of power.

The parallelism between celestial hierarchy and earthly hierarchy is, after all, already announced in the opening of the treatise on angels and repeated more than once in the text; it is then taken up almost in the same terms in the *Ecclesiastical Hierarchy*. "Power, which loves men and introduces us to mystery," writes the Pseudo-Dionysius, "reveals the celestial hierarchies to us and establishes our hierarchy in such a way that it is linked to their ministry [*sylleitourgon*] through the resemblance with its celestial form" (*Celestial Hierarchy*, 124a, p. 16). "For thus our hierarchy," repeats the treatise on the earthly hierarchy, "reverently arranged in ranks fixed by God, is like the Celestial hierarchies, preserving, so far as man can do, its Godlike characteristics and Divine imitation" (*Ecclesiastical Hierarchy*, 536d, p. 88).

In both treatises, however, the hierarchy is in itself the principle that brings about the work of salvation and deification: the "Divinity [. . .] bequeathed the Hierarchy for the salvation and deification of all rational and intelligent beings" (ibid., 376b, p. 52). Hierarchy is essentially the activity of government, which as such implies an "operation" (*energeia*), a "knowledge" (*epistēmē*), and an "order" (*taxis*) (*Celestial Hierarchy*, 164d, p. 21; see *Ecclesiastical Hierarchy*, 372a, p. 50: hierarchy as *theourgikē epistēmē*). And its origin and its archetype is the Trinitarian economy: "The origin of this hierarchy is the Triad—the Fountain of Life, the Essence of Goodness, the One Cause of things that be—from which all being and good come to things [. . .] it is the real salvation of Beings through its rational design" (ibid., 373c, p. 52). For this reason—that is, insofar as it is a "Divine imitation" (*Celestial Hierarchy*, 164d, p. 21) and a "likeness of God" (ibid., 165a), the hierarchy (whether it be earthly or celestial) is essentially triadic. It gives the cadence to the internal articulation of that divine government of the world that, via two characteristic terms (the first invented and the second derived from Proclus), the apocryphal author defines as *thearchia* (divine power or government, a concept that is more powerful than the modern "theocracy") and *diakosmēsis* (ordered arrangement, *oikonomia*).

א *The hierarchy (the "sacred power") of the Pseudo-Dionysius is in this sense an unfolding of the concept of* diakosmēsis *in Proclus (see* Elements of Theology, prop. 144 and 151). Diakosmeō *means "to govern by ordering" (or "to order by governing"); in the same way, in the concept of "hierarchy" it is impossible to distinguish between "ordered arrangement" and "government."*

6.5. At this point the strategy of the apocryphal author begins to reveal itself. The intricate mystagogical framework and initiatory vocabulary, drawn from Neoplatonism, are given their meaning and real function by an apparatus that is ultimately governmental. *Thearchia*, whose triadic manifestation is the hierarchical government of the world, is ineffable, unnameable, and suprasubstantial; it is the invisible principle of power. The providential *oikonomia* is fully translated into a hierarchy, into a "sacred power" that penetrates and traverses the divine as well as the human world, from the celestial principalities to the nations and peoples of the earth:

> For the Angels, as we have already previously said, complete the whole series of celestial minds, as being the last Order of the heavenly Beings, who possess the Angelic characteristic. Yea, rather, they are more properly named Angels by us than those of higher degree. Especially because their Hierarchy is occupied in making known, and is more particularly concerned with the things of the world. For the very highest Order, as being placed in the first rank near the Hidden One, we must consider as directing in spiritual things in a more hidden fashion than the Order itself. But the second Order, which is composed of the holy Lordships and Powers and Authorities, directs the Hierarchy of the Principalities and Archangels and Angels more clearly indeed than the first Hierarchy, but more hiddenly than the Order after it. We must bear in mind that the more revealing Order of the Principalities, Archangels, and Angels presides through each other over the Hierarchies among men, in order that the instruction, and conversion, and communion, and union with God may be in due order, and, in short, that the procession from God vouchsafed in a manner becoming His goodness to all the Hierarchies, and passing to all

in common, may be in a most sacred regularity. Hence, the sacred scripture has assigned our Hierarchy to Angels, naming the distinguished Michael the Archon of the Jewish people and others over other peoples. For the Most High established borders of nations according to the number of Angels of God. (*Celestial Hierarchy*, 260a–b, pp. 34–35)

This is absolutely clear in the most theologically dense treatise, on *The Divine Names*. Toward the end of the book, when analyzing the names that express God's sovereignty (Saint of saints, King of kings, Ruling still and eternally, Lord of lords, God of gods), the apocryphal author defines regality (*basileia*) as the "appointment [*dianemēsis*] of all bound [*horos*], order [*kosmos*], law [*thesmos*] and rank [*taxis*]" (*The Divine Names*, 969b, p. 86). It is an original definition that, in contrast with the traditional ones (the Aristotelian, the Judeo-Christian, or the neo-Pythagorean), understands regality as an essentially hierarchical principle. If other names (for instance, "holiness" and "Lordship") express the superiority and the perfection of power, nevertheless it is regality understood as an ordering, distributing, and hierarchizing element that expresses most effectively the essence of the "All-transcendent Cause" (ibid., 969c):

> [. . .] from it [. . .] have sprung forth and have been imparted [*dianenemētai*] to all things the unsullied perfection [*akribeia*] of spotless purity; every order [*diataxis*] and all ordered government [*diakosmēsis*] which expels all disharmony and inequality and disproportion, and converts to Itself the things found worthy to participate in It; [. . .] But the Scriptures give the names Holy, King, Lord, God, to the first Orders in each hierarchy through which the secondary ranks, receiving the gifts from God, bring the unity of their participation into multiplicity through their own diversity, and this variety the First Orders, in their Providential divine activity, bring together into their own unity. (Ibid., 969d–972b, pp. 86–87)

According to the postulate of the governmental machine with which we are now familiar, an absolutely transcendent thearchy beyond every cause acts in truth as a principle of immanent order and government. That apophatic theology has here the function of cover and serves, in fact, to found a governmental hierarchy is evident in the function of acclamation and liturgy that belongs to the divine names, with which the ineffable god must—in apparent contrast with his unsayability—ceaselessly be celebrated and his praises sung. We "must praise [*hymnein*, to sing with hymns and praise] Him of innumerable Names as Holy of Holies and King of kings, reigning in Eternity, and eternally [. . .] Lord of lords, God of Gods [. . .] these things must be celebrated absolutely" (ibid., 969a–c, p. 86). Ineffable sovereignty is the hymnological and glorious aspect of power that, according to a paradigm that we have already encountered in Peterson, cherubims, seraphims, and Thrones celebrate by singing the *Sanctus*:

> For some of them [angels], to speak after the manner of men, proclaim as a "voice of many waters," "Blessed is the glory of the Lord, from His place." But others cry aloud that frequent and most august word of God, "Holy, Holy, Holy, Lord of Sabaoth, the whole earth is full of His glory." (*Celestial Hierarchy*, 212b, p. 30)

For this reason the apocryphal author can refer the final exposition of the angelological doctrine back to a lost or fictitious treatise he had composed, which bears the name *The Divine Hymns* (*Peri tōn theiōn hymnōn*) (ibid.). The angel that shouts out the hymn of praise, is, however, in accordance with its dual nature, at once contemplative and ministerial, an essential part of the providential machine that carries out the divine government of the world:

> [The thearchy] is alone and one of three-fold subsistence, sending forth His most kindly forethought to all created things, from the supercelestial minds to the lowest of the earth; as principle and cause of all creation, and containing all things supernaturally in His resistless embrace. (Ibid., 212c, p. 31)

The hierarchy is a hymnology.

א *Hugo Ball was the first to grasp the true character of the Pseudo-Dionysius's angelology. Even if Schmitt's statement that Ball sees Dionysius as a "monk who subordinates himself to the priest, who therefore gives precedence to the priest's hierarchical-ecclesiastical office over every ascetic endeavor, however great, and over all martyrdom" (Schickel, p. 51) is not entirely correct, it reflects the idea of the hierarchical superiority of the ecclesiastical hierarchy that is at the heart of Ball's book* Byzantinisches Christentum *(1923), in which the figure of the Pseudo-Dionysius is analyzed at length.*

6.6. The parallels between celestial and worldly bureaucracy are not an invention of the Pseudo-Dionysius. If already in Athenagoras the angels are defined by means of terms and images drawn from the language of administration (see § 2.8 above), the analogy is clearly affirmed in the passage of the *Adversus Praxean* by Tertullian that we have already analyzed (see § 2.11 above: "Therefore, if the divine monarchy is also administered by so many 'legions' and 'armies of angels' [. . .]": *Against Praxeas*, 3, p. 32) and in Clement of Alexandria: "Also the grades of the Church, of bishops, presbyters, deacons, are imitations of the angelic glory, and of that *oikonomia* which, the Scriptures say, awaits those who, following the footsteps of the apostles, have lived in perfection of righteousness" (*The Stromata*, Book VI, Chapter XIII, p. 505).

After the Pseudo-Dionysius, these parallels become commonplace and, as in Tertullian, are extended to profane power. A "sacred rule, which is what the term 'hierarchy' means, exists among men and among angels," writes Thomas Aquinas (*Summa Theologiae*, q. 108, a. 1, 3, p. 121). Exactly the same as in the case of the angels, the orders of ecclesiastical functionaries are distinguished according to the three functions of purification (*purgare*), enlightenment (*illuminare*), and perfection (*perficere*) (ibid., a. 2, 3, p. 125). But the civil hierarchies also have to be articulated according to orders and degrees:

> The very meaning of hierarchy, then, demands a distinction of orders that has its explanation on the basis of differing offices and acts. This is illustrated in the case of a city, where there are classes of people differing according to their varying activities—judges, soldiers, peasants and the like are distinct classes. Yet, while within the one city there are such classes, all are reducible to three, in the sense that any organized group is made up of a beginning, and middle and an end. Hence in cities there are three classes of people: some are at the top, the upper class; some are at the bottom, the common people; some are in between, the middle class [*populus honorabilis*]. So too, then, in each of the angelic hierarchies there are orders, distinct on the basis of diverse acts and offices [. . .] (Ibid., a. 2, p. 127)

Having established the centrality of the notion of hierarchy, angels and bureaucrats tend to fuse, exactly as they do in Kafka's world. Not only are celestial messengers organized according to offices and ministries, but worldly functionaries in turn assume angelic qualities and, in the same way as angels, become capable of cleansing, enlightening, and perfecting. Moreover, following an ambiguity that characterizes the history of the relation between spiritual power and secular power, the paradigmatic relation of angelology and bureaucracy runs now in one direction, now in another. Sometimes, as in Tertullian's writings, the administration of the worldly monarchy is the model of the angelic ministries, whereas at others the celestial bureaucracy furnishes the archetype for the worldly.

What is decisive, however, is that long before the terminology of civil administration and government was developed and fixed, it was already firmly constituted in angelology. Not only the concept of hierarchy but also that of ministry and of mission are, as we have seen, first systematized in a highly articulated way precisely in relation to angelic activities.

℟ *In a short article published in 1928, which did not fail to catch Kantorowicz's attention, Franz Blatt had already demonstrated how, in the manuscripts of the patristic texts, the two terms* mysterium *and* ministerium *obstinately tend to merge. Exemplary among the numerous cases cited is a passage from Jerome's Eighteenth Letter in which (in relation to the seraphims) some codices reveal the* lectio difficilior: *"in diversa mysteria mittantur," while others (where it is not possible to think that an error might have been made by the scribe) have the more obvious "in diversa ministeria mittantur." Blatt certainly hits the target with his suggestion that the evolution from "ministry" to "mystery" can be explained by the fact that, particularly in the case of the priest who officiates the mass (which is at once sacrament and service), the two terms coincide perfectly (Blatt, p. 81). But the origin of the confusion is older and depends on the Pauline expression "economy of the mystery" and its inversion in a "mystery of the economy" of which we have already spoken in relation to Hippolytus and Tertullian. It is not surprising then that the first conscious interplay—at once alliterative and conceptual—between the two terms was in the Vulgate of 1 Corinthians 4:1, where* hypēretas Christou kai oikonomous mystēriōn theou *is rendered "ministros Christi et dispensatores mysteriorum Dei." The administration (the "economy") is essentially concerned with the arcane, while, on the other hand, mystery can only be dispensed administratively and "economically." It is this link—which is absolutely constitutive of the economy of the Trinity—that explains the frequent and deliberately promiscuous use of the terms* mysterium *and* ministerium *from the early Fathers to late Scholasticism (an instructive example can be found in Marius Victorinus,* In Epistolam ad Ephesios, II, 4, 12, *in* PL, 8, 1275c: "dono Christi instituta sunt hujusmodi et mysteria et ministeria"; *see the observations made by Benz, p. 153).*

In the same letter of Jerome's that we have already cited, it is possible to note one of the first testimonies to the metonymic evolution that will lead the term ministerium *(which signifies "service, assignment") to assume the modern administrative significance of "set of functionaries and offices." Jerome asks: "Quando [Deus] Thronos, Dominationes, Potestates, Angelos, totumque ministerium coeleste condiderit?" (Hieronymus,* Epistolae, *I, 18, 7, in* PL, *22, 365). Just as the angelic bureaucracy anticipates the human in its hierarchical perfection, so the "celestial ministry" precedes the earthly ministry that inherits from its theological model its own arcane character.*

6.7. Toward the end of Question 108, shortly before moving on to discuss the order of demons, Aquinas makes a sudden digression to ask if the hierarchies and orders of angels will remain even after the Day of Judgment. The question is by no means to be taken for granted nor is it avoidable. Indeed, once the history of the world and its creatures has reached its end and the elect, as well as the damned, have received either eternal bliss or eternal punishment, what is the purpose of the existence of the orders of angels? How can we imagine inoperative angels?

The problem was complicated further by the fact that, in a passage of the First Letter to the Corinthians (15:24), Paul appeared to indicate the elimination or deactivation of the ranks of angels at the time of the parousia: "Then comes the end, when he [Christ] hands over the Kingdom to God the Father, after he has rendered inoperative [*katargēsēi;* Latin: *evacuaverit*] every ruler and every authority and power." The return of the messianic Kingdom to the hands of the Father implies the consummation of the historical task of redemption. In his commentary on Paul's Epistles, Aquinas had already discussed the problem of the end of government and of the function of angels from this viewpoint, distinguishing between "glory" and "execution," between those angels who direct and those who execute:

> *After he does away with every principality, power and virtue,* that is, when all dominion both human and angelic shall have ceased, then we shall be immediately under God [*immediate erimus sub Deo*] [. . .] But will not the orders of angels remain distinct? I answer yes, as to the eminence of glory [*ad eminentiam gloriae*], by which one is superior to another, but not as to the efficacy of their executive government toward us [*ad efficaciam executionis ad nos*]. Therefore, he says that those angels whose names concern the execution will be rendered inoperative, namely, principalities, powers and virtues. He does not name those angels who belong to the higher hierarchy, because they are not executors [. . .] neither does he say that their dominations will

> be rendered inoperative, because although they belong to the executive, they do not perform the activity themselves, but direct and command. (Aquinas, *Commentary on the First Epistle to the Corinthians*, Chapter 15, l. 3)

Even on the last day, the function of the angels is, in some ways, still thinkable; not only, according to Matthew 25:31, will they witness the Last Judgment, but they will also be "sent in every place to gather up the resurrected" (Daniélou, p. 131). Moreover, according to Origen, the resurrected will be "sustained by the angels" and "carried upon their shoulders" (ibid., pp. 133–134). But when the last of the blessed has risen to heaven and the last of the damned repelled into hell, what will happen to the celestial ministers?

In the treatise *De gubernatione mundi*, the aporia is fully revealed. The *oikonomia*, the providential government of the world, is not eternal but is completed on the Day of Judgment. "The purpose of the angelic offices is to lead men to salvation. Accordingly the angelic offices and so their orders will not go on after judgment day" (*Summa Theologiae*, I, q. 108, a. 7, 3, p. 151). The Kingdom that will follow is what we might call radically without government. But how can one think a Kingdom without any possible Government?

Aquinas draws certain subtle distinctions in order to resolve this aporia. It is a case of nothing less than separating the hierarchy from its function in an attempt to think the possibility of power surviving its exercise. In the same way that the function of the leader of an army is different in battle and in the triumph that follows it, so the hierarchy and its glory can remain even beyond the government to which they were assigned:

> We can take into account two elements in the angelic orders, the distinction of ranks and the carrying out of ministries. As shown, a distinction of ranks among them exists on the basis of their differences in grace and nature. Both differences will last forever; any natural difference would be removable only by destroying the nature; a difference in glory corresponding to a difference in prior merits will also last forever. The carrying out of offices will, after judgment day, in some way continue and in another way stop. It will stop in regard to offices having as their purpose the leading of others to the end; it will continue in the way appropriate to those in possession of the end. The duties of an army's ranks, for example, are different in battle and in victory. (Ibid., pp. 151–153)

The hierarchy, which appeared to be tightly linked to the exercise of an office or ministry, gloriously outlives it.

6.8. The problem Aquinas is trying to overcome is, in the final analysis, that of the end of the *oikonomia*. The history of salvation, which was the concern of the machine of the providential government of the world, is entirely exhausted. What happens now to the machine? What happens to the billions of angels that, perfectly ordered in nine lines within the celestial hierarchy, have at each instant from the creation to the Day of Judgment fulfilled their tireless ministry? For some of these Aquinas's verdict is inexorable: "At the final consummation Christ will bring Principalities and Powers to naught as far as leading others to the end is concerned, since once one is attained, there is no need to strive for it" (ibid., p. 153). The statement in the *Questions on Providence* by Matthew of Acquasparta is yet more categorical:

> The final consummation allows for neither the cooperation of creatures nor any possible ministry. In the same way that God is the immediate beginning of all creatures, in the same way he is immediately their end, *alpha* and *omega* [. . .] Therefore, all administration will cease. All angelic ministries will cease, since it was ordered to conduct men to their end, and once this end has been reached, it must end. All hierarchical operations will cease, all subordination and all superiority, as the Apostle says (in 1 Corinthians 15:24). (Matthew of Acquasparta, p. 316)

The cessation of the governmental machine feeds back into the Trinitarian economy itself. If the latter was constitutively tied to the action of God and his practice of providential government of the world, how can one think of God as inoperative? If the Trinitarian economy had been able to reconcile in a single God the Gnostic division between *deus otiosus* and *deus actuosus*, the cessation of every activity seems to put back in question the very meaning of that economy. For this reason Saint Jerome, in the epistle to Pope Damasus, commenting upon Isaiah (6:2–3), in which it is said that the seraphims covered with their wings the head and feet of the Lord, catches a glimpse of a sign of the impossibility of thinking what precedes the creation of the world or follows its end:

> What will happen after the consummation of the century? After humanity has been judged, what life can there be? Will there still be another earth? Will new elements and a new world be created? [. . .] Isaiah wants to say that what there was before the world and what there will be after it cannot be told [. . .] We know only what is in between and has been revealed through Scripture: when the world was created and when man was created, the flood,

the law, and how starting with the first man all the world was filled, until in the last age the Son of God was incarnated for our salvation. Everything else was hidden by the two Seraphims, who covered their head and feet. (Hieronymus, *Epistolae*, I, 18, 7, in *PL*, 22, 365)

It is like saying that of God we can know and think only the economy, the Government, not the Kingdom or the inoperativity; and yet the Government is nothing but the brief interval running between the two eternal and glorious figures of the Kingdom.

It is now comprehensible why, in the theological tradition that finds its most extreme representative in Peterson, the perfect cipher of Christian citizenship is constituted by the song of praise, and the pleromatic figure of the political is bestowed upon the angels who have become inoperative. The doctrine of Glory as the final end of man and as the figure of the divine that outlives the government of the world is the answer that theologians give to the problem of the end of the economy. The angelic ministries survive the universal judgment only as a hymnological hierarchy, as contemplation and praise of the glory of the divine. With every providential operation exhausted and with all administration of salvation coming to an end, only song remains. Liturgy survives only as doxology.

ℵ *That the problem of how to think the inoperative figure of divinity represents, in Christian theology, a veritable* crux, *is proven by the difficulty encountered—since Irenaeus and Augustine—by the attempts to answer the blasphemous question par excellence: "What was God doing before He made heaven and earth? [. . .] Why did He not continue to do nothing forever as He did before?" Already Augustine—who in the* Confessions *(Book 11, § 10, p. 240) relates the question in this form, attributing it to men* pleni vetustatis suae—*mentions the ironic reply, which in truth betrays incredible embarrassment: "He was getting hell ready for people who pry too deep [*alta (. . .) scrutantibus gehennas parabat*]" (ibid., § 12, p. 241). Eleven centuries later, as testimony to the persistence of the problem, Luther takes it up again in the following form: "He sat in the forest, cutting rods to beat those who ask impertinent questions."*

The question—which, it is no coincidence, derives from pagans and Gnostics, for whom it posed no difficulty—was particularly embarrassing for Christians, precisely because the Trinitarian economy was essentially a figure of action and government. It corresponded perfectly, a parte ante, *to the ques-*

tion regarding the state not only of God but also of the angels and the blessed after the world's end.

Hence glory is what must cover with its splendor the unaccountable figure of divine inoperativity. *Even if it can fill entire volumes (as in the case of Balthasar), the* theologia gloriae *is what we might call a blank page in the arguments of the theologians. For this reason its typical form is that of mysticism, which—in the face of the glorious figure of power—can do nothing except fall silent. In every other case,* scrutator maiestatis obtunditur a gloria, *as Luther stated in his incisive formula.*

In Judaic circles, where God has not taken the oikonomia *within himself, the question regarding the inoperativity of God is much less embarrassing. According to the Midrash (Tehillim, 90, 391), two thousand years before he created the heavens and the earth, God created seven things (the Torah, the throne, paradise, hell, the celestial sanctuary, the name of the Messiah, and the voice that cries: "Repent, ye sons of men"). In the subsequent two thousand years—always according to this Midrash, which thus answers the question preemptively—he has consulted the Torah, has created other worlds, and has discussed with the letters of the alphabet which of them should be the agent of creation.*

6.9. The evacuation of the angelic ministries after the Judgment demonstrates that the divine government of the world is structurally limited in time; that the theological economy is essentially finite. The Christian paradigm of government, like the vision of history that supports it, lasts from the creation until the end of the world. The modern conception of history that takes up without reservation the theological model in many of its aspects, finds itself for this reason in a contradictory situation. On the one hand, it abolishes the eschatology and infinitely prolongs the history and the government of the world; on the other hand, it finds that the finite character of its paradigm returns ceaselessly (which is as evident in Kojève's interpretation of Hegel as it is in the problem of the end of the history of being in the later Heidegger).

The principle according to which the government of the world will cease with the Last Judgment has only one important exception in Christian theology. It is the case of hell. In Question 89, Thomas Aquinas asks himself whether the demons will execute the sentence of the damned ("Utrum daemones exequentur sententiam iudicis in damnatos"). Against the opinion of those who held that, with the Judgment, all function of government and ministry would cease, Aquinas instead claims that the demons will carry out their judicial function as executors of the infernal punishments for all eternity. In the same way as he had argued that the angels would lay down their ministries but would eternally maintain their order and their hierarchies, so now he writes that "so, too, will order be observed in punishments, men being punished by demons, lest the Divine order, whereby the angels are placed between the human nature and the Divine, be entirely set aside" (*Summa Theologiae*, Supplement, q. 89, a. 4).[1] In other words, hell is that place in which the divine government of the world survives for all eternity, even if only in a penitentiary form. And while the angels in paradise will abandon every form of government and will no longer be ministers but only assistants, despite conserving the empty form of their hierarchies, the demons, meanwhile, will be the indefectible ministers and eternal executioners of divine justice.

However, this means that, from the perspective of Christian theology, the idea of eternal government (which is the paradigm of modern politics) is truly infernal. Curiously, this eternal penitentiary government, this penal colony that knows no expiation, has an unexpected theatrical implication. Among the questions Aquinas poses with regard to the condition of the blessed, is whether they are able to witness the punishments of the damned ("Utrum beati qui erunt in patria, videant poenas damnatorum"). He is aware that the horror and the *turpitudo* of a similar spectacle is not suitable fare for saints; and yet, with a psychological candor in the face of the sadistic implications of his arguments that it is not easy for us moderns to accept, he affirms without reservations that "the happiness of the saints may be more delightful to them [. . .] [if] they are allowed to see perfectly the sufferings of the damned" (ibid., Supplement, q. 94, a. 1). In addition to this, the blessed and the angels with whom they contemplate it are not allowed to feel compassion before this atrocious spectacle, but only enjoyment, insofar as the punishment of the damned is the expression of the eternal order of divine justice ("et hoc modo sancti de poenis impiorum gaudebunt, considerando in eis ordinem divinae justitiae, et suam liberationem, de qua gaudebunt": ibid., a. 3).

The "spectacle of suffering," whose solidarity with the power of the *ancien régime* Foucault has demonstrated, finds here its eternal root.

Threshold

That angelology directly coincides with a theory of power, that the angel is the figure of the government of the world par excellence is already evident from the simple fact that the angelic names are identified with those of worldly powers: *arkai, exousiai, kyriotētes* (*principatus, potestates, dominationes* in the Latin translation). This is evident in Paul, in whose Letters it is not always easy to distinguish the names of the angels from those of the worldly authorities. After all, the hendiadys *arkai kai exousiai* is commonly used, in the Greek of that time, as a way of indicating human powers in a generic way (so in Luke 12:11, Jesus's followers are dragged into the synagogue before "magistrates, and powers [*epi* (. . .) *tas arkas kai tas exousias*]," and in Titus 3:1, Paul counsels the members of the community to be "subject to *arkais exousiais*"). In the Letter to the Colossians as well, where the cult of angels is certainly in question, it is not clear whether the "principalities and powers" over which the Messiah has triumphed via the cross (Colossians 2:15) are angelic or human powers. And even in the celebrated verse of 1 Corinthians 15:24, the destruction of "all rule and all authority and power" that the Messiah brings about when he hands back the kingdom to God can refer equally well to worldly powers and to the angels. In other passages, in which the terms unequivocally denote angelic powers, these are seen as ambiguous demonic powers. So the Letter to the Ephesians, which opens with the luminous image of the resurrected Messiah whom God places on his right-hand side, "far above all principality, and power, and might, and dominion" (Ephesians 1:21), ends with the evocation of angels themselves as "the rulers of the darkness of this world" (*kosmokratores tou skotou toutou*): "For we wrestle not against flesh and blood, but against principalities, against powers, against the rulers of the darkness of this world, against spiritual wickedness in high places" (Ephesians 6:12).

The intercourse between the angels and the worldly powers is more intimate and essential, and derives, first, from the fact that, insofar as they are figures of the divine government of the world, they are immediately also the "princes of this world" (1 Corinthians 2:6). The worldly and angelic powers become indistinguishable in Paul because they both stem from God. The celebrated passage in Romans 13:1–5, on the divine origin of every *exousia* ("there is no power but of God"), should be read from this perspective, and in it one also finds its corrective. Pauline angelol-

ogy is, in fact, in agreement with the critique of law and authority that
it founds. For authority, like law (which "was ordained by angels": Gala-
tians 3:19; see also Hebrews 2:2), was given "for sin" (Romans 8:3), and its
power ceases with the arrival of the Messiah. No "angel" nor any "power"
(*arkē*) can separate us from "Christ Jesus our Lord" (Romans 8:38–39),
because "we shall judge angels" as well (1 Corinthians 6:3). George B.
Caird has observed that the ambiguity of the angelic powers, like that of
the law and of every power, resides in the fact that what had been given
provisionally and for sin pretends to be valid absolutely.

> But when the law is isolated and exalted into an independent system of reli-
> gion, it becomes demonic. The corruption of the law is the work of sin, and
> in particular the sin of self-righteousness [. . .] All legalism is self-assertion, a
> claim that we can establish our own righteousness, that we can save ourselves
> by our own moral and spiritual attainments. (Caird, p. 41)

But this demonic radicalization of the law and of angelic ranks also in
some ways constitutes a hypostasis of fury and divine justice that the
cabalists will call *Din*, rigor, and that in Paul appears as "indignation and
wrath" (*orgē kai thymos*: Romans 2:5–8). The angels, as a cipher for the
divine power of government of the world, also represent the dark and
demonic aspect of God, which, as such, cannot simply be expunged.

Pauline messianism must be seen from this perspective. It acts as a corrective to the demonic hypertrophy of angelic and human powers. The
Messiah deactivates and renders inoperative the law as well as the angels
and, in this way, reconciles them with God (*katargeō*[2] is the technical
term that Paul uses to express the relation between the Messiah and the
power of angels and men; I translate *argos* as "inoperative" and not simply
as "I destroy"). (One reads in Colossians 1:15–20 that all things, "whether
they be thrones, or dominions, or principalities, or powers," have been
created through the Messiah, and through him they will be reconciled
with God.)

The theme of the law no longer applied, but studied, that in Kafka's
novels goes hand in hand with that of the constantly inoperative angel-
functionaries, here reveals its messianic pertinence. The ultimate and glorious telos of the law and of the angelic powers, as well as of the profane
powers, is to be deactivated and made inoperative.

§ 7   The Power and the Glory

7.1. The caesura that divides the nature of angels and articulates their orders into those of assistants and administrators, into choristers of glory and ministers of government corresponds to a dual figure of power that we must now interrogate. Perhaps only in the tension between *gloria* and *gubernatio*, the articulation of Kingdom and Government, which we have attempted patiently to reconstruct by means of the history of the theological-economic paradigm, attains at one and the same time both its full intelligibility and its maximum opacity. Intelligibility, because never as in the opposition between assistants and ministers has the difference between Kingdom and Glory become so effective; opacity, because what is a politics that would not be of government but of liturgy, not of action but of hymn, not of power but of glory?

To answer this question we must first identify the secret thread that unites Peterson's 1935 text on angels to the dissertation that the young theologian, not yet converted to Catholicism, publishes in 1926 under the title *Heis Theos. Epigraphische, formgeschichtliche und religionsgeschichtliche Untersuchungen.* Years later, confronting similar themes, Kantorowicz called Peterson's dissertation "fundamental." The subtitle, which brings together a philological category with concepts drawn from theological studies is, from this point of view, misleading. It is neither a properly theological study nor is it, despite the imposing critical apparatus and the extraordinary erudition, a case of a solely historical-philological investigation. The disciplinary field in which the dissertation is to be placed remains obscure and so requires some preliminary considerations.

In 1934, in the introduction to his book on the formation of imperial

167

Roman ceremonials, Andreas Alföldi lamented that, while the study of the rational-juridical aspects of the imperial State had produced works of the caliber of Mommsen's *Staatsrecht*, the investigation of its ceremonial and religious aspects was left to works of dubious scientific value such as *Culte impérial* by the abbot Beurlier (Alföldi, p. 5). In the same way, in the introduction to his book on the *Laudes Regiae* (1946), Ernst Kantorowicz observed that the study of liturgical sources of political history remained, till the beginning of the twentieth century, the prerogative of theologians and of Church historians who, as parties to the case, were not necessarily the most trustworthy sources (Kantorowicz 1946, p. vii).

Although composed by a theologian (who could nonetheless claim Franz Boll, Eduard Norden, and Richard Reitzenstein as his teachers), Peterson's dissertation broke with this tradition insofar as it is concerned entirely with the relations between political ceremonies and ecclesiastical liturgy, via the examination of the exhortation *Heis theos*. In the same way that Carl Schmitt was able to confirm many years later, "an enormous amount of material from literary sources and epigraphic evidence is laid out with perfect objectivity, and no judgment for or against any theological standpoint or any specific dogmatic creed can be found" (Schmitt 2008a, p. 61). In other words, it was the case of a first step en route to a science that is still lacking today; one that is dedicated to the history of the ceremonial aspects of power and right; a sort of political archaeology of liturgy and protocol, which we can inscribe here—albeit provisionally—under the heading of "archaeology of glory." It would therefore be valuable for us to follow carefully the development of Peterson's dissertation in order to uncover its results and strategies.

7.2. The inquiry opens with the patient cataloguing of an imposing mass of findings, particularly epigraphic ones, in which the expression *heis theos* appears (sometimes it is expanded in a Binitarian and Trinitarian sense in the expressions *Heis theos kai Christos* or *Heis theos kai Christos autou kai to hagion pneuma*). Peterson deploys a twofold strategy in the face of the dominant interpretations that linked this material to liturgical formulae and that, in the final analysis, were to be understood as professions of faith. On the one hand, he decisively denies that the formulae in question contain anything like a profession of faith; on the other hand, he ascribes them in an equally resolute fashion to the sphere of acclamations: "The formula *Heis theos* is an acclamation, but not a profession of faith"

(Peterson 1926, p. 302). This, however, means pushing back the origin of these essentially Christian expressions to a more obscure foundation in which they overlap with the acclamations of the pagan emperors and with the cries that greeted the epiphany of Dionysius in the Orphic rituals, with the exorcisms of the magical papyruses and the formulae of the Mithraic, Gnostic, and Manichean mysteric cults. It also means posing the problem of the origin and significance of the acclamations and their relation with Christian liturgy.

What is an acclamation? It is an exclamation of praise, of triumph ("Io triumphe!"), of laudation or of disapproval (*acclamatio adversa*) yelled by a crowd in determinate circumstances. The acclamation was accompanied by a gesture of raising the right hand (testified in both pagan and Christian art) or, in theaters and circuses, by applause and the waving of handkerchiefs. Here the acclamation could be directed, as testified by Cicero (*Letters to Atticus*, vol. 1, 1.16, pp. 149–163), not only to athletes and actors, but also to the magistrates of the republic and, later, to the emperor. The arrival of the sovereign in a city would give way to a ceremonial parade (the *adventus*), generally accompanied by solemn acclamations. The acclamation could assume a variety of forms that Peterson examines in detail: the desire for victory (*nika, vincas*), of life and fertility (*vivas, floreas, zēs, felicissime*), of long life (*polla ta etē, eis aiōnas, de nostris annis augeat tibi Iuppiter annos*), of strength and salvation (*valeas, dii te nobis praestent, te salvo salvi et securi sumus*), of invocation and prayer (*kyrie, kyrie sōzōn, kyrie eleēson*), and of approval and praise (*axios, dignum et iustum esti, fiat, amen*). The acclamations were often ritually repeated and, at times, modulated. A Christian testimony provides us with the details of an *acclamatio adversa* in the Circo Massimo:

> Pars maior populi clamabant, dicentes: Christiani tollantur! Dictum est duodecim. Per caput Augusti, christiani non sint! Spectantes vero Hermogenianum, praefectum urbis, item clamaverunt decies: Sic, Auguste, vincas! [. . .] Et statim discesserunt omnes una voce dicentes: Auguste, tu vincas et cum diis floreas!

Augustine himself informs us of the Christian use of acclamatory formulae of the type *axios, dignum est* when describing in a letter the ceremony for the designation of his successor Heraclius as bishop of Hippo:

> A populo acclamatum est: Deo gratias, Christo laudes; dictum est vicies ter-

ties. Exaudi Christe, Augustino vita; dictum est sexies decies [. . .] Bene meritus, bene dignus; dictum est quinquies. Dignus et iustus est; dictum est sexies [. . .] Fiat, fiat; dictum est duodecies. (Augustine, *Letters*, 213, 5–8)

It is essential to an understanding of the importance of acclamations that, as Peterson notes, "they were in no way irrelevant, but they could acquire a juridical meaning in certain circumstances" (Peterson 1926, p. 141). Peterson refers us to the article "*Acclamatio*," in the *Realencyclopädie der Classischen Altertumswissenschaft*, commonly called the Pauly-Wissowa; but Mommsen, in his *Staatsrecht*, pointedly recognized the decisive juridical value of acclamations in Roman public law. In the first place, he noted the acclamation with which, in the republican era, the troops accorded the victorious commander the title of *imperator* (Mommsen, vol. 1, p. 124) and, in the imperial epoch, invested him with the title of Caesar (ibid., vol. 2, p. 841). The acclamation of the senators, in the imperial era in particular, could also be used to give the status of decision to a message from the emperor (ibid., vol. 3, pp. 949–950), and, in the electoral meetings, it could act as a substitute for the votes of individual voters (ibid., p. 350).

It is this juridical value of the acclamation that, at a crucial point, Peterson emphasizes while stating, alongside the thesis of the pagan origin of many Christian acclamations, the essential link that unites law and liturgy. In relation to the formulae *dignum et iustum est* (which appears, in addition to the rituals of elections and ecclesiastic depositions, at the beginning of the anaphora of the Mass as well), Peterson—after criticizing modern juridical science for failing to grasp correctly the meaning of acclamations—suggests that the formula is not to be considered (as had been suggested) to be a shorter type of electoral procedure. Instead, in accordance with a habit that the Church takes up from the profane *ecclesia*, it "expresses, in the form of acclamation, the people's *consensus*" (Peterson 1926, p. 177). This consensus has, however, a juridical significance that throws a new light on the connection between law and liturgy. Referring to the works of P. Cagin on the tradition of doxological acclamations that registered the analogy with the acclamations for the election of the emperor Gordian (*Aequum est, iustum est! Gordiane Auguste, dii te servent feliciter!*), Peterson writes:

> Cagin is certainly correct when, in an incisive chapter, he concludes his analysis with the observation that the first word of the anaphora *vere dignum* is nothing other than a reply to the acclamation of the people: *Dignum et ius-*

tum est. But neither Cagin nor others have sufficiently clarified the fact that, through the acclamation *axion kai dikaion,* both the liturgy and the hymn (*Te deum, Gloria,* etc.) are given a juridical foundation. In other words, *the adoption of the public ceremonial ("leitourgia") of the "Eucharistia" in the anaphora or the hymn can only occur in the juridical form of an acclamation by the people ("laos") and the priest.* (Ibid., p. 178)

7.3. In 1927, in an article entitled "Referendum and Petition for a Referendum" (but in German the two corresponding technical terms—*Volksentscheid* and *Volksbegehren*—literally mean "popular decision" and "request from the people"), Schmitt referred to Peterson's book, which had been published just a year earlier, specifically in relation to the political meaning of acclamations. In this text Schmitt opposes the individual vote by secret ballot that characterizes contemporary democracies to the immediate expression of the united people that characterizes "pure" or direct democracy and, at the same time, links in constitutive fashion people and acclamation.

Individual secret voting, which is not preceded by any sort of public debate procedurally regulated, annihilates precisely the specific possibilities of the united people. In fact, the real activity, capacity, and function of the people, the center of all popular expression, the original democratic phenomenon, what even Rousseau indicated as being a real democracy, is acclamation, the cry of approval or rejection from the united masses. The people acclaim a leader, the army (identical here with the people) a general or emperor, citizens or rural communities a proposal (where the question remains open as to whether what is acclaimed is a leader or the content of a proposal); the people cries "up with" or "down with," it exults or complains, takes up arms and calls another leader; it consents to a deliberation with any word or withholds its acclamation with silence. A fundamental piece of research by Erik Peterson that, with regard to its scientific significance, far surpasses the particular area of its subject matter, has described the *acclamatio* and its forms in the early Christian period. (Schmitt 1927, pp. 33–34)

Just as for Peterson the acclamations and liturgical doxologies express the juridical and public character of the Christian people (*laos*), so for Schmitt the acclamation is the pure and immediate expression of the people as constituent democratic power. "This people," he had written some lines earlier, "possesses constituent power, is the subject of *pouvoir constituant,* and hence is something essentially different from the people that

[. . .] exerts certain authorities in the form prescribed by the constitution, that is, elects the *Reichstag* or the president of the Reich, or becomes active in the case of a referendum" (ibid., p. 32). For this reason, by shifting Peterson's thesis into the profane sphere, Schmitt is able to push it to the extreme by affirming that the "acclamation is an eternal phenomenon of all political communities. There is no state without a people, and no people without acclamations" (ibid., p. 34).

Schmitt's strategy is clear: drawing from Peterson the notion of a constitutive function of the liturgical acclamation, he assumes the habits of a theorist of pure or direct democracy in order to pitch it against Weimar liberal democracy. In the same way that the faithful who utter the doxological formulae exist alongside the angels in the liturgy, so the acclamation of the people in its immediate presence is the opposite of the liberal practice of the secret ballot, which denudes the sovereign subject of his constituent power.

> This scientific discovery of the acclamation is the starting point for an explanation of the procedure of direct or pure democracy. One must not ignore the fact that, wherever there is public opinion as social reality and not merely as a political pretext, in all the decisive moments in which the political meaning of a people can be affirmed, there first appear acclamations of approval or refusal that are independent of the voting procedure, because through such a procedure their genuineness could be threatened, insofar as the immediacy of the people united, which defines this acclamation, is annulled by the isolation of the single voter and by the secrecy of the ballot. (Ibid., p. 34)

7.4. The historians of liturgy know that the primitive Christian liturgy issues from the union of psalmodic and doxological elements with the Eucharistic celebration. In this way, textbooks of liturgy distinguish to this day between *liturgia epaenetica*, or of laudation, and Eucharistic liturgy. A careful examination of the Eucharistic liturgy demonstrates, however, that, in it, acclamations, doxologies, and Eucharistic sacrifice are so closely interwoven that they are actually indiscernible. In Nicolas Cabasilas's fourteenth-century treatise on the divine liturgy, in which the author summarizes the thought of the Eastern Church on the order of divine mysteries, Eucharistic consecration is distinguished from the hymns of praise, from prayers, from the readings of the sacred texts, and from "all that which is said and done before and after the consecration" (Cabasilas, p. 57). And yet, both of these aspects of the liturgy in reality form a "single body" and contribute to the same end, which is the sanctifying of the faithful. "The entire mystagogy," writes Cabasilas, "is a single narrative body [*sōma hen historias*], which conserves from beginning to end its harmony and integrity, in such a way that each of its gestures and formulae makes its common contribution to the whole" (ibid., p. 129). Liturgy and *oikonomia* are, from this perspective, strictly linked, since as much in the songs and the acclamations of praise as in the acts of the priest, it is always only "the economy of the Savior [*oikonomia tou Sōtēros*] that is meant" (ibid., p. 61). In the same way as the offer of bread and wine, the doxologies and the songs are, according to the words of the psalmist (Psalm 50:14–15), a "sacrifice of praise": "Offer unto God thanksgiving; and pay thy vows unto the most High [. . .] I will deliver thee, and thou shalt glorify me" (Cabasilas, p. 58).

Consider the liturgy of the Gallic Mass as it was celebrated from the sixth to the eighth century (but any form of the ancient liturgy, from the *Traditio apostolica* to the description of the anaphora in Saint Cyril of Alexandria's *Catachesis*, could serve the same purpose). The Mass began with a preamble in song, in which the bishop would approach the altar, accompanied by a psalmodic antiphone and by the doxology *Gloria Patri*. From our standpoint, it is a case of a series of acclamations:

> *Alleluja! Benedictus qui venit, alleluja,*
> *in nomine Domini: Alleluja! Alleluja!*
> *Deus Dominus, et illuxit nobis.*
> *In nomine Domini.*
> *Gloria et honor Patri et Filio et Spiritui Sancto*
> *in saecula saeculorum. Amen.*
> *In nomine Domini.*

Immediately afterward, the *Trisagion*, the solemn song of praise, was performed in Greek and Latin, and the faithful answered with the acclamation: *Amen*. Then three young boys would together sing the acclamation *Kyrie eleison*, followed by the song *Benedictus* in two alternating choruses.

But the Eucharistic liturgy was at the time, as with the contemporary ritual, so thick with interspersed doxologies and acclamations that a separation of the different elements cannot be conceived. The formulation called *immolatio* that opened the consecration was a tissue of acclamations: *Vere aequum et iustum est: nos tibi gratias agere, teque benedicere, in omni tempore, omnipotens aeterne Deus* [. . .] *exaudi per Christum Domi-*

num nostrum. Per quem majestatem tuam laudant angeli [. . .] The *immo-latio* was followed by the intonation of the triple *Sanctus* and the formula *Vere sanctus, vere benedictus Dominus noster Jesus Christus Filius tuus.*

We shall now examine the substantial presence of acclamations in the liturgy from the standpoint of Peterson's dissertation. If his thesis is correct, we should view the doxological-acclamatory element not only as that which connects the Christian liturgy with the pagan world and Roman public law, but also as the veritable juridical foundation of the "liturgical," which is to say public and "political," character of the Christian celebrations. The term *leitourgia* (from *laos*, the "people") signifies etymologically "public service," and the Church has always tried to underline the public character of liturgical worship in contrast to private devotions. Only the Catholic Church—as the *Enchiridia liturgica* traditionally emphasize—can perform the legitimate worship of God (*cultum legitimum aeterno patri persolvere*: Radó, p. 7). Peterson's thesis can in this sense be said to provide the basis for the public character of the liturgy through the acclamations of the people united in an *ekklēsia*. The two terms (*laos* and *ochlos*) that, in the Septuagint and the New Testament, designate the people are, in the tradition of public law, contrasted with one another and rearticulated in the terms of *populus* and *multitudo*:

> The *laos* that takes part in the *eucharistia* is *laos* only to the extent that it has juridical capacity. Think of Cicero's *Republic*, I, 25: "Populus autem non omnis hominum coetus quoquo modo congregatus, sed coetus multitudinis iuris consensu et utilitatis communione sociatus." [. . .] If the juridical acts of the *laos* in later times were limited simply to the rights of acclamation, this changes nothing in the fact that one can speak in an originary way of a *populus* (*laos*) or of an *ekklēsia* only where there is, for a people, the possibility of performing juridical actions. Someone who one day wants to write a history of the "laicized" [*Laie*] (*laos*) will have to pay attention to all the contexts hinted at here and, at the same time, understand that the *laos* is precisely the *ochlos*, insofar as it must utter liturgical acclamations. Hence, when the *laos* proffers liturgical acclamations, it binds itself to its statute of ecclesiastic law in the same way in which in public law the *laos* receives its statute precisely through the right to proffer its *ekboēsis* (acclamation) to the *despotēs* in the profane *ekklēsia*. (Peterson 1926, p. 179)

Characteristically, it is in a footnote that Peterson interprets the *amen* that intermittently appears in the liturgical celebration as an acclamation in the technical sense, one through which the multitude of the faithful constitutes itself as the "people" (*laos*) (ibid., note 2). When Justin (*The First Apology*, 65, 3, p. 64) informs us that, at the end of the prayer and the Eucharist, "all the people present express their assent by saying *Amen* [*pas ho parōn laos euphēmei legōn: Amēn*]," what is in question is precisely the technico-juridical meaning of the acclamation that constitutes the "publicity" of the liturgy; or more precisely, the "liturgical" character of the Christian Mass.

ℵ *An analysis of the terms that in the New Testament—and, in particular, Paul's Letters—refer to the people can shed light on Peterson's antimessianic strategy. The term* dēmos, *which is so important for our understanding of the* polis, *hardly appears. The people are referred to by the term* ochlos (*as many as 175 times in the New Testament; it is, moreover, translated into Latin by* turba; *in the Vulgate, alongside* turba *and* populus, *one can find the terms* plebs *and* multitudo; massa, *which would be a good translation of* ochlos, *has, since Augustine, had the negative meaning of carrier of the original sin: "ea damnatione, quae per universam massam currit": Augustine,* On Nature and Grace, *§ 8.9, p. 28) or with* plēthos (*which appears frequently in Luke) and, in a sense that corresponds to the term that in the Septuagint recurrently designates the chosen people, with* laos (*which occurs 142 times). Peterson relates the impolitical* ochlos *to the theological meaning of* laos: *the* ochlos *becomes* laos; *it becomes "politicized" through liturgy. To do this, he must ignore the peculiar usage adopted by Paul. It is in fact significant that Paul never uses the term* ochlos *and uses* laos *only twelve times, and always with reference to biblical citations (for example, with reference to Hosea in Romans 9:25: "my non-people"). Hēmeis, that is, "we," is the term by which Paul refers to the messianic community in the technical sense, often in opposition to* laos (*as in Romans 9:24) or to Jews and Greeks (as in 1 Corinthians 1:22–24: "For the Jews require a sign, and the Greeks seek after wisdom: But we [*hēmeis de] preach Christ crucified"). In the cited passage from the First Letter to the Corinthians, the pronoun "we" is qualified immediately by "those who are called" (*autois de tois klētois). *In Paul, the messianic community as such is anonymous and appears to be situated on an undifferentiated threshold between public and private.*

7.5. In 1934 and 1935, Andreas Alföldi published the results of his research on the forms and insignia of the imperial Roman ceremonial in the *Römische Mitteilungen*. Abandoning the stereotype already to be found in classical sources according to which the imperial ceremonial, thought to be alien to the traditional sobriety of Roman politics, had been introduced by Diocletian according to the model provided by the rituals of Persian courtiers, Alföldi demonstrates instead how it gradually developed from the last years of the republic and from the first years of the principality in accordance with a paradigm into which several different traditions certainly flowed, but which was substantially theological. In order to understand the "theologico-sacred" character that the relationship between the sovereign and his subjects begins to assume in Rome, it is by no means necessary to more or less arbitrarily draw upon the Eastern model of divine monarchy. "The principality had raised the head of State infinitely higher than the senators, who pray and celebrate sacrifices for his well-being, swear on his name, invoke him as the son of God, and celebrate his birthday and other private festivities as a public ceremonial. The *auctoritas* that, according to their declaration, raises the *principes* above all others, had assumed a religious hue, as had the sacred title of *Augustus* that they bore" (Alföldi, p. 29).

Alföldi minutely reconstructs, from within this perspective, the introduction of the *proskynēsis* (adoration), which already in the republican era appears as the gesture of the suppliant who falls upon his knees before the powerful and, little by little, becomes an integral part of the imperial ritual. The senators and the higher-ranking knights kissed the emperor on each cheek (*salutatio*); but with time they were only allowed to kiss once they had kneeled before him; until the moment when, in Byzantium, the *salutatio* ended up always including the *adoratio*, the kissing of the knees and hands.

Of particular interest is the broad treatment of the costumes and insignia of power that Alföldi significantly dedicates to the memory of Theodor Mommsen, as though he were completing the missing part of the *Staatsrecht* with his own analysis of the ceremonial. Although Alföldi does not always seem to be entirely aware of this, the field of research that opens up here is one in which what is at stake is the very way in which that field will be defined. He shows how the imperial costume, which at the beginning of the principality simply coincides with the toga of the Roman citizen, progressively assumes the characteristics of the robes that the victorious magistrate would wear in the triumphal cortege and, later, as a constant feature from the time of Commodus, the military uniform with *paludamentum* and armor (*lorica*). At the same time, as demonstrated by numerous sculptures, the crown of laurel of the *vir trium-phalis* became a technical attribute of sovereignty, which would later be replaced, especially on coins, by the *corona radiata* (which in contrast to the laurel crown seems never actually to have been worn). In analogous fashion, the *sella curulis* upon which the consuls sat became the seat of the prince who, in isolating himself on a *podium* from at least the time of Caligula, progressively transforms its function into that of a throne (*basileios thronos, hedra basilikē*).

What is decisive, however, is the technico-juridical significance of these transformations. Indeed, it is not a case of a simple passion for luxury and pomp, or merely a desire to distinguish oneself from ordinary citizens, but of a veritable sphere that is constitutive of sovereignty. The difficulty scholars encountered in defining this sphere is evident in their necessarily vague use of terms such as "ceremonial," "insignia or signs of domination" (*Herrschaftszeichen*), and "symbols of power or of the state" (*Machtsymbole, Staatssymbolik*). We already see this in the way Mommsen observes that, from the third century onward, "the purple clothing of war becomes the symbol of monarchy" (Mommsen, vol. I, p. 433). But what does "symbol" mean here? The technical meaning of objects such as the *fasces lictoriae* in Roman public law or of the crown in medieval law have been known for some time, and yet, a juridical theory able to precisely define their sphere and value is still lacking.

Let us consider the problem of the *mutatio vestis* that leads the emperor to substitute the toga of the citizen with the *paludamentum insigne* of the military commander. To understand this process (as Alföldi does) simply as a consequence of the growing primacy of the army in contrast to the authority of the senate; or to speak, in relation to the ceremonial, of an opposition between law and power, still says nothing about its specific meaning. For we know that already in the republican era, the opposition between toga and *paludamentum* corresponded to the distinction between the *pomerium* and the rest of the territory and so immediately had implications for public law. Under no circumstances could the magistrate enter Rome in military dress, having rather to *sumere togam* before crossing the frontier. So the fact that the emperor would wear his purple *paludamentum* in the city did not so much indicate the factual predominance of the army but mainly signaled a lack of determination of the formal difference between consular power and proconsular power, *pomerium* and territory, the laws of peace and the laws of war. The *mutatio vestis* has, therefore, an immediate performative effect in public law. Only from this perspective can one understand how in Byzantium the ceremonial of the emperor's robes was assigned to a particular office, called *mētatōrion*, in which high-ranking functionaries would be scrupulously attentive to the fact that to each situation there would correspond the correct garb. Only if we understand the legal significance of the color purple as the insignia of sovereignty is it possible to comprehend how, beginning in the fourth century, the production of the color purple was nationalized and its possession by a private person could result in the crime of lese majesty (Alföldi, p. 169).

Analogous remarks can be made in relation to the complicated protocol that regulates, in addition to the *proskynēsis*, the relation between the erect and the seated posture in the public appearances of the emperor. In this case as well, rather than see in the posture merely the symbolic expression of rank, it is necessary to understand that it is the posture that immediately establishes the hierarchy. In the same way that for the Pseudo-Dionysius the divinity is not manifested in the hierarchy but is itself *ousia* and *dynamis*—glory, substance, and power of the celestial and worldly hierarchies (*Ecclesiastical Hierarchy*, 378a)—so imperial sovereignty is, in its very behavior, in its gestures as in its apparel, both hierarchical ceremonial and insignia.

7.6. Ernst Percy Schramm, a historian who became known even outside the strictly academic field through his edition of Adolf Hitler's *Tischrede*, dedicated a monumental study to the insignia and symbols of power. In the preface and the introduction to the three volumes of *Herrschaftszeichen und Staatssymbolik*, he insists on the need to rescue the field of his research from those "romantics—or worse still—those who seek in the signs of sovereignty what they imagine to be the 'spirit of the Middle ages'" (Schramm, vol. 1, p. ix) and to abandon, because of their ambiguity, terms like "insignia" and "symbol," preferring instead the—hardly more precise—"signs of dominion" (*Herrschaftszeichen*) and "symbolism of the state" (*Staatssymbolik*) (ibid.).

Despite the fact that Schramm returns more than once to terminological and methodological questions, and speaks, following the Warburgian *Pathosformeln*, of "formulae of majesty" (*Majestätsformeln*) and of "model-images" (*Bildmodel*), the book is in fact an immense poem dedicated to the signs of power. In the course of the work, which runs to nearly twelve hundred pages, hardly anything escapes the meticulous, ekphrastic passion of the author and the scrupulousness of the cataloguing by his collaborators: from the triumphal *trabea* of the Roman emperor to the mitre and tiara of the pontiffs and the sovereigns; from the holy lance of the Germanic and Lombard kings to the bells (*tintinnabula*) that adorn the gowns of the churchmen and kings; from the infinite forms of the royal and imperial crowns, to the rich phenomenology of the throne in all of its varieties—from the *cathedra Petri* to the thrones of the English, the Aragones, the Poles, the Swedish, the Sicilians.

Of particular interest is the section on monograms and seals, including that of Theodoric the Great concerning which Schramm makes an observation that is worth developing. He writes: the "monogramatic *nomen regium* [. . .] represents force and law as well as an effigy might: the monogram does not simply explain the image; it rather renders the king present [*stellt* (. . .) *den König dar*] on its own" (ibid., vol. 1, p. 226). In the second volume, the section on flags (*bandum, vandum, banière*) and standards deserves particular attention. Here the character and special performative force of insignia appear with a clarity that, unfortunately, Schramm does not seem to be fully aware of. He refers to the works of a historian of law, Carl Erdmann, who had demonstrated that the particular power of the flag does not lie in its markings or the colors that it contains, but springs from the thing itself. For this reason, "like the crown, the king's flag must not be lost; just as the king's honor can be harmed through the crown, so it can be through the flag [. . .] the flag can substitute for the sovereign, it shows where his peace reigns and how far his power extends" (ibid., vol. 2, p. 653).

At the beginning of his work, Schramm stated his wish that "from what has been, until now, the arbitrary and subjective treatment of the signs of power," there might be born a science as exact and rigorous as that to which we have become accustomed in historical research. At the end of the book, where Schramm attempts to set out the *Grundbegriffe* (Schramm, vol. 3, p. 1098) that guided his work, it is clear that his wish has not been fully realized. In the same way that in the frontispiece to the first volume he had framed his research in light of Goethe's definition of the symbol ("the symbol is the thing without being the thing and yet it is the thing: an image condensed in the mirror of the mind and yet identical with the object"), so he now evokes a passage from Hegel, who defines the symbolic as "something obscure, which becomes ever more obscure the more forms we learn to understand" (Schramm, vol. 3, p. 1065). Schramm never entirely escapes the obscurity and ambiguity of these concepts. The science of the signs of power still awaits its foundation.

7.7. Karl von Amira, a historian who would compromise himself by a relationship to Nazism and whom Schramm cites in his investigation, advanced a science called "the archaeology of right." A clear example of Amira's genealogical method is his work on hand gestures in the miniatures of the medieval code known as *Sachsenspiegel,* whose exuberant mimicry had been compared to the gesticulations of the Neapolitans as described by de Jorio. In the debate between those who, like Jacob Grimm, considered miniature figures exclusively from the perspective of the history of art, as a "symbolism of the artist" (*Simbolyk des Künstlers*), and those who instead saw in them the expression of a genuinely juridical mimicry, Amira resolutely takes the middle path by mobilizing the resources of both disciplines. He thereby distinguishes between authentic gestures (*echte Handgebärden*), in which the hand immediately symbolizes a spiritual process, and inauthentic gestures, where the hand is only the "instrument of a symbol" that is intended not for the effective expression of a will but is to make visible a social attribute of the person (Amira, p. 168). Amira fixes his attention on the former alone, in order to verify the extent to which each time the gestures of the miniatures can be ascribed with certainty to juridical symbolism.

The distinction between authentic (or pure) gestures and inauthentic ones suggests a conceptual direction for the investigation that Amira, who is only preoccupied with identifying the juridical uses of gesture, does not pursue. One of the most interesting mimetic categories to be found in the work is the gesture that accompanies discourse, the linguistic gesture (*Redegestus*). In this case a gesture that derives from the *ingens manus,* which expressed the special efficacy of imperial power (the open hand that is raised along with the forearm in such a way as to more or less form a right angle with the arm), merges with the gestures that, according to ancient rhetoric, should accompany the *actio* of the orator in order then to become fixed in the gesture of the *Logos* of benediction—which was to assume such an important function in Christian liturgy and iconography (the *benedictio latina,* with thumb, index, and middle finger distended and the other two fingers folded against the palm, or the variant known as the *benedictio graeca* with the little finger distended as well). Quintilian, who in his *Institutiones oratoriae* minutely describes the linguistic gesture in all its variants, writes, in relation to its unquestionable efficacy, that it is the hands themselves that speak ("ipsae loquuntur": II, 3, 85). It would be impossible to define more precisely the power of a linguistic gesture that is irreducible to a scansion or to a mere emphasizing of the discourse: there where the gestures become words, the words become facts. We find ourselves in the presence of a phenomenon that corresponds, even if apparently through an inverse process, to the insoluble interweaving of words and facts, of reality and meaning that defines the sphere of language that linguists call performative and that has attained philosophical status through Austin's book *How to Do Things with Words* (1962). The performative is indeed a linguistic utterance that is also, in itself, immediately a real fact, insofar as its meaning coincides with a reality that it produces.

But in what way does the performative realize its peculiar efficacy? What allows a certain syntagma (for example, "I swear") to acquire the status of a fact, negating the ancient maxim according to which words and actions are separated by an abyss? Linguists do not tell us, as if here they found themselves before a final, magical layer of language. In order for us to answer these questions, it is necessary to begin by reminding ourselves that the performative is always constituted through a suspension of the normal, denotative character of language. The performative verb is necessarily constructed with a *dictum* that, considered in itself, has the nature of a pure statement without which it remains empty and without effect ("I swear" has value only if it is followed or preceded by a *dictum*— for example, "that yesterday I was in Rome"). It is this normal denotative character of the *dictum* that is suspended and, in some way, transformed at the very moment that it becomes the object of a performative phrase.

This means, in all truth, that the performative utterance is not a sign but a signature [*segnatura*], one that marks the *dictum* in order to suspend its value and displace it into a new nondenotative sphere that takes the place of the former. This is the way we should understand the gestures and signs of power with which we are occupied here. They are signatures that inhere in other signs or objects in order to confer a particular efficacy upon them. It is not therefore by chance that the spheres of right and the performative are always strictly conjoined and that the acts of the sovereign are those in which gesture and word are immediately efficacious.

7.8. The insignia of power did not exist only in the imperial age. There was an object in the Roman republic that sheds light on the peculiar nature of the insignia with particular force. It is the *fasces lictoriae*, to which curiously neither Alföldi nor Schramm refer. Their history, which begins with the monarchy, reaches its apogee in the republican era and continues into the imperial era, although increasingly obscured. It is well known that, like the *laudes regiae*, they were provisionally resurrected in the twentieth century. The fasces were elm or birch rods about 130 centimeters in length, bound together with a red strap into which an axe was inserted laterally. They were assigned to a special corporation, half *apparitores* and half executioners, called *lictores*, who wore the fasces on their left shoulder. In the republic, the period about which we have most information, the fasces were the prerogative of the consul and the magistrate who had *imperium*. The lictors, twelve in number, had to accompany the magistrate on every occasion, not just on public occasions. When the consul was at home, the lictors waited in the vestibule; if he went out, even if only to the spa or the theater, they invariably accompanied him.

To define the fasces as the "symbol of *imperium*," as has sometimes been the case, tells us nothing about their nature or their specific function. So little does the word *symbol* characterize them that they in fact served to actually inflict capital punishment in its two forms: flogging (the rods) and decapitation (the axe). Thus we begin to understand the nature of the fasces only when we examine in detail the manner in which they were linked to the *imperium*. It immediately defines the nature and the effectiveness of the *imperium*. If, depending on the specific circumstance, a consul did not exercise his *imperium*, he lost his right to the fasces. (In 19 BC the senate conferred on Augustus, who at that time was without consular *imperium*, the right to the fasces; this marked the beginning of an involution that would be fully achieved only in the imperial age.) What is particularly significant is the circumstance that the axe was to be removed from the fasces of the magistrate when he found himself within the *pomerium*, because here the *ius necis* inhering in the *imperium* was limited by the right belonging to each Roman citizen to appeal to the people against the death penalty. For the same reason, the magistrate had to lower the fasces before the popular assemblies.

The fasces do not symbolize the *imperium*; they execute and determine it in such a way that to each of its juridical articulations there corresponds a material articulation of the fasces, and vice versa. For this reason, *fasces attollere* signifies the magistrate's entering office, just as the breaking open of the fasces corresponds to his dismissal. This connection between the fasces and the *imperium* was so immediate and absolute that no one could stand between a magistrate and his lictor (except for a prepubescent son who, according to Roman law, was already subjected to the *ius necisque potestas* of the father). For the same reason, in some sense the lictor was without an existence of his own: not only did his garments conform to that of the magistrate he accompanied (military *sagum* outside the *pomerium*, a toga within the walls), but the very term "lictor" is synonymous with "fasces."

Particularly instructive is the relationship between the fasces and a phenomenon that had a decisive significance for the formation of imperial power. We are speaking of the case of the triumph, whose relation to acclamations we have already noted. The ban on the magistrate's being able to display the fasces with the axe inside Rome had two important exceptions: the dictator and the triumphant general. This means that triumph implies an indetermination of the difference *domi-militiae*, which from the standpoint of public law distinguishes the territory of the city from that of Italy and the provinces. We know that the magistrate who had asked for the triumph to be accorded him had to wait for the decision of the senate outside the *pomerium*, in the Campo Martius; otherwise he would forever forfeit the right to the triumph, which was due only to the victorious general who effectively possessed *imperium*, that is, who was accompanied by the fasces. Fasces and *imperium* once again demonstrate here their consubstantiality. At the same time, the triumph is revealed to be the seed from which imperial power will develop. If the triumph can be technically defined as the extension within the *pomerium* of prerogatives belonging to the *imperator* that are only valid outside it, the new imperial power will be defined precisely as the extension and fixing of the triumphal right in a new figure. Moreover, if, as in Mommsen's penetrating formulation, the centralization of the *imperium* in the hands of the prince transforms the triumph into a right reserved for the emperor (*kaiserliches Reservatrecht*: Mommsen, vol. 1, p. 135), conversely, the emperor may be defined as the one who has the monopoly on triumph and who permanently possesses its insignias and prerogatives. One phenomenon, the *ius triumphi*, which is usually analyzed as if it concerned merely the formal apparatus and pomp of power, instead shows itself to be the original juridical core of an essential transformation of Roman public law.

What appeared to be merely a question of clothing and splendor (the purple gown of the triumphant general, the crown of laurels that encircles his brow, the axe as a symbol of the power of life and death) becomes the key to understanding the decisive transformations of the constitution. Thus the way is cleared for a more precise understanding of the meaning and nature of the insignia and of the acclamations and, more generally, of the sphere that we have defined with the term "glory."

7.9. In the first half of the tenth century, Constantine VII Porphyrogenitus gathered in an ample treatise the traditions and prescriptions relating to the imperial ceremony (*basileios taxis*). In the introduction, Constantine presents his task as the "most intimate and desirable, because through a praiseworthy ceremony, imperial power appears better ordered and majestic" (Constantine Porphyrogenitus, *Le livre des cérémonies*, I, p. 1). It is clear, however, from the beginning, that the end of this gigantic choreography of power is not merely aesthetic. The emperor writes that it is a case of placing at the heart of the royal palace a kind of optical device, a "clear and well-polished mirror, so that, in carefully contemplating the image of imperial power in it [. . .] it is possible to hold its reins with order and dignity" (ibid., I, p. 2). Never has the ceremonial folly of power reached such an obsessive liturgical scrupulousness as it does in these pages. There is not a gesture, garment, ornament, word, silence, or place that is not ritually fixed or meticulously catalogued. The *incipit* of the chapters announces, for each one, what "must be observed" (*hosa dei paraphylattein*) for this or the other occasion, what must be "known" (*isteon*), and what acclamations (*aktalogia*) are to be expressed for each festival, procession, and assembly. An infinite hierarchy of functionaries and other people involved in the various tasks, divided into the two great classes of the "bearded ones" and the "eunuchs," watches over the protocol to ensure that it is observed at every moment. The *ostiarii* announce the entrance of the dignitaries, and the silentiaries regulate the silences and the euphemias before the sovereign; the manglavites and the members of the *Hetaireia* escort him during the solemn processions; dieticians and dressers (*bestētores*) provide personal care; and the cartularies and the prothonotaries follow its signatures and the chancellory. Emperor Constantine's opening description of the coronation ceremony reads as follows:

When all is ready, the emperor departs the Augusteion, wearing his *skaramangion* and purple *sagion*, escorted by his personal staff, and proceeds as far as the vestibule called *Onopodion*; here he receives the first homage of the patricians. The Master of Ceremonies says: "Acclaim [*Keleusate*]!" and they exclaim: "Many good years [*Eis pollous kai agathous chronous*]!" Then they all proceed down as far as the great Konsistorion, and within the Konsistorion the consuls and the rest of the senators assemble. The sovereigns stand in the *kiborion*, while all the senators together with the patricians prostrate themselves. As they rise, the sovereigns give a sign to the Praipositos of the Sacred Cubicle and the silentiaries intone: "Acclaim!" and they wish him "Many good years!" And then the group of sovereigns moves toward the cathedral, passing through the Scholae, and the factions, properly attired, are standing in their assigned places, making the sign of the cross.

And when the emperor has entered the Horologion, the curtain is raised and he goes into the *mētatōrion*; he changes into the *divītision* and the *tzitzakion*, and throws over them the *sagion*; then he enters with the patriarch. He lights candles on the silver doors, walks through the central nave, and he proceeds to the *sōlea*; he prays before the holy gates, and, having lit other candles, he ascends the ambo together with the patriarch. The patriarch recites a prayer over the mantle, and, when he is finished, the servants of that room take up the mantle and dress the sovereign up with it. The patriarch recites a prayer over the sovereign's crown, and, when the prayer is complete, he takes in his hands the crown [*stemma*] and places it on the head of the emperor, and immediately the people [*laos*] thrice cry out with the acclamation [*anakrazei*] "Holy, Holy, Holy [*Hagios, Hagios, Hagios*]! Glory in the heavens [*Doxa en hypsistois*] to God and peace on earth!" And other people cry out: "Many years to the emperor [*autokratoros*] and to the great king!" and what follows. Wearing the crown he goes down and enters the *mētatōrion* and sits on the royal seat [*sellion*], and the dignitaries [*ta axiōmata*] enter, prostrating themselves and kissing his knees. First come the magistrates. Second the patricians and generals; third the swordbearers [*protospatharî*]; fourth the *logothete*, the *domestikos* of the excubitors, of the *hikanatoi* and of the numbers [*noumeroi*], the senatorial swordbearers [*spatharioî*], and the consuls. Fifth come the swordbearers; sixth the squires; seventh the counts [*komētes*] of the Scholae; eighth the Candidates of the cavalry; ninth the scribes [*skribōnoî*] and domestics; tenth the secretaries, the dressers, and the silentiaries; eleventh the imperial *mandatores* and candidates of the infantry; twelfth the counts of the *arithmos*, of the *hikanatoi*, the tribunes and counts of the fleet.

To all the Praipositos says: "Acclaim!" and they exclaim "Many happy years!" [...] (Ibid., I, p. 47)

7.10. It is hardly necessary to underline the central role that acclamations play in imperial ceremonies and liturgy. In Constantine's treatise, insofar as they constitute an essential part of every ceremony, they, when not undertaken by the master of ceremonies or by the silentiaries, are entrusted to the special functionaries called the *kraktai* (literally, the "shriekers") who, acting like chief *claques* (or, rather, like the presbyters who start to sing the psalmody in the liturgical celebration), articulate them along with the people in the guise of responses. So, in the procession for Christ's birth, at the moment when the sovereigns arrive at the *Lychni*

> [...] the *kraktai* cry: "*Polla, polla, polla* [Many, many, many ('years': is implied)]," and the people [*laos*] reply "*Polla etē, eis polla* [Many years and many more]." And once again the *kraktai*: "Many years [*chronoi*] for you divine sovereign"; and the people thrice cry: "Many years to you." Then the *kraktai*: "Many years to you, attendants of the Lord," and the people call out three times: "Many years to you." Then the *kraktai* cry: "Many years to [such-and-such] autocrat of the Romans"; and for three times the people reply: "Many years to you." The *kraktai*: "Many years to you [such-and-such] august dignitary of the Romans," and thrice the people reply: "Many years to you" [...] (Ibid., I, 2, p. 30)

What is significant, if at first disconcerting, is that the same ritualizing of acclamations takes place for the horse racing in the hippodrome. The shriekers cry out here as well: "Many many many" and the people reply, just as they do in the Christmas ceremony: "Many years, and many more," substituting the name of the race winner for that of the emperor. In Byzantium, beginning already in the Justinian era, the two factions into which the spectators are divided in the hippodrome, the Blues and Greens, have a strong political character and even constitute, so to speak, the only form of political expression left to the people. Therefore, it is not surprising that sporting acclamations are invested with the same process of ritualization that defines the acclamations of the emperors. Under Justinian's rule there was even an uprising that shook the city for almost a week, which had as its slogan a sporting acclamation (*nika*, "win!"; exactly as today, in Italy, an important political faction draws its name from an acclamation heard in the stadiums).[1]

Alföldi shows that to these acclamations in Byzantine hippodromes there correspond, in even earlier times, analogous acclamations in Rome, which sources describe to us in detail. Despite involving thousands of men applauding, these acclamations did not occur by chance, but were, in the words of an attentive witness such as Cassius Dio, "a chorus that was accurately prepared [*hōsper tis akribōs choros dedidagmenos*]" (Alföldi, p. 81). It is with acclamations of the same type that the crowds in the stadiums will later turn to the emperor and empress, in what must have appeared an extraordinary piece of choreography that traversed and animated the mass of spectators like a wave of color:

> Immediately a jubilant roar resounds: with a thousand voices the common people wish the princes good fortune. "Long life to Justin and to the august Sophia," they acclaim all around. The applause and cries of joy reverberate, and the crowds alternate in answering one another. All together they raise their right arm and all together bring it down. In the whole stadium the people *certatim micat* (flashes, palpitates) and dense waves of white sleeves (*manicis albentibus*) are produced. Songs are sung and songs are added to the movement [. . .] (Ibid., p. 82)

Alföldi, who dedicates considerable space to the analysis of the political significance of acclamations, does not however manage to define its specific nature. On the whole, in the emergence of the acclamatory and ceremonial aspect of power, and in the contemporaneous raising up of the sovereign above the community of citizens, Alföldi sees an element that is in some ways antagonistic to law:

> Alongside the juridical formulation of the power of the prince we can also see another formative principle of imperial omnipotence, which is not objective and rational, but subjective and imaginary. In it, it is not reason but sentiment that is expressed. (Ibid., pp. 186–187)

And yet, he has to admit shortly afterward that one cannot correctly understand phenomena such as acclamations as long as one sees in them only a form of purely subjective adulation:

> It is entirely misguided to glimpse here something like ephemeral individual adulation, since the praise is beginning to end bound objectively. The official discourses of the prince, like the acclamations directed at him, betray the same formal constraints as do works of poetry or art. (Ibid., p. 188)

At the end of his 1935 study, he appears to oppose—in the process that

leads to the constitution of the imperial State—right (*Recht*) and power
(*Macht*), which are "incorporated into the army and the senate respectively, and confer on the empire real power [*Gewalt*] and formal sanction" (ibid., p. 272). But the simple opposition of violence and formal
sanction leaves in the shadows the decisive fact that we are dealing here
with two procedures of legitimation that, in the last instance, are both
presented in the form of acclamations. The opposition between a juridical and a religious element is equally insufficient (ibid., p. 186), because
the acclamation is precisely the point at which they appear to coincide
without remainder. More pertinent is Alföldi's observation, with regard to
the purple robes of the emperor, which unfortunately he fails to develop,
that what "founds sovereignty juridically is no longer the *auctoritas* of the
Optimates nor the *consensus* of the people, but this consecrated symbol of
power [*dieses geheiligte Machtsymbol*]" (ibid., p. 169).

In other words, the acclamation points toward a more archaic sphere
that brings to mind the one that Gernet used to call, using an infelicitous
term, prelaw, in which terms that we customarily consider juridical appear to act in a magic-religious manner. More than a chronologically earlier stage, we must here think of something like a threshold of indistinc-
tion that is always operative, where the juridical and the religious become
truly indistinguishable. A threshold of this type is that which elsewhere
we have called *sacertas*, in which a double exception, from both human
and divine law, allows a figure to emerge, *homo sacer*, whose relevance for
Occidental law and politics we have attempted to reconstruct. If we now
call "glory" the uncertain zone in which acclamations, ceremonies, liturgies, and insignia operate, we will see a field of research open before us
that is equally relevant and, at least in part, as yet unexplored.

7.11. Kantorowicz has dedicated an exemplary study to the history
of one liturgical acclamation: the *Laudes Regiae*, published in 1946 but
largely written between 1934 and 1940 when the scholar, who as a twenty-
year-old had fought against the revolutionary workers' councils in Munich, figured among the "displaced foreign scholars"[2] (and it is with this
title that, while at Berkeley, he received a special subsidy to complete his
research). The book reconstructs the history of a particular acclamation—
specifically a *laude* or *laetania*, which begins with the phrase "Christus
vincit, Christus regnat, Christus imperat"—that was in use in the Gaul-
Frankish Church beginning with the eighth century and spread from here

to the whole of Europe in various forms. The peculiarity of this long acclamation, which concerns Christ the victor, king, and emperor, is that it unites the divinity not only with the names of the saints, but also with those of the pontiff and the emperor. Having called upon Christ the victor three times, the hymn of praise passes on to the repeated acclamatory *exaudi* phrase, and acclaims the pontiff and then the emperor with a phrase of the type *vita* ("Leoni summo pontifici et universali pape vita/Carolo excellentissimo et a deo coronato atque magno et pacifico regi Francorum et Longobardorum ac Patricio Romanorum vita et victoria"). After a lengthy list of names of angels and saints (acclaimed with a phrase of the type "Sancte Gabrihel, Sancte Silvestre tu illum adiuva"), the acclamation unexpectedly mentions the functionaries and the imperial army ("omnibus iudicibus vel cuncto exercitui Francorum vita et victoria"). At this point, the *tricolon*, "*Christus vincit (. . .) regnat (. . .) imperat*," is once again repeated three times and then followed by a series of Christological acclamations of a "military" type (*Rex regum, gloria nostra, fortitudo nostra, victoria nostra, arma nostra invictissima, murus noster inexpugnabilis*, etc.), whose origin Kantorowicz traces back to the pagan imperial acclamations in the *Historia Augusta*. There then follows a series of doxologies and hymns of praise to the second person of the Trinity; and, finally, the invocation of *Christe eleison* and the closing acclamations *Feliciter feliciter feliciter, tempora bona habeas, multos annos*, which, as we know, made up part of the acclamations to the Roman emperors.

The acclamation, which promiscuously united heaven and earth, angels and functionaries, emperor and pontiff, was destined to play an important role at the point where profane power and spiritual power, courtly and liturgical protocol met. It is particularly instructive to follow, with Kantorowicz, the incessant comings and goings of the acclamations between the two spheres. It emerges and is fully comprehensible only in the context of what Kantorowicz calls "Carolingian political theology" (Kantorowicz 1946, p. 59). This begins to develop with Pepin as a restoration of biblical regality (*Regnum Davidicum*) against the Roman Empire, and culminates in the introduction of the biblical rite of real unction. In this manner, the Carolingian kings effect a form of liturgization of secular power; it is in this context that one should place the appearance of the *Laudes Regiae*. They "represent an early and most remarkable example of the hierarchical-theocratic tendency. In this artfully composed chant the orders of dignitaries on earth, both secular and ecclesiastical, and the series of celestial intercessors reflect, and merge into, each other" (ibid., pp. 61–62).

In following the successive development of the *Laudes* in Roman liturgy, Kantorowicz demonstrates that they contain elements that indubitably stem from pagan acclamations. Indeed, the imperial ceremony of pagan Rome had been progressively "litanized" and transformed into the form of divine service for which the acclamations were a constitutive element. In the tight interweaving of the religious and the profane, acclamations, which contained improvised elements at the very beginning, became increasingly formalized in a process in which ecclesiastical liturgy and profane protocol mutually reinforced one another.

> No matter how much the liturgical language had originally borrowed from that of the court, the language of the court ceremonial stiffened as the terms became filled with ecclesiastical spirit and echoed the language of the liturgy. The formula of dismissing the court dignitaries, *Ite missa est*, became all the more solemn as it now matched the words of the dismissal in church, and a change such as that of the invocation *Exaudi Caesar!* to *Exaudi Christe!* is likewise indicative of the shift from a "Here and Now" to a transcendency beyond time and motion. (Ibid., p. 66)

It is in this context that the *laudes* became part of the ritual of imperial coronation in the West. In Byzantium in 450, Flavius Marcianus had himself crowned in a ceremony where, in addition to the acclamation by the senate and the army, an essential role was reserved for the Church. But in the West, the coronation of the sovereign only passed into the hands of the clergy with Pepin and Charlemagne. "Recognition by the Church, therefore, gradually gained so much in importance and esteem that the assent of the other king-creating powers, above all that of the acclaiming people, was more or less overshadowed by sacerdotal functions" (ibid., pp. 78–79). In the solemn coronation ceremony of Charlemagne that took place in Rome on Christmas Day, AD 800, the *laudes* played an essential part, whose technical-legal significance Kantorowicz tries, at times a little uncertainly, to define. Of course,

> [. . .] in the High Mass which followed the consecration [. . .] the chant inevitably elicited the vision that not only the visible Church acclaimed, confirmed and recognized the new ruler, but also that through the Church the Heavens consented to the new *Deo coronatus*. The chant implied that the new king was acclaimed also by the choirs of angels and saints, as well as by Christ

himself, who, in his quality as Victor, King, and Commander, recognized the new *christus* of the Church as his fellow ruler. (Ibid., p. 82)

According to Kantorowicz, it is not a case of a mere allegory but, to the extent that one can speak of "realism" in medieval culture, of a perfectly "realistic" conception. Nothing better than a miniature in the manuscript of the *Laudes* shows in what way one should understand their admirable efficacy: the artist depicts the king, with a crown, scepter, and globe, seated on a throne formed by a large X, which constitutes the initial of the *tricolon Xristus vincit*: the *regale carmen* is the very throne of majesty.

However great the importance of the acclamations, for Kantorowicz it does not have a constitutive value, but only a recognitional one.

> The laudes acclamation, representing the recognition of the king's legitimacy, was an accessory manifestation, impressive by its festal and solemn character, but not indispensable; for legally the liturgical acclaim added no new element of material power which the king had not already received earlier by his election and coronation [. . .] By means of this chant, the Church professed and publicly espoused the king in a solemn form. However, the weight of this profession or espousal cannot be measured by legal standards. (Ibid., p. 83)

And with an implicit but unequivocal polemical reference to Peterson, Kantorowicz denies that this recognition stems from the people:

> "People" and "Church" are not the same thing. The laudes, representing the recognition of the ruler on the part of the visible and invisible Church, therefore cannot be regarded as an "acclamation on the part of the people" and even less so as "the people's consent." [. . .] Besides, the laudes were sung by the clergy, not by the people. (Ibid., p. 82)

Nevertheless, there is an important exception to this restriction on the juridical value of the *laudes*: the coronation of Charlemagne in Rome. In his description of the ceremony, Kantorowicz comes as close as possible to a veritable theory of the juridical-constitutional meaning of acclamations.

> This event was extraordinary in every respect, and it was extraordinary also with reference to the ceremonial [. . .] However, even through the dimness of the extant accounts the two acclamations seem to be discernible, those of the people and those of the Church. It is a question of interpreting the two main sources with regard to whether or not we are to make a distinction, on the one hand, between the hails of the "faithful Romans" who, after the

pope had placed the crown on Charlemagne's head, shouted their "Karolo, piissimo Augusto a Deo coronato, magno et pacifico imperatori, vita et victoria," and, on the other hand, the chant of the laudes proper, in which this hail was repeated by the Roman *clergy* [. . .] The shouts of the Romans and the laudes, as they then followed one after the other without a break, seem to have formed one single tumultuous outburst of voices in which it is idle to seek the particular cry which was "constitutive" and legally effective. (Ibid., p. 84)

7.12. What is at stake in Kantorowicz's interpretation of the *laudes regiae* is political theology. It unites the 1946 book with the following one, *The King's Two Bodies* (1957), whose subtitle is *A Study in Medieval Political Theology*. The latter attempted to reconstruct, through a history of the idea of the mystical body of the king, the formation of a veritable "myth of the state," just as the former reconstructed imperial ideology through the history of acclamations where liturgical elements and profane ones were indissolubly interwoven.

Thus, the analysis of the theological-political meaning of the *laudes* predominates over the analysis of their strictly juridical value. This is evident in the concluding chapter of the book dedicated to "the laudes in modern times." Between the thirteenth and the sixteenth centuries, the use of the *laudes* in liturgy and in coronation ceremonies began to fall away everywhere. But they arise again unexpectedly in the course of the 1920s, revived by theologians and musicologists at precisely the moment in which, "with the irony of which History is so fond" (ibid., p. 184), the European political scene was dominated by the emergence of totalitarian regimes. They play an important role in the convergent itineraries of Pius XI, elected pontiff in February 1922, and Benito Mussolini, who takes power in October of that same year. "Fascist challenges were answered, without closing the door completely, by the papal counterchallenges when Pius XI, at the end of the Holy Year 1925, instituted the new feast of 'Christ the King'" (ibid.). In the solemn mass for this festival, the song *Christus vincit* [. . .] *regnat* [. . .] *imperat* was revived in a new rendering that immediately became popular. From this moment onward, according to the constant oscillation between the sacred and the profane that characterizes the history of acclamations, the *laudes* shifted from the faithful to fascist militants, who—among other things—used them in the course of the Spanish Civil War. Even earlier, in 1929, the fascist minister for education included the *laudes regiae* in an official collection of "patriotic songs," in which the acclamation *vita* of the original text assumed the form *Regi nostro Victorio Dei gratia feliciter regnante pax, vita et salus perpetua; Duci Benito Mussolini italicae gentis gloriae pax, vita et salus perpetua.*

Recounting this new and extreme version of the *laudes* at the end of his book, Kantorowicz observes that acclamations are "indispensable to the emotionalism of a Fascist regime" (ibid., p. 185). And in a footnote on Nazi acclamations he launches a final, ironic attack on Peterson, writing that the acclamation *Ein Reich, ein Volk, ein Führer*, declared in Vienna in 1938 on the occasion of the annexation of Austria, "leads via Barbarossa [. . .] to the *Heis theos* so brilliantly discussed by Peterson" (ibid., p. 185, note 23). The attempt to exclude the very possibility of a Christian "political theology," so as to found in glory the only legitimate political dimension of Christianity, comes dangerously close to the totalitarian liturgy.

7.13. The works of Kantorowicz, as well as those by Alföldi and Schramm, show that the relation between the theological and the political is not univocal, but always runs in both directions. Jan Assmann, an Egyptologist who, after having worked on Egyptian doxologies, investigated—on Jacob Taubes's suggestion—political theology in Egypt and in Judaism, reformulated the Schmittian theorem according to which all "significant concepts of the modern theory of the state are secularized theological concepts" (Schmitt 2005, p. 36), by turning it into the axiom "the significant concepts of theology are theologized political concepts" (Assmann, p. 20). Every inversion of a thesis remains, however, in some sense implicitly in agreement with the original. More interesting than taking sides with one thesis or the other is, however, to try to understand the functional relationship that links the two principles. Glory is precisely the place at which this bilateral (or bi-univocal) character of the relation between theology and politics clearly emerges into the light. Louis Bréhier, one of the first scholars to become interested in the interrelations between imperial cult and ecclesiastical liturgy, observed, not without irony, that "when the pope goes to Constantinople, in the course of the sixth and seventh centuries, the emperor adores him, but at the same time he adores the emperor. In the same way, in the tenth century, the emperor and the patriarch adore one another when they meet at Saint Sophia" (Bréhier and Batiffol, p. 59).

More original—or better, more decisive—than the opposition between theology and politics, spiritual power and profane power, is the glory within which they coincide. What, from the perspective of Schmitt's political theology (or of its reversal in Assmann), appeared as a clear distinction between two principles that find their point of contact in secularization (or sacralization), from the perspective of glory—and of the economic theology of which it forms a part—crosses a threshold of indetermination where it is not always easy to distinguish between the two elements. The theology of glory constitutes, in this sense, the secret point of contact through which theology and politics continuously communicate and exchange parts with one another.

In a passage from *Joseph and His Brothers*, a novel that caused such labor among scholars of myth, Thomas Mann observes that—in a phrase that is Assmann's starting point—religion and politics are not two fundamentally distinct things but that, on the contrary, they "exchange clothes." It is possible, however, that this exchange can take place only because underneath the garments there are no body and no substance. Theology and politics are, in this sense, what results from the exchange and from the movement of something like an absolute garment that, as such, has decisive juridical-political implications. Like many of the concepts we have encountered in our investigation, this garment of glory is a signature [*segnatura*] that marks bodies and substances politically and theologically, and orientates and displaces them according to an economy that we are only now beginning to glimpse.

א *In two exemplary studies, Albrecht Dieterich (*Eine Mithrasliturgie, *1903) and Eduard Norden (*Agnostos theos, *1913) developed a doctrine of the forms of doxology and prayer (see Norden, p. 261). Norden's work shows how literary elements and forms deriving from diverse traditions, profane as well as religious (Stoic, Judaic, mystico-hermetic, etc.), converge in Christian doxological formulations. This is formally consistent with the concrete examples detailed in Alföldi, Schramm, and Kantorowicz's investigations. The doxologies, both profane and religious, have the same morphological structure; but this still does not say anything about the strategies they pursue or the function they have to perform.*

Threshold

The scholars who have been concerned with the ceremonial aspects of power—and Kantorowicz is certainly the most lucid among them—seem to hesitate before the question, which is difficult to sidestep: What is the relation that so intimately links power to glory? If power is essentially force and efficacious action, why does it need to receive ritual acclamations and hymns of praise, to wear cumbersome crowns and tiaras, to submit itself to an inaccessible ceremony and an immutable protocol—in a word, why does something that is essentially operativity and *oikonomia* need to become solemnly immobilized in glory? Ammianus Marcellinus was astonished to observe the fixity of Emperor Constantius II during his solemn *adventus* to Rome, and he compared him not to a living creature nor to a god, but to a *figmentum*, a sort of statue "with a rigid neck, who held his eyes fixed before him, without looking left or right, like a figment in human form" (Alföldi, p. 274). The simple instrumental explanation that states that this is a stratagem of the powerful to justify their ambition or a mise-en-scène to produce reverential fear and obedience in the subjects, while it can occasionally get somewhere near the truth, is certainly not able to account for the deep and original connection that involves not only the political sphere but also the religious one. If one bears in mind the complicated choreography, the economic expense, and the imposing symbolic apparatus that were mobilized as much in Byzantium in the ninth century as in Berlin in the twentieth, the mere exhibition of arms would certainly have been more appropriate for the task. And ceremonial glory is frequently experienced by someone who receives it as a painful obligation that even the sovereign, who is above the law, must submit to as one does to a veritable *lex ceremoniarum*. According to the words of the pontiff to Charles V at the moment he offers his feet to be kissed: "I suffer against my will the kissing of my feet, but I am forced by the law of the ceremonial" ("*invitus passus sum osculari pedes meos, sed lex ceremoniarum ita cogit*": Kantorowicz 1946, p. 180, note 3).

Instrumental explanations—like the sociological theory that understands ceremonies as a sort of symbolic mise-en-scène of a whole society (Schenk, pp. 506–507)—do not take us much further than the late Baroque antiquarians who saw in it the consequence of original sin, which had produced inequality between men and the creation of a sort of *theatrum ceremoniale* in which the powerful enacted the signs of their wickedness (Lünig, pp. 1–70).

In the following pages we shall try to grasp the connection between power and glory in the exemplary case of acclamations and liturgical doxologies. We shall try to make strategic use of Luther's warning, that glory blinds those who try to penetrate majesty, by not asking the questions: What is glory? What is power? Instead, we shall pursue what is a more humble aim only in appearance: to investigate the forms of their relations and their operations. We shall, in other words, interrogate not glory but glorification, not *doxa* but the *doxazein* and the *doxazestai.*

§ 8   The Archaeology of Glory

8.1. The studies on glory in the field of theology were knocked off course for a long time by the apparently commanding work of Hans Urs von Balthasar, *Herrlichkeit. Eine theologische Aesthetik*. Despite the clear etymological connection between the German term *Herrlichkeit* and the sphere of domination and power (*Herrschaft, herrschen*), Balthasar chose to orientate his study of glory in terms of aesthetics. "We here attempt," he writes in the foreword to the first volume, "to develop a Christian theology in the light of the third transcendental, that is to say: to complement the vision of the true and the good with that of the beautiful (*pulchrum*)" (Balthasar 1982, p. 9). In contrast to Protestantism, which had deaestheticized theology, he proposed to restore it to the aesthetic rank that belongs to it. He of course recognized that the *kabhod*, glory in its original biblical sense, presupposed the idea of "lordship" and "sovereignty"; however, for him, it was a case of transferring these concepts into the sphere of beauty—or, rather, of an aesthetics characterized heavily by Kantian references:

> It is a case of envisioning the revelation of God, and God can only be truly recognized in his lordship and sovereignty, in what Israel calls *kabhod* and the New Testament calls glory, despite all the question marks concerning human nature and the cross. This means: God comes to us primarily not as teacher ("the true"), nor as "redeemer" with many ends for us ("the good"), but to show and radiate himself, the glory of his eternal trinitarian love, in the "disinterestedness" that true love has in common with beauty. (Balthasar 1965, p. 27)

Balthasar is aware of the risk inherent in such a project, that of "aestheticizing theology"; but he thinks he can sufficiently guard against it by shifting the emphasis from the adjective to the substantive and distinguishing in this sense a "*theological aesthetics*" from an "*aesthetic theology*," in which "the attribute will inevitably be understood in the worldly, limited, and, therefore, pejorative sense" (Balthasar 1982, p. 79).

One may doubt, of course, whether the effectiveness of such a purely verbal precaution is sufficient. In the 1930s, Walter Benjamin, recognizing in fascism the project of an "aestheticizing of politics," placed in opposition to it a "politicization of art" (not of aesthetics). In contrast to Balthasar's attempt to "aestheticize glory" and to transfer a genuinely "political" concept (from Peterson's perspective it in fact defined the specifically "public" character of liturgy) into the sphere of beauty, our reading of glory will never forget the context to which it belongs from the start. In the Bible, neither *kabhod* nor *doxa* is ever understood in an aesthetic sense: they are concerned with the terrifying appearance of YHVH, with the Kingdom, Judgment, and the throne—all things that can be defined "beautiful" only from a perspective that it is hard not to call aestheticizing.

8.2. The syntagma "glory of God" (*kabhod YHVH*) is a fundamental concept of Judaism. Immediately after the treatment of the names of God in the *Guide of the Perplexed*, Maimonides defines its meaning and, at the same time, its contextual problematic, through a tripartite structure:

> Similarly *kabhod* is sometimes intended to signify the created light that God causes to descend in a place in order to confer honor upon it in a miraculous way: *And the glory of Y.H.V.H. abode upon mount Sinai, and [the cloud] covered it, and so on* [Exodus 24:16]; *And the glory of Y.H.V.H. filled the tabernacle* [Exodus 40:34]. The expression is sometimes intended to signify his true essence and true reality [. . .] as when he says, *Show me, I pray Thee, Thy glory* [Exodus 33:18], and was answered: *For man shall not see Me and live* [Exodus 33:20]. This answer indicates that the *glory* that is spoken of here is His essence [. . .] *Kabhod* is sometimes intended to signify the glorification of Him [. . .] by all men. In fact all that is other than God [. . .] glorifies Him. For the true way of glorifying Him consists, in apprehending His greatness. Thus everybody who apprehends His greatness and His perfection, honors Him according to the extent of his apprehension [. . .] It is in view of this notion being named *glory* that it is said, *The whole earth is full of His glory* [Isaiah 6:3], this being equivalent to the dictum, *And the earth is full of His praise* [Habakkuk 3:3], for praise is called *glory*. Thus it is said: *Give glory to the Lord your God* [Jeremiah

13:16]; and it is said: *And in His temple all say: Glory* [Psalm 29:9] [. . .] Understand then the equivocality with reference to *glory* and interpret the latter in every passage in accordance with the context. (Maimonides, *The Guide of the Perplexed*, Book I, Chapter 64, pp. 156–157)

Of the three points at which Maimonides articulates the meaning of *kabhod*, the first refers to the episode in Exodus 40:34, in which "the glory of *Y.H.V.H.*" appears to the Jews as consuming fire, surrounded by a cloud that only Moses can penetrate. The second, in which the term would designate the essence of God, is actually derived from the same context. While speaking to Moses, *YHVH* covers him with his hand so as to prevent him from seeing his blinding *kabhod*, but the skin and face of Moses nevertheless receive such splendor that the Jews are unable to look at him, and he must place a veil over his face. With a characteristic gesture, Maimonides derives the second meaning of the term—which the biblical passage in no way suggests—from the fact that the *kabhod*, in its first sense as "created light," does not simply reveal *YHVH* but hides him to the same degree. This impossibility of seeing forms the basis of the second meaning, that of *kabhod* as God's "true reality" hidden behind the *kabhod* understood as "created light."

The third meaning—that of praise by creatures—insofar as it designates a certain human praxis (even though Maimonides extends glorification to include inanimate creatures who "bespeak" the *kabhod* of God in their own way), is the only concrete meaning. But this time as well Maimonides uses it to derive the second meaning inasmuch as praise presupposes the greatness and perfection of the divine being. In some way then, the *glorification* stems from the *glory* that, in truth, it founds.

It is interesting to note how Maimonides' strategy can be found repeated without significant variations in modern studies of this question, both Jewish and Christian. Works of lexicography and monographs both end up distinguishing the same three meanings, more or less, as Maimonides, at times specifying more precisely the second meaning in terms of "power" [*potenza*], "greatness," "weight" (this last being the etymological meaning of the Semitic root *kbd*). The relation, established by Maimonides, between the *kabhod* as "created light" and *kabhod* as the being of God, is developed by modern theologians, Christian and Jewish, in the sense of binding glory to the "manifestation" of God, to the divine essence insofar as it is made visible and perceptible.

This meaning of *kabhod*, which in the final instance is identified with

YHVH himself, is then opposed to the "objective" meaning of "glorification": "There is also a *kabhod* that creatures offer to God. It can be described as the 'objective' *kabhod* of YHWH" (Stein, p. 318—the medieval theologians, more correctly named this glory "subjective"). This *kabhod*, which is expressed in acclamations and hymns of praise, is at times presented as the natural and joyous reply of men to the manifest glory of God. At other times it resembles the honor that is bestowed upon the profane powers and cannot easily be related to the *kabhod*-being of God, as it was for Maimonides. In this case, modern scholars aim precisely at leaving out this objective meaning (ibid., p. 323).

However, for the ancients as well as for the moderns, the problem is precisely to justify—or at times to conceal—the double meaning, the homonymy and ambiguity of *kabhod*: at once glory and glorification, objective and subjective *kabhod*, divine reality and human praxis.

א *In the rabbinical tradition, the* kabhod YHVH *is related to the* Shekinah *(literally, "habitation," "residence") that expresses the presence of God among men. Hence, where the biblical passage states: "The Lord is in this place" (Genesis 28:16), the* Targum *translates this as "Truly the Glory of the* Shekinah *dwells in this place." And in the* Alphabet of Rabbi Akiba *one can read: "{At that hour God looked and saw his throne and his* Kabhod *and his* Shekinah}" *(quoted in Scholem 1997). Even Maimonides relates glory to the verb* shakan *(to reside) and with* Shekinah, *which for him does not mean manifestation, but only "[God's] abode in a place"* (Maimonides, The Guide of the Perplexed, *Book 1, Chapter 25, p. 55).*

In the same way, Sa'adiah Ga'on—and along with him Yehudah Halewi and the other medieval philosophers—identify Shekinah *with* kabhod: *"{The bright apparition that proves to the prophet the authenticity of the revelation God made to him is a light that was created: it is called* kabhod *in the Bible and* Shekinah *in the rabbinic tradition}" (quoted in Scholem 1990). The* Shekinah *is not identical with God but, as with the* kabhod *in its first meaning of the term according to Maimonides, it is one of his free creations, which precedes the creation of the world.*

א *In the Old Testament and in rabbinical Judaism, the* kabhod *assumes a particular meaning in eschatology. This will coincide with the full revelation of the glory of God, which will appear in Zion as a cloud and a canopy (Isaiah 4:5). In the* Deutero-Isaiah, *it will appear not only to the Jews but to "all flesh"* (*"And the glory of the LORD shall be revealed, and all flesh shall see it together": Isaiah 40:5). According to Habakkuk 2:14: "For the earth shall be filled with the knowledge of the glory of the LORD [YHWH], as the waters cover the sea." Ezekiel's terrible vision, which with its winged "living creatures" and its throne of sapphire would so profoundly influence Christian apocalypticism, is presented by the prophet as a vision of glory: "This was the appearance of the likeness of the* kabhod *of the LORD. And when I saw it, I fell upon my face, and I heard a voice of one that spake" (Ezekiel 1:28).*

8.3. The Septuagint translates *kabhod* with *doxa*, and this Greek term (which the Vulgate will translate as "glory") thereby becomes the technical term for glory in the New Testament. But as occurs with any translation, in this passage the biblical *kabhod* undergoes a profound transformation. What was originally an element external to God, one that signified his presence, became—in conformity with the new theological context— an expression of the internal relations of the Trinitarian economy. This means that between *oikonomia* and *doxa* there is a constitutive nexus, and that it is not possible to understand economic theology if one does not at the same time give an account of this connection. In the same way that Christian theology had dynamically transformed biblical monotheism by dialectically opposing within it the unity of substance and of ontology (the *theologia*) to the plurality of persons and practices (the *oikonomia*), so the *doxa theou* defines the operation of reciprocal glorification between the Father and the Son (and, more generally, between the three persons). The Trinitarian economy is constitutively an economy of glory.

We can perhaps say that this glorious economy appears nowhere with the same clarity as in the Gospel of John. It melodically resonates from one end of the text to the other—in the same way that it does, with a different tone, in the Letters of Saint Paul—and achieves its most vibrant expression in Jesus's prayer before his arrest: "Father, the hour is come; glorify [*doxason*] thy Son, that thy Son also may glorify [*doxasēi*] thee [. . .] I have glorified thee on the earth: I have finished the work which thou gavest me to do. And now, O Father, glorify thou me with thine own self with the glory which I had with thee before the world was" (John 17:1–5). A little earlier, when the betrayal was predicted, the same theme was announced in the words of Jesus to his disciples, who sat around him at the table: "Now is the Son of man glorified [*edoxasthē*], and God is glorified [*edoxasthē*] in him. If God be glorified in him, God shall also glorify him in himself, and shall straightaway glorify him" (John 13:31–32).

One is struck in these passages by the perfect circularity of the economy that they describe. The work—the economy of salvation—that Jesus has accomplished upon earth is, in truth, the glorification of the father—that is, an economy of glory. But it is, to the same extent, the glorification of the son through the work of the father. And this doxological circle is marked not only by the insistent repetition of forms of the same verb, but seems to be perfectly completed in the idea that glory precedes the very creation of the world and thus defines the Trinitarian relationship from the beginning ("glorify thou me with thine own self with the glory which I had with thee before the world was"). In Jewish messianism, the name ("*chem*" is a concept intimately linked to that of glory) is part of the five (or seven) things created before the world; but John, who takes up this Jewish motif, turns it into the doxological nucleus of the intradivine relation. And while the economy of salvation that was entrusted to the son is accomplished in time, the economy of glory has neither beginning nor end.

However, the economy of glory in John's Gospel includes men as well. Referring to those to whom he revealed the name of the father (that is, the glory), Jesus adds: "And all mine are thine, and thine are mine; and I am glorified [*dedoxasmai*] in them" (John 17:10). And immediately afterward he expands upon this: "And the glory which thou gavest me I have given them" (John 17:22). Thus to the glorious economy of the Trinity corresponds the reciprocal glorification of men and God.

א *The term that in Homeric Greek corresponds to the semantic sphere of glory is not* doxa *but* kleos. Kleos, *which is a term etymologically connected with the sphere of words and of "that which is heard" (*klyō*), is not a property of the gods, and indeed it results from the activity of a special category of men: the poets. They of course need the cooperation of divine beings, the Muses, who push them to "sing about the* kleos *of men" (Homer,* The Odyssey, *Book 8, 73); but the glory that they confer and that can get "through heaven" (ibid., 74) is their jealously guarded and exclusive competence. For this very reason, it is not a case of knowledge, so much as of something that exhausts itself entirely within the sphere of the word. "We poets," says Homer, "hear the* kleos *and we know nothing" (Homer,* Iliad, *Book 2, 486).*

Gregory Nagy has shown how the Iliad *and the* Odyssey *are first of all po-*

ems of the kleos *of Achilles and Odysseus and that it is precisely the theme of glory that unites the two poems. If Achilles, the best of the Achaeans, is the one who exchanges return and life for glory ("there is no* nostos *for me, but there will be eternal* kleos*": Homer,* Iliad, *Book 9, 413), Odysseus had both return and glory (Nagy, p. 29). But it is once again the poets who bestow glory. Both the Phaecian singer in the* Odyssey *(8, 72–82) and the poet of the* Theogony *present themselves as masters of glory, who look as much to the past as to the future ("that I might spread the fame [*kleioimi*] of past and future": Hesiod,* Theogony, *p. 12).*

The Homeric world has therefore a figure of glory that is entirely the work of man, mere glorification. For this reason, many centuries later, a Roman poet was able to push this "glorifying" strain of poetry to the limit, writing that not just heroes, but "the gods too (if I may be allowed to say so) exist through poetry; even the majesty of one so great has need of the voice of someone to celebrate it" ("Di quoque carminibus, si fas est dicere, fiunt / tantaque maiestas ore canentis eget": Ovid, The Pontic Epistles, *Book IV, 8, 55–56, p. 455).*

8.4. In the Second Letter to the Corinthians, Paul takes up again the *kabhod* of Exodus 29ff., in order to found, by meticulously building up a series of optical images, his theory of glory. The—provisional—glory that illuminates Moses' face after he received the tablets of the law from God (which were defined, following Paul's implacable critique of the law, as a "ministration of death," *diakonia tou thanatou*: 2 Corinthians 3:7) is incomparably less than that which results from the "ministration of redemption" that the Messiah brought to mankind. Nevertheless the members of the messianic community (the term "Christian" is unknown to Paul) have no need to place a veil (*kalymma*) over their faces, as Moses does—a veil that "even unto this day, when Moses is read [. . .] is upon their heart" (2 Corinthians 3:15). In fact, the Messiah involves the deactivation of the veil (*hoti en Christōi katargeitai*: 2 Corinthians 3:14). When the Jews are converted, the veil will be removed from them as well. "But we all, with open face [*anakekalymmenōi prosōpōi*] beholding as in a glass [*katoptrizomenoi*] the glory of the Lord, are changed into the same image from glory to glory [*apo doxēs eis doxan*], even as by the Spirit of the Lord" (2 Corinthians 3:18).

The economy of glory is expressed here in solely optical terms. And it is the same image that Hebrews 1:3 specifies further. The son is *apaugasma*, that is, at once reflection and radiation of God's glory (the verb *apaugazein* in fact means as much "to irradiate, to emit luminous rays" as much as it means "to reflect irradiating rays"). This is why in 2 Corinthians 4:6, God shines the light on Christ's face (*en prosōpōi Christou*), "the light of the knowledge of the glory of God."

The optical phenomenology of glory unfolds in the following way: God, "the Father of glory" (Ephesians 1:17), radiates his glory onto the face of Christ who reflects it and radiates in turn like a mirror onto the members of the messianic community. The celebrated eschatological verse 1 Corinthians 13:12 should be read in this light: the glory that we now see enigmatically in a mirror (*di' esoptrou en ainigmati*), we will go on to see face-to-face (*prosōpon pros prosōpon*). In the present, we await the "glorious appearing" (Titus 2:13), in the same way as all that which is created impatiently waits to be "delivered from the bondage of corruption into the glorious liberty of the children of God" (Romans 8:13).

In contrast to John, here the stress lies not on the reciprocal glorification of Father and Son, but on the radiation of glory by the Father onto the Son and to the members of the messianic community. At the heart of Paul's gospel lies not the Trinitarian economy but messianic redemption.

8.5. It is necessary to explode the commonly held view, frequently repeated in the lexicons, that a theory of glory is lacking in the Church Fathers of the first centuries after Christ. Precisely the opposite is true. That is, as could be expected, it is precisely those authors who develop the theology of the economy who also produce the elements for a theology of glory. This is particularly true in the case of Irenaeus. In the fourth book of *Against Heresies*, he takes up, through the canonical citation from Exodus 33:20 ("there shall no man see me [God], and live"), the biblical theme of the unknowability of *kabhod* (of the "marvelous glory," *anexēgētos doxa*: Irenaeus, *Against Heresies*, Book 4, Chapter 20, § 5, p. 366). But, to the unknowability of the biblical God he opposes the revelation of God by way of the prophetic Spirit and, above all, through the son, the true "exegete," "administrator" or "dispenser," and singer of glory:

> From the beginning the Son is the interpreter [*exēgētēs*] of the Father, since from the beginning he has been with him. It is by his song that the prophetical visions, and the diversities of gifts, and his own ministries, and his Father's glorification [*doxologia*], have been orderly and systematically revealed unto

mankind, in meet time to profit withal. And so the Word [*Logos*] became the dispenser of the father's grace for the good of men, and for their sake He wrought such mighty and manifold *economies*, on the one side revealing God to men, on the other, presenting man unto God: and as He guards the invisibility of the Father, lest at any time man should become a despiser of God, and that he might always have something to grow toward, so on the other hand through many and manifold economies He reveals God unto men, lest men altogether falling away from God, should cease to be at all. For the glory of God is a living Man, and the life of man is to see God. (Ibid., § 7, pp. 368–369)

In this extraordinary passage the glorification performed by the *Logos* is described in the same "economic" terms with which Irenaeus had described the economy of salvation. Not only does the economy of salvation presuppose the economy of glory, but the latter is the "exegesis" of what would otherwise remain "indescribable," as much in the life of the deity as in the world of men. Glory is, in other words, the economy of economies; that which, inasmuch as it interprets the economies (*tas oikonomias exegeito*), reveals how much *YHVH* remained unknown in the *kabhod*:

Therefore, if neither Moses saw God, nor Elias, nor Ezekiel, who did see many of the celestial things, and if the things which they did see were resemblances of the Lord's glory and prophecies of things to come; it is plain that the Father indeed is invisible, concerning whom also the Lord said, *No man hath God seen at any time.* But his word [*Logos*], at his own pleasure, and for the profit of such as behold, revealed the brightness of the Father and has interpreted the economies (as the Lord has said, "*The Only Begotten God, who is in the Bosom of the Father, He hath interpreted Him*": John 1:18). (Ibid., § 11, p. 372)

א *Important cues for a theology of glory can also be found in the* Adversus Praxean *by Tertullian, that is, precisely in the incunabulum of economic theology. Tertullian not only knows perfectly well that what was, in the economy of salvation (*in ipsa oikonomia: Against Praxeas, § 23, p. 91), a lessening and diminution for the son would have resulted in an economy of glory that was the complete opposite ("gloria tamen et honore coronaturus illum in caelos resumendo": ibid., p. 92); but also, through the strategic citation of John, he glimpses in glory the inseparable relation that ties the Father to the Son, the irrevocable abode of the Son in the Father: "Jesus said: 'And God will glorify Him in Himself,' that is, the Father, the Son whom He 'having Him in Him-*

self,' though He has been sent forth to earth, will later glorify by resurrection" (*ibid., p. 94*).

8.6. The most condensed exposition of a theology of glory in the writings of the Church Fathers of the first centuries is to be found in the digression—which almost forms a *peri doxēs* treatise—that Origen inserts in the thirty-second book of his commentary on the gospel according to John. The theme of glory appears to him so important that, at the end of the digression, the author feels he must thank God because, despite the inadequacy of his arguments, what he wrote appears to him to be "well above his abilities [*pollōi meizosin tēs hemeteras axias*]" (Origen, *Commentaire*, p. 345). He begins by taking his leave of the pagan, purely acclamatory meaning of the term (glory as "praise by the multitude": ibid., p. 329), to which he opposes not only the canonical passage from Exodus on the *kabhod* of God that is revealed to Moses, but also the interpretation of this passage that Paul makes in the Second Letter to the Corinthians (2 Corinthians 3:7–11). The interpretation of these passages that Origen proposes is a perfect example of his exegetical method, which distinguishes the literal from the anagogical (or spiritual) meaning:

> If, from the corporeal standpoint, a divine epiphany is produced under the tent and in the temple and on the face of Moses after he spoke with God, from the anagogical point of view one could speak of the "vision of the Glory of God," that which is known and is seen in God with an entirely purified intellect. The intellect that has been purified and has overcome all material things so as to carefully contemplate God, becomes divine through that which it contemplates. One can say that that is what the glorification of the face of him who has contemplated God consists in. (*Commentaire*, pp. 333–335)

In other words, Origen interprets glory in terms of knowledge and, immediately afterward, applies this exegesis to the passage in John according to which "the son of man has been glorified and God has been glorified through him" (ibid., p. 335). The specific and ingenuous contribution made by Origen is to read into this passage nothing less than the process of divine self-knowledge:

> Thus, knowing the Father, the Son has been glorified through his very knowledge, which is the greatest good and leads to perfect knowledge since it is that with which the Son knows the Father. I believe, however, that he has been glorified by his knowledge, since it is in this way that he comes to know him-

self [. . .] All this glory, through which the Son of man is glorified, was glorified by a gift of the Father. And of all the elements that lead to the full glory of man, the principal one is God insofar as he is not glorified simply because he is known *by* the Son, but is glorified *in* [*en*] his Son. (Ibid., pp. 335–337)

The process of reciprocal glorification between father and son coincides with God's self-knowledge, which is to be understood as an *autosophia* (ibid.), and this process is so intimate that the glorification cannot be said to be produced by the son but only *in* the son. At this point it is clear why the "economy of passion" (*hē oikonomia tou pathos*) is able to coincide perfectly with the glorious economy through which the son reveals the father (*ek tēs oikonomias apokalyptein ton patera ho hyios*: ibid., p. 343):

> For this reason, when Jesus arrived at the economy in accordance with which he was to be raised above the world and, once recognized, to be glorified by the glory of those who would go on to glorify him, he spoke these words: "Now the Son of man has been glorified"; and since "no man knoweth the Father, save the Son who reveals him" and the Son was about to reveal the Father through an economy, for this reason "God as well was glorified in him." (Ibid.)

The economy of passion and the economy of revelation coincide in glory, and the latter (or, rather, glorification) defines the set of Trinitarian relations. The trinity is a doxology.

8.7. Modern theologians distinguish, as we have seen, between "economic trinity" (or trinity of revelation) and "immanent trinity" (or trinity of substance). The former defines God in his praxis of salvation through which he reveals himself to men. The immanent trinity instead refers to God as he is in himself. We rediscover here, in the opposition between two trinities, the fracture between ontology and praxis, theology and economy that we have seen constitutively marking the formation of economic theology (see § 3.4 above). To the immanent trinity there correspond ontology and theology; to the economic there correspond praxis and *oikonomia*. Our investigation has tried to reconstruct the way in which these original polarities have, at different levels, developed into the polarities of transcendent order and immanent order, Kingdom and Government, general providence and special providence, which define the operation of the machine of the divine government of the world. The economic trinity (Government) presupposes the immanent trinity (the Kingdom), which justifies and founds it.

It comes as no surprise, therefore, that immanent trinity and economic trinity, distinguished at the very beginning, are then perpetually reunited and articulated together by the theologians and that it is precisely this articulation that is at stake in theology. The "economic Trinity *is* the immanent Trinity, and vice versa" (Moltmann, p. 160): this is the principle that must guide all attempts to think their relation. The work of sacrifice and salvation, which is in question in economic theology, cannot be erased in the immanent trinity.

> If the central foundation of our knowledge of the Trinity is the cross, on which the Father delivered up the Son for us through the Spirit, then it is impossible to conceive of any Trinity of substance in the transcendent primal ground of this event, in which cross and self-giving are not present. (Ibid.)

That is, there are not two different trinities, but a single trinity that is, at once, a single divine story of salvation and a single economy. And yet, this identity should not be understood as "the dissolution of the one in the other" (ibid.). According to the complex mechanism that, as we have seen, marks the relations between theology and economy from the beginning—and, then, the functioning of the governmental machine—the two trinities, though intimately articulated, remain distinct. What is in question is rather the reciprocity of their relations.

> What this thesis is actually trying to bring out is the interaction between the substance and the revelation, the "inwardness" and the "outwardness" of the triune God [. . .] From the foundation of the world, the *opera trinitatis ad extra* correspond to the *passiones trinitatis ad intra*. (Ibid.)

Glory is the place where theology attempts to think the difficult conciliation between immanent trinity and economic trinity, *theologia* and *oikonomia*, being and praxis, God in himself and God for us. For this reason, the doxology, despite its apparent ceremonial fixity, is the most dialectical part of theology, in which what can only be thought of as separate must attain unity.

> Real theology, which means the knowledge of God, finds expression in thanks, praise and adoration. And it is what finds expression in doxology that is the real theology. There is no experience of salvation without the expres-

sion of that experience in thanks, praise and joy. An experience which does not find expression in this way is not a liberating experience [. . .] So God is not loved, worshipped and perceived merely because of the salvation that has been experienced, but for his own sake. That is to say, praise goes beyond thanksgiving. God is recognized, not only in his goodly works but in his goodness itself. And adoration, finally, goes beyond both thanksgiving and praise. (Ibid., pp. 152–153)

In glory, economic trinity and immanent trinity, God's praxis of salvation and his being are conjoined and move through each other. From here stems the indissoluble knot that binds together doxological elements in the strict sense and the Eucharistic mimesis that one finds in liturgy. Praise and adoration directed toward the immanent trinity presuppose the economy of salvation, just as in John, the Father glorifies the Son and the Son glorifies the Father. *The economy glorifies being, as being glorifies the economy.* And only in the mirror of glory do the two trinities appear to reflect into one another; only in its splendor do being and economy, Kingdom and Government appear to coincide for an instant. Hence the Council of Nicaea, in order to avoid all risk of separating the Son from the Father, the economy from the substance, felt the need to insert into the symbol of faith the formula *phōs ek phōtos,* "light of light." For this reason, Augustine, while seeking obsessively to eliminate all risk of subordination by the trinity, takes up an image of light and glory (Augustine, *On the Trinity,* Book 4, Chapter 20, § 27).

א *Given that glory is the place in which the movement of the Trinitarian economy has to reveal itself in full, it is also the place in which the risk of non-coincidence between being and praxis and of a possible asymmetry in the relation between the three divine persons is at its highest. It comes as no surprise then that it is precisely in the excursus on glory that Origen seems to adopt a subordinationalist position that could make him appear as a precursor to Arius. Having commented upon the reciprocal glorification of Father and Son in John, he prudently puts forward the idea of a self-glorification of the Father that is independent of the one that he receives from the Son:*

I wonder whether God can be glorified in a way that is independent of his being glorified by the Son, since he has the advantage of being glorified in himself; through the contemplation of himself he rejoices in his own knowledge and vision with an indescribable satisfaction and joy that are greater than that of the Son, since he finds his joy and satisfaction in himself—as far as it is possible to express such ideas with respect to God. Indeed, I use these terms that cannot really be applied to God, because I lack the unspeakable words. (Origen, *Commentaire*, pp. 337–339)

That subordinationalism is rejected from the beginning as an intolerable heresy is not so much and not only because it implies a superiority of the Father over the Son (in the Gospels, Jesus frequently attributes to the Father just such a superiority), but also and above all because it endangers the functioning of the Trinitarian apparatus, which is founded upon a perfect interpersonal circulation of glory between immanent trinity and economic trinity.

It is still with reference to the passage in John that Augustine, in On the Trinity, *warns against every attempt to introduce an asymmetry into glory so as to found upon it the superiority of one person over another.*

But here also let them wake up if they can, who have thought this, too, to be testimony on their side, to show that the Father is greater than the Son, because the Son hath said, "Father, glorify me." Why, the Holy Spirit also glorifies Him. Pray, is the Spirit, too, greater than He? [. . .] Whence it may be perceived that all things that the Father hath are not only of the Son, but also of the Holy Spirit, because the Holy Spirit is able to glorify the Son, whom the Father glorifies. But if he who glorifies is greater than he whom he glorifies, let them allow that those are equal who mutually glorify each other [*invicem*]. (Augustine, *On the Trinity*, Book 2, Chapter 4, § 6, pp. 47–48)

The economy of glory can only function if it is perfectly symmetrical and reciprocal. All economy must become glory, and all glory become economy.

8.8. Theology never manages truly to get to the bottom of the fracture between immanent trinity and economic trinity, between *theologia* and *oikonomia.* This is demonstrated in the very glory that was supposed to celebrate their reconciliation. It is marked by a fundamental dissymmetry in which only the economic trinity is completed at the end of days, but not the immanent trinity. After the Last Judgment, when the economy of salvation is complete and "God may be all in all" (1 Corinthians 15:28), the economic trinity will be reabsorbed by the immanent trinity and "what remains is the eternal praise of the triune God in his glory" (Moltmann, p. 161). The paradisiacal liturgy ends up in doxology; it knows no mass but only the hymn of praise. In this asymmetry of glory, the "anarchic"—and, at the same time, generated—character of the Son reemerges, putting in question the laboriously achieved result of the long and acrimonious dispute with Arianism. The economy is anarchical and, as such, has no foundation in God's being; and yet, the Father has generated the Son before the eternal times. This is the "mystery of the economy," whose darkness glory is not able completely to dispel in its light. To the original paradox of a generated anarchy, at the end of days, there corresponds that of an economic—and yet finite—anarchy. (The attempt to think, at one and the same time, an infinite being and its finite history—and hence, the figure of being that survives its economy—forms precisely the theological inheritance of modern philosophy, which achieves its most extreme form in the last works of Heidegger.)

Of course, the operation of glory—or at least its pretension—is to express the pleromatic figure of the trinity, in which economic trinity and immanent trinity are once and for all securely articulated together. But it can only fulfill this task by continuously dividing what it must conjoin and each time reconjoining what must remain separated. For this reason, just as in the profane sphere glory was an attribute, not of Government but of the Kingdom, not of the ministers but of the sovereign, so the doxology refers ultimately to the being of God, not to his economy. And yet, just as we have seen that the Kingdom is nothing but that which remains if one removes Government, and the Government that which remains if the Kingdom removes itself, in such a way that the governmental machine always consists in the articulation of these two polarities, equally, one could say that the theo-doxological machine results from the correlation between immanent trinity and economic trinity, in which each of these two aspects glorifies the other and stems from the other. Government glorifies the Kingdom, and the Kingdom glorifies Government. But the center of the machine is empty, and glory is nothing but the splendor that emanates from this emptiness, the inexhaustible *kabhod* that at once reveals and veils the central vacuity of the machine.

8.9. The aporias implicit in every theology of glory are evident in the work of the Protestant theologian who lies at the origin of Balthasar's attempt to aestheticize doxology. In a decisive passage of his *Church Dogmatics*, Karl Barth inserts a brief treatise on glory, which the Catholic theologian takes up and expands upon in his masterpiece. Even though the stylistic form of the work of the two theologians is very different, their aim is substantially the same. Barth is perfectly well aware that glory refers to "His freedom, majesty and sovereignty" (Barth, p. 641). For him it defines "His competence to make use of His omnipotence [. . .] and to exercise His lordship [*Herrschaft*]" (ibid.). Abruptly shifting his analysis of glory into the "immediately proximate" (ibid.) sphere of beauty, he uses this concept as a supplement (*Hilfsbegriff*: ibid, p. 653) to confront what appears to him a "blind spot" (ibid., p. 650) in the theological conception of glory. That is to say, it is a case of nothing less than the neutralization of the idea that the glory and sovereignty of God are reducible to the *brutum factum* of his omnipotence and his force.

> Or can we say positively of the method of God's glory, of His self-glorification, only that it has the whole omnipotence of God behind it, that it persuades [*überzeugt*] and convinces [*überführt*, literally, "it guides us from above"] by ruling, mastering [*herrscht*] and subduing [*überwältigt*] with the utterly superior force [. . .]? [. . .] When the Bible uses the term "glory" to describe the revelation and knowledge of God, does it not mean something other and more than the assertion of a brute fact? [. . .] We have seen that when we speak of God's glory we do emphatically mean God's "force." Yet the idea of "glory" contains something which is not covered by that of "force." For the idea of "kingdom" which precedes the other two concepts in the doxology of the Lord's Prayer seems to say something of wider range than can be described by "force" alone. Light too, has force and is force, but it is not this that makes it light. Has not and is not God more than is covered by the idea of force when He has and is light and is glorious? (Ibid.)

We find here, as we find at the hidden root of all aestheticisms, the need to cover and dignify what is in itself pure force and domination. Beauty names precisely the "supplementary element" that enables one to think glory beyond the *factum* of sovereignty, to "depoliticize" the lexis of *Herrlichkeit* (that Barth, not by chance, had up to this point expressed with the technical terms of political sovereignty and government: *herrschen*, *führen*, *walten*), transferring it into the sphere of aesthetics.

> If we can say that God is beautiful, to say this is to say how He enlightens and convinces and persuades us. It is to describe not merely the naked fact of His revelation or its power [*Gewalt*] but the shape and form in which it is a fact and is power. (Ibid.)

Barth is perfectly aware of the impropriety and inadequacy of the term "beauty," which inevitably refers one to the profane sphere "of pleasure, desire, and enjoyment" (ibid., p. 651); and yet the risk of aestheticism ("drohende Ästhetizismus": ibid., p. 652) is precisely the price to be paid if one is to detach the theory of glory from the sphere of *Gewalt*, of power. That beauty should become the designation, at once improper and absolutely inevitable, of glory, means that the problem of the relation between immanent trinity and economic trinity, between ontology and *oikonomia* will have to be related to the aesthetic sphere as well. God's glory and freedom are not an "abstract freedom or sovereignty" (ibid., p. 659). The being of God is not "self-enclosed and pure divine being" (ibid.); what makes him divine and real is his being nothing other than the being of the Father, the Son, and the Holy Spirit. "His being [. . .] is not form in itself but the concrete form of the triune being of God" (ibid.). The trinity of God is, in this sense, "the secret of His beauty" (ibid., p. 661). The decisive moment of the transferral of the biblical *kabhod* into the neutral sphere of aesthetics, which only a few years later Balthasar will consider to have been fully achieved, takes place here.

8.10. There is also another reason behind the aestheticization of glory. It allows one to confront the problem that, in the history of theology, is—at one and the same time—ever present and always eluded by new means. We are speaking of that glory that the theologians define as *subiectiva, seu formalis* (or, external); that is, the glorification that men (and with them the angels) owe to God. Inasmuch as it constitutes the doxological nucleus of liturgy, it enjoys a lustrous prestige and self-evidence; however, despite the specifications and arguments of the theologians, it certainly cannot be said that its rationale is equally clearly illuminated.

As long as there has been glory there has been glorification; and this not only in the profane sphere. The *kabhod* that YHVH has inasmuch as he is "king of glory" (*melek ha-kabhod*) is also something that men owe him. "Give *kabhod* to YHWH, give him thanks" is the cry that ceaselessly resounds among the sons of Israel. It culminates in Isaiah's *trisagion* (Isaiah 6:3), where "the whole earth is full of his [God's] glory." It is the glorifying *kabhod* that liturgy formalizes in doxology proper, which in the synagogue takes the form of the *Kaddish*, which exalts, blesses, and praises the name of YHVH.

In the great eschatological doxology of Revelation 4:3, which we shall need to consider below, and in Paul's Letters one discovers early testimonies of the Christian doxologies concerning he who, as "lord" or "father" of glory is, or should be, already firmly in possession of it (both in the form of the prescription "Glorify!," *doxasate*—1 Corinthians 6:20—as well as in the form of ritual doxologies of the type found in Hebrews 13:21, "To whom be glory for ever and ever. Amen"). In this case as well, the Church formalizes glorification, in ritual fashion, as much in the daily duty of prayer as in liturgy.

One should note the singular explanation for this dual figure of glory that is supplied by the theologians. Subjective glory is nothing but the joyous response of man to the objective glory of God. We do not praise God because he has any need of it (he is already filled with glory). Nor do we praise him because it is useful for us. "The only reason for praising God is that he is worthy of praise" (Mascall, p. 112). Through a perfectly circular line of argument, subjective glory is due to objective glory, because the latter is worthy of glory. That is: glorification is due to glory because in some sense it derives from it.

This vicious circle is what is crystallized in the thirteenth century by the scholastic definition provided by William of Auvergne:

> A very early meaning of the glory of God is nothing but his extremely eminent magnificence and nobility, and this is the glory of God in himself or close to himself, for which reason praise, glorification, and every form of worship are owed him. Another meaning of what is named the glory of God is that through which he is glorified, that is, honored, preached about, praised, and adored by the elect and by all men. (William of Auvergne, *De retributionibus sanctorum*, p. 320)

א *As we have already seen with regard to the term "order," which means as much a transcendent relation with God* (ordo ad Deum) *as a property immanent in creatures* (ordo ad invicem), *so glory is at once an essential attribute of God and something that creatures owe to him and that expresses their relation to him. Moreover, in the same way that the dual meaning of the term "order" ultimately ends up befitting the very essence of God, so the ambiguity of the term "glory" makes of it the name that defines God's most intimate nature. In this sense, both terms are signatures* [segnature] *rather than concepts.*

8.11. Not even Barth's treatise manages to escape the circularity of glory. On the contrary, it takes an extreme form in which the Lutheran tradition's reservations with respect to the theology of glory are set aside. Barth's treatise begins with the statement that, in the New Testament, glory indicates the honor that God himself enjoys, as well as the glory that he receives from creatures. This co-existence of two contradictory mean-ings in the same term is, however, "absolutely necessary" (Barth, p. 670). Glory and the hymn of praise that the creatures bestow upon God are, in fact, nothing but the "echo" (*Widerhall*: ibid.) that answers the glory of God. Rather, insofar as it has its foundation in glory, glorification "can only be understood in the proper and decisive sense as the work of God's glory" (ibid.). Furthermore, the being and liberty of creatures essentially depend upon the act of glorification and thanksgiving. "The creature be-comes free for the glory of God not because it could and wanted to do so but because it only did so through the glory of God" (ibid., p. 671). And they do not merely thank, but "*are* themselves thankfulness [*Dank*]" (ibid.). The circularity of glory here attains its ontological formulation: becoming free for the glorification of God means to understand oneself as constituted, in one's very being, by the glory with which we celebrate the glory that allows us to celebrate it. "It does not belong to the essence of the creature to have or to be the power to glorify God. This ability is God's [. . .] God gives Himself to the creature [. . .] And the creature to whom God gives Himself may praise Him" (ibid.). The liberation of crea-tures from their "powerlessness" is manifested in glorification and "results in the praise of God" (ibid., p. 672).

If creatures are essentially the glorification of glory, a glory that divine glory bestows upon itself, it is clear that the life of creatures culminates in obedience (*Lebensgehorsam*: ibid., p. 674). "It has no alternative but to thank and praise God. And in this thanks and praise it has nothing else to offer God but itself—nothing more and nothing less" (ibid.). The preem-inent location for this service is the Church. At the end of his treatise, and in singularly lofty tones that seem more suited to a Catholic theologian, Barth celebrates the Church as the proper space of glory. Certainly the Church is not identified, as it is in Peterson, with the community of an-gels and the blessed who celebrate the glory of God in the heavens (ibid., p. 675). However, the Church is the form in which we are "surrounded by the glory of God, and in which we participate in it" (ibid., p. 676).

It should now be clear in what sense the preliminary exclusion from the theory of glory of any reference to the political sphere is misleading. For as we have seen already with respect to Peterson, after the repression of politics in theology, it reappears—as is the case with all forms of repres-sion—in an improper form in doxology. Such an absolute reduction of creatures to their glorifying function is clearly reminiscent of the behavior demanded of their subjects by the profane powers in Byzantium and in the Germany of the 1930s, which Barth voluntarily abandoned. Here, as well, the highest dignity and the highest freedom are to be found in the glorification of the sovereign. Here, as well, the glorification is due to the sovereign not because he needs it but, as his resplendent insignia, his throne, and crown reveal, because he is glorious in himself. The circularity of the paradigm is the same in both cases.

8.12. The paradox of glory has the following form: glory is the exclusive property of God for eternity, and it will remain eternally identical in him, such that nothing and no one can increase or diminish it; and yet, glory is glorification, which is to say, something that all creatures always incessantly owe to God and that he demands of them. From this paradox follows another one, which theology pretends to present as the resolution of the former: glory, the hymn of praise that creatures owe to God, in reality derives from the very glory of God; it is nothing but the necessary response, almost the echo that the glory of God awakens in them. That is (and this is the third formulation of the paradox): everything that God accomplishes, the works of creation and the economy of redemption, he accomplishes only for his glory. However, for this, creatures owe him gratitude and glory.

The paradox, in its three forms, culminates in post-Tridentine and Baroque theology, that is, when the theory of profane sovereignty achieves a new configuration. We could say that the first formulation of the paradox implodes in the motto of Ignatius of Loyola, which became something similar to the insignia of the Society of Jesus: *Ad maiorem Dei gloriam.* There has been much discussion of the origin and meaning of this motto, which perfectly summarizes Ignatius's intentions when he decided to abandon worldly honors for the honor of God. One thing that is clear is that he takes the paradox of glory to its extreme, since the human activity of glorification now consists in an impossible task: the continual increase of the glory of God that can in no way be increased. More precisely—and perhaps this is the real meaning of the motto—the impossibility of increasing the inner glory of God translates into an unlimited expansion of the activity of external glorification by men, particularly by the members of the Society of Jesus. What cannot be increased—glory in the first sense of the term—demands the infinite increase of glory in the exterior and subjective sense. This means, on the one hand, that the nexus of glory

and glorification has now been severed and that the worldly work of glorification relies on the glory of God, which should justify it. On the other
hand, it means that glorification begins to react on glory, and the idea
begins to form that the action of men can start to influence divine glory
and increase it. In other words, while the difference between glory and
glorification begins to become indeterminate, the accent shifts progressively from the former onto the latter.

The manifesto for the primacy of glorification over glory can be found
in the booklet *De perfectionibus moribusque divinis* (1620), by Leonard
Lessius, a Jesuit theologian who had an enduring influence on the theology of glory between the seventeenth and eighteenth centuries. Under the
heading *De ultimo fine*, he poses the following simple question: "What
benefit could God draw from the creation and from the government of
the world?" The answer that is at first glance surprising is, logically speaking, entirely consistent. God, "being infinitely perfect and in every way
blessed," can draw no benefit for himself from the multiplicity, variety,
and beauty of creatures, which are as though "suspended over nothingness
by the beam of divine light" (Lessius, p. 513). The purpose of the creation
and the government of the world must, therefore, be "something external
[*quid extrinsecum*], such as having children similar to himself, who participate in his glory and his blessedness" (ibid.).

Lessius is certainly aware of the distinction between internal glory—
which is the same as the splendor and excellence of the divinity himself
(that is the objective internal glory) and amounts to the knowledge, love,
and enjoyment that God has within himself (formal internal glory)—and
external glory. But the specific contribution of his manifesto springs from
its overturning of the relation between the two glories. God cannot have
created the world in order to acquire or increase his internal glory, which
he already possesses *plenissime*. So his purpose cannot be anything but the
acquiring and increasing of his external glory.

> Glory is not necessarily an intrinsic good. The glory of kings and princes,
> which mortals so value and desire, consists in external things, in the splendor
> of the courts, in the magnificence of their palaces, in military power, and
> the like. Even if no internal increase in divine glory is possible, neverthe-
> less an extrinsic increase is possible through the addition of those things in
> which the glory of persons consists: that is, an increase in the sons of God by
> whom glory is recognized, loved, and praised. In this sense, the glory of God
> is greater; in this sense, it can be said that it is increased. This is the glory that

God wanted to acquire for himself through all his external works. (Ibid., pp. 516–517)

Lessius also ruthlessly sacrifices to the logical coherence of this vainglorious God the idea of God's love for creatures. Since every creature "is nothing when compared to him" and since "the glory of God is more important than any of the creatures' goods," God's actions must "necessarily advance his glory rather than the perfection of his creatures" (ibid., p. 538). It is of this external glory that God is jealous (as testified to in Isaiah 48:11: "I will not give my glory unto another"); and it is this glory that man must propose as the end of all his actions (Lessius, p. 539).

Without the preliminary comprehension of this theory of glory, it is difficult to fully understand the post-Tridentine politics of the Church, the fervor of the missionary orders, and the imposing activity *ad maiorem Dei gloriam*—and, at the same time, the notoriety—of the Society of Jesus. Once again, in the dimension of glory, the Church and the profane power enter into a durable threshold of indetermination, in which it is difficult to measure the reciprocal influences and the conceptual exchanges. At the same time as the sovereign territorial state begins to adopt the figure of the "government of men," the Church, setting aside its eschatological preoccupations, increasingly identifies its own mission with the planetary government of souls, not so much for their salvation, as for the "increased glory of God." The indignant reaction of a twentieth-century Catholic philosopher in the face of this God who is merely egotistical, a sort of "eternal Caesar," who only uses men "as an instrument to demonstrate to himself his glory and power," stems from this.

א *It is against the background of the theory of glory from the Baroque era that one can understand how such usually sober-minded thinkers as Malebranche or Leibniz have been able to think the glory of God in terms of his self-satisfaction with his own perfection. Malebranche calls glory "the love that God has for himself," and he pushes the principle according to which God acts only for his own glory to the point at which he ends up denying that the reason for the incarnation is nothing but the will to redeem humanity from sin. Through the incarnation of the Word, God receives a "glory of infinite splendor," and for this reason Malebranche denies that "the Fall was the only cause of the Incarnation of the Son of God" (Malebranche 1923, dialogue 9, § 5, p. 232).*

Equally unedifying is the idea of glory that, following Bayle, Leibniz ascribes to God in his Theodicy:

"God," [Bayle] says, "the Being eternal and necessary, infinitely good, holy, wise and powerful, possesses from all eternity a glory and a bliss that can never increase or diminish." This proposition of M. Bayle's is no less philosophical than theological. To say that God possesses "glory" when he is alone, that depends upon the meaning of the term. One may say, with some, that glory is the satisfaction one finds in being aware of one's own perfections; and in this sense God possesses it always. But when glory signifies that others become aware of these perfections, one may say that God acquires it only when he reveals himself to intelligent creatures; even though it be true that God thereby gains no new good, and it is rather the rational creatures who thence derive advantage, when they apprehend aright the glory of God. (Leibniz, § 109, p. 183)

It is enough to confront these conceptions of glory with what Spinoza writes in the scholium to Proposition 36 of Book V of the Ethics *to measure the abyss that separates them.*

8.13. The title of Lessius's brief treatise (*De ultimo fine*) refers to the condition of the blessed after the Last Judgment. In paradisiacal blessedness, when the work of salvation is complete and "all the movements and ministries" (Lessius, p. 549) have been deactivated, nothing will be left to the angels and the blessed but the contemplation, love, and celebration of the glory of God. They will simply "contemplate his infinite beauty, exult in his glory with ineffable joy, with perpetual praise, benediction, and thanksgiving" (ibid.).

One of the most important points to be discussed with regard to glory is, in fact, precisely the "glory of the elect," that is, the condition of the blessed in paradise. Not only does this imply a transformation of the body that, according to Paul's teaching (1 Corinthians 15:44), now becomes a "glorious body," but the whole rational creature, with its intelligence and will, must participate in the glory of God as the highest good. The heated debate that divides theologians from the time of the early Scholastics concerns the character of this participation. According to Thomas Aquinas and the Dominicans, the element that defines paradisiacal blessedness is the intellect, which is to say, knowledge or the "beatific vision" of God. According to Bonaventure and the Franciscans, blessedness is instead defined as an operation of the will, that is, love.

In 1951, a young Oxford theologian, Eric L. Mascall, published, in a French journal that brought together the writings of theologians such as Jean Daniélou and intellectuals of various backgrounds (among whom were Maurice de Gandillac and Graham Greene), an article that took up the question of blessedness from a perspective that cannot but interest us closely here. According to Mascall, neither knowledge nor love can define in a satisfactory fashion the supreme purpose of man. Not only is knowledge essentially egotistic because it concerns, above all, our enjoyment of God, but it is not ultimately useful either to men or to God—at least not in the postjudicial condition. As far as love is concerned, it cannot be truly disinterested either, because, as Saint Bernard reminded us, to love God without thinking of our happiness at the same time, is a psychological impossibility (Mascall, p. 108).

> The only thing that can define the first and essential element of our blessed state is neither the love nor the knowledge of God but only his *praise*. The only reason to love God is that he is worthy of praise. We do not praise him because it is good for us, although we find our good in it. We do not praise him because it is good for him, because in fact our praise cannot benefit him. (Ibid., p. 112)

The praise that is in question here is, of course, first and foremost doxology and glorification:

> Praise is superior both to love and to knowledge, although it can include both and transform them, because praise does not concern itself with interest but only with glory [. . .] In the worship that on earth we bestow on God, the first place is due to praise as well [. . .] And what scripture allows us to glimpse of celestial worship always shows us praise. The vision of Isaiah in the temple, the song of the angels in Bethlehem, the celestial liturgy of the fourth chapter of Revelation repeat the same thing: *Gloria in excelsis deo* [. . .] "Our Lord and God, you are worthy of receiving glory, honor, and power." (Ibid., p. 114)

Here we discover all the elements of the theory of glory with which we have become familiar. The specific value of glory as the ultimate purpose of man lies, curiously, in the fact that ultimately neither God nor men need it or draw any utility from it. And yet, in contrast to Lassius, praise is not extrinsic to God. "The archetype of all praise can be found within the Trinity itself, within the eternal filial response of the word to God his Father" (ibid., p. 115). God is, in other words, literally composed of praise, and, by glorifying him, men are admitted to participate in his most intimate existence. But if things stand thus, if the praise that men give God is intimate and consubstantial with him, then doxology is, perhaps, in some way a necessary part of the life of the divinity. Basil used the term *homotimos* ("of the same glory") as a synonym for *homousios*, the technical term that in the Nicene symbolism denoted consubstantiality, suggesting thereby a proximity between the glory and the being of God. Perhaps the distinction between internal glory and external glory serves precisely to cover over this intimate link between glorification and the substance of the divinity. What appears in God when the distinction breaks down is something that theology absolutely does not want to see, a nudity that must be covered by a garment of light at any cost.

8.14. Catholic liturgy contains a doxology that bears the curious name of *improperia*, that is, reproaches. It appears for the first time in liturgical texts of the ninth century, but is probably older still. The peculiarity of this doxology is that it is introduced by an antiphon in which God turns to his people and reproaches them: "Popule meus, quid feci tibi aut in quo contristavi te? Responde mihi" (My people, what have I done to you, in what way have I displeased you? Answer me). In other versions, the complaint comes from Christ himself: "Quid ultra debui facere tibi, et non feci?" (What more should I have done that I have not done already?). Only at this point do the deacons respond from the altar, singing the great hymn of praise, *trisagion: Agios ho Theos, agios ischyros, agios athanatos, eleēson hēmas.*

It is decisive in this case that it is God himself who is demanding praise. In the legend contained in the Greek menology, he does not limit himself to uttering reproaches but provokes an earthquake that does not stop until the people and the emperor sing together the doxology "Sanctus Deus, sanctus fortis, sanctus et immortalis, miserere nobis." Lassius's theory, which suggested that the purpose of the divinity's actions could only be that of glorification, is confirmed here. Moreover, according to the anaphora of Basil's liturgy "it is deserving and just, and fitting the greatness of your sanctity, to praise you, sing to you, bless you, adore you, offer up thanks to you, glorify you"; but God appears to need this praise and adoration, to the point of requesting from men the acclamation "three times holy" (*trisagios phonē*) that he already receives from the seraphims in heaven. If, as is recited in John Chrysostom's liturgy, the power of the Lord is incomparable and unrepresentable (*aneikastos*) and his glory surpasses all comprehension (*akataléptos*), why utter it and represent it incessantly in the doxologies? Why call him "sovereign" (*despotēs*); why invoke the "ranks and armies" (*tagmata kai stratias*) of angels and archangels in "the service of his glory" (*leitourgian tēs doxēs*)? The answer that, in the form of an acclamation of the type, *axios*, monotonously accents the anaphora—*hoti prepei soi pasa doxa*, "because all glory is suited to you"—suggests that the *prepei* ("fits, is suited") hides a more intimate necessity: the acclamation has a sense and value that escape us and that we should pursue.

8.15. In the Western Church, the hymn of praise par excellence, the *doxologia maxima*, is the *Te Deum*, the tradition of which has, without any real evidence, been traced back to Ambrose and Augustine. The historians of liturgy who have long debated its authorship, time of composition, and place of origin are more or less in agreement in considering it to contain three parts, which at a certain point were firmly bound together to form its twenty-nine verses: the first (verses 1–13) and oldest is a hymn to the Trinity, probably composed in the Ante-Nicene era; the second (verses 14–21), which is entirely Christological, is probably more recent since it seems to bear witness to the anti-Arian polemics; and the last (verses 22–29) concludes the hymn with a series of quotations from the Psalms.

Scholars, who are as usual entirely concerned with questions of chronology and attribution, omit to say what is nevertheless obvious beyond any possible doubt: whatever its origin might be, the *Te Deum* is formed from start to finish by a series of acclamations in which the Trinitarian and Christological elements are inserted into a substantially uniform doxological and epenetic context. Verses 1–10 appear to have no other purpose than to assure the divinity of the praise and glory that surrounds him on all sides, on earth as in heaven, in the past as in the present:

> *Te Deum laudamus te Dominum confitemur*
> *Te aeternum patrem omnis terra veneratur*
> *Tibi omnes angeli Tibi caeli et universae potestates*
> *Tibi Cherubim et Seraphim incessabili voce proclamant*
> *Sanctus sanctus sanctus Dominus Deus Sabaoth*
> *Pleni sunt caeli et terra maiestatis gloriae tuae*
> *Te gloriosus apostolorum chorus*
> *Te prophetarum laudabilis numerus*
> *Te martyrum candidatus laudat exercitus*
> *Te per orbem terrarum sancta confitetur Ecclesia.*

The mention given to the persons of the Trinity, which follows this meticulous enumeration of the names and functions of the glorifiers, seems to be aimed above all at specifying the one to whom the praise is directed, reiterating it in the form of doxological attributes:

> *Patrem immensae maiestatis*
> *Venerandum tuum verum et unicum Filium*
> *Sanctum quoque paraclytum Spiritum.*

However, even in the following Christological verses, which certainly contain doctrinal elements, as in the formula *hominem suscipere*, Christ is first invoked in eschatological terms as the "king of glory," and it is as such that the faithful who glorify him ask in exchange to be allowed to participate in his eternal glory:

> *Tu rex gloriae Christe*
> *Tu patris sempiternus es filius*
> *Tu ad liberandum suscepisti hominem non horruisti virginis uterum*
> *Tu devicto mortis aculeo aperuisti credentibus regna caelorum*
> *Tu ad dexteram Dei sedes in gloria patris*
> *Iudex crederis esse venturus*
> *Te ergo quaesumus tuis famulis subveni quos pretioso*
> *sanguine redimisti*
> *Aeterna fac cum sanctis tuis in gloria munerari.*

In the final antiphon, one is struck by the biblical citations that assure us that the service of glory will be eternal and ceaseless, day after day, age after age:

> *Per singulos dies benedicimus te*
> *Et laudamus nomen tuum in saeculum et in saeculi saeculum.*

Even more evident is the acclamative structure of the other great doxology, the *Gloria* that the most ancient documents—such as the *Constitution of the Apostles* (AD 380)—attribute to the Matins. In this case the text is nothing more than an uninterrupted collage of acclamations of every type: of praise, benediction, thanks, supplication:

> *Gloria in excelsis Deo*
> *et in terra pax*
> *hominibus bonae voluntatis*

Laudamus te
benedicimus te
adoramus te
glorificamus te
gratias agimus tibi
propter magnam gloriam tuam
Domine Deus rex caelestis
Deus pater omnipotens
Domine Fili unigenite Jesu Christe
Cum Sancto Spiritu
Domine Deus agnus Dei
Filius patris, qui tollis peccata mundi
Miserere nobis [. . .]

As we have seen, Peterson, Alföldi, and Kantorowicz have shown that liturgical acclamations often have a profane origin, that the formulae of the liturgy of glory are derived from the acclamations of the imperial ceremonials. It is, however, probable that the exchange took place in both directions. We know, for example, that both the *Te Deum* and the *Gloria* have had an extraliturgical use, the former on the battlefields (at Las Novas de Tolosa and in Liège in 1213) and the latter at the time of the discovery of the body of the martyr Mallosus and of the arrival of Pope Leo III at the court of Charlemagne. In all these instances, it was a case of a sudden explosion of triumph and jubilation, as is often the case with acclamations. But how can one explain, beyond the relation between profane and religious ceremonials, the massive presence of acclamations in the Christian liturgy? Why must God be continually praised, even if the theologians (at least up to a certain point in history) never tire of assuring us that he has no need of it? Does the distinction between internal and external glory, which reciprocally respond to one another, really constitute a sufficient explanation? Does it not rather betray the attempt to explain the unexplainable, to hide something that it would be too embarrassing to leave unexplained?

8.16. Marcel Mauss's unfinished doctoral thesis on prayer, which was only published in 1968, has rightly been called "one of the most important works" (Mauss 1968, p. 356) that the great French anthropologist has left us. He begins by noting—and his observations of 1909 interestingly remind one of Kantorowicz's analogous considerations on the situation of liturgical studies almost forty years later—the singular poverty of scientific literature on such an important question. Philologists, who are more used to analyzing the meaning of words than their efficacy, were put off by the unquestionably ritualistic character of prayer; the anthropologists, solely occupied with the study of primitive cultures, put to one side what appeared to them to be a late product in the evolution of religions. Therefore, once again the subject was abandoned and left in the hands of theologians and philosophers of religion whose theories are, for obvious reasons, "the account they give of their experiences [which] is in no way scientific" (Mauss 2003, p. 29).

Mauss's thesis comes to a sudden end after 175 pages, when presumably he was about to draw the final consequences from his analysis of the oral rites of an Australian people, the Arunta, which he had chosen as his *terrain de recherche*; but both in the previous pages and in an almost contemporaneous series of articles, he leaves no doubt as to the hypothesis that guided his research. Prayer—even when it takes the form of praise or a hosanna—is, above all, an oral rite and, therefore, like all rites, an "effective act" that concerns sacred things and acts upon them. As such, it is

> also efficacious and with a *sui generis* efficacy, for the words of prayer can give rise to the most extraordinary phenomena. Certain early rabbis, by saying the appropriate *berakâ* (blessing), could change water into fire and the great kings, by using certain formulae, could change impious Brahmins into insects which were then devoured by towns that had been changed into ant hills. Even when all efficacy seems to have disappeared from prayer which has become pure adoration, or when all power seems to be confined to a god, as in Catholic, Jewish or Islamic prayer, it is still efficacious because it causes the God to act in a certain way. (Ibid., p. 54)

It is not always easy, from this perspective, to distinguish between magic and religion: "There are all sorts of degrees between incantations and prayers, as there are generally between the rites of magic and those of religion" (ibid., p. 55). Nevertheless, Mauss distinguishes magical rites from religious ones because, while the former appear to be endowed with an immanent power, the latter produce their effects only through the intervention of divine powers, which exist outside the rite itself. "Thus the Indian performs a magic rite when, in hunting, he believes that he is able to stop the sun by placing a stone at a certain height in a tree, whereas Joshua performed a religious rite when, in order to stop the same sun, he

invoked the omnipotence of Jahweh" (ibid., p. 53). And while the aim of
spells and magical rituals is not to influence sacred beings, but to produce
an immediate effect upon reality, prayer "on the contrary, is above all
a means of acting upon sacred beings; it is they who are influenced by
prayer, they who are changed" (ibid., p. 56). Before turning to his field-
work, he defines prayer as follows: "*Prayer is a religious rite which is oral
and bears directly on the sacred*" (ibid., p. 57).

A work that had considerable influence on Mauss's thought, and of
which he wrote a review only a year after it was published, was *La doctrine du sacrifice dans le Brâhmanas* (1899). The author, Sylvain Levi, who
had been his indology teacher in Paris, wanted to show that the oldest
Brahmin religion "had no moral qualities" and that sacrifice is essentially
defined by its material effects: "It resides completely in the acts and ends
with them, and it consists entirely in the scrupulous observance of rites"
(Mauss 1968, p. 353). The most surprising result of Levi's research was,
however, that Indian sacrifice is not simply an effective action, as are
all rites; it does not limit itself to merely influencing the gods; it creates
them:

> According to the theologians of the Vedic era, the gods, like the demons, are
> born from sacrifice. It is thanks to it that they have ascended to the heavens,
> in the same way as the one who carries out a sacrifice still does. They gather
> around the sacrifice; they are a product of the sacrifice that they share among
> themselves, and it is this distribution that determines the way in which they
> share the world. Moreover, sacrifice is not only the author of the gods. It is a
> god itself or, rather, the god par excellence. It is the master, the indeterminate,
> infinite god, the spirit from which everything proceeds, that ceaselessly dies
> and is reborn. (Ibid.)

Thus, both sacrifice and prayer present us with a theurgical aspect in
which men, by performing a series of rituals—more gestural in the case
of sacrifice, more oral in that of prayer—act on the gods in a more or less
effective manner. If this is true, the hypothesis of a primacy of glorification over glory should be considered in a new light. Perhaps glorification
is not only that which best fits the glory of God but is itself, as effective
rite, what produces glory; and if glory is the very substance of God and
the true sense of his economy, then it depends upon glorification in an
essential manner and, therefore, has good reason to demand it through
reproaches and injunctions.

א *In peremptorily advancing his idea of the theurgical character of prayer, Mauss was taking up an idea that Émile Durkheim—with whom he enjoyed close intellectual and familial relations—had put forward in his* Elementary Forms of Religious Life. *Durkheim writes:*

> It is necessary, then, to refrain from believing, with Smith, that the cult was instituted only for the benefit of men and that the gods have no use for it. They still need it as much as their faithful do. No doubt, the men could not live without gods; but on the other hand, the gods would die if they were not worshipped. Thus the purpose of the cult is not only to bring the profane into the communion with sacred beings but also to keep the sacred beings alive, to remake and regenerate them perpetually. (Durkheim, p. 350)

8.17. The idea that there is a close relationship between human behaviors—in particular oral rites—and the glory of God is present in rabbinical literature as well as in the Kabbalah. Charles Mopsik dedicated to this theme an exemplary study whose subtitle is significant: *Les rites qui font Dieu* (The Rites That Make God) (1993). That the Kabbalah contained theurgical elements was well known; Mopsik, however, demonstrates through the analysis of an extraordinary quantity of texts not only that it is one of its absolutely central motifs but also that analogous themes are already clearly present in early rabbinical literature. Alongside texts that repeat the by now familiar principle that observance of worship "neither helps nor harms God," as we have seen through the discussion of the Christian tradition, one also finds numerous testimonies that point decisively in the opposite direction. Already in the Midrash on Lamentations we can read that "when the Israelites carry out the will of the blessed Saint, whoever he may be, they strengthen the force of the Power above, as it is written, 'let the power of my lord be great' (Numbers 14:17). And when they do not carry out the will of the Saint, may he be blessed, they weaken the strength from above and, in this way, they also walk without strength before he who persecutes them" (in Mopsik, p. 53). According to other rabbinical sources, prayers and laudations have the remarkable power of crowning YHVH with a regal diadem that the angel Sandalphon weaves for him by invoking his name in what appears to be a veritable coronation ceremony, in which God, as the Midrash states, "forces himself to receive a crown from his servants." But Mopsik is able to demonstrate with ease that YHVH's very regality seems to depend in some way on the prayers of the just (ibid., p. 58).

In the Kabbalah, this theurgical conception attains its full stature. A direct relationship between worship and glory, identified with the *sefirah* Malkut (the Kingdom), is at the center of the thinking of Shem Tov ibn Shem Tov as much as of Meir ibn Gabbai, a Spanish kabbalist who dedicated his principal work to this relationship, *The Book of Sacred Worship* (1531). Shem Tov, taking up again the Midrash on Lamentations, argues that ritual practices provoke an "overflowing" of the celestial world onto the terrestrial:

> The forms of the lower world in fact have their root in the superior reality, because man is an upside-down tree, the roots of which are in the air. If man is united with the Glory of the Name and sanctifies himself and concentrates, he will be able to bring about the overflowing into the higher glory, in the same way as when one lights a fire or a lamp to illuminate the home. But if man neglects to worship the divine and despairs of it, this causes the reabsorption of the divine light that was shining on the lower beings. (In Mopsik, p. 260)

For his part, Ibn Gabbai, forcing a rabbinical expression that means "for the needs of the temple," announces a veritable theurgical theorem in the form: "Worship is 'a need of the one who is Highest'" (ibid., p. 365). Adopting a bold musical metaphor, the relationship of worship and glory is compared to that of two musical instruments tuned by the same tuning fork, "so that, through the vibration of a chord in one of them, we bring about a corresponding vibration in the other" (ibid., p. 367).

In the great texts of the medieval Kabbalah, the statement of the theurgical character of worship turns on the interpretation of Psalms 119:126, in which the verse that can mean "it is time for thee, Lord, to work" is interpreted as though it meant "it is time to make God" (Mopsik, p. 371). In the face of the extreme consequences of such an exegesis, scholars have asked how it is possible that such a radical thesis, which implies that man was, ultimately, "the creator of the creator"—or at least he who sustains his being and perpetually "fixes" him—could have emerged within a religion that never stopped denouncing the vanity of the pagan gods, created by men. And yet, in the tripartite form of "making the Name," "making the Saturday," and "making God," such a thesis is formulated beyond any doubt in the cabalists of Gerona and in the *Zohar* as much as in the Kabbalah after the expulsion from Spain: "He who observes a commandment below, affirms it and makes it above" (Azriel of Gerona in Mopsik, p. 558).

To make, here, does not necessarily mean to create *ex novo*: the idea is, rather, that without ritual practices, the divine pleroma loses its strength and decays; that God, in other words, needs to be continually restored and repaired by the pity of men, in the same way that he is weakened by their impiety. On the basis of the close link between worship and glory that we have already observed, the cabalists speak in this sense of a "restoration of glory."

> Carrying out commandments below, one carries them out above, and their archetype awakens so as to restore the superior Glory [...] It is a case of the restoration of Glory, the secret of the glorious Name [...] The right below awakens the right above and together they restore and make the superior Glory and augment and intensify his energy [...] (Gabbai in Mopsik, p. 602)

This conception is so solid, diffuse, and coherent that, at the end of his investigation, Mopsik, evoking Durkheim's thesis on the divine need of worship, discreetly suggests that he might have been influenced by the Kabbalah: "Durkheim, who was the son of a rabbi, began his studies at the Rabbinical School in Paris. Let us leave to the historians of sociology the task of drawing conclusions from this, if it is right to do so" (Mopsik, p. 648).

8.18. It was not our intention to formulate hypotheses on the theurgic origins of the doxologies and acclamations, nor was it to announce scientific mythologems on the genesis of glory. As we have seen, sociologists, anthropologists, and historians of religion have, in part, already effectively confronted this problem. For us the task is rather to try, once again, to understand the functioning of the governmental machine, whose bipolar structure we have tried to define in the course of our investigation and which was the reason for the archaeology of glory that we have sketched out. The analysis of the theology of glory is only the shadow that our inquiry into the structure of power casts over the past. That doxologies and acclamations are, in the final instance, concerned with producing and augmenting glory is, of course, something that interests us. It is not necessary to share Schmitt's thesis on secularization in order to affirm that political problems become more intelligible and clear if they are related to theological paradigms. On the contrary, we have tried to show that this comes about because doxologies and acclamations in some sense constitute a threshold of indifference between politics and theology. Just as liturgical doxologies produce and strengthen God's glory, so the profane acclamations are not an ornament of political power but found and justify it. And just as the immanent trinity and economic trinity, *theologia* and *oikonomia* constitute, within the providential paradigm, a bipolar machine from whose distinction and correlation stems the government of the world, so Kingdom and Government constitute the two elements or faces of the same machine of power.

However, beyond merely registering this correspondence, our interest lies in understanding its operation. In what way does liturgy "make" power? And if the governmental machine is twofold (Kingdom and Government), what function does glory play within it? For sociologists and anthropologists it always remains possible to turn to magic as the sphere that, bordering upon rationality and immediately preceding it, allows one to explain that which we do not understand about the society in which we live as ultimately a magical survival. We do not believe in the magical power of acclamations and of liturgy, and we are convinced that not even theologians or emperors really believed in it. If glory is so important in theology it is, above all, because it allows one to bring together within the governmental machine immanent trinity and economic trinity, the being of God and his praxis, Kingdom and Government. By defining the Kingdom and the essence, it also determines the sense of the economy and of Government. It allows, that is, for us to bridge that fracture between theology and economy that the doctrine of the trinity has never been able to completely resolve and for which only the dazzling figure of glory is able to provide a possible conciliation.

8.19. In Christian liturgy, *amen* is the acclamation par excellence. Already in the biblical usage of this term, which belongs to the semantic sphere of stability and fidelity, it is used as the acclamation of consensus or in response to a doxology (*berakhah*) and, later, in the synagogue, as the response to a benediction. This anaphoric function of *amen*, which must always refer to a word that precedes it—which, typically, must not be enunciated by the one who says *amen*—is essential. The enunciation of this acclamation was so important in Judaism that in the Talmud (b Tractate Shabbat, 119b) one finds the phrase: "He who answers *amen* with all his strength opens the doors of paradise for himself." Paul's frequent use of the word at the end of a doxology (Romans 1:25: "Blessed for ever.

Amen") is perfectly coherent with this tradition, which we find in the most ancient Christian liturgy, particularly in the acclamation at the end of the prayer of the Eucharist (*omnes respondent: amen*). After what we have seen regarding the particular relation that unites glory with the divine essence, we will not be surprised that in the Talmud, to the question "What does *amen* mean?" (b Tractate Shabbat, 119b) one may reply "God, the faithful king" (*el melek ne'eman*); and that an analogous identification of divinity and acclamation can be found in Revelation 3:14 where Christ is defined as "the Amen, the true witness" (*ho Amēn, ho martys ho pistos*).

It is interesting to follow the story of the translation of this term—or rather, of its nontranslation into Greek and Latin. The Septuagint, which frequently renders it as *genoito* (let it be) and sometimes with *alēthōs* (truly), frequently leaves it untranslated (as in Nehemiah 8:6: "And all the people answered, Amen"). The New Testament limits itself to transcribing it into Greek letters, although in some passages *alēthōs* and *nai* appear to presuppose an *amēn*. On the other hand, the Latin translations of the Old Testament, following the *genoito* of the Septuagint, render *amen* as *fiat*.

Augustine, on more than one occasion, poses the problem of the appropriateness of translating the term into Latin. He is aware of the quasi-juridical value of the acclamation, which significantly he compares to some institutions of Roman law ("Fratres mei, amen vestrum subscriptio vestra est, consensio vestra est, adstipulatio vestra est": "My brothers, your amen is your signature [*firma*], your consensus, your agreement as guarantors to a contract": Augustine, *Sermons,* fragment 3). In the small treatise on translation contained in *De doctrina christiana,* he distinguishes the two terms *amen* and *halleluiah,* which are not translated but could be, from interjections such as *hosanna* and *racha,* which, since they express a feeling rather than a concept, "are said to be untranslatable into another tongue" (Augustine, *On Christian Doctrine,* Book 2, Chapter 11, § 16, p. 641). He notes, however, that the term *amen* has remained untranslated "propter sanctiorem auctoritatem," on account of the more sacred authority that attaches to it (ibid.) ("authority," another term that derives from the lexicon of law). And in relation to the doxologies, Isidore takes up Augustine's observation, stating that "it is not permitted for Greek, Latin, or barbarian to translate these two words, *alleluia* and *amen,* wholly into their own language" (Isidore, *The Etymologies,* 6, 19–20, p. 147).

The constant tendency to transform acclamations that, originally, may even have been spontaneous, into ritual formulae is present in profane liturgies just as much as it is in religious ones. It goes hand in hand with a desemanticization of the terms through which the acclamations are expressed; like the *amen*, they are often intentionally left in the original language. Numerous testimonies reveal how, already in the fourth century, the faithful appeared to understand *amen* as a simple formula that marked the end of a prayer and not as an acclamation that answers to a doxology.

As in the case of every acclamation, its effect and function are more important than the comprehension of its meaning. The audience who, today, in a French or American concert hall cry out "bravo," might not know its precise meaning or the grammar of the Italian term (not varying it even if it is said of a woman or to more than one person), but they know perfectly well the effect that the acclamation must produce. It rewards the actor or virtuoso and obliges him to return to the stage. Those who know about show business go so far as to claim that actors need applause in the same way that one needs nourishment. This means that, in the sphere of doxologies and acclamations, the semantic aspect of language is deactivated and appears for a moment as an empty rotation; and, yet, it is precisely this empty turning that supplies it with its peculiar, almost magical, efficacy: that of producing glory.

א *It has often been noted that in the Gospels Jesus uses* amen *in a way that has no parallel in the Old Testament nor in rabbinical literature; he uses it not as a liturgical response but instead at the beginning of his statements, in expressions of the form:* Amēn amēn legō ymin *[. . .] (in the Vulgate:* Amen amen dico vobis*). It is possible to glimpse in this particular use something like a self-conscious messianic transformation of acclamation into affirmation, of the doxology that approves and repeats into a position that, at least in appearance, innovates and transgresses.*

8.20. Among the manuscripts that Mauss left unfinished at the time of his death, there is a study of the notion of nourishment (*anna*) in the Brahmana, the theological part of the Veda. Among the notions—at once "curiously abstract and surprisingly coarse" (Mauss, *Manuscript,* p. 1)—invented by the Brahmins of the Vedic era, "nourishment" is one of the most primitive. Already in the Rig-Veda one of the aims of sacrifice is to obtain nourishment, the juice and strength that food contains; and among the gods, there are two whose principal attribute is that of nourishing themselves: "Agni, the god of fire, who is nourished by the combustible, and Indra, the god who drinks *soma*, who is nourished by the sacrifice of this ambrosia (*amrita*), this essence of immortality" (ibid., pp. 3–4). But it is in the Brahmana that the doctrine of nourishment attains a theological and "almost philosophical" (ibid., p. 18) consistency. The *anna* is no longer the nourishment of this or that god; it is "nourishment in general, *anna*-in-itself, *annadya*, the edible, and the possession of what is edible" (ibid., p. 8). The *annadya* thereby becomes one of the qualities that define the *kshatra*, regal power. Not only does the king, to whom sacrifices are offered, become the "lord of nourishment"; we also see the gradual birth of a veritable "cult of nourishment" in India, having the character of a public cult, in the course of which nourishment "becomes the object of a kind of divinization" (ibid., p. 14). The *anna*, stripping itself of its material qualities, becomes the principle of life, the force that maintains and augments life; "one might almost say that nourishment is the vital breath and spirit" (ibid., p. 20). Insofar as it is the living principle and the active and spiritual essence, nourishment can be common to men as much as it is to the gods, and "sacrifice is nothing but the nourishment of the gods" (ibid., p. 24) in which men participate and from which they also draw nourishment. It is precisely in developing this idea of nourishment that Mauss is able to recount the tale of the formation, beyond the pantheon of the divine persons, of the idea of Prajapati, of a "unique, cosmic existence, of a God, male and firstborn, at once sacrifice and offering" (ibid., p. 28). On the last page, just before the manuscript abruptly breaks off, in the course of describing the cultural function of the Prajapati, Mauss appears to intentionally evoke, without ever naming, the Christian sacrifice: the body of Prajapati is "the matter of the universal feast [. . .] the supreme host that nourishes this entire world"; he is the nourishment-god who, in saying "there is no other nourishment than me," offers himself up as a sacrifice for the life of his creatures (ibid., p. 29). "The divine essence," concludes Mauss, "was, from this point of view, a food, nutrition itself. God was food" (ibid.).

Among the papers that refer to the incomplete study of nourishment in the Brahmana, there is a brief article, "Anna-Viraj," in which the theory of *anna* is taken in an unexpected direction. The *viraj* is a metrical Vedic form composed of three feet of ten syllables each (the title could be translated as "nourishment-hymn"). The Brahmana regards this metrical form as itself possessing a fundamental and specific nutritional virtue. "The ideal of the Brahmins was to compose through a collection of hymns, of songs [. . .], a male life, a bird, animal, or man and offer this supreme mystical food to the eating god, creator of the world" (Mauss 1974, p. 594). What is decisive here is that the hymn, the *viraj*, does not simply produce the food, but *is* food in-itself. In order to assure at all costs the presence of nourishment, the Brahmins would employ the rites of mantra composed with this meter; and lacking these, verses and formulae from other sources would be transposed, prosodically, into the form of the *viraj*. "Arbitrary pauses after every ten syllables; interruptions with musical cries repeated ten times; any expedient, barbarous or refined, is used to force songs intended to be sung in other forms into the procrustean bed of the *viraj*" (ibid., p. 595). The link between the metrical form and its nutritious character is so essential that the Brahmin theologians affirm without reserve that if one sings the hymn in the form of the *viraj*, "that is because the *viraj* has ten syllables, because the *viraj* is nutrition" (ibid., p. 597). The link is so intimate that Mauss, in the unfinished manuscript on the notion of nutrition, appears to suggest that the speculations on the *anna*-nutrition could precisely enable one to comprehend the sense of the prosodic structure of the Veda: "These hymns, songs, meters, these things expressed through numbers, these numbers, these rhythmical gestures, veiled words, cries that mean nutrition and are arranged, in relation to others, like food is arranged within the body or near it, all is part of a system of which we will discover the explanation when we have carried out the history of the ideas and the symbols concerning food" (Mauss, *Manuscript*, pp. 15–16).

In the theology of the Brahmana, the gods nourish themselves with hymns, and men, who ritually sing the *viraj*, provide for the gods' nourishment in this way (and indirectly provide for their own as well). This perhaps permits us to unexpectedly shed some light on the essence of liturgy. Just as in the case of the Eucharistic sacrifice, the god who offers himself as nourishment to men can do so only in the context of the doxological canon, so in the Brahmana, the metrical form of the hymn must be ritually fixed since it amounts to the food of god. And vice versa.

8.21. That the ultimate purpose of the word is to celebrate is a recurrent theme in the poetic tradition of the West. The specific form of celebration in this tradition is the hymn. The Greek term *hymnos* is derived from the ritual acclamation that was shouted out during the marriage ceremony: *hymēn* (frequently followed by *hymenaios*). It does not correspond to a definite metrical form, but, from the time of the most ancient attestations in the so-called Homeric hymns, it refers above all to the song in honor of the gods. This, in any case, is its content in Christian hymnology, which flourishes in the fourth century, if not earlier, with Ephrem the Syrian, Ambrose, Hilary, and Prudentius among the Latin speakers, and Gregory of Nazianzus and Synesius from the Eastern Church. Isidore defines it in tripartite form: praise, the object of praise (God), and song:

> Hymnus est canticus laudantium, quod de Graeco in Latino laus interpretatur, pro eo quod sit carmen laetitiae et laudis. Proprie autem hymni sunt continentes laudem Dei. Si ergo sit laus et non sit Dei, non est hymnus; si sit et laus et Dei laus, et non cantetur, non est hymnus. Si ergo et in laudem Dei dicitur et cantatur, tunc est hymnus.

> (The hymn is the song of he who praises, which in Greek means "praise," because it is a poem of joy and praise. But hymns in the proper sense are those that contain praise of God. If, therefore, there is praise but not of God, it is not a hymn; if there is praise of God, but it is not sung, it is not a hymn. If, on the other hand, it is in praise of God and is sung, only then is it a hymn.) (Isidore, *The Etymologies*, 6, 19, 17)

Sacred hymnology begins its irreversible decline at the end of the Middle Ages. The Franciscan *Laudes creaturarum*, despite not being fully part of the hymnological tradition, constitutes the last great example of it and, at the same time, marks its end. Modern poetry is more elegiac than hymnological, despite some important exceptions in the German tradition in particular (as well as in the Italian, as is the case with Manzoni's *Sacred Hymns*).

In the poetry of the 1900s, Rilke is a case apart. He dressed up an indubitably hymnological intention in the garb of elegy and lament. The almost liturgical aura of sacredness that has always surrounded the *Duino Elegies* is probably owed to this contamination of elements, to this spurious attempt to grasp a dead poetic form. Their hymnological character, in the technical sense, is evident from the first verse, which calls into question the angelic hierarchies ("Who, if I cried out, would hear me among the angelic orders?": Rilke 2000, p. 5), that is, precisely those who must share the hymn with men ("For the reason why we recite this doxology is to share in the singing [*koinōnoi tēs hymnōdias* (. . .) *genōmetha*] of the angelic armies," writes Cyril of Jerusalem in his *Mystagogic Catechesis*, p. 183). The angels, to whom Rilke addresses his hymn of praise ("Praise the world to the Angel": Rilke 2000, 9, 53, p. 55), which they sing along with him, remain to the end the privileged interlocutors of the poet ("may I emerge singing praise and jubilation to the assenting angels [*zustimmenden Engeln*] who join in the song": ibid., 10, 1–2, p. 59). And in the *Sonnets to Orpheus*, which Rilke considered to be an essential companion to the *Elegies* and almost a kind of esoteric exegesis of the same, he clearly announces the hymnological (that is, celebratory) vocation of his poems: "Rühmen, das ists!," "Praising, that's it!" (Rilke 1987, 7, 1, p. 15). The eighth sonnet thus supplies the key to the elegiac titles of his hymns: the lamentation (*Klage*) can exist only in the sphere of celebration ("Nur im Raum der Rühmung darf die Klage / gehn [. . .]": ibid., 8, 1–2) just as in the tenth elegy the hymn passes with equal necessity into the sphere of the lament.

Furio Jesi, who has dedicated some exemplary studies to Rilke's work, in a planned preface to an edition of the *Elegies* that would never see the light of day, overturns the customary critical accounts that glimpse in the *Elegies* an exceptionally rich doctrinal content. He asks whether it makes sense to speak of "content" in this case. He proposes to bracket out the doctrinal content of the *Elegies* (which is in any case a sort of rehash of the clichés of Rilke's poetry) and to read them as a series of rhetorical possibilities that keep the poet from remaining silent. The poet wants to speak, but what wants to speak within him is the unknowable. For this reason,

> The discourse that resonates has no content: it is a pure will to discourse. The content of the voice of the secret that ultimately resonates is nothing other than the fact that "the secret speaks." For this to occur, it is necessary that the modalities of discourse are emptied out of all content, and that this is done in a totalizing manner in order to bring to an end all the activity that has gone before, all the words uttered, at a single point. The organization of the multitude of Rilkean commonplaces, even of the oldest, in the context of the *Elegies*, follows from this. But so does the necessity for there to be somewhere for the content of these *topoi* to flow, so that in the *Elegies* they are able to echo in vain [. . .] (Jesi, p. 118)

Jesi's definition of the *Elegies* as a poem that has nothing to say, as a pure "asseveration of the semantic nucleus of the word" (ibid., p. 120), is valid—in truth—for the hymn in general; that is, it defines the most profound intention of every doxology. At the point where it perfectly coincides with glory, praise is without content; it culminates in the *amen* that says nothing but merely assents to and concludes what has already been said. And what the *Elegies* lament and, at the same time, celebrate (according to the principle that lamentation can take place only in the sphere of celebration) is precisely the incurable absence of the content of the hymn, the turning in the void of language as the supreme form of glorification. The hymn is the radical deactivation of signifying language, the word rendered completely inoperative and, nevertheless, retained as such in the form of liturgy.

א *In the final years of his poetic production, between 1800 and 1805, Hölderlin composed a series of often fragmentary and unfinished poems that have traditionally been called "hymns." And in the technical sense they are hymns, because their content is fundamentally concerned with the gods and demigods (here, the latter can be said to take the place of the angels in some way). Nevertheless, because of a decisive shift, what these hymns celebrate is not the presence of the gods but their departure. In other words, Hölderlin's late hymns are the symmetrical inverse of Rilke's elegies: whereas the latter are hymns dressed up as elegies, Hölderlin writes elegies in the form of hymns. This sober inversion, this irruption of elegy into an alien context, is marked metrically by the breaking of the hymn's rhythm. The particularly fierce prosodic fragmentation that characterizes Hölderlin's hymns has not escaped the notice of the critics. It is precisely in order to underline this tearing apart of the syntactic structure that Adorno called his reading of Hölderlin's final literary productions "Parataxis." Norbert von Hellingrath, who in 1913 edited the first philologically accurate posthumous edition of Hölderlin's writings, had registered this prosodic breaking more thoroughly. He drew on Alexandrine philology—in particular the work of Dionysius of Halicarnassus—the poetological distinction between* harmonia austera *and* harmonia glaphyra *(or austere connection—whose greatest exemplar is Pindar—and elegant connection—literally "hollow," derived from* glaphy, *"cave") and translated it into modern terms such as* harte *and* glatte Fügung, *hard articulation and flat articulation. In his comments on Hölderlin's translation of Pindar's fragments, he writes: "We can render this Greek terminology with 'hard articulation' and 'flat articulation' and establish that it is realized through the hard or flat character of the syntactical articulation of single elements in the three parallel strata of the poem: the rhythm of the words, the* melos, *and the sound" (Hellingrath, pp. 20–21). It is not so much the parataxis itself that defines the hard articulation as that, in it, single words are isolated from their semantic context to the point of constituting a sort of autonomous unity, whereas in the case of the flat articulation, the images and the syntactic context subordinate and link together a number of words. "The hard articulation does all it can to emphasize the word itself, imparting it to the listener and tearing it, as much as possible, from the associative context of the images and feelings to which it belonged" (ibid., p. 23).*

The broken prosody and the almost aprosody of Hölderlin's late hymns could not be characterized more precisely. The single words—sometimes even simple conjunctions such as aber, *"but"—are isolated and jealously wrapped up in themselves; and the reading of the verse and the strophe is nothing but a succession of scansions and caesura in which all discourse and all meaning appear to break up and retract, as in a sort of prosodic and semantic paralysis. In this "staccato" of rhythm and thought, the hymn exhibits the elegy—that is, the lament for the taking leave of the gods or, rather, for the impossibility of the hymn—as its only proper content. Poetry's bitter tendency to isolate words, which the Alexandrines used to call "free style," can be defined as "hymnical." It rests on the fact that every doxology is ultimately concerned with the celebration of the name, that is, with the enunciation and repetition of the divine names. In hymn, all names tend to be isolated and become desemanticized in the proper names of the divine. In this sense, every poem presupposes the hymn—however distant they are—which is to say, it is only possible against the backdrop and within the horizon of the divine names. In other words, poetry is a field of tensions traversed by the currents of the* harmonia austera *and the* harmonia glaphyra, *and at whose polar extremes there stand, on the one hand, hymn, which celebrates the name and, on the other hand, elegy, which is the lament for the impossibility of proffering the divine names. Breaking the hymn, Hölderlin shatters the divine names and, at the same time, takes leave of the gods.*

The most extreme form of the hymnical isolation of the word in modern poetry may be found in the work of Mallarmé. Mallarmé has enduringly sealed French poetry by giving a genuinely hymnical purpose to an unheard of exasperation of harmonia austera. *The latter disarticulates and breaks the metrical structure of the poem to such an extent that it literally explodes in a handful of names without links, disseminated across the page. Isolated in a "vibratile suspension" from their syntactic context, the words, restored to their status of* nomina sacra, *are exhibited—in Mallarmé's words—as "ce qui ne se dit pas du discourse," as that which in language tenaciously resists the discourse of meaning. This hymnological explosion of the poem is the* Coup de dés. *In this unrecitable doxology, the poet, in a gesture that is at once an initiation and an epilogue, has constituted modern lyric poetry in the form of an a-theological (or rather, theo-alogical) liturgy, in comparison to which the celebratory intention of Rilke's elegy seems decidedly belated.*

8.22. The special relation that ties glory to inoperativity is one of the recurrent themes of economic theology that we have tried to reconstruct. Inasmuch as it names the ultimate ends of man and the condition that follows the Last Judgment, glory coincides with the cessation of all activity and all works. It is what remains after the machine of divine *oikonomia* has reached its completion and the hierarchy of angelic ministries has become completely inoperative. While in hell something like penal administration is still in operation, paradise not only knows no government, but also no writing, reading, no theology, and even no liturgical celebration—besides doxology, the hymn of glory. Glory occupies the place of postjudicial inoperativity; it is the eternal *amen* in which all works and all divine and human words are resolved.

In Judaism, inoperativity as the dimension most proper to God and man is given a grandiose image in the Sabbath. Indeed, the festivity of the Jews par excellence has its theological foundation in the fact that it is not the work of creation that is considered sacred but the day on which all work ceases (Genesis 2:2–3; Exodus 20:11). Thus, inoperativity is the name of what is most proper to God ("{Only God truly posses inoperative [*anapauesthai*] being}": Philo, *On the Cherubim*, § 90, p. 89; "{The Sabbath, which means inoperativity [*anapausis*], belongs to God}": ibid., § 87, p. 89) and, at the same time, that which is awaited in eschatology ("They should not enter into my inoperativity [*eis tēn katapausin mou*]": Psalms 95:11).

In Paul's Letters, in particular the Epistle to the Hebrews, the eschatological theme of inoperativity is introduced through a Midrash on Psalm 95:11. Paul (or whoever is the author of the epistle) calls "sabbatism" (*sabbatismos*: Hebrews 4:9) the inoperativity and beatitude that await the people of God.

> Let us therefore fear, lest, a promise being left us of entering into his inoperativity [*katapausis*], some of you will be excluded from it. For unto us was the gospel preached, as well as unto them: but the word preached did not profit them, not being mixed with faith in them that heard it. For we who have believed do enter into inoperativity, as He said, *As I have sworn in my wrath,*

if they shall enter into my inoperativity: although the works were finished from the foundation of the world. For He spake in a certain place of the seventh day on this wise, *And God did rest the seventh day from all His works.* And in this place again, *they shall not enter into my inoperativity.* Seeing therefore it remaineth that some must enter therein, and they to whom it was first preached entered not in because of their lack of obedience: Again, He limiteth a certain day, saying in David, Today, after so long a time; as it is said, *Today if ye will hear His voice, harden not your hearts.* For if Joshua had given them inoperativity, then would He not afterward have spoken of another day? There remaineth therefore a sabbatism to the people of God. For he that is entered into His inoperativity, he also hath ceased from his own works, as God did from His. (Hebrews 4:1–10)

The link that Paul, developing a biblical and rabbinical motif, establishes between the eschatological condition, Sabbath, and inoperativity profoundly marks the Christian conception of the Kingdom. In his commentary on the Epistle to the Hebrews, John Chrysostom identifies without reservation inoperativity, sabbatism, and the Kingdom of heaven: "For [Paul] said not inoperativity but 'Sabbath-keeping'; calling the kingdom 'Sabbath-keeping,' by the appropriate name" (John Chrysostom, *Homilies on the Epistle to the Hebrews* 6, § 2, p. 654); "What other inoperativity [*katapausis*] then is there, except the kingdom of Heaven [*basileia tōn ouranōn*], of which the Sabbath was an image and type [*eikōn kai typos*]?" (ibid., 6, § 7, p. 651). Sabbatism is the name of eschatological glory that is, in essence, inoperativity. *The Clementine Homilies*, a text strongly influenced by Judeo-Christian traditions, defines God himself as Saturday and inoperativity. In an extremely dense theological passage, after attributing to God the name "nothing" (*to ouden*) and linking him to the void, the author writes: "This is the mystery of the Sabbath [*hebdomados mystērion*]. He Himself is the inoperativity of all things [*tōn holōn anapausis*]" (Clement of Alexandria, *The Clementine Homilies*, Chapter 17, § 10, pp. 320–321). And in the Pseudo-Dionysius, in the passage that we have already cited on hymnology, glory, the hymnical, and inoperativity are tightly conjoined and the hymns of the angels are defined as "divine places of thearchical inoperativity [*theioi topoi tēs thearchikēs* (. . .) *katapauseōs*]" (*Celestial Hierarchy*, 7, 57).

It is in Augustine that this theme becomes a problem or, more precisely, the supreme theological problem, that of the eternal Saturday ("sabbatum non habens vesperam," "the Saturday that does not set"), which concludes—in a sublime and, at the same time, tortured glimpse—*The City of God*, that is, the work that contains his most extreme meditation on theology and politics. Immediately, the problem is clearly announced in all its simplicity: "How the saints shall be employed when they are clothed in immortal and spiritual bodies [*Quid acturi sint in corporibus inmortalibus atque spiritalibus sancti*]?" (*The City of God*, Book XXII, Chapter 29, p. 691). Augustine realizes that one cannot properly speak either of "action" or *otium* and that the problem of the final inoperativity of creatures surpasses the intelligence of both men and angels. What is in question is "'the peace of God which,' as the apostle says, 'passeth all understanding'" (ibid.).

The vision of this "peace" is, for Augustine, so difficult to conceive that, on the one hand, he is keen to qualify it by stating that it will not only be intellectual, because we will see God through the senses of our glorious body. On the other hand, he forgets that what is in question is precisely a "peace" and appears to maintain that on the eternal Saturday we will see God govern a new heaven and a new earth (ibid.). But he quickly returns to the decisive question, that of the unthinkable nature of the inoperativity of the blessed. It is a case of a new state that knows no acedia (*desidia*) or need (*indigentia*), and whose movements, which it is impossible even merely to imagine, will nevertheless be full of glory and decorum (ibid., XXII, 30). He finds no other adequate expression for the blessed inoperativity, which is neither a doing nor a not-doing, than a "becoming Sabbath" of the resurrected in which they are identified with God:

> "Be inoperative and know that I am God [*vacate et videte quoniam ego sum Deus*]." There shall be the great Sabbath which has no evening [. . .] For we shall be the Sabbath, when we shall be filled and replenished with God's blessing and sanctification. There shall we be inoperative [*vacantes*], and know that He is God [. . .] But when we are restored by Him and perfected with greater grace, we shall be eternally inoperative [*vacabimus in aeterno*] to see that He is God, for we shall be full of Him when He shall be all in all. (Ibid., p. 695)

Here, in a stuttering attempt to think the unthinkable, Augustine defines the final condition as a sabbatism to the nth degree, a making the Sabbath take rest in the Sabbath, a resolving of inoperativity into inoperativity:

> After this period God shall be inoperative on the Sabbath, when He shall make inoperative in itself that very Sabbath that we shall be [*cum eundem*

diem septimum, quod nos erimus, in se ipso Deo faciet requiescere] [. . .] Suffice it to say that this shall be our Sabbath, which shall be brought to a close, not by an evening, but by the Lord's day, as an eighth and eternal day [. . .] There we shall be inoperative [*vacabimus*] and see, see and love, love and praise. This is what shall be in the end without end. For what other end do we propose to ourselves than to attain to the kingdom of which there is no end? (Ibid., p. 696)

And only at this point, in the full glory of the Sabbath, where nothing is in excess and nothing is lacking, Augustine can conclude his work and pronounce his *amen*:

I think I have now, by God's help, discharged my obligation in writing his large work. Let those who think I have said too little, or those who think I have said too much, forgive me; and let those who think I have said just enough join me in giving thanks to God. Amen. (Ibid.)

8.23. If the postjudicial condition coincides with the supreme glory ("vera ibi gloria erit": *The City of God*, p. 696) and if glory in the century of centuries has the form of an eternal Sabbath, what remains to be investigated is precisely the meaning of this intimacy between glory and sabbatism. At the beginning and the end of the highest power there stands, according to Christian theology, a figure not of action and government but of inoperativity. The indescribable mystery that glory, with its blinding light, must hide from the gaze of the *scrutatores maiestatis* is that of divine inoperativity, of what God does before creating the world and after the providential government of the world is complete. It is not the *kabhod*, which cannot be thought or looked upon, but the inoperative majesty that it veils with its clouds and the splendor of its insignia. Glory, both in theology and in politics, is precisely what takes the place of that unthinkable emptiness that amounts to the inoperativity of power. And yet, precisely this unsayable vacuity is what nourishes and feeds power (or, rather, what the machine of power transforms into nourishment). That means that the center of the governmental apparatus, the threshold at which Kingdom and Government ceaselessly communicate and ceaselessly distinguish themselves from one another is, in reality, empty; it is only the Sabbath and *katapausis*—and, nevertheless, this inoperativity is so essential for the machine that it must at all costs be adopted and maintained at its center in the form of glory.

In the iconography of power, profane and religious, this central vacuity of glory, this intimacy of majesty and inoperativity, found its exemplary symbol in the *hetoimasia tou thronou*, that is, in the image of the empty throne.

The adoration of an empty throne has ancient roots and can be found in the Upanishads. In Mycenaean Greece, the throne discovered in the so-called Throne Room in Knossos is, according to the archaeologists, an object of worship and not a seat designed to be used. The bas-relief in the Medici Villa in Rome, which represents the empty throne from the front and surmounted by a crown surrounded by towers, appears to testify to a cult of the throne in the rites of the Magna Mater (Picard, p. 11). A cult of the throne for political ends, dating back to the fourth century BC about which we are well informed is that of the empty throne of Alexander, established in Cynda by Eumenes, the commander in chief of the Macedonian troops in Asia, in 319–312 BC. Claiming inspiration from Alexander himself who appeared to him in a dream, Eumenes fitted out the royal tent with an empty golden throne at its center on which rested the crown, scepter, and sword of the deceased monarch. Before the empty throne stood an altar on which officers and soldiers spread incense and myrrh before performing a ritual *proskynēsis*, as though Alexander had been present.

The first record of this oriental custom in Rome is to be found in the *sella curulis*—the seat usually allocated to the republican magistrates in office—which the senate awarded to Caesar to be exhibited at the games, empty and adorned with a golden crown encrusted with precious stones. In Augustus's epoch, both the written testimonies and his image as it is reproduced on coins show that the golden throne of the *divus Iulius* was constantly exhibited at the games. We know that Caligula had an empty throne placed on the Capitoline Hill, in front of which the senators were made to perform the *proskynēsis*. Alföldi provides reproductions of coins that clearly demonstrate that under Titus and Domitian, the empty *sellae* of the emperors, surmounted by a crown, had by then been transformed into thrones as objects of devotion similar in every way to the *pulvinaria* and the *lectisternia* upon which the gods were represented. Cassius Dio (72, 17, 4) tells us that, for Commodus, whether he was present or absent, theaters were fitted out with the symbols of Hercules: a golden throne, a lion skin, and a club.

However, the cultual meaning of the empty throne culminates in Christianity, in the grandiose eschatological image of the *hetoimasia tou thronou*, which adorns the triumphal arches and apses of the paleo-Christian and Byzantine basilicas. So the fifth-century mosaic on the arch of Saint Sixtus III in Santa Maria Maggiore in Rome shows an empty throne encrusted with multicolored stones, on which rests a cushion and a cross; next to it one can make out a lion, an eagle, a winged human figure, some fragments of wings, and a crown. In the church of San Prisco in Capua, another mosaic represents the empty throne, between a winged bull and an eagle, resting on which is a scroll fastened with seven seals. In the Byzantine basilica of Santa Maria Assunta in Torcello, the *hetoimasia* in the mosaic of the Last Judgment shows a throne with a cross, a crown, and a sealed book, accompanied above it by seraphims with six wings and, on either side, by two large figures of angels. In Mystras, in the church of Saint Demetrius, a fresco of the thirteenth century exhibits an empty throne suspended from the air, draped in purple, and surrounded by six acclaiming angels; just above it, in a crystalline transparent rhombus, there is a book, an amphora, a snow-white bird, and a black bull.

Historians usually interpret the image of the empty throne as a symbol of regality, both divine and profane. "The value of the throne," writes Picard, "never appears with as much force as it does when the throne is empty" (Picard, p. 1). This interpretation, which is certainly simplistic, could be developed in the terms of Kantorowicz's theory of the "two bodies" of the king, which suggests that the throne, like the other insignia of regality, refers more to the office and the *dignitas* of the sovereign than to his person.

A similar explanation cannot, however, provide an account of the empty throne in the Christian *hetoimasia*. This must first be referred back to its eschatological context in Revelation 4:1–11. Here the apostle has inseparably conjoined the originary paradigm of all Christian liturgical doxologies with an eschatological vision that takes up again the motifs of the hallucinatory prophecies of Isaiah 6:1–4 and Ezekiel 1:1–28. The image of the throne, upon which, in Isaiah, YHVH sits and in Ezekiel, a "likeness as the appearance of a man" (1:26), is derived from both of these passages. From Ezekiel the "four living creatures" (1:5) with the faces of a lion, a bull, a man, and an eagle (which from the time of Irenaeus would be identified with the evangelists); from Isaiah, the song of the *Trisagion* ("holy holy holy is the Lord omnipotent"), which makes here its first appearance in Christian doxology. It is decisive, however, that while in the apocalyptic text, the anonymous being who sits on the throne "was to look upon like a jasper and a sardine stone" (Revelation 4:3), in the representations of the *hetoimasia tou thronou* the throne is absolutely empty—aside from the book (which in the text lies "in the right hand of him that sat"), the crown, and, later, the symbols of the crucifixion.

The term *hetoimasia*, like the verb *hetoimazō*, and the adjective *hetoimos* is, in the Greek of the Septuagint, a technical term that, in the Psalms, refers to YHVH's throne: "{The LORD prepared His throne in Heaven}" (Psalms 102:19); "Justice and judgment are the *hetoimasia* of thy throne" (89:14); "Thy throne is established (*hetoimos*) of old" (93:2). *Hetoimasia* does not mean the act of preparing and fitting out something, but the readiness of the throne. The throne has always been ready and has always awaited the glory of the Lord. According to rabbinical Judaism, the throne of glory is, as we have seen, one of the seven things that YHVH created before the creation of the world. In the same sense, in Christian theology the throne has been ready for all eternity because the glory of God is co-eternal with it. *The empty throne is not, therefore, a symbol of regality but of glory.* Glory precedes the creation of the world and survives its end. The throne is empty not only because glory, though coinciding with the divine essence is not identified with it, but also because it is in its innermost self-inoperativity and sabbatism. The void is the sovereign figure of glory.

8.24. The apparatus of glory finds its perfect cipher in the majesty of the empty throne. Its purpose is to capture within the governmental machine that unthinkable inoperativity—making it its internal motor—that constitutes the ultimate mystery of divinity. And glory is as much the objective glory that exhibits the inoperativity of the divinity, as it is the glorification in which human inoperativity celebrates its eternal Sabbath. The theological and profane apparatuses of glory coincide here, and, following the aims that have governed our investigation, we can make use of it as the epistemological paradigm that will enable us to penetrate the central mystery of power.

We can now begin to understand why doxology and ceremonials are so essential to power. What is at stake is the capture and inscription in a separate sphere of the inoperativity that is central to human life. The *oiko-nomia* of power places firmly at its heart, in the form of festival and glory, what appears to its eyes as the inoperativity of man and God, which cannot be looked at. Human life is inoperative and without purpose, but pre-

cisely this *argia* and this absence of aim make the incomparable operativity [*operosità*] of the human species possible. Man has dedicated himself
to production and labor [*lavoro*], because in his essence he is completely
devoid of work [*opera*], because he is the Sabbatical animal par excellence.
And just as the machine of the theological *oikonomia* can function only if
it writes within its core a doxological threshold in which economic trinity
and immanent trinity are ceaselessly and liturgically (that is, politically)
in motion, each passing into the other, so the governmental apparatus
functions because it has captured in its empty center the inoperativity of
the human essence. This inoperativity is the political substance of the Occident, the glorious nutrient of all power. For this reason festival and idle-
ness return ceaselessly in the dreams and political utopias of the Occident
and are equally incessantly shipwrecked there. They are the enigmatic rel-
ics that the economic-theological machine abandons on the water's edge
of civilization and that each time men question anew, nostalgically and in
vain. Nostalgically because they appear to contain something that belongs
to the human essence, but in vain because really they are nothing but the
waste products of the immaterial and glorious fuel burnt by the motor of
the machine as it turns, and that cannot be stopped.

ℵ *Aristotle has written on the idea of the constitutive inoperativity of hu-*
manity as such in a passage from the Nichomachean Ethics *(1097b). When he*
comes to define happiness as the ultimate end of the science of politics, Aristotle
poses the question of what "the function of man" is (to ergon tou anthropou)
and he evokes the idea of a possible inoperativity of the human species:

> For just as for a flute-player, a sculptor, or any artist, and, in general, for all
> things that have a function [*ergon*] or activity [*praxis*], the good and the "well"
> is thought to reside in the function, so would it seem to be for man, if he
> has a function. Have the carpenter, then, and the tanner certain functions or
> activities, and has man none? Is he naturally functionless [*argon*]? (Aristotle,
> *Nichomachean Ethics*, 1097b, 25–30, vol. 2, p. 1735)

The idea is immediately dropped and the work of man is identified with that
particular "operativity" (energeia) *that is life according to the* logos. *But the*
political relevance of the theme of an essential inoperativity of man as such did
not escape Averroes, who makes power [potenza] *and not the act of thought*
what determines the specific character of the human species, or Dante, who
in De Monarchia *(I, 3) places it at the heart of his doctrine of the multitude.*

8.25. We can now try to answer the questions that without ever having been explicitly formulated have accompanied our archaeology of glory from the beginning: Why does power need inoperativity and glory? What is so essential about them that power must inscribe them at all costs in the empty center of its governmental apparatus? What nourishes power? And finally, is it possible to think inoperativity outside the apparatus of glory?

If by following the epistemological strategy that has orientated our investigation we reformulate our first three questions above on the plane of theology, Judaism and the New Testament agree on a single answer: *chayye 'olam, zōē aiōnios,* eternal life. First of all these syntagmas name what is due to the just in the future eon. In this sense, *zōē aiōnios* appears for the first time in the Septuagint as the translation of *chayye 'olam* in Daniel 12:2, where it is written that "many of them that sleep in the dust of the earth shall awake, some to everlasting life, and some to shame and everlasting contempt." Here, "everlasting," or "eternal," as is clear in both the Hebrew *'olam,* which indicates the divine world and the eschatological reality, and the Greek *aiōn* ("the *aiōn,*" writes John of Damascus, "was created before heaven and before time"), does not have a merely temporal significance but designates a special quality of life and, more precisely, the transformation that human life undergoes in the world to come. Hellenic Judaism defines it, therefore, as "{true life}" (*alēthinē zōē*: Philo, *The Special Laws* 1, § 32, pp. 536–537) or "{incorruptible life}" (*aphthartos zōē*: ibid., *On the Giants,* § 15; *On Flight and Finding,* § 59, pp. 153 and 326, respectively) or even "carefree life" (*zōē amerimnos*). The rabbinical tradition describes this future life in opposition to the present life and, at the same time, in a singular contiguity with it; that is, as a deactivation of biological functions and bad instincts: "In the world to come there will be no eating and drinking, nor any generation and reproduction. There will be no commerce and trade, quarrels, envy or hostility; the just will sit with their crowns on their heads and will be refreshed by the splendor of the *shekinah*" (Talmud, b Berakhot, 17a).

The crown that the just wear upon their heads is derived from the diadem that is owed to the triumphant *imperator* or athlete as a symbol of victory and expresses the glorious quality of eternal life. It is this same symbol of a "crown of glory" (*stephanos tēs doxēs*) or a "crown of life" (*stephanos tēs zōēs*) that in the New Testament becomes the technical term for the glory of the blessed: "Be thou faithful unto death, and I will give thee a crown of life" (Revelation 2:10); "Ye shall receive a crown of glory that fadeth not away" (1 Peter 5:4); and "He shall receive the crown of life" (James 1:12).

Paul uses this symbol on more than one occasion to describe the eschatological situation of the just, who are compared to athletes running a race ("they do it to obtain a corruptible crown; but we an incorruptible": 1 Corinthians 9:25; "I have fought a good fight, I have finished my course, I have kept the faith: Henceforth there is laid up for me a crown of righteousness, which the Lord, the righteous judge, shall give me at that day": 2 Timothy 4:7–8). For him, however, the theme of eternal life not only indicates a future condition but the special quality of life in messianic time (*ho nyn kairos,* the time-of-now), that is, the life in Jesus the Messiah ("unto eternal life by Jesus Christ our Lord": Romans 5:21). This life is marked by a special indicator of inoperativity, which in some ways anticipates the sabbatism of the Kingdom in the present: the *hōs mē,* the "as not." In the same way that the Messiah has brought about the law and, at the same time, rendered it inoperative (the verb that Paul uses to express the relation between the Messiah and the law—*katargein*—literally means "to render *argos*," inoperative), so the *hōs mē* maintains and, at the same time, deactivates in the present all the juridical conditions and all the social behaviors of the members of the messianic community:

> But this I say, brethren, the time is short: it remaineth, that both they that have wives be as though they had none [*hōs mē*]; and they that weep, as though they wept not; and they that rejoice, as though they rejoiced not; and they that buy, as though they possessed not; and they that use this world, as not abusing it: for the fashion of this world passeth away. (1 Corinthians 7:29–31)

Under the "as not," life cannot coincide with itself and is divided into a life that we live (*vitam quam vivimus,* the set of facts and events that define our biography) and a life for which and in which we live (*vita qua vivimus,* what renders life livable and gives it a meaning and a form). To live in the Messiah means precisely to revoke and render inoperative at each instant every aspect of the life that we live, and to make the life for which we live, which Paul calls the "life of Jesus" (*zōē tou Iesou—zōē* not *bios!*) appear within it: "For we which live are always delivered unto death for Jesus's sake, that the life also of Jesus might be made manifest in our mortal flesh" (2 Corinthians 4:11). The messianic life is the impossibility that life might coincide with a predetermined form, the revoking of every *bios* in order to open it to the *zōē tou Iesou*. And the inoperativity that takes place here is not mere inertia or rest; on the contrary, it is the messianic operation par excellence.

By contrast, in the future eon, when the just will enter into the inoperativity of God, the eternal life is, for Paul, placed decisively under the sign of glory. The celebrated passage in 1 Corinthians 15:35–55—the interpretation of which is the source of so much endeavor for the theologians from Origen to Thomas Aquinas—in truth says nothing more than this: that the bodies of the just will be resurrected in glory and will be transformed into glory and into the incorruptible spirit. What in Paul is left intentionally indeterminate and generic ("It is sown in dishonor; it is raised in glory: it is sown in weakness; it is raised in power: it is sown a natural body; it is raised a spiritual body") is articulated and developed into a doctrine of the glorious body of the blessed by the theologians. In accordance with an apparatus that has by now become familiar to us, a doctrine of glorious life that isolates eternal life and its inoperativity in a separate sphere comes to substitute that of the messianic life. Life, which rendered all forms inoperative, itself becomes a form in glory. Impassivity, agility, subtlety, and clarity thereby become the characters that define the life of the glorious body according to the theologians.

8.26. In the scholium to Proposition 36 of Book V of the *Ethics*, Spinoza unexpectedly evokes the idea of glory in relation to the mind's love for God. The proposition had shown that the intellectual love of the mind for God is nothing other than the love with which God loves himself and that, therefore, the mind's love for God is not distinct from God's love of men. It is at this point that the scholium develops a theory of glory that mobilizes and condenses in a few, vertiginous lines the theological motifs of the Jewish *kabhod* and Christian *doxa*:

> From this we clearly understand in what our salvation or blessedness or freedom consists, namely, in the constant and eternal love toward God, that is, in God's love toward men. This love or blessedness is called Glory in the Holy Scriptures, and rightly so. For whether this love be related to God or to the mind, it can properly be called spiritual contentment, which in reality cannot be distinguished from glory. For insofar as it is related to God, it is pleasure (if we may still use this term) accompanied by the idea of himself, and this is also the case insofar as it is related to the mind. (Spinoza, *Ethics,* Book V, Proposition 36, pp. 378–379)

Moreover, pushing to the limit the correspondence between glory and glorification, inner glory and outer glory, glory names here a movement internal to the being of God, which proceeds as much from God toward men as from men toward God. But we also discover here the Sabbatical connection between glory and inoperativity (*menuchah, anapausis, katapausis*—here rendered with the term *acquiescentia*, which was unknown in classical Latin), understood here in a specific way. Inoperativity and glory are, here, the same thing: "Acquiescentia [. . .] revera a gloria [. . .] non distinguitur."

In order to fully grasp the sense of this radicalization of the theme of glory and inoperativity it will, therefore, be necessary to return to the definition of *acquiescentia* contained in the demonstration of Proposition 52 of the fourth book. "Self-contentment" [*acquiescentia in se ipso*] writes Spinoza, "is the pleasure arising from man's contemplation of himself and his power of activity" (ibid., Book IV, Proposition 52, proof, p. 347). What does Spinoza mean when he writes of "man's contemplation of himself and his power of activity"? What is an inoperativity that consists in contemplating one's own power [*potenza*] to act? And how, from this perspective, are we to understand an inoperativity that "cannot be distinguished from glory"?

Philo had written that the inoperativity of God does not mean inertia or inactivity [*aprassia*], but a form of action that implies neither suffering nor effort:

> In fact, only God, among existing things, is inoperative [*anapauomenon*], and by "inoperativity" I do not mean "inactivity" (since that which is by its nature energetic, that which is the cause of all things, can never desist from doing what is most excellent), but I mean an energy [*energeian*] completely free from labor [*aponōtatēn*], without any feeling of suffering, and with the most perfect ease [*eumareias*]; for one may say, without impropriety, that the sun and moon, and the entire heaven, inasmuch as they are not endowed with independent power, and are continually in a state of motion and agitation, [do suffer] [. . .] and the most undeniable proofs of their labor are the yearly seasons [. . .] God is subject to no labor [. . .] and that which has no participation in weakness, even though it moves everything, cannot possibly cease to enjoy inoperativity for ever. So that rest and inoperativity are the appropriate attributes of God alone. (Philo, *On the Cherubim*, § 87–90, p. 89)

Spinoza describes as "contemplation of [. . .] power" what one might describe as an inoperativity within the operation itself, that is, a sui generis "praxis" that consists in rendering all specific powers of acting or doing inoperative. The life, which contemplates its (own) power to act, renders itself inoperative in all its operations, and lives only (its) livability. We write "own" and "its" in parentheses, because it is only through the contemplation of power, which renders all specific *energeia* inoperative, that something like an experience of one's "own" and a "self" becomes possible. "Self," subjectivity, is what opens itself as a central inoperativity in every operation, like the live-*ability* of every life. In this inoperativity, the life that we live is only the life through which we live; only our power of acting and living, our act-*ability* and our live-*ability*. Here the *bios* coincides with the *zōē* without remainder.

One can therefore understand the essential function that the tradition of Western philosophy has assigned to contemplative life and to inoperativity: properly human praxis is sabbatism that, by rendering the specific functions of the living inoperative, opens them to possibility. Contemplation and inoperativity are, in this sense, the metaphysical operators of anthropogenesis, which, by liberating the living man from his biological or social destiny, assign him to that indefinable dimension that we are accustomed to call "politics." Opposing the contemplative life to the political as "two *bioi*" (Aristotle, *Politics*, 1324a, p. 2102), Aristotle deflected politics and philosophy from their trajectory and, at the same time, delineated the paradigm on which the economy-glory apparatus would model itself. The political is neither a *bios* nor a *zōē*, but the dimension that the inoperativity of contemplation, by deactivating linguistic and corporeal, material and immaterial praxes, ceaselessly opens and assigns to the living. For this reason, from the perspective of theological *oikonomia* the genealogy of which we have here traced, nothing is more urgent than to incorporate inoperativity within its own apparatuses. *Zōē aiōnios*, eternal life, is the name of this inoperative center of the human, of this political "substance" of the Occident that the machine of the economy and of glory ceaselessly attempts to capture within itself.

א *A model of this operation that consists in making all human and divine works inoperative is the poem. Because poetry is precisely that linguistic operation that renders language inoperative—or, in Spinoza's terms, the point at which language, which has deactivated its communicative and informative functions, rests within itself, contemplates its power of saying* [potenza di

dire] *and in this way opens itself to a new possible use. In this way, Dante's*
La Vita Nuova *and Leopardi's* Canti *are the contemplation of the Italian
language, Arnauld Daniel's sestina the contemplation of the Provençal language, Hölderlin's hymns or the poems of Bachmann the contemplation of
the German language,* Les Illuminations *of Rimbaud the contemplation of
the French language, and so on. And the poetic subject is not the individual
who wrote these poems, but the subject that is produced at the point at which
language has been rendered inoperative and, therefore, has become in him and
for him, purely sayable.*

   *What the poem accomplishes for the power of saying, politics and philoso-
phy must accomplish for the power of acting. By rendering economic and biological operations inoperative, they demonstrate what the human body* can
do; *they open it to a new, possible use.*

   א *It is only from the perspective opened by this genealogy of government
and of glory that Heidegger's decision to pose the question of technology as the
ultimate problem of metaphysics acquires its proper significance and, at the
same time, reveals its limits. The* Ge-stell, *which Heidegger defines as the essence of technology, "the complete orderability of all that is present" (Heidegger
1994, p. 54), the activity that arranges and accumulates things and even men
as resources* (Bestand), *is nothing other than that which, from within the
horizon of our investigation, appears as* oikonomia; *that is, as the theological
apparatus of the government of the world. "Orderability"* (Bestellbarkeit) *is
nothing other than governmentality; and that which, on the theological plane,
is presented as that which must be ordered and guided toward salvation, arranges itself, on the plane of technology, as a resource to sustain the* Ge-stell.
The term Ge-stell *corresponds perfectly (not only in its form: the German*
stellen *is equivalent to* ponere, *that is, to place) to the Latin term* dispositio,
which translates the Greek oikonomia. *The* Ge-stell *is the apparatus of the
absolute and integral government of the world.*

   *The failure of Heidegger's attempt to resolve the problem of technology is
also evident here. Insofar as technology is not, in itself, "anything technological" (ibid., p. 57), but is the epochal figure of the unveiling-veiling of being,
it rests in the final analysis on ontological difference in the same way that, in
theology, the economy-government is founded in the economy of the Trinity.
Therefore, the problem of technology is not something that can be decided by
men, and the self-refusal of the world that takes place in the Ge-stell is the "supreme mystery of being" (ibid., p. 107), just as the "mystery of the economy" is*

the most intimate mystery of God. For this reason men cannot but correspond (entsprechen) to this mystery in a dimension in which philosophy appears to pass into religion and which, in its very name (Kehre), repeats the technical term for conversion (in German, Bekehrung). Salvation (Rettung), which grows in the danger of technology, does not signify an action but a bringing back into the essence, a guarding (in die Hut nehmen), a preserving (wahren) (ibid., p. 102).

Heidegger cannot resolve the problem of technology because he was unable to restore it to its political locus. The economy of being, its epochal unveiling in a veiling is, like economic theology, a political mystery that corresponds to power's entering into the figure of Government. And the operation that resolves this mystery, which deactivates and renders inoperative the technological-ontological apparatus, is political. It is not a guarding of being and of the divine but an operation that, within being and the divine, deactivates its economy and accomplishes it.

Threshold

Here, the investigation that has led us from the *oikonomia* to glory may come to a halt, at least provisionally. It has brought us into proximity with the center of the machine that glory envelops with its splendor and songs.

The essential political function of glory, of acclamations and doxologies appears to have declined. Ceremonies, protocols, and liturgies still exist everywhere, and not only where monarchical institutions persist. In receptions and solemn ceremonies, the president of the republic continues to follow protocol rules the observance of which is ensured by special functionaries, and the Roman pontiff continues to sit on the *cathedra Petri* or on the *sedia gestatoria* and wears paraments and tiaras, whose meaning is largely lost to the memory of the faithful.

Generally speaking, however, ceremonies and liturgies tend today to be simplified; the insignia of power reduced to a minimum; crowns, thrones, and scepters kept in glass cases in museums or treasuries; and the acclamations that had such great importance for the glorious function of power appear everywhere to have almost disappeared. It is certainly true that it was not so long ago that, in the field of what Kantorowicz called the "emotionalism" of fascist regimes, acclamations played a decisive function in the political life of certain great European states: perhaps never has an acclamation, in the technical sense of the word, been expressed with so much force and efficacy as was "Heil Hitler" in Nazi Germany or "Duce duce" in fascist Italy. And yet these uproarious and unanimous cries that resounded yesterday in the piazzas of our cities appear today to be part of a distant and irrevocable past.

But is it really so? Taking up again in 1928, in his *Constitutional Theory*, the theme of his article, written a year earlier, "Referendum and Petition for a Referendum," Schmitt specifies the constitutive function of acclamation in public *law* and does so precisely in the chapter dedicated to the analysis of the "theory of democracy."

> "People" is a concept that becomes present only in the *public* sphere [*Öffentlichkeit*]. The people appear only in the public, and they first produce the public generally. People and public exist together: no people without public and no public without the people. By its *presence*, specifically, the people initiate the public. Only the present, truly assembled people are the people and produce the public. The correct idea that supports Rousseau's famous thesis that the people cannot be represented rests on this truth. They cannot be represented, because they must be *present*, and only something absent, not something present, may be represented. As a present, genuinely assembled people, they exist in the pure democracy with the greatest possible degree of identity: as [*ekklēsia*] in the market of Greek democracy; in the Roman forum; as assembled team or army; as a local government of a Swiss Land [. . .] The genuinely assembled people are first a people, and only the genuinely assembled people can do that which pertains distinctly to the activity of this people. They can *acclaim* in that they express their consent or disapproval simply by calling out, calling higher or lower, celebrating a leader or a suggestion, honoring the king or some other person, or denying the acclamation by silence or complaining [. . .] When indeed only the people are actually assembled for whatever purpose, to the extent that it does not only appear as an organized interest group, for example, during street demonstrations and public festivals, in theaters, on the running track, or in the stadium, this people engaged in acclamation is present, and it is, at least potentially, a political entity. (Schmitt 2008b, p. 272)

Schmitt's contribution here is not only to have established an indissoluble link between acclamations and democracy as well as between acclamations and the public sphere but also that of identifying the forms in which it can subsist in contemporary democracies, in which "genuine popular assemblies and acclamations are entirely unknown" (ibid., p. 273). In contemporary democracies, acclamations survive, according to Schmitt, in the sphere of public opinion and only by setting out from the constitutive nexus of people—acclamation—public opinion is it possible to reintegrate into its rights the notion of publicity, which is today "rather obscure, [but] is essential for all political life, especially for modern democracy" (ibid., p. 272).

> *Public opinion is the modern type of acclamation.* It is perhaps a diffuse type, and its problem is resolved neither sociologically nor in terms of public law. However, its essence and political significance lie in the fact that it can be understood as an acclamation. There is no democracy and no state without public opinion, as there is no state without acclamation. (Ibid., p. 275)

Of course, Schmitt is conscious of the essential risks that democracy is exposed to, from such a perspective, with the manipulation of public opinion; but, in accordance with the principle that the ultimate criterion of the political existence of a people is its capacity to distinguish friend from enemy, he maintains that, while that capacity exists, such risks are not decisive:

> In every democracy, there are parties, speakers, and demagogues, from the [*prostatai*] of the Athenians up to the *bosses* in American democracy. Moreover, there are the press, films, and other methods of psycho-technical handling of great masses of people. All that escapes a comprehensive set of norms. The danger always exists that invisible and irresponsible social powers direct public opinion and the will of the people. (Ibid.)

More than the singular linking (which is already present in the 1927 article) of acclamations to the genuine democratic tradition—they appear to belong rather to the tradition of authoritarianism—what we wish to focus on is the suggestion that the sphere of glory—of which we have attempted to reconstitute the meaning and archaeology—does not disappear in modern democracies, but simply shifts to another area, that of public opinion. If this is true, the problem of the political function of the media in contemporary society that is so widely debated today acquires a new meaning and a new urgency.

In 1967, Guy Debord—in what appears to us a truism today—diagnosed the planetary transformation of capitalist politics and economy as an "immense accumulation of *spectacles*" (Debord, p. 12) in which the commodity and capital itself assume the mediatic form of the image. If we link Debord's analysis with Schmitt's thesis according to which public opinion is the modern form of acclamation, the entire problem of the contemporary spectacle of media domination over all areas of social life assumes a new guise. What is in question is nothing less than a new and unheard of concentration, multiplication, and dissemination of the function of glory as the center of the political system. What was confined to the spheres of liturgy and ceremonials has become concentrated in the media and, at the same time, through them it spreads and penetrates at each moment into every area of society, both public and private. Contemporary democracy is a democracy that is entirely founded upon glory, that is, on the efficacy of acclamation, multiplied and disseminated by the media beyond all imagination. (That the Greek term for glory—*doxa*—is the same term that today designates public opinion is, from this standpoint, something more than a coincidence.) As had always been the case in profane and ecclesiastical liturgies, this supposedly "originary democratic phenomenon" is once again caught, orientated, and manipulated in the forms and according to the strategies of spectacular power.

We are now beginning to better understand the sense of the contemporary definitions of democracy as "government by consent" or "consensus democracy"[1] and the decisive transformation of the democratic institutions that is at stake in these terms. In 1994, following the verdict of the German Federal Court that rejected the appeal to the unconstitutional nature of the ratification of the Maastricht Treaty, a debate took place in Germany between an illustrious scholar of constitutional law, Dieter Grimm, and Jürgen Habermas. In a brief article (significantly entitled in the interrogative, "Braucht Europa eine Verfassung?," "Does Europe Need a Constitution?"), the German constitutional theorist intervened in the discussion, which was particularly animated in Germany, between those who believed the treaties that had led to European integration had formal constitutional value and those who instead believed that an actual constitutional document would be required. He underlined the irresolvable difference between international treaties, whose juridical foundation lies in the agreement between states, and constitutions that presuppose the constitutive act of the people.

[. . .] It is inherent in a constitution in the full sense of the term that it goes back to an act taken by or at least attributed to the people, in which they attribute political capacity to themselves. There is no such source for primary Community law. It goes back not to a European people but to the individual member states, and remains dependent on them even after its entry into force. (Grimm, p. 290)

Grimm had no nostalgia for the nation-state model or for that of the national community whose unity is in some sense presupposed in a substantial form or "rooted in ethnic origin" (ibid., p. 297); but he could not but register that the lack of a European public opinion and of a common language makes the formation even of something like a common political culture impossible, at least for now.

This thesis, which lucidly reflected the principles of modern public law, substantially coincided with the position of those sociologists, such as Lepsius, who, in more or less the same years, while distinguishing between *ethnos* (national collectivity based upon descent and homogeneity) and *dēmos* (the people as "nation of citizens"), had affirmed that Europe did not yet posses a common *dēmos* and cannot therefore constitute a politically legitimate European power.

To this conception of the necessary relationship between people and constitution, Habermas opposes the thesis of a popular sovereignty that is entirely emancipated from a substantial subject-people (constituted by "members of a collectivity who are physically present, participating, and involved") and fully resolved in the communicative forms without subject that, according to his idea of publicity, "regulate the flows of the political formation of public opinion and will" (Habermas, p. xxxix [2]). Once popular sovereignty dissolves itself and is liquefied in such communicative procedures, not only can the symbolic place of power no longer be occupied by new symbols of identity, but the objections of constitutionalists to the possibility that something like a "European people"—correctly, that is communicatively, understood—can exist, also fall away.

It is well known that in subsequent years a "European constitution" was drafted, with the unexpected consequence—which should have been anticipated—that it was rejected by the "citizens as people" ["*popolo dei cittadini*"] who were asked to ratify what was certainly not an expression of their constituent power. The fact is that, if to Grimm and the theorists of the people-constitution nexus one could object that they still harked back to the common presuppositions of language and public opinion, to Habermas and the theorists of the people-communication one could easily object that they ended up passing political power into the hands of experts and the media.

What our investigation has shown is that the holistic state, founded
on the immediate presence of the acclaiming people, and the neutralized
state that resolves itself in the communicative forms without subject, are
opposed only in appearance. They are nothing but two sides of the same
glorious apparatus in its two forms: the immediate and subjective glory
of the acclaiming people and the mediatic and objective glory of social
communication. As should be evident today, people-nation and people-
communication, despite the differences in behavior and figure, are the
two faces of the *doxa* that, as such, ceaselessly interweave and separate
themselves in contemporary society. In this interlacing of elements, the
"democratic" and secular theorists of communicative action risk finding
themselves side by side with conservative thinkers of acclamation such
as Schmitt and Peterson; but this is precisely the price that must be paid
each time by theoretical elaborations that think they can do without archaeological precautions.

That "government by consent"[3] and the social communication on
which, in the last instance, consensus rests, in reality hark back to acclamations is what can be shown even through a summary genealogical
inquest. The first time that the concept of "consensus" appears in the
technical context of public law is in a crucial passage from Augustus's
Res gestae divi Augusti, where he briefly summarizes the concentration
of constitutional powers in his person: "In consulatu sexto et septimo,
postquam bella civilia extinxeram, per consensum universorum potitus
rerum omnium" ("In my sixth and seventh consulates, after putting out
the civil war, {having obtained everybody's consent, I assumed all pow-
ers}": *Res gestae divi Augusti*, § 34). The historians of Roman law ques-
tioned the foundation of this extraordinary concentration of powers in
public law. Mommsen and Kornemann, for example, maintain that it was
no longer based on the function of the triumvirate, but upon a state of
exception of a certain kind (*Notstandkommando*) (Kornemann, p. 336). It
is peculiar, however, that Augustus unequivocally founds it upon consent
("per consensum universorum"), and also that immediately beforehand
he specifies the ways in which that consent manifested itself: "Twice I triumphed with an ovation, and three times I enjoyed a *curule* triumph and
twenty-one times I was named emperor [*Bis ovans triumphavi, tris egi curulis triumphos et appellatus sum viciens et semel imperator*]" (*Res gestae divi
Augusti*, § 4). For a historian such as Mommsen, who had never heard

of "communicative action," it was certainly not easy to relate the notion of consensus back to a foundation in public law; but if one understands the essential link that ties it to acclamation, consensus can be defined without difficulty, paraphrasing Schmitt's thesis on public opinion, as the "modern form of acclamation" (it matters little that the acclamation is expressed by a physically present multitude, as in Schmitt, or by the flow of communicative procedures, as in Habermas). In any case, consensual democracy, which Debord called "the society of the spectacle" and which is so dear to the theorists of communicative action, is a glorious democracy, in which the *oikonomia* is fully resolved into glory and the doxological function, freeing itself of liturgy and ceremonials, absolutizes itself to an unheard of extent and penetrates every area of social life.

Philosophy and the science of politics have omitted to pose the questions that appear decisive in every way, whenever the techniques and strategies of government and power are analyzed, from a genealogical and functional perspective: Where does our culture draw the criterion of politicality—mythologically and in fact? What is the substance—or the procedure, or threshold—that allows one to confer on something a properly political character? The answer that our investigation suggests is: glory, in its dual aspect, divine and human, ontological and economic, of the Father and the Son, of the people-substance and the people-communication. The people—whether real or communicational—to which in some sense the "government by consent"[4] and the *oikonomia* of contemporary democracies must hark back, is, in essence, acclamation and *doxa*. Establishing whether, as we have tried to show liminally, glory covers and captures in the guise of "eternal life" that particular praxis of man as living being [*vivente uomo*] that we have defined as inoperativity, and whether it is possible, as was announced at the end of *Homo Sacer I*, to think politics—beyond the economy and beyond glory—beginning from the inoperative disarticulation of both *bios* and *zōē*, is the task for a future investigation.

Appendix: The Economy of the Moderns

1. *The Law and the Miracle*

1.1. In the second half of the seventeenth century, the question of providence assumed in France the forms that Pascal ridicules in his *Provincial Letters*. Due to the increasing interest in all areas for governmental practices and for the theory of power, the debate among theologians also focused on the ways in which providence governs (and hence on nature and on grace, which are its principal instruments) and on the relation between government and the governed (to what extent providence obligates rational creatures and in what sense they remain free with respect to the grace they receive). According to Pascal's testimony, what irreducibly divides Jesuits, Molinists, Thomists, and Jansenists is precisely the question of "sufficient" grace and "effective" grace; that is, the ways in which God intervenes in the government of the second causes.

> Their differences on the subject of sufficient grace is chiefly this. The Jesuits maintain there is a general grace bestowed upon all mankind, but in a sense subordinated to free will, so that this grace is rendered effective or ineffective as the world chooses, without any additional assistance from God. It does not need anything external to itself to make its operations effectual. On this account it is distinguished by the word *sufficient*. In contrast, the Jansenists affirm that no grace is actually sufficient unless it is also effective. That is, all principles that do not determine the will to act effectively are insufficient for action because, they say, no one can act with effective grace. (Pascal 2003, pp. 245–246)

Although Jesuits and Thomists are in agreement in condemning the Jansenists, great confusion also reigns among them with regard to the definition of grace (whether sufficient or effective)—the instrument par excellence of providential government. Indeed, the Thomists call sufficient that grace that is not sufficient, since it is not enough to determine action. "That is to say, all men have grace enough, and all have not grace enough—this grace is sufficient and it is insufficient; that is to say, it is nominally sufficient and really insufficient" (ibid., pp. 247–248). "Where are we now?" Pascal continues ironically.

> Which side am I to take here? If I deny sufficient grace, I am a Jansenist. If I admit it with the Jesuits in such a sense that there is no necessity for efficacious grace, I am, you tell me, a heretic. If I agree with you, I fly against common sense. I am a madman, say the Jesuits. What then am I to do in this inevitable situation of being either considered a madman, a heretic, or a Jansenist? (Ibid., p. 248)

In reality, what hides behind an apparently terminological question is the very way in which we are to conceive the divine government of the world, and, in a more or less witting way, the theologians are in fact discussing politics. The providential government of the world is derived from a difficult balance between the action of governing (grace, in its various forms) and the free will of governed individuals. If Cornelius Jansen's position is unacceptable to the Church, this is because, in affirming that grace is always efficacious and, as such, invincible, he destroys the freedom of men and transforms the activity of providence into an absolute and impenetrable government that—like the government of the large baroque states, with their mysteries and their "reasons"—saves the elect and condemns the others to eternal damnation through its will.

1.2. It is in this context that Malebranche publishes in 1680—fifteen years after the vociferous debate surrounding the publication of the *Provincial Letters*—his *Treatise on Nature and Grace*. In this text he gives a new formulation to the doctrine of general providence and special providence, of first causes and secondary causes, which would exert a lasting influence not only among theologians but also and above all on philosophers, to whom it was explicitly directed ("pour lesquels j'ai écrit le Traité": Malebranche 1979, p. 146). Since it is a case of nothing less than an absolutization of divine government, which radically transforms the sense of secondary causes (now conceived of as occasional causes), it is worth following the summary exposition that Malebranche gives of his doctrine in the *Eclaircissements* appended to the treatise.

The subject of providential action is the divine will. Therefore, Malebranche begins by distinguishing the general wills from the particular wills.

> I say that God acts by general wills, when he acts in consequence of general laws which he has established. For example, I say that God acts in me by general will when he makes me feel pain at the time when I am pricked; because in consequence of the general and efficacious laws of the union of the soul and the body which he has established, he makes me feel pain when my body is ill disposed. In the same way, when a ball strikes a second one, I say that God moves the second by a general will, because he moves it in consequence of the general and efficacious laws of the communication of motion—God having generally established at the moment that the two bodies strike, the motion is divided between the two according to certain proportions; and it is through the efficacy of this general will that bodies have the power to move each other. (Malebranche 1992, p. 195).

It will, on the other hand, be said that God acts with a particular will if this produces its effects independently of a general law. If God makes me feel the pain of a prick without a cause having acted on my body, within me or outside me, and if a body begins to move without being struck by another, this could be the effect of a particular will, that is, of a miracle.

Malebranche's strategy consists in more or less completely excluding from providence the particular wills and reducing the problem of the divine government of the world to the terms of the relationship between general will and the causes that he defines as occasional (in other words, he transforms secondary causes into occasional ones).

> When one sees that an effect is produced immediately after the action of an *occasional* cause, one must judge that this effect is produced by the efficacy of a general will. A body moves immediately after having been struck: the collision of the bodies is the action of the *occasional* cause; thus this body moves by a general will. A stone falls on the head of a man and kills him; and this stone falls like all others, I mean that its movement continues nearly according to the arithmetical progression 1, 3, 5, 7, 9, etc. That supposed, I say that it moves by the efficacy of a general will, or according to the laws of the communication of motion, as it is easy to demonstrate. (Ibid., p. 197)

But also when an effect is produced without there being an occasional cause (if, for example, a body moves without having been knocked by another), we cannot be sure whether it is a particular will or a miracle that has intervened. One can suppose, in fact, that God has established a general law according to which the angels have the power to move bodies with their will; the particular angelic will will act as an occasional cause of the will of God and the mechanism of providential government will in all cases be the same.

> Thus one can often be assured that God acts by general wills; but one cannot in the same way be assured that he acts by particular wills even in the most attested miracles. (Ibid.)

The fact is that, according to Malebranche, it conforms better to divine wisdom to act according to simple and general ways than through a multiplicity of particular wills. In this way he formulates a kind of Ockham's razor with respect to miracles: miracles, like entities, *non sunt multiplicanda extra necessitatem.* If one sees the rain fall on a field that was much in need of it, it is not necessary to verify whether or not it also fell on neighboring fields or on the roads that did not need it, "for one must not, without necessity, have recourse to miracles" (ibid., p. 200).

> For, since there is more wisdom in executing his plans by simple and general means than in complex and particular ways [. . .] one must do this honor to God, to believe that this way of acting is general, uniform, constant, and proportioned to the idea that we have of an infinite wisdom. (Ibid., pp. 200–201)

The paradigm of providential government is not the miracle but the law; not the particular will but the general.

This is also the only reasonable way to account for the evils that seem to us to be irreconcilable with what we suppose to be the designs of providence. God has established as a general law that we should feel a pleasant sensation when we enjoy the fruits that are suited to nourishing our bodies. If we feel that same sensation when we eat poisoned fruit, this does not mean that God departs from the law that he has established through a particular will. On the contrary:

> [. . .] since a poisoned fruit excites in our brain motions like those which good fruit produces therein, God gives us the same feeling, because of the general laws which unify the soul and the body—in order that it be wakeful

to its preservation. In the same way God gives those who have lost an arm feelings of pain with respect to this arm only by a general will [. . .] Thus it is certain that rains which are useless or harmful to the fruits of the earth are necessary consequences of the general laws of the communication of motion which God has established to produce the effects in the world [. . .] (Ibid., pp. 198–199)

The Stoic theory of collateral effects is here taken up against and inscribed within the divine government of the world that is dominated by general laws, the order of which corresponds perfectly to that which the natural sciences are just beginning to decipher.

A wise man must act wisely; God cannot deny himself; his ways of acting must bear the character of his attributes. Now God knows all, and foresees all; his intelligence has no limits. Thus his way of acting must bear the character of an infinite intelligence. Now to choose occasional causes, and to establish the general laws to execute some work, indicates a knowledge infinitely more extensive, than to change his wills at every moment, or to act by particular wills. Thus God executes his plans by general laws, whose efficacy is determined by occasional causes. Certainly it requires a greater breadth of mind to create a watch which, according to the laws of mechanism, goes by itself and regularly—whether one carries it oneself, whether one holds it suspended, whether one shakes it as one pleases—than to make one which cannot run correctly if he who has made it does not change something in it at every moment according to the situation it is placed in [. . .] Thus to establish general laws, and to choose the simplest ones, which are at the same time the most fruitful, is a way of acting worthy of him whose wisdom has no bounds; and by contrast to act by particular wills indicates a limited intelligence [. . .] (Ibid., pp. 210–211)

This is not, for Malebranche, to deny or play down the power of providence; on the contrary, it now coincides so perfectly with the order of the world that it is no longer necessary to distinguish it from nature; nature is nothing other than "the general laws which God has established to construct or to preserve his work by very simple means, by an action which is uniform [and] constant" (ibid., p. 196). Every other conception of nature, for instance, that of pagan philosophers, is a "chimera." But this nature, in which God "does all in all things" (ibid.), to the extent that he acts only through the general wills and laws, is in no way distinguishable from that of modern science. For this reason Fénelon, commenting on

Malebranche's treatise, perceptively observes that "his God must coincide with the order of the world," which "could not violate this order without ceasing to be God" (Fénelon, p. 342).

1.3. What is in every way decisive is the function that Malebranche gives to Christology in providential government. He interprets the Trinitarian *oikonomia* in the sense that Jesus Christ, after his sacrifice, where he acted as the *meritorious* cause of redemption, was constituted by the Father as the *occasional* cause of grace and, as such, he executes and renders effective in its particulars the grace that God established through his general laws. "Thus he himself applies and distributes his gifts, as *occasional* cause. He disposes of everything in the house of God, like a well-loved son in the house of his father" (Malebranche 1992, p. 201). In other words, he is an integral part of the governmental machine of providence, and occupies the place of the determining node that articulates its execution in every area and for all individuals. It is in this sense that, according to Malebranche, one must understand both the affirmation in the Gospel that states that to Christ has been given "omnis potestas in coelo et in terra" (Matthew 28:18), and that of Paul according to which Christ is the head of the Church of which the faithful are members (Ephesians 4:6). The words of Paul

> [. . .] do not simply say that Jesus Christ is the *meritorious* cause of all graces: they express even more distinctly the notion that Christians are members of the body of which Jesus Christ is the head; that it is in him that we believe and that we live a wholly new life; that it is through his internal working *kat' energeian*, that his Church is formed, and that he has thus been established by God as the sole *occasional* cause who, by his different desires and different efforts, distributes the graces which God as true cause diffuses in men. (Malebranche 1992, p. 203)

Christ acts, in other words, as the chief of the executive of a *gubernatio* of which God is the supreme legislator. But, just as the *oikonomia* did not imply the division of the divinity, in the same way the power [*potenza*] assigned to Christ does not involve a division of sovereignty. For this reason Malebranche is able to speak, with respect to Christ, of a "sovereign power" ("puissance souveraine de cause occasionnelle": Malebranche 1979, p. 148, even if this was given to him by the father) and, at the same time, to define its function simply as "ministry":

Jesus Christ, as a man, is the head of the Church, and it is he who distributes among its members the grace that sanctifies. But since he only has this power as a consequence of the general laws that God has established in him in order to execute his great design, the eternal temple, one can truly say that it is God, and only God, who gives inner grace, although he only gives it in truth through the ministry of Jesus Christ, who—as a man—determines the efficacy of the divine will through his prayers and his desires. (Malebranche 1979, p. 185)[1]

In this sense, Christ is compared to the angels that, in the Bible, act as "ministers of God" (ibid., p. 183). In the same way as the angels gave the Old Law, of which they were ministers, so Christ "is the angel of the New Law" (ibid., p. 186) and, as "minister" of it, he has been elevated above the angels (ibid., p. 187).

ℵ *Even in Malebranche the definition of the providential role of the angels betrays a "ministerial," that is, genuinely governmental, preoccupation. Not only are the angels the envoys and ministers of God, but their action—which coincides with the area traditionally assigned to miracles—provides, within the system of laws and general wills, something like the paradigm of the state of exception, which allows Malebranche to formulate in new terms his critique of miracles. According to Malebranche, there are in the Old Testament many places that testify to miraculous events, but these must not be interpreted as being caused by the particular wills of God that are contrary to his general laws. Instead, they should be understood as the consequence of a general will through which he has communicated his power to the angels: "I believe I can prove with the authority of Sacred scripture that the angels have received from God a power over the present world; that God executes their wills and, through them, his designs, according to certain general laws, in such a way that everything that appears miraculous in the Old Testament in no way proves that God acts in accordance with particular wills" (ibid., pp. 182–183). So-called miracles are the consequence of a general law with which God has given to his angelic ministers the power to act in apparent violation of another general law (for instance, that of the communication of movements). The exception is, in other words, not a miracle (a particular will outside the system of general laws), but the effect of a general law that confers on the angels a special power of government. Miracles are not outside the legal system but represent a particular case in which a law is not applied so that another law, through which God delegates his sovereign power to the angels in view of the best possible government, can be.*

Schmitt's theory of the state of exception—which, though suspending the application of some norms, is not situated outside the global legal order—corresponds perfectly to the model of angelic power to be found in the Treatise.

1.4. What is at stake in the treatise is the definition of the best possible government. The difficulty that the task runs into (the same as that with which Jansen struggles) is the conciliation of two propositions that are in apparent contradiction with one another: "God wants all men to be saved" and "Not all men are saved." It is nothing less than a contrast in God between the will, which wishes that all men, even the wicked, will be saved, and the wisdom that cannot but choose the most simple and general laws for this end. The best government will therefore be that which is able to find the most economic relationship between will and wisdom or, as Malebranche writes, between the wisdom that has order and constancy in its sights, and fecundity (which demands that the Church be broader and more numerous):

> God loves men and wants them all to be saved; he wants to sanctify them all; he wants his work to be beautiful; that his Church be the broadest and the most perfect. But God loves his wisdom infinitely more, because he loves it invincibly with a natural and necessary love. He cannot therefore dispense with acting in a manner that is most wise and worthy of himself; he must follow the behavior that corresponds best to his attributes. But by acting in ways that are most simple and worthy of his wisdom, his work cannot be more beautiful or greater than it is. For if God had been able to make his Church greater and more perfect than it is, by following other equally simple paths, it would mean that by acting as he did, he did not intend to execute the work that was most worthy of him [. . .] The wisdom of God, which prevented him from complicating his paths and carrying out miracles at each instant, obliges him to act in a general, constant, and uniform way. For this reason he does not save all men, although in reality he wishes them all to be saved. Despite loving his creatures, he only does for them what his wisdom enables him to do; and, although he wants a broad and perfect Church, he does not make it absolutely greater and more perfect but the greatest and most perfect in relation to the paths that are most worthy of him. For, once again, God does not form his designs other than by comparing the means with the work that they can execute. And when he knew that there was a better relationship

between wisdom and fecundity, between certain means and certain works, then, to speak as humans do, he took the decision, chose his paths, and established his decrees. (Ibid., p. 171)

Bayle had already begun to ask how such statements could be in accord with the commonly accepted notions of the nature and omnipotence of the supreme being. In his *Réponse aux questions d'un provincial*, which Leibniz cites in his *Theodicy*, he writes:

These [notions] teach us that all things not implying contradiction are possible for him, that consequently it is possible for him to save people whom he does not save: for what contradiction would result supposing the number of the elect were greater than it is? They teach us [. . .] that [. . .] he has no will which he cannot carry out. How, then, shall we understand that he wills to save all men and that he cannot do so? (Leibniz, § 223, pp. 266–267)

In reality, Malebranche's theses become fully comprehensible only if one places them on their true terrain, which is that of the government of the world. In question is not the abstract point regarding the omnipotence or impotence of God, but the possibility of the government of the world, that is, of *an ordered relation between general laws and particular occasional causes.* If God, as the possessor of sovereignty, acted from start to finish according to particular wills, infinitely multiplying his miraculous interventions, there would be neither government nor order but only chaos and what one might call a pandemonium of miracles. For this reason, as sovereign, he must *reign* and not *govern*; he must fix the laws and the general wills and allow the contingent play of occasional causes and particular wills their most economical execution:

A God that knows everything must not disturb the simplicity of his paths. An immutable being must always maintain uniform behavior. A general cause must not act through particular wills. The government of God must bear the signs of his attributes, unless the immutable and necessary order does not force him to change it; because, with respect to God, order is an inviolable law; he loves it invincibly and will always prefer it to the arbitrary laws with which he executes his designs. (Malebranche 1979, p. 188)

But what results from the relationship between general will and occasional causes, between Kingdom and Government, God and Christ is an *oikonomia* in which what is at stake is not so much whether men are good or evil, but in what way the damnation of many can be reconciled in an ordered way with the salvation of few, and the evil nature of some people is nothing but the collateral effect of the goodness of others.

א *In Leibniz's polemic with Bayle, from which resulted his* Essais de Théodicée sur la bonté de Dieu, la liberté de l'homme et l'origine du mal, *he evokes the name of Malebranche on more than one occasion and declares himself in agreement with his theory of the general wills, which he claims— rightly or wrongly—to have fathered. He writes:*

> The excellent author of *The Search for Truth*, having passed from philosophy to theology, published finally an admirable treatise on Nature and Grace. Here he showed in his way [. . .] that the events which spring from the enforcement of general laws are not the object of a particular will of God [. . .] I agree with Father Malebranche that God does things in the way most worthy of him. But I go a little further than he, with regard to "general and particular acts of will." As God can do nothing without reasons, even when he acts miraculously, it follows that he has no will about individual events but what results from some general will. (Leibniz, § 204–206, pp. 254–256)

The proximity of his theory of preestablished harmony and of the best of possible worlds to Malebranche's system seemed to Leibniz so great that it led him to remind his readers that he had been the first to elaborate it:

> While I was in France I showed to M. Arnauld a dialogue I had composed in Latin on the cause of evil and the justice of God [the *Confessio philosophi*]; it was not only before his disputes with Father Malebranche, but even before the book on *The Search for Truth* appeared. (Ibid., § 211, p. 260)

The very idea of "theodicy" is, in fact, already present in Malebranche: "It is not enough," he writes, "to have it understood that God is powerful and that he makes his creatures do what he wishes. It is necessary, if possible, to justify his wisdom and his goodness" (Malebranche 1979, p. 174). Like Malebranche, Leibniz also affirms that God always chooses the most simple and general paths,

> [. . .] which it is easiest to explain, and which also are of greatest service for the explanation of other things [. . .] And even though the system of Pre-established Harmony were not necessary otherwise, because it banishes superfluous miracles, God would have chosen it as being the most harmonious [. . .] It is as if one said that a certain house was the best that could have

been constructed at a certain cost. One may, indeed, reduce these two conditions, simplicity and productivity, to a single advantage, which is to produce
as much perfection as possible: thus Father Malebranche's system in this point
amounts to the same as mine. (Leibniz, § 208, p. 257)

The consequences that Leibniz drew from his system with regard to the prob-
lem of the origin and necessity of evil are well known. Divine wisdom em-
braces all possible worlds, compares them, and weighs them up in order to
penetrate the major or minor degree of perfection. It sets them out and dis-
tributes them in an infinity of possible universes, each of which contains an
infinity of creatures:

The result of all these comparisons and deliberations is the choice of the best
from among all the possible systems, which wisdom makes in order to satisfy
goodness completely; and such is precisely the plan of the universe as it is.
(Ibid., § 225, pp. 267–268)

But the choice of the best possible world has a price, which is the quantity of
evil, of suffering, and damnation that is contained within it as the necessary
attendant effect. Once again Malebranche is called upon to justify the provi-
dential choice in the name of general laws:

But one must believe that even sufferings and monstrosities are part of order;
and it is well to bear in mind not only that it was better to admit these defects
and these monstrosities than to violate general laws, as Father Malebranche
sometimes argues, but also that these very monstrosities are in the rules, and
are in conformity with general acts of will, though we are not capable of
discerning this conformity. It is just as sometimes there are appearances of
irregularity in mathematics which issue finally in a great order when one has
finally got to the bottom of them: that is why I have already in this work
observed that according to my principles all individual events, without exception, are consequences of general acts of will. (Ibid., § 241, pp. 276–277)

Even the most beautiful minds have zones of opacity in which they get lost to
the point that a much weaker mind can ridicule them. This is what occurred
to Leibniz with Voltaire's caricature of his position in Candide. *In the case of*
Leibniz this defeat has two reasons. The first is juridical-moral, and concerns
the justificatory intent that is expressed in the very title, Theodicy. *The world*
as it is does not require justification but saving; and, if it does not require
saving, it needs justifying even less. But to want to justify God for the way in
which the world is amounts to the worst misunderstanding of Christianity

that one can imagine. The second and more important reason has a political character, and concerns his blind faith in the necessity of the law (of the general will) as the instrument of the government of the world. According to this aberrant idea, if the general law requires as a necessary consequence that Auschwitz takes place, then also "monstrosities are within the rules," and the rule does not become monstrous for this reason.

1.5. The influence of Malebranche on Rousseau's political theory has been widely documented (Bréhier, Riley, Postigliola). However, scholars have merely reconstructed the considerable terminological debts and the remarkable influences that run between them, but they have rarely investigated the structural analogies that accompanied and made possible the shift from the theological context to the political one. In particular, the monograph by Patrick Riley, *The General Will Before Rousseau*, has traced a broad genealogy of the notions of *volonté générale* and *volonté particulière*, which leads from the theology of the eighteenth century up to the *Contract social*. Rousseau did not invent these notions but drew them from theological debates on grace where, as we have seen, they had a strategic function in the conception of the providential government of the world. Riley demonstrates that the general will in Rousseau can be defined without any doubt as a secularization of the corresponding category in Malebranche and that, more generally, French theological thought, from Arnaud to Pascal, from Malebranche to Fénelon, has left substantial traces in all of Rousseau's work. But to what extent this might also determine the displacement of an entire theological paradigm into a political dimension is something that remains outside Riley's study. That the transfer of a notion from the field of theology to the field of politics might imply some unexpected consequences and, hence, something like an "unforgivable omission," in the case of Rousseau, was not lost on Alberto Postigliola (Postigliola, p. 224). But he limits himself to showing that the notion of "general will" in Malebranche is synonymous with the divine attribute of infinity, which renders problematic, if not contradictory, its shift into the profane sphere of Rousseau's city in which the generality can only be finite. We will attempt to show instead that with the notions of *volonté générale* and *volonté particulière* the entire governmental machine of providence is transferred from the theological to the political sphere, thereby compromising not only some points of Rousseau's *économie publique*, but giving it its fundamental structure; that is to say, the relationship between sovereignty and government, law and executive power. Through the *Social Contract* the republican tradition inherited without reservations a theological paradigm and a governmental machine of which it is still far from becoming conscious.

1.6. In the course of the 1977–1978 lectures *Securité, territoire, population*, Foucault defined in a few, extremely dense lines, the fundamental structure of Rousseau's political project (Foucault, pp. 106–108). He seeks here to demonstrate that the problem of sovereignty did not leave the stage at the moment the art of government came to the fore in European politics. On the contrary, never is it posed with such urgency as it is at this time: although up until the seventeenth century one limited oneself to deducing a paradigm of government from the theory of sovereignty, it then became an inverse process; given the growing primacy of the arts of government, it became a case of discovering the juridical form and theory of sovereignty that were able to sustain and found this primacy. It is at this stage that he illustrates his thesis via a reading of Rousseau and, in particular, of the relationship between the 1775 article on "Political Economy" in the *Encyclopedia* and the *Social Contract*. The problem with the article lies, according to Foucault, in the definition of an "economy" or an art of government that is no longer modeled on the family, but that has the common aim of governing in the best possible way and with maximum efficacy in order to make men happy. When Rousseau writes the *Social Contract*, the problem will instead be precisely that of

> how, with notions like those of "nature," "contract," and "general will," one can give a general principle of government that will allow for both the juridical principle of sovereignty and the elements through which an art of government can be defined and described [. . .] The problem of sovereignty is not eliminated; on the contrary, it is made more acute than ever. (Foucault, p. 107)

Let us attempt to advance Foucault's analysis in light of the results of our investigation. To begin with, he has come as close as he possibly can to the intuition of the bipolar character of the governmental machine, although the methodological decision to set aside the analysis of the juridical universals prevents him from articulating it fully. Rousseau's theory of sovereignty is certainly a function of a theory of government (or of "public economy," as he sometimes defines it); but the correlation between the two elements is, in Rousseau, still more intimate and tight than it appears in Foucault's brief analysis and is entirely founded upon the theological model that he adopts from Malebranche and the French theorists of providence.

What is decisive from this point of view is the distinction and articulation of sovereignty and government, which is at the basis of Rousseau's political thought. "I urge my readers also," he writes in his article on the *Economie politique*, "to distinguish carefully *public economy*, about which I am to speak, and which I call *government*, from the supreme authority, which I call *sovereignty*—a distinction that consists in the one having the legislative right and in certain cases obligating the body of the nation itself, while the other has only the executive power and can obligate only private individuals" (Rousseau 1992, p. 142). In the *Social Contract* the distinction is restated as the articulation between general will and legislative power on the one hand, and government and executive power on the other. That for Rousseau the distinction has a strategic relevance is proved by the fact that he forcefully denies that it is a case of division and presents it instead as an internal articulation of one indivisible supreme power:

> For the same reason that sovereignty is inalienable it is indivisible; for the will is either general, or it is not; it is either that of the body of the people, or that of only a part of it. In the first case, this declared will is an act of sovereignty and constitutes law; in the second case, it is only a particular will, or an act of magistracy—it is at most a decree. But our politicians, being unable to divide sovereignty in its principle, divide it in its object. They divide it into force and will, into legislative power and executive power; into rights of taxation, of justice, and of war; into internal administration and foreign relations—sometimes conflating all of these branches, and sometimes separating them. They make the sovereign into a fantastic being, formed of disparate parts; it is as if they created a man from several different bodies, one with eyes, another with arms, another with feet, and nothing else. The Japanese conjurors, it is said, cut up a child before the eyes of the spectators; then throwing all its limbs into the air, they make the child come down again alive and whole. Such almost are the jugglers' tricks of our politicians; after dismembering the social body, by magic worthy of the circus, they recombine its parts, in any unlikely way. This error arises from their not having formed clear ideas about the sovereign authority, and from their regarding as elements of this authority what are only emanations from it. (Rousseau 2002, p. 171)

In the same way as in the paradigm of providence, general providence and special providence do not stand in contrast with each other nor do they represent a division within the one divine will; and, as in Malebranche, the occasional causes are nothing but the particular actualization of God's general will, so in Rousseau, the government, or executive power, claims to coincide with the sovereignty of law from which it nevertheless distinguishes itself as its particular emanation and actualization. The concept of emanation, utilized by Rousseau, has not failed to surprise his commentators; but the choice of term is all the more significant if one returns it to its original context, which is that of the emanative causes of Neoplatonism, which were incorporated into the theory of creation and providence through the work of Boethius, Johannes Scotus Eriugena, the *Liber de causis*, and Jewish theology. Precisely because of this origin, in Rousseau's time the term did not have a good press. In the article by Diderot, "Kabbalah," in the *Encyclopaedia*, the emanative paradigm was defined as the "axis around which the entire philosophical Kabbalah and system of emanations turn, according to which it is necessary that all things emanate from the divine essence." And even more critical judgments could be found in the entry "Emanation," which, having restated the link with the Kabbalah, warned that "this theory leads straight to pantheism." Introducing the term at a delicate point in his system, Rousseau must have calculated the implications of his choice. This did not hark back to the Kabbalah but to Christian theology, in which the term referred first to the procession of persons in the Trinitarian economy (until the seventeenth century this was, in fact, the only meaning of the French term *émanation*) and to the theory of causes in the creationist and providential paradigm. In this context, the term implied that the divine principle has not been diminished nor is it divided by its Trinitarian articulation and by its activity of creation and conservation of the world. It is in this sense that Rousseau uses the term; in order to exclude, in contrast to those thinkers whom he ironically calls *les politiques*, that sovereignty is in some way divisible. And yet, just as in the case of the Trinitarian economy and in the theory of providence, what cannot be divided is articulated through the distinctions *sovereign power/government, general will/particular will, legislative power/executive power*, which mark within it a series of caesurae that Rousseau tries carefully to minimize.

1.7. Through these distinctions the entire economic-providential apparatus (with its polarities *ordinatio/executio,* providence/fate, Kingdom/Government) is passed on as an unquestioned inheritance to modern politics. What was needed to assure the unity of being and divine action, reconciling the unity of substance with the trinity of persons and the government of particulars with the universality of providence, has here the strategic function of reconciling the sovereignty and generality of the law with the public economy and the effective government of individuals. The most nefarious consequence of this theological apparatus dressed up as political legitimation is that it has rendered the democratic tradition incapable of thinking government and its economy (today one would instead write: economy and its government, but the two terms are substantially synonymous). On the one hand, Rousseau conceives of government as the essential political problem; on the other hand, he minimizes the problem of its nature and its foundation, reducing it to the activity of the execution of sovereign authority. The ambiguity that seems to settle the problem of government by presenting it as the mere execution of a general will and law has weighed negatively not only upon the theory, but also upon the history of modern democracy. For this history is nothing but the progressive coming to light of the substantial untruth of the primacy of legislative power and the consequent irreducibility of government to mere execution. And if today we are witnessing the government and the economy's overwhelming domination of a popular sovereignty emptied of all meaning, this perhaps signifies that Occidental democracies are paying the political price of a theological inheritance that they had unwittingly assumed through Rousseau.

The ambiguity that consists in conceiving government as executive power is an error with some of the most far-reaching consequences in the history of Western political thought. It has meant that modern political thought becomes lost in abstractions and vacuous mythologems such as the Law, the general will, and popular sovereignty, and has failed to confront the decisive political problem. *What our investigation has shown is that the real problem, the central mystery of politics is not sovereignty, but government; it is not God, but the angel; it is not the king, but ministry; it is not the law, but the police—that is to say, the governmental machine that they form and support.*

ℵ *The two sovereignties, the dynastic and the popular-democratic, refer to two completely different genealogies. The dynastic sovereignty of divine right is derived from the theological-political paradigm; the popular-democratic is derived from the theological-economic-providential paradigm.*

ℵ *Rousseau does not hide the fact that the fundamental articulations of his political system derive from a theological paradigm. In the article on* Political Economy, *he affirms that the principal difficulty of the system that he proposes is that of reconciling "public freedom and the government's authority" (Rousseau 1992, p. 145). This difficulty has been removed, writes Rousseau, by the "most sublime of all human institutions, or rather by a divine inspiration, which teaches mankind to imitate here below the unchangeable decrees of the Deity" (ibid.). In other words, the sovereignty of the law, to which Rousseau refers, imitates and reproduces the structure of the providential government of the world. Just as in Malebranche, for Rousseau the general will, the law, subjugates men only in order to make them freer, and in immutably governing their actions does nothing but express their nature. And just as in letting oneself be governed by God they do nothing but let their own nature take its course, so the indivisible sovereignty of the Law guarantees the coincidence of the governing and the governed.*

The agreement with Malebranche's thought also appears forcefully in the third Letter from the Mountain in relation to the critique of miracles. Rousseau closely connects the miracle with the exception (it is "a real and visible exception to [God's] Laws": Rousseau 2001, p. 173) and firmly criticizes the necessity of miracles to faith and revelation. In question is not so much whether God "can" carry out miracles, so much as—through a perhaps conscious return to the distinction between absolute power and ordering power—whether God "wants" to do so (ibid.). It is interesting to observe that Rousseau, despite denying the necessity of miracles, does not exclude them entirely, but conceives them as exceptions. Schmitt's theory, which sees in miracles the theological paradigm of the state of exception (Schmitt 2005, p. 49), finds its confirmation here.

2. *The Invisible Hand*

2.1. The term *oikonomia* disappears from the theological language of the West in the course of the Middle Ages. Certainly, its equivalents *dispo-*

sitio and *dispensatio* continue to be used, but they progressively lose their technical meaning and merely designate in a generic way the divine activity of the government of the world. The humanists and erudite scholars of the seventeenth century are not ignorant of the theological meaning of the Greek term, which is defined with sufficient clarity in Étienne Chauvin's and Johann Kaspar Suicer's lexicons (1682, particularly in the meaning of the "incarnation of the word of God") and in the theological compendia such as Petavius's *De theologicis dogmatibus* (1644–1650). However, when in the course of the eighteenth century, the term reappears in the Latinate form *oeconomia* and especially in its equivalents in other European languages with the meaning that is familiar to us: "activity of management and government of things and people," it appears to spring, as it were, *ex novo* already formed in the heads of the *philosophes* and the *économistes*, without any essential relation either to classical economics or to its theological past. It is well known that the economics of the moderns is not derived from Aristotelian economics, nor from the medieval treatises of *Oeconomica* that refer to it, and even less to the moralizing tradition of works such as Menius's *Oeconomia christiana* (Wittenberg, 1529) or Battus's (Antwerp, 1558), which have as their object the behavior of the Christian family. But the more or less subterranean connections that might link the economics of the moderns to the paradigm of the theological *oikonomia* and the divine government of the world have been left almost entirely unexplored. It is not our intention to reconstruct the specifics of these links, but it seems clear that a genealogical inquiry into economics could usefully focus on the relation to the theological paradigm, whose essential traits we have sought to delineate. We will merely give a few summary indications here that others might wish to complete.

2.2. In 1749 Linneaus publishes in Uppsala his *Specimen academicum de oeconomia naturae*. Given the strategic function that the syntagma "economy of nature" will perform in the birth of modern economics, it is worthwhile dwelling on the definition he gives of it at the beginning of his book:

> By "economy of nature" we mean the wise disposition [*dispositio*] of natural beings, established by the sovereign Creator, according to which they tend to common ends and execute reciprocal actions. Everything contained within the limits of this universe loudly celebrates the wisdom of the Creator. Everything that falls within our senses, everything that is presented to our mind

and deserves observation combines, through its disposition, to manifest the glory of God; that is, to produce ends that God wanted as the purpose of all his works.

However surprising this conception may appear in an author we are accustomed to think of as the founder of modern scientific taxonomy, the derivation of the syntagma from the economic-providential tradition is here obvious and beyond doubt. *Oeconomia naturae* simply means—in perfect accordance with the theological paradigm that is familiar to us— the wise and providential *dispositio* that the creator has impressed upon his creation and through which he governs it and leads it to its ends, in such a way that an apparent evil in reality agrees with the general good. Moreover, from the start of the 1740s, Linneaus writes a series of short works that have this idea at their heart. In *Curiositas naturalis* (1748), an inhabitant of the moon falls unexpectedly to earth and observes in astonishment the terrible and disordered struggle of all against all that appears to reign on this planet. But as he observes events in an increasingly careful manner, the citizen of the moon begins to decipher—beneath the apparently cruel chaos—the immutable order of general laws in which he recognizes the intention and hand of a divine creator. The experiment is taken up again in 1760 in the more substantial and pondered *Dissertatio academica de politia naturae*. The "economy of nature" cedes its place to a *politia naturae*, but this, according to the terminology of *Policeywissenschaft* that has by this time become consolidated, means simply knowledge and government of the order and internal constitution of human society. In this book a moon-dweller is also thrown to earth naked as Adam in the middle of wars and horrifying slaughter. Once again, however, he gradually achieves an understanding of the hidden order that governs the reciprocal relations between creatures and moves them according to a perfectly circular motion.

> One can rationally conclude that there is a necessary *politia* in the natural realm. A realm without government, without order, and without control would gradually fall into ruin. In a state, we call *politia* the direction and just administration of the whole; and this conception cannot but be confirmed if one follows as far as possible the chain of nature.

It is in the knowledge of this "natural police" that man's true vocation consists:

Man who is himself the eye and mind of the earth, always taking care to observe with astonishment the economy of the creator, discovers that he is the only being that must venerate God by observing the perfection of his work.

2.3. The concept of an "economy of nature," in what contemporaries called *la secte économiste*—that is, the Physiocrats—is entirely in agreement with these premises. The influence of Malebranche upon Quesnay is well documented (see Kubova in Quesnay, vol. 1, pp. 169–196), and, more generally, the influence of the model of the providential order on Physiocratic thought does not require proof. And yet, there has not been sufficient reflection on the curious circumstance that the modern science of economics and government has been constituted on the basis of a paradigm that had been developed within the horizon of the theological *oikonomia* and whose concepts and signatures [*segnature*] it is possible to precisely document.

The concept of "order," which we have seen to play an essential role in the constitution of the divine government of the world, has a particular relevance in this regard. It is at the center of Quesnay's thinking even before the 1750s, when he composes the celebrated *Tableau économique* (1758) and the articles "Fermiers" and "Grains" of the *Encyclopaedia* (1756). Well before taking on the form with which we are familiar, the term "economy" had established itself already in the first half of the eighteenth century in the syntagma "animal economy." However, animal economy is not a social science but a branch of medicine, which broadly corresponds to physiology. In 1736, Quesnay, who remained a medical doctor until the end of his life, composes the *Essay physique sur l'économie animale*, where the latter is defined in terms of an immanent order that forcefully calls to mind a paradigm of government. The animal economy, he writes, does not designate the animal as such, but

> [. . .] the order, the mechanism, the set of functions and movements that support animal life, the perfect and universal exercise of which, if executed faithfully, with alacrity and ease, constitutes the most flourishing state of health, in which the smallest disturbance is itself an illness.

It is sufficient to transfer this order of the "state of health" to the political state, from nature to society, in order that it be immediately converted into a paradigm of government. The *gouvernement économique d'un royaume* is nothing but the *ordre naturel plus avantageux*, and this results from the immutable laws that the Supreme Being has established for the formation and conservation of his work. Economy for Quesnay means order, and order founds government. For this reason the 1762 edition of the *Dictionnaire de l'Académie* can record as the meaning of the term *économie* "the order through which a political body principally subsists" (the 1798–1799 edition adds, "in this case it is called political economy"). Also here, as in Thomas Aquinas, order operates as a signature [*segnatura*] that serves to relate the theological order of the universe to the immanent order of human society; the general laws of providence and nature with the set of particular phenomena. Quesnay writes:

> Men cannot penetrate the designs for the construction of the universe of the Supreme Being; they cannot raise themselves to the destined ends of the immutable rules that he has established for the formation and conservation of his work. Nevertheless, if these rules are examined with care, one will realize that the physical causes of physical harm are the same as the causes of physical good; that rain, which irritates the traveler, fertilizes the earth. (Quesnay, vol. 2, p. 73)

(The example of the rain that is at once benign and destructive is, not coincidentally, what Malebranche uses to define the mechanism of providence.)

This substantially theological idea of a natural order impressed upon things is so clearly present in the thought of the *économistes* that the science that we call "political economy" could have been called the "science of order." This is the name that Le Trosne persistently gives it in his treatise *De l'ordre social* (1777), whose biblical epigraph taken from the book of Psalms leaves no doubt as to the origin of the concept. Despite the fact that Le Trosne is the first of the *économistes* to develop a theory of value that overcomes the limits of Physiocracy, his system rests upon unequivocally theological foundations. Indeed, through the concept (or rather, the signature [*segnatura*]) of "order" and the "economic truths" that it implies, he attempts to make it possible to comprehend and govern the politics that had "seemed to try to appear impenetrable up to that point" (Le Trosne, p. VIII).

> The science of administration presented nothing but facticious, arbitrary, and variable rules; and, since it could not achieve trust, to achieve respect it adopted the mysterious obscurity of the oracles. (Ibid., p. IX)

But as soon as men glimpse the "science of order," the mysteries dissipate and are replaced by the knowledge of the economy through which human societies have been established according to the same laws that support the physical world:

> There exists *a natural, immutable, and essential order* instituted by God in order to govern civil societies in the way most advantageous to sovereigns and subjects; men have by necessity partly conformed to it; otherwise any association between them would become impossible. And if societies are not as happy as they should be and as they should desire to be, that is because the disorders and evils that they undergo stem from the fact that, of that order, they merely know some general principles without understanding it as a whole, without drawing from it the practical consequences that follow from it, and moving away from it on some essential points. This order, which is so important to discover and understand, has a *physical basis* and is derived, through a chain of necessary relations, from the laws of physical order; these are the only means of growth for sustenance, riches, and populations and, consequently, for the prosperity of empires and for the measure of happiness that the social state entails. (Ibid., pp. 302–303)

The "economic science" of the Physiocrats is nothing but the "application" and transposition of the natural order into the "government of societies" (ibid., p. 318); but the *physis* in question is that which results from the paradigm of the divine government of the world, that is, from the ensemble of relations that exists between general laws and particular cases, between first causes and secondary causes, between ends and means, the calculation of which is the object of that "invention that is so important and ingenious" (ibid., p. 320) that is the *tableau économique*. The use of the syntagma *gouvernement de l'ordre*, to which the eighth discourse (*De l'évidence et la possibilité du gouvernement de l'ordre*) of Le Trosne's treatise is dedicated, is decisive. Here the genitive is, at once, subjective and objective; in the same way as in Thomas Aquinas, order is not an externally imposed schema, it is the being of God himself, which founds the government of the world and, at the same time, the dense network of immanent relations that, by linking the creatures together, renders them governable.

Political economy is constituted, in other words, as a social rationalization of providential *oikonomia*. It is not by chance, therefore, that the epigraph on the frontispiece of Le Mercier de la Rivière's treatise on the *Ordre naturel et essential des sociétés politiques* (1767) situates the new science with the words of Malebranche: "Order is the inviolable law of the Spirits and nothing is regulated if it does not conform to it."

2.4. Christian Marouby has demonstrated the importance of the concept of "economy of nature" in Adam Smith (Marouby, pp. 232–234). When it appears for the first time in the *Theory of Moral Sentiments* (1759), its links with the providential paradigm are entirely explicit. Not only does Smith avail himself of it to express the link that the "Author of nature" has established between the final causes and secondary causes, ends and means (Smith 2002, Part 1, § II, Chapter 5, note), but, more generally, he underlines on more than one occasion the affinity between his conception and the providential paradigm. Smith calls upon the "ancient Stoics": "The ancient Stoics were of the opinion that, as the world was governed by the all-ruling providence of a wise, powerful, and good God, every single event ought to be regarded as making a necessary part of the plan of the universe, and as tending to promote the general order and happiness of the whole: that the vices and follies of mankind, therefore, made as necessary a part of this plan as their wisdom or their virtue; and by that eternal art which educes good from ill, were made to tend equally to the prosperity and perfection of the great system of nature" (ibid., Part 1, § II, Chapter 3, p. 44). But Perrot has demonstrated the influence that French authors such as Mandeville, Malebranche, Pierre Nicole, and Pascal exercised over his thinking (Perrot, p. 348). Perrot believes that the celebrated passage according to which "it is not from the benevolence of the butcher, the brewer, or the baker that we expect our dinner, but from their regard to their own interest," derives from Nicole and Pascal; and it is from this perspective that one should investigate the celebrated image of the invisible hand.

It appears, as is well known, twice in Smith's work: the first time in the *Theory of Moral Sentiments* and, the second, in Chapter 2 of the fourth book of the *Wealth of Nations*:

> As every individual [. . .] directing that industry in such a manner as its produce may be of the greatest value, he intends only his own gain, and he is in this, as in many other cases, led by an invisible hand to promote an end which was no part of his intention. Nor is it always the worse for the society that it was no part of it. (Smith 1976, p. 477)

That the metaphor has a biblical origin is not in doubt. Even if the im-

mediate derivation is to be sought in all probability in the authors chronologically closer to Smith, our investigation into the genealogy of the
providential economic paradigm has led us by chance to this image on
more than one occasion. According to Augustine, God governs and administers the world, from the great to the small things, with an occult
hand sign ("omnia, maxima et minima, occulto nutu administranti": Augustine, *The Literal Meaning of Genesis*, 3, 17, 26); in Salvian's treatise on
the government of the world, empires and provinces, but also the smallest
details of private homes are led by "quasi quadam manu et gubernaculo"
(Salvian, *On the Government of God*); Thomas Aquinas (*Summa Theologiae*, q. 103, a. 1, ad 2, p. 5) speaks in the same way of a *manus gubernatoris*
that governs the created without being seen; in Luther (*De servo arbitrio*),
the creature is itself a hand (*Hand*) of the hidden God; finally, in Bossuet,
"Dieu tient du plus haut des cieux les rênes de tous les royaumes; il a tous
les coeurs en sa main" (Bossuet 1936, Part III, Chapter 7, pp. 1024–1025).

But the analogy is even stronger and deeper than the image of the "invisible hand" allows us to infer. Didier Deleule has magisterially analyzed
the link between Hume and Smith's thought and the birth of economic
liberalism. He opposes the "naturalism" of Hume and Smith to the "providentialism" of the Physiocrats who are direct tributaries, as we have seen, of
a theological paradigm. To the idea of an original divine design, comparable
to a project developed in the brain, Hume opposes, as we have seen, that
of an absolutely immanent principle of order, which functions instead as a
"stomach," rather than as a brain. "Why," he makes Philo ask, "can an ordered system not be woven out of a stomach rather than a brain"? (Deleule,
pp. 259 and 305, note 30). If it is probable that the Smithian image of the
invisible hand is to be understood, in this sense, as the action of an immanent principle, our reconstruction of the bipolar machine of the theological
oikonomia has shown that there is no conflict between "providentialism"
and "naturalism" within it, because the machine functions precisely by cor-
relating a transcendent principle with an immanent order. Just as with the
Kingdom and the Government, the intradivine trinity and the economic
trinity, so the "brain" and the "stomach" are nothing but two sides of the
same apparatus, of the same *oikonomia*, within which one of the two poles
can, at each turn, dominate the other.

Liberalism represents a tendency that pushes to an extreme the su-
premacy of the pole of the "immanent order-government-stomach" to
the point that it almost eliminates the pole "transcendent God-kingdom-

brain." But by doing so it merely plays off one side of the theological machine against the other. And when modernity abolishes the divine pole, the economy that is derived from it will not thereby have emancipated itself from its providential paradigm. In the same way, in modern Christian theology, there are forces that cast Christology into a near a-theological drift; but in this case as well, the theological model is not overcome.

2.5. In the *Theodicy*, Leibniz relates the opinion of certain cabalists according to which Adam's sin consisted in his separating the divine Kingdom from its other attributes, thereby making a dominion within a dominion:

> With the Hebrew Cabalists, *Malcuth* or the Kingdom, the last of the Sephiroth, signified that God controls everything irresistibly, but gently and without violence, so that man thinks he is following his own will while he carries out God's. They said that Adam's sin had been *truncatio Malcuth a caeteris plantis*, that is to say, that Adam had cut back the last of the Sephiroth, by making a dominion for himself within God's dominion [. . .] but that his fall had taught him that he could not subsist of himself, and that man must be redeemed by the Messiah. (Leibniz, § 372, p. 348)

According to Leibniz, Spinoza (who in the *Theologico-Political Treatise* again takes up the image of the *imperium in imperio* in order to criticize the modern idea of freedom), in his system, had done nothing but take the cabalist thesis to its extreme point.

The *oikonomia* of the moderns is this *truncatio Malcuth* that, taking for itself a sovereignty separated from its divine origin, in truth maintains the theological model of the government of the world. It establishes an *oikonomia* in the *oikonomia*, leaving intact the concept of government that conformed to this model. For this reason, it does not make sense to oppose secularism and the general will to theology and its providential paradigm; what is needed is, rather, an archaeological operation like the one that we have attempted here, one that, by moving upstream to a time before the separation that took place and that turned the two poles into rival but inseparable brothers, undoes the entire economic-theological apparatus and renders it inoperative.

That the two poles of this apparatus are not antagonistic, but remain secretly in agreement until the end, is evident in the thinking of the theologian who has brought the providential standpoint to such an extreme that it appears to resolve itself completely and without remainder in the image of the world of modernity. In his *Traité du libre arbitre* Bossuet tries at all costs to reconcile human freedom with the divine government of the world. God, he writes, wishes for all eternity that man be free, and not only potentially but in the actual and concrete exercise of his freedom.

> What is there more absurd than to say that man is not free because God wants him to be unfree? Should one not instead say, on the contrary, that he is free because God wants him so; and that, just as it comes about that we are free as a consequence of the decree that states that we are free, in the same way we freely execute this or that action as a consequence of the same decree that extends to the particulars? (Bossuet 1871, Chapter 8, p. 64)

The divine government of the world is so absolute and it penetrates creatures so deeply, that the divine will is annulled in the freedom of men (and the latter in the former):

> It is not necessary that God, to make us conform with his decree, places within us anything other than our own determination or that he places it within us through others. Just as it would be absurd to say that our own determination takes away our freedom, equally it would be to affirm that God takes it from us through his decree; and just as our will, deciding to choose one thing rather than another, does not take away the power to choose, one must conclude in the same way that God does not take it from us either. (Ibid., p. 65)

At this point, theology can resolve itself into atheism, and providentialism into democracy, because *God has made the world just as if it were without God and governs it as though it governed itself.*

> One can in fact say that God makes us just as we would be were we able to be on our own; because he makes us in all the principles and states of our being. Therefore, it is true to say that the state of our being is to be all that God wishes us to be. In the same way he makes man be what man is; and body be what body is; and thought be what thought is; and passion be what passion is; and action be what action is; and necessary be what necessary is; and free be what free is; and free in action and exercise what free in action and exercise is [. . .] (Ibid.)

In this grand image, in which the world created by God is identified with the world without God, and where contingency and necessity, freedom and slavery all merge into one another, the glorious center of the governmental machine appears clearly. Modernity, removing God from the world, has not only failed to leave theology behind, but in some ways has done nothing other than to lead the project of the providential *oikonomia* to completion.

Notes

Preface

1. In English in the original [*Translator's note*].

Chapter 2

1. *Governare le bestie* could be rendered in English as "to attend to the animals," or, more literally, "to govern animals" [*Translator's note*].

Chapter 5

1. In English in the original [*Translator's note*].

Chapter 6

1. The Supplement to Questions 89 and 94 Agamben refers to does not appear in the English translation of the *Summa*. A translation of these passages can, however, be found at http://www.newadvent.org/summa/5.htm [*Translator's note*].

2. The King James Bible uses "fail" for *katargeō*, as in 1 Corinthians 13:8 [*Translator's note*].

Chapter 7

1. Agamben is here referring to *Forza Italia*—literally "Go Italy!" or "Come on Italy!"—the party Silvio Berlusconi founded in 1993 and led until its dissolu-

tion into *Il Popolo della Libertà* (The People of Freedom) in 2008 [*Translator's note*].

2. In English in the original [*Translator's note*].

Chapter 8

1. In English in the original [*Translator's note*].
2. The English translation omits this passage from the 1990 Suhrkamp edition [*Translator's note*].
3. In English in the original [*Translator's note*].
4. In English in the original [*Translator's note*].

Appendix

1. The English translation of the *Eclaircissements* appended to Malebranche's *Treatise on Nature and Grace* is only partial. This passage and the subsequent ones are unavailable. Page references refer to the French original [*Translator's note*].

References

Alexander of Aphrodisias. 1931. *On Destiny.* Translated by A. Fitzgerald. London: The Scholartis Press.

Alexander of Aphrodisias. 1999. *La provvidenza. Questioni sulla provvidenza.* Edited by S. Fazzo and M. Zonta. Milan: Rizzoli.

Alexander of Hales. 1952. *Glossa in quatuor libros sententiarum Petri Lombardi.* Florence: Quaracchi.

Alföldi, Andreas. 1970. *Die monarchische Repräsentation im römischen Kaiserreiche.* Darmstadt: Wissenschaftliche Buchgesellschaft.

Amira, Karl von. 1905. *Die Handgebärden in den Bilderhandschriften des Sachsenspiegels.* Abhandlungen der Bayerischen Akademie der Wissenschaften, Philosophisch-Philologische und Historische Klasse, vol. 23, no 2.

Apuleius. 1909. *Apologia.* Translated by H. E. Butler. Oxford: Clarendon Press.

Aristides. 1951. *The Apology of Aristides the Philosopher.* In *The Ante-Nicene Fathers,* vol. X. Translated by Rev. D. M. Kay. Grand Rapids, MI: Wm. B. Eerdmans Publishing.

Aristotle. 1945. *Aristotle's Politics.* Edited by J. A. Smith and W. D. Ross. Oxford: Clarendon Press.

Aristotle. 1951. *De mundo.* In *The Works of Aristotle,* vol. III. Edited by J. A. Smith and W. D. Ross. Oxford: Clarendon Press.

Aristotle. 1953. *Aristotle's Metaphysics.* Revised with introduction and commentary by W. D. Ross. Oxford: Clarendon Press.

Aristotle. 1966. *Oeconomica.* Translated by E. S. Forster. In *The Works of Aristotle,* vol. X. Oxford: Clarendon Press.

Aristotle. 1984. *Nichomachean Ethics.* In *The Complete Works of Aristotle,* vol. 1. Translated by J. Barnes. Princeton: Princeton University Press.

Arius. 1957. *Letter to Alexander.* In Athanasius, *Select Works and Letters, The*

Nicene and Post-Nicene Fathers, vol. IV. Edited by A. Robertson. Grand Rapids, MI: Wm. B. Eerdmans Publishing.

Assmann, Jan. 2000. *Herrschaft und Heil. Politische Theologie in Altägypten, Israel und Europa*. Munich: Carl Hanser Verlag.

Athenagoras. 1956. *Embassy for the Christians; The Resurrection of the Dead*. Edited by J. Quasten and J. C. Plumpe. London: Longmans, Green & co.

Aubin, Paul. 1963. *Le problème de la conversion. Étude sur un terme commun à l'hellénisme et au christianisme des trois premiers siècles*. Paris: Beauchesne.

Augustine. 1847–1848. *Expositions on the Book of Psalms*. Vols. 1–5. Translated by J. H. Thomas. Oxford: J. Parker.

Augustine. 1873. *On the Trinity*. Translated by Rev. A. W. Hadden. Edinburgh: T. & T. Clark.

Augustine. 1952. *The City of God*. Translated by M. Dods. In *The Confessions, The City of God, On Christian Doctrine*. Chicago: Encyclopaedia Britannica.

Augustine. 1952. *On Christian Doctrine*. Translated by J. F. Shaw. In *The Confessions, The City of God, On Christian Doctrine*. Chicago: Encyclopaedia Britannica.

Augustine. 1992. *On Nature and Grace*. In *Four Anti-Pelagian Writings*. Translated by J. A. Mourant and W. J. Collinge. Washington, DC: Catholic University of America Press.

Augustine. 2002. *The Literal Meaning of Genesis*. In *On Genesis*. Translated by E. Hill. Hyde Park, NY: New City Press.

Augustine. 2002. *A Refutation of the Manichees*. In *On Genesis*. Translated by E. Hill. Hyde Park, NY: New City Press.

Augustine. 2006. *Confessions*. Translated by F. J. Sheed. Indianapolis: Hackett.

Augustine. 2007. *On Order*. Translated by S. Borruso. South Bend, IN: St. Augustine's Press.

Austin, John L. 1962. *How to Do Things with Words*. Oxford: Clarendon.

Ball, Hugo. 1923. *Byzantinisches Christentum. Drei Heiligenleben*. Munich: Duncker & Humboldt.

Balthasar, Hans Urs von. 1965. *Rechenschaft*. Einsiedeln: Johannes Verlag.

Balthasar, Hans Urs von. 1982. *The Glory of the Lord*. Vol. 1. Translated by E. Leiva-Merikakis. Edinburgh: T. & T. Clark.

Barth, Karl. 1957. *Church Dogmatics*. Vol. 2, *The Doctrine of God*, first half volume. Edited by G. W. Bromiley and T. F. Torrance. Edinburgh: T. & T. Clark.

Basil. 1952. *Letters and Select Works*. In *The Nicene and Post-Nicene Fathers*, vol. VIII. Translated by Rev. B. Jackson. Grand Rapids, MI: Wm. B. Eerdmans Publishing.

Bayle, Pierre. 1704–1707. *Réponse aux questions d'un provincial*. 5 vols. Rotterdam.

Bengsch, Alfred. 1957. *Heilsgeschichte und Heilswissen. Eine Untersuchung zur*

Struktur und Entfaltung des theologischen Denkens im Werk "Adversus haereses" des heiligen Irenäus. Leipzig: St. Benno-Verlag.

Benz, Ernst. 1932. *Marius Victorinus und die Entwicklung der abendländischen Willenmetaphysik.* Stuttgart: Kohlahmmer.

Blatt, Franz. 1928. "Ministerium-Mysterium." In *Archivum Latinitatis Medii Aevi*, 4, pp. 80–81.

Blumenberg, Hans. 1985. *The Legitimacy of the Modern Age.* Cambridge, MA: MIT Press.

Boethius. 1969. *The Consolation of Philosophy.* Translated by V. E. Watts. Harmondsworth, UK: Penguin.

Bossuet, Jacques Bénigne. 1871. *Traité du libre arbitre.* In *Œuvres choisies*, vol. IV. Paris: Gallimard.

Bossuet, Jacques Bénigne. 1936. *Discours sur l'histoire universelle.* In *Œuvres.* Paris: Gallimard.

Bréhier, Émile. 1938–1939. "Les lectures malebranchistes de J.-J. Rousseau." In *Révue internationale de philosophie*, 1 (October), pp. 98–142.

Bréhier, Louis, and Pierre Batiffol. 1920. *Les survivances du culte impérial romain, à propos des rites shintoïstes.* Paris: Picard.

Cabasilas, Nicolas. 1967. *Explication de la divine liturgie.* In *Sources chrétiennes*, 4bis. Paris: Cerf.

Caird, George B. 1956. *Principalities and Powers. A Study in Pauline Theology. The Chancellor's Lectures for 1954 at Queen's University, Kingston, Ontario.* Oxford: Clarendon Press.

Carchia, Gianni. 1997. "Elaborazione della fine. Mito, gnosi, modernità." *Contro tempo*, 2, pp. 18–28.

Christ, Felix (editor). 1967. *Oikonomia: Heilsgeschichte als Thema der Theologie. Oscar Cullmann zum 65. Geburtstag gewidmet.* Hamburg-Bergstedt: Herbert Reich.

Cicero. 1965. *Letters to Atticus.* Edited by D. R. Shackleton Bailey. Cambridge: Cambridge University Press.

Clement of Alexandria. 1934. *The Excerpta ex Theodoto of Clement of Alexandria.* Edited with translation, introduction, and notes by R. P. Casey. London: Christophers.

Clement of Alexandria. 1951. *The Clementine Homilies.* In *The Ante-Nicene Fathers*, vol. VIII. Translated by Rev. T. Smith. Grand Rapids, MI: Wm. B. Eerdmans Publishing.

Clement of Alexandria. 1962. *Exhortation to the Heathen.* In *The Ante-Nicene Fathers*, vol. II. Edited by Rev. A. Roberts and J. Donaldson. Grand Rapids, MI: Wm. B. Eerdmans Publishing.

Clement of Alexandria. 1962. *The Stromata, or Miscellanies.* In *The Ante-Nicene*

Fathers, vol. II. Edited by Rev. A. Roberts and J. Donaldson. Grand Rapids, MI: Wm. B. Eerdmans Publishing.

Coccia Emanuele. 2006. "Il bene e le sue opere in un trattato anonimo della fine del sec. XIII." In *Etica e conoscenza nel XIII e XIV secolo*. Edited by I. Zavattero. Arezzo: Università degli Studi di Siena.

Constantine Porphyrogenitus. 1935. *Le livre des cérémonies*. Vol. I. Paris: Les Belles Lettres.

Costa, Pietro. 1969. *Iurisdictio. Semantica del potere politico nella pubblicistica medievale. 1100–1433*. Milan: Giuffrè.

Courtenay, William. 1990. *Capacity and Volition. A History of the Distinction of Absolute and Ordained Power*. Bergamo: P. Lubrina.

Cyril of Jerusalem. 2000. In E. Yarnold, *Cyril of Jerusalem*, containing Cyril's *Mystagogic Catechesis*. London: Routledge.

D'Alès, Adhémar. 1919. "Le mot 'oikonomia' dans la langue théologique de saint Irénée." In *Revue des études grecques*, 32, pp. 1–9.

Daniélou, Jean. 1990. *Les anges et leur mission d'après les Pères de l'église*. Chevetogne: Éditions de Chevetogne.

Dante. 1990. *The Banquet*. Translated by R. H. Lansing. New York: Garland Publishing.

Debord, Guy. 1994. *The Society of the Spectacle*. Translated by D. Nicholson-Smith. New York: Zone Books.

Deleule, Didier. 1979. *Hume et la naissance du libéralisme économique*. Paris: Aubier Montaigne.

Dieterich, Albrecht. 1903. *Eine Mithrasliturgie*. Leipzig: Teubner.

Diodorus Siculus. 1939. *The Library of History*. Translated by C. H. Oldfather. London: Heinemann.

Dionysius, the Areopagite. 1894. *The Celestial and Ecclesiastical Hierarchy*. Translated by Rev. J. Parker. London: Skeffington & Son.

Dionysius, the Areopagite. 1957. *The Divine Names*. Translated by C. Rolt. London: Unwin Brothers.

Doornick, Stefan von. 1891. *Die summa über das Decretum Gratiani*. Giessen: Kessinger.

Dörrie, Heinrich. 1970. "Der König. Ein platonische Schlüsselwort, von Plotin mit neuem Sinn erfüllt." In *Revue internationale de philosophie*, 24, pp. 217–235.

Durant, Will. 1947. *The Story of Philosophy*. London: Ernest Benn.

Durkheim, Émile. 1995. *The Elementary Forms of Religious Life*. Translated by K. E. Fields. New York: The Free Press.

Eunomius. 1987. *Expositio Fidei / The Confession of Faith*. In *The Extant Works*. Translated and edited by R. P. Vaggione. Oxford: Clarendon.

Eusebius. 1903. *Preparation for the Gospel*. Translated by E. H. Gifford. Oxford: E Typographeo Academico.

Eusebius. 1927. *The Ecclesiastical History and the Martyrs of Palestine*. Edited by H. J. Lawlor and J. E. L. Oulton. London: Society for Promoting Christian Knowledge.

Eusebius. 1957. *Letter of Eusebius of Caesarea to the People of His Diocese*. In Athanasius, *Select Works and Letters, The Nicene and Post-Nicene Fathers*, vol. IV. Edited by A. Robertson. Grand Rapids, MI: Wm. B. Eerdmans Publishing.

Fénelon, François. 1997. *Réfutation du système du père Malebranche*. In *Œuvres*. Paris: Gallimard.

Flasch, Kurt. 1956. *"Ordo dicitur multipliciter." Eine Studie zur Philosophie des "ordo" bei Thomas von Aquin*. Phil. Dissertation. Frankfurt.

Foucault, Michel. 2009. *Security, Territory, Population. Lectures at the Collège de France 1977–1978*. Translated by G. Burchell. New York: Picador.

Gass, Wilhelm. 1874. "Das Patristische Wort 'oikonomia.'" In *Zeitschrift für wissenschaftliche Theologie*.

Gernet, Louis. 1981. *The Anthropology of Ancient Greece*. Baltimore: Johns Hopkins University Press.

Giles of Rome. 1986. *On Ecclesiastical Power*. Translated by R. W. Dyson. Woodbridge, UK: The Boydel Press.

Gogarten, Friedrich. 1953. *Verhängnis und Hoffnung der Neuzeit. Die Säkularisierung als theologisches Problem*. Stuttgart: Vorwerk.

Gregory of Nazianzus. 1952. *Select Orations*. In *The Nicene and Post-Nicene Fathers*, vol. VII. Translated by C. G. Browne and J. E. Swallow. Grand Rapids, MI: Wm. B. Eerdmans Publishing.

Gregory of Nyssa. 1972. *The Great Catechism*. In *The Nicene and Post-Nicene Fathers*, vol. V. Translated by W. Moore and H. A. Wilson. Grand Rapids, MI: Wm. B. Eerdmans Publishing.

Grimm, Dieter. 1995. "Does Europe Need a Constitution?" In *European Law Journal*, 3, no. 95.

Habermas, Jürgen. 1991. *The Structural Transformation of the Public Sphere. An Inquiry into a Category of Bourgeois Society*. Translated by T. Burger. Cambridge, MA: MIT Press.

Harnack, Adolf. 1924. *Marcion. Das Evangelium vom fremden Gott. Eine Monographie zur Geschichte der Grundlegung der katholischen Kirche*. Leipzig: Hinrichs.

Heidegger, Martin. 1962. *Kant and the Problem of Metaphysics*. Translated by R. Taft. Bloomington: Indiana University Press.

Heidegger, Martin. 1994. *Bremer und Freiburger Vorträge*. Frankfurt: Klostermann.

Hellingrath, Norbert von. 1936. *Hölderlin-Vermächtnis. Forschungen und Vorträge. Ein Gedenkbuch zum 14. Dezember 1936*. Munich: Bruckmann.

Hesiod. 2004. *Theogony, Works and Days*. Translation, introduction, and notes by A. N. Athanassakis. Baltimore: Johns Hopkins University Press.

Hippolytus of Rome. 1977. *Contra Noetum*. Introduced, edited, and translated by R. Butterworth. London: Heythrop Monographs.

Hobbes, Thomas. 1983. *De Cive*. Oxford: Clarendon Press.

Ibn Rushd [Averroes]. 1984. *Ibn Rushd's Metaphysics*. Translated by C. Genequand. Leiden: Brill.

Ignatius of Antioch. 1946. *The Epistles of St. Clement of Rome and St. Ignatius of Antioch*. Translated by J. A. Kleist. Westminster, MD: The Newman Press.

Irenaeus. 1868. *Against Heresies*. In *The Writings of Irenaeus*. Translated by Rev. A. Roberts and Rev. W. H. Rambaut. Edinburgh: T. & T. Clark.

Isidore of Seville. 2006. *The Etymologies*. Translated, with introduction and notes by S. A. Barney, W. J. Lewis, J. A. Beach, and O. Berghof. Cambridge: Cambridge University Press.

Jesi, Furio. 1999. "Rilke, Elegie di Duino. Scheda introduttiva." In *Cultura tedesca, 12*.

John Chrysostom. 1889. *Homilies on the Epistle to the Hebrews*. In *Nicene and Post-Nicene Fathers*, vol. XIV. Translated by Rev. F. Gardiner. Grand Rapids, MI: Wm. B. Eerdmans Publishing.

John Chrysostom. 1961. *Sur la providence de Dieu*. Edited by A.-M. Malingrey. In *Sources chrétiennes*, 79. Paris: Cerf.

John of Damascus. 1973. *Exposition of the Orthodox Faith*. In *The Nicene and Post-Nicene Fathers*, vol. IX. Translated by Rev. S. D. F. Salmond. Grand Rapids, MI: Wm. B. Eerdmans Publishing.

Justin. 1867. *The First Apology*. In *Translations of the Writings of the Fathers down to A.D. 325*. Edited by Rev. A. Roberts and J. Donaldson. Edinburgh: T. & T. Clark.

Justin. 1881. *Iustini philosophi et martyris opera quae feruntur omnia*. Edited by J.C. T. Otto. Vol. 3, *Opera Iustini subditicia. Fragmenta Pseudo-Iustini*, t. 2, "Corpus apologetarum Christianorum saeculi secundi." Jenae.

Justin. 2003. *Dialogue with Trypho*. Translated by Rev. T. B. Falls. Washington, DC: The Catholic University of America Press.

Kantorowicz, Ernst. 1946. *Laudes Regiae. A Study in Liturgical Acclamations and Medieval Ruler Worship*. Berkeley: University of California Press.

Kantorowicz, Ernst. 1957. *The King's Two Bodies. A Study in Medieval Political Theology*. Princeton: Princeton University Press.

Kantorowicz, Ernst. 2005. *I misteri dello Stato*. Edited by G. Solla. Genoa: Marietti.

Kolping, Adolf. 1948. *Sacramentum Tertullianeum. Erster Teil: Untersuchungen über die Anfänge des christlichen Gebrauches der Vokabel "Sacramentum."* Münster: Regensberg.

Kornemann, Ernst. 1905. "Zum Streit un die Entstehung des Monumentum Ancyranum." In *Klio*, 5, pp. 317–322.

Krings, Hermann. 1940. "Das Sein und die Ordnung. Eine Skizze zur Ontologie des Mittelalters." In *Deutsche Vierteljahrsschrift für Literaturwissensschaft und Geistesgeschichte*, 18, pp. 233–249.

Krings, Hermann. 1941. *Ordo. Philosophisch-historische Grundlegung einer abendländischen Idee*. Halle: Niemeyer.

Leibniz, Gottfried Wilhelm von. 1951. *Theodicy. Essays on the Goodness of God, the Freedom of Man, and the Origin of Evil*. Edited with an introduction by A. Farrer. Translated by E. M. Huggard. London: Routledge & Kegan Paul.

Lessius, Leonardus. 1861. *De perfectionibus moribusque divinis libri 14*. Freiburg.

Le Trosne, Guillaume François. 1777 [1980]. *De l'ordre social. Ouvrage suivi d'un traité élementaire sur la valeur, l'argent, la circulation, l'industrie & le commerce intérieure & extérieure*. Paris [Munich: Kraus Reprint].

Lillge, Otto. 1955. *Das patristische Wort "oikonomia." Seine Geschichte und seine Bedeutung*. Dissertation. Erlangen.

Longinus. 1935. *Longinus on the Sublime*. Translated by W. R. Roberts. Cambridge: Cambridge University Press.

Löwith, Karl. 1953. *Weltgeschichte und Heilsgeschehen. Die theologischen Voraussetzungen der Geschichtsphilosophie*. Stuttgart: W. Kohlhammer.

Lübbe, Hermann. 1965. *Säkularisierung. Geschichte eines ideenpolitischen Begriffs*. Freiburg: Alber.

Lünig, Johann Christian. 1719. *Theatrum ceremoniale historico-politicum*. Leipzig.

Maccarone, Michele. 1959. *Il sovrano "Vicarius Dei" nell'Alto Medioevo*. Leiden: Brill.

Maimonides, Moses. 1963. *The Guide of the Perplexed*. Translated by S. Pines. Chicago: University of Chicago Press.

Malebranche, Nicolas. 1923. *Dialogues on Metaphysics and on Religion*. Translated by M. Ginsberg. London: George Allen & Unwin.

Malebranche, Nicolas. 1979. *Traité de la nature et de la grâce*. In *Œuvres*, vol. 2. Paris: Gallimard.

Malebranche, Nicolas. 1992. *Treatise on Nature and Grace*. Translated by P. Riley. Oxford: Clarendon Press.

Marcus Aurelius. 1887. *The Meditations of Marcus Aurelius*. Translated by J. Collier. London: Walter Scott.

Markus, Robert A. 1954. "Pleroma and Fulfilment. The Significance of History in St. Irenaeus' Opposition to Gnosticism." In *Vigiliae Christianae*, 8, no. 4.

Markus, Robert A. 1958. "Trinitarian Theology and the Economy." In *Journal of Theological Studies*, 9.

Marouby, Christian. 2004. *L'économie de la nature. Essai sur Adam Smith et l'anthropologie de la croissance.* Paris: Seuil.

The Martyrdom of Polycarp. 1954. In *The Apostolic Fathers II.* Translated by K. Lake. London: William Heinemann.

Mascall, Eric L. 1951. "Primauté de la louange." In *Dieu vivant,* 19.

Matthew of Acquasparta. 1956. *Quaestiones disputatae de productione rerum et de providentia.* Bibliotheca Franciscana 17. Florence: Quaracchi.

Mauss, Marcel. 1968. *Œuvres.* Vol. 1. Paris: Les Éditions de Minuit.

Mauss, Marcel. 1974. *Œuvres.* Vol. 2. Paris: Les Éditions de Minuit.

Mauss, Marcel. 2003. *On Prayer.* Translated by S. Leslie. New York: Durkheim Press.

Mauss, Marcel. *Manuscript.* [Quotations refer to the handwritten transcription that was kindly lent to me by Claudio Rugafiori.]

Melandri, Enzo. 2004. *La linea e il circolo.* Macerata: Quodlibet.

Moingt, Joseph. 1966. *Théologie trinitaire de Tertullien.* 3 vols. Paris: Aubier.

Moltmann, Jürgen. 1981. *The Trinity and the Kingdom of God.* Translated by M. Kohl. London: SCM Press.

Mommsen, Theodor. 1969. *Römisches Staatsrecht.* 5 vols. Graz: Akademische Druck.

Mondzain, Marie-José. 1996. *Image, icône, économie. Les source byzantines de l'imaginaire contemporain.* Paris: Seuil.

Mopsik, Charles. 1993. *Les grandes textes de la cabale. Les rites qui font Dieu.* Lagrasse: Verdier.

Nagy, Gregory. 1979. *The Best of the Achaens. Concepts of the Hero in Archaic Greek Poetry.* Baltimore: Johns Hopkins University Press.

Napoli, Paolo. 2003. *Naissance de la police moderne. Pouvoir, normes, société.* Paris: La Découverte.

Nautin, Pierre (editor). 1949. Hippolyte. *Contre les hérésies.* Paris: Cerf.

Negri, Antonio, and Michael Hardt. 2000. *Empire.* Cambridge, MA: Harvard University Press.

Norden, Eduard. 1913. *Agnostos theos. Untersuchungen zur Formengeschichte religiöser Rede.* Leipzig: Teubner.

Origen. 1973. *On First Principles.* Translated by G. W. Butterworth. Gloucester, MA: Peter Smith.

Origen. 1983. *Philocalie, 1–20, sur les écritures et la Lettre à Africanus sur l'histoire de Suzanne.* In *Sources chrétiennes,* 302. Paris: Cerf.

Origen. 1992. *Commentaire sur S. Jean.* In *Sources chrétiennes,* 385. Paris: Cerf.

Origen. 1998. *Homilies on Jeremiah: Homily on 1 Kings 28.* Translated by J. C. Smith. Washington, DC: The Catholic University of America.

Ovid. 1851. *The Pontic Epistles.* In *The Fasti, Tristia, Pontic Epistles, Ibis, and Halieuticon.* Translated by H. T. Riley. London: H. G. Bohn.

Pascal, Blaise. 1962. *Pensées*. Paris: Seuil.

Pascal, Blaise. 2003. *Letters Written to a Provincial*. In *The Mind on Fire*. Edited by J. M. Houston. Vancouver: Regent College Publishing.

Perrot, Jean-Claude. 1992. *Une histoire intellectuelle de l'économie politique. 17–18 siècle*. Paris: Éditions de l'École des Hautes Études en Sciences Sociales.

Peters, Edward. 2001. *Limits of Thought and Power in Medieval Europe*. Aldershot, UK: Ashgate.

Peterson, Erik. 1926. *Heis Theos. Epigraphische, formgeschichtliche und religiongeschichtliche Untersuchungen*. Göttingen: Vandenhoeck und Ruprecht.

Peterson, Erik. 1994. *Ausgewählte Schriften*. Vol. 1, *Theologische Traktate*. Würzburg: Echter.

Peterson, Erik. 1995. *Ausgewählte Schriften*. Vol. 2, *Marginalien zur Theologie und andere Schriften*. Würzburg: Echter.

PG: Patrologiae cursus completus. Series Graeca. 1857–1866. Edited by Jacques-Paul Migne. Paris.

Philip the Chancellor. 1985. *Summa de bono*. 2 vols. Bern: Editiones Francke Bernae.

Philo. 1993. *The Works of Philo*. Translated by C. D. Yonge. Peabody, MA: Hendrickson Publishers.

Photius. 1986. *Photii Epistulae et Amphilochia*. Vol. 4. Edited by L. G. Westerink. Leipzig: Teubner.

Picard, Charles. 1954. "Le trône vide d'Alexandre dans la cérémonie de Cyunda et le culte du trône vide à travers le monde gréco-romain." In *Cahiers archéologiques*, VII, pp. 1–18.

PL: Patrologiae cursus completus. Series Latina. 1844–1855. Edited by Jacques-Paul Migne. Paris.

Plato. 2002. *Letters*. In *The Collected Dialogues*. Edited by E. Hamilton and H. Cairns. Princeton: Princeton University Press.

Plutarch. 1959. *On Fate*. In *Moralia VII*. Edited by P. H. De Lacy and B. Einarson. Cambridge, MA: Harvard University Press.

Pohlenz, Max. 1948. *Die Stoa. Geschichte einer geistigen Bewegung*. 2 vols. Göttingen: Vandenhoeck & Ruprecht.

Postigliola, Alberto. 1992. *La città della ragione—per una storia filisofica del settecento francese*. Rome: Bulzoni.

Prestige, George L. 1952. *God in Patristic Thought*. London: SPCK.

Proclus. 1833. *Two Treatises of Proclus*. Translated by T. Taylor. London: William Pickering.

Proclus. 1963. *The Elements of Theology*. Translated by E. R. Dodds. Oxford: Clarendon Press.

Proclus. 2004. *Tria Opuscula. Provvidenza, libertà, male*. Edited by F. F. Paparella. Milan: Bompiani.

Puech, Henri Ch. 1978. *En quête de la Gnose*. Paris: Gallimard.

Quesnay, François. 1968. *Quesnay et la physiocratie*. 2 vols. Paris: Institut National d'Études Démographiques.

Quidort. 1614. *Fratris Johannis de Parisiis . . . de potestate regia et papali*. In Melchior Goldast, *Monarchiae sacri Romani imperii, sive Tractatuum de iurisdictione imperiali seu regia et pontificia seu sacerdotalis*, vol. 2. Frankfurt.

Radó, Polycarpus. 1966. *Enchiridion liturgicum complectens theologiae sacramentalis et dogmata et leges*. Rome: Herder.

Res gestae divi Augusti. 2009. Translated by A. E. Cooley. Cambridge: Cambridge University Press.

Richter, Gerhard. 2005. *Oikonomia. Der Gebrauch des Wortes Oikonomia im Neuen Testament, bei den Kirchenvätern und in der teologischen Literatur bis ins 20. Jahrundert*. Berlin: de Gruyter.

Rigo, Antonio (editor). 2004. *Gregorio Palmas e oltre. Studi e documenti sulle controversie teologiche del XIV secolo bizantino*. Florence: Olschki.

Riley, Patrick. 1988. *The General Will Before Rousseau. The Transformation of the Divine into the Civic*. Princeton: Princeton University Press.

Rilke, Rainer Maria. 1987. *Sonnets to Orpheus*. Translated by D. Young. Middletown, CT: Wesleyan University Press.

Rilke, Rainer Maria. 2000. *Duino Elegies*. Translated by E. Snow. New York: North Point Press.

Ross, William D. 1953. *Aristotle's Metaphysics*. Oxford: Clarendon Press.

Rousseau, Jean-Jacques. 1992. *Discourse on Political Economy*. In *Collected Writings of Rousseau*, vol. III. Translated by J. R. Bush, R. D. Masters, C. Kelly, and T. Marshall. Hanover, NH: University Press of New England.

Rousseau, Jean-Jacques. 2001. *Letters Written from the Mountain*. In *The Collected Writings of Rousseau*, vol. IX. Translated by J. R. Bush and C. Kelly. Hanover, NH: University Press of New England.

Rousseau, Jean-Jacques. 2002. *The Social Contract*. In *The Social Contract and the First and Second Discourses*. Edited by S. Dunn. New Haven, CT: Yale University Press.

Salvian. 1977. *The Writings of Salvian, the Presbyter*. Translated by J. F. O'Sullivan. Washington, DC: The Catholic University of America Press.

Santillana, Giorgio De. 1963. "Fato antico e fato moderno." In *Tempo presente*, VIII, no. 9–10.

Scarpat, Giuseppe. 1959. "Introduction" to Tertullian, *Adversus Praxean*. Turin: Loescher.

Schelling, Friedrich Wilhelm Joseph. 1977. *Philosophie der Offenbarung. 1841/42*. Frankfurt: Suhrkamp.

Schenk, Gerrit Jasper. 2003. *Zeremoniell und Politik. Herrschereinzüge im spätmittelalterlichen Reich*. Cologne: Böhlau.

Schickel, Joachim. 1993. *Gespräche mit Carl Schmitt*. Berlin: Merve.

Schmitt. Carl. 1927. *Volksentscheid und Volksbegehren. Ein Beitrag zur Auslegung der Weimarer Verfassung und zur Lehre von der unmittelbaren Demokratie.* Berlin: Walter de Gruyter.

Schmitt, Carl. 1933. *Staat, Bewegung, Volk. Die Dreigliederung der politischen Einheit.* Hamburg: Hanseatische Verlagsanstalt.

Schmitt, Carl. 2003. *Nomos of the Earth in the International Law of the Jus Publicum Europaeum.* Translated by G. L. Ulmen. New York: Telos Press.

Schmitt, Carl. 2005. *Political Theology: Four Chapters on the Concept of Sovereignty.* Translated and with an introduction by G. Schwab. Chicago: University of Chicago Press.

Schmitt, Carl. 2008a. *Political Theology II: The Myth of the Closure of Any Political Theology.* Edited by M. Hoelzl and G. Ward. Cambridge: Polity Press.

Schmitt, Carl. 2008b. *Constitutional Theory.* Translated and edited by J. Seitzer. Durham, NC: Duke University Press.

Scholem, Gershom. 1990. *Origins of the Kabbalah.* Translated by A. Arkush. Princeton: Princeton University Press.

Scholem, Gershom. 1997. *On the Mystical Shape of the Godhead.* Translated by J. Neugroschel. New York: Schocken Books.

Schramm, Ernst Percy. 1954–1965. *Herrschaftszeichen und Staatssymbolik. Beiträge zu ihrer Geschichte vom dritten bis zum sechzehnten Jahrhundert.* 3 vols. Stuttgart: Anton Hiersemann.

Schürmann, Reiner. 1990. *Heidegger on Being and Acting: From Principles to Anarchy.* Bloomington: Indiana University Press.

Seibt, Klaus. 1994. *Die Theologie des Markell von Ankyra.* Berlin: de Gruyter.

Senellart, Michel. 1995. *Les arts de gouverner. Du "regimen" médiéval au concept de gouvernement.* Paris: Seuil.

Silva Tarouca, Amadeo de. 1937. "L'idée d'ordre dans la philosophie de Saint Thomas d'Aquin." In *Revue néoscholastique de philosophie,* 40, pp. 341–384.

Simonetti, Manlio (editor). 1986. *Il Cristo.* Vol. II, *Testi teologici e spirituali in lingua greca dal IV al VII secolo.* Milan: Fondazione Valla/Mondadori.

Smith, Adam. 1976. *An Enquiry into the Nature and Causes of the Wealth of Nations.* Chicago: University of Chicago Press.

Smith, Adam. 2002. *Theory of Moral Sentiments.* Cambridge: Cambridge University Press.

Spinoza, Benedict. 2002. *Ethics.* In *Complete Works.* Translated by S. Shirley. Indianapolis: Hackett Publishing.

Stein, Bernhard. 1939. *Der Begriff KEBOD JAHWEH und seine Bedeutung für die Alttestamentliche Gotteserkenntnis.* Emsdetten: Heim.

Stoicorum veterum fragmenta (SVF). 1903. Edited by Hans von Arnim. Vols. II–III. Leipzig: Teubner.

Suárez, Francisco. 1858. *Opera omnia.* Vol. 3. Paris: Vives.

The Targum Onqelos to Genesis. 1988. Translated by B. Grossfeld. Edinburgh: T. & T. Clark.

Tatian. 1867. *Address of Tatian to the Greeks*. In *The Writings of Tatian and Theophilus; and The Clementine Recognitions*. Translated by Rev. B. P. Pratten, Rev. M. Dods, and Rev. T. Smith. Edinburgh: T. & T. Clark.

Taubes, Jacob. 1987. *Ad Carl Schmitt. Gegenstrebige Fügung*. Berlin: Merve.

Tertullian. 1948. *Tertullian's Treatise Against Praxeas*. Edited by E. Evans. London: SPCK.

Tertullian. 1972. *Adversus Marcionem*. Edited and translated by E. Evans. Oxford: Clarendon Press.

Theodoret. 1969. *Dialogues (The "Eranistes" or "Polymorphus" of the Blessed Theodoretus, Bishop of Cyrus)*. Translated with notes by Rev. B. Jackson. In *The Nicene and Post-Nicene Fathers*, vol. III. Grand Rapids, MI: Wm. B. Eerdmans Publishing.

Theodoret of Cyrus. 2001. *Commentary on the Letters of Saint Paul*. 2 vols. Translated with an introduction by Robert Charles Hill. Brookline, MA: Holy Cross Orthodox Press.

Theophilus of Antioch. 1970. *Ad Autolycum*. Edited and translated by R. M. Grant. Oxford: Clarendon Press.

Thomas Aquinas. 1961. *Commentary on the Metaphysics of Aristotle*. Translated by J. P. Rowan. Chicago: Regnery.

Thomas Aquinas. 1964–1981. *Summa Theologiae*. Edited and translated by Th. Gilby et al. London: Blackfriars.

Thomas Aquinas. 1975. *Summa contra Gentiles*. Translated by A. C. Pegis, J. F. Anderson, V. J. Bourke, and Ch. J. O'Neil. London: University of Notre Dame Press.

Thomas Aquinas. 1979. *On Kingship to the King of Cyprus*. Revised translation, introduction, and notes by I. Th. Eschmann. Westport, CT: Hyperion Press.

Thomas Aquinas. 1996. *Commentary on the Book of Causes*. Translated by V. A. Guagliardo, C. R. Hess, and R. C. Taylor. Washington, DC: The Catholic University of America Press.

Thomas Aquinas. 1997. *On the Government of Rulers: De regimine principum*. Translated by J. M. Blythe. Philadelphia: University of Pennsylvania Press.

Torrance, Thomas. 1967. "The Implications of Oikonomia for Knowledge and Speech of God in Early Christian Theology." In *Oikonomia. Heilgeschichte als Thema der Theologie. Oscar Cullmann zum 65. Geburstag gewidmet*. Edited by Felix Christ. Hamburg-Bergstedt: Herbert Reich.

Troeltsch, Ernst. 1925. *Glaubenslehre. Nach Heidelberger Vorlesungen aus den Jahren 1911 und 1912*. Munich: Duncker & Humblot.

Verhoeven, Theodorus L. 1948. *Studiën over Tertullianus' "Adversus Praxean." Voornamelijk betrekking hebbend op Monarchia, Oikonomia, Probola in ver-*

band met de Triniteit. Amsterdam: N. V. Noord-Hollandsche Uitgevers Maatschappij.

Vernant, Jean-Pierre. 1972. "Ebauches de la volonté dans la tragédie grecque." In Various Authors, *Psychologie comparative et art. Hommage à Ignace Meyerson.* Paris: PUF.

Weston, Jessie L. 1920. *From Ritual to Romance.* Cambridge: Cambridge University Press.

William of Auvergne. 1570. *De Retributionibus sanctorum.* In *Opera omnia,* vol. 2. Paris.

Wolff, Christian. 1995. *Natürliche Gottesgelahrtheit nach beweisender Lehrart abgefasset.* In *Gesammelte Werke,* ser. I, vol. 23.5. Hildesheim: Olms.

Xenophon. 1923. *Memorabilia and Oeconomicus.* Translated by E. C. Marchant. London: Heinemann.

Crossing Aesthetics

Paul Celan, *The Meridian*

Bernard Stiegler, *Technics and Time, 3: Cinematic Time and the Question of Malaise*

Giorgio Agamben, *The Sacrament of Language: An Archeology of the Oath*

Peter Fenves: *The Messianic Reduction: Walter Benjamin and the Shape of Time*

Giorgio Agamben, *Nudities*

Hans Blumenberg, *Care Crosses the River*

Bernard Stiegler, *Taking Care of Youth and the Generations*

Ruth Stein, *For Love of the Father: A Psychoanalytic Study of Religious Terrorism*

Giorgio Agamben, *"What is an Apparatus?" and Other Essays*

Rodolphe Gasché, *Europe, or the Infinite Task: A Study of a Philosophical Concept*

Bernard Stiegler, *Technics and Time, 2: Disorientation*

Bernard Stiegler, *Acting Out*

Susan Bernstein, *Housing Problems: Writing and Architecture in Goethe, Walpole, Freud, and Heidegger*

Martin Hägglund, *Radical Atheism: Derrida and the Time of Life*

Cornelia Vismann, *Files: Law and Media Technology*

Jean-Luc Nancy, *Discourse of the Syncope: Logodaedalus*

Carol Jacobs, *Skirting the Ethical: Sophocles, Plato, Hamann, Sebald, Campion*

Cornelius Castoriadis, *Figures of the Thinkable*

Jacques Derrida, *Psyche: Inventions of the Other*, 2 volumes, edited by Peggy Kamuf and Elizabeth Rottenberg

Mark Sanders, *Ambiguities of Witnessing: Literature and Law in the Time of a Truth Commission*

Sarah Kofman, *The Sarah Kofman Reader*, edited by Thomas Albrecht, with Georgia Albert and Elizabeth Rottenberg

Susannah Young-ah Gottlieb, ed. *Hannah Arendt: Reflections on Literature and Culture*

Alan Bass, *Interpretation and Difference: The Strangeness of Care*

Jacques Derrida, *H. C. for Life, That Is to Say . . .*

Ernst Bloch, *Traces*

Elizabeth Rottenberg, *Inheriting the Future: Legacies of Kant, Freud, and Flaubert*

David Michael Kleinberg-Levin, *Gestures of Ethical Life*

Jacques Derrida, *On Touching—Jean-Luc Nancy*

Jacques Derrida, *Rogues: Two Essays on Reason*

Peggy Kamuf, *Book of Addresses*

Giorgio Agamben, *The Time that Remains: A Commentary on the Letter to the Romans*

Jean-Luc Nancy, *Multiple Arts: The Muses II*

Alain Badiou, *Handbook of Inaesthetics*

Jacques Derrida, *Eyes of the University: Right to Philosophy 2*

Maurice Blanchot, *Lautréamont and Sade*

Giorgio Agamben, *The Open: Man and Animal*

Jean Genet, *The Declared Enemy*

Shosana Felman, *Writing and Madness: (Literature/Philosophy/Psychoanalysis)*

Jean Genet, *Fragments of the Artwork*

Shoshana Felman, *The Scandal of the Speaking Body: Don Juan with J. L. Austin, or Seduction in Two Languages*

Peter Szondi, *Celan Studies*

Neil Hertz, *George Eliot's Pulse*

Maurice Blanchot, *The Book to Come*

Susannah Young-ah Gottlieb, *Regions of Sorrow: Anxiety and Messianism in Hannah Arendt and W. H. Auden*

Jacques Derrida, *Without Alibi*, edited by Peggy Kamuf

Cornelius Castoriadis, *On Plato's 'Statesman'*

Jacques Derrida, *Who's Afraid of Philosophy? Right to Philosophy 1*

Peter Szondi, *An Essay on the Tragic*

Peter Fenves, *Arresting Language: From Leibniz to Benjamin*

Jill Robbins, ed. *Is It Righteous to Be?: Interviews with Emmanuel Levinas*

Louis Marin, *Of Representation*

Daniel Payot, *The Architect and the Philosopher*

J. Hillis Miller, *Speech Acts in Literature*

Maurice Blanchot, *Faux pas*

Jean-Luc Nancy, *Being Singular Plural*

Maurice Blanchot / Jacques Derrida, *The Instant of My Death / Demeure: Fiction and Testimony*

Niklas Luhmann, *Art as a Social System*

Emmanual Levinas, *God, Death, and Time*

Ernst Bloch, *The Spirit of Utopia*

Giorgio Agamben, *Potentialities: Collected Essays in Philosophy*

Ellen S. Burt, *Poetry's Appeal: French Nineteenth-Century Lyric and the Political Space*

Jacques Derrida, *Adieu to Emmanuel Levinas*

Werner Hamacher, *Premises: Essays on Philosophy and Literature from Kant to Celan*

Aris Fioretos, *The Gray Book*

Deborah Esch, *In the Event: Reading Journalism, Reading Theory*

Winfried Menninghaus, *In Praise of Nonsense: Kant and Bluebeard*

Giorgio Agamben, *The Man Without Content*

Giorgio Agamben, *The End of the Poem: Studies in Poetics*

Theodor W. Adorno, *Sound Figures*

Louis Marin, *Sublime Poussin*

Philippe Lacoue-Labarthe, *Poetry as Experience*

Ernst Bloch, *Literary Essays*

Jacques Derrida, *Resistances of Psychoanalysis*

Marc Froment-Meurice, *That Is to Say: Heidegger's Poetics*

Francis Ponge, *Soap*

Philippe Lacoue-Labarthe, *Typography: Mimesis, Philosophy, Politics*

Giorgio Agamben, *Homo Sacer: Sovereign Power and Bare Life*

Emmanuel Levinas, *Of God Who Comes to Mind*

Bernard Stiegler, *Technics and Time, 1: The Fault of Epimetheus*

Werner Hamacher, *pleroma—Reading in Hegel*

Serge Leclaire, *Psychoanalyzing: On the Order of the Unconscious and the Practice of the Letter*

Serge Leclaire, *A Child Is Being Killed: On Primary Narcissism and the Death Drive*

Sigmund Freud, *Writings on Art and Literature*

Cornelius Castoriadis, *World in Fragments: Writings on Politics, Society, Psychoanalysis, and the Imagination*

Thomas Keenan, *Fables of Responsibility: Aberrations and Predicaments in Ethics and Politics*

Emmanuel Levinas, *Proper Names*

Alexander García Düttmann, *At Odds with AIDS: Thinking and Talking About a Virus*

Maurice Blanchot, *Friendship*

Jean-Luc Nancy, *The Muses*

Massimo Cacciari, *Posthumous People: Vienna at the Turning Point*

David E. Wellbery, *The Specular Moment: Goethe's Early Lyric and the Beginnings of Romanticism*

Edmond Jabès, *The Little Book of Unsuspected Subversion*

Hans-Jost Frey, *Studies in Poetic Discourse: Mallarmé, Baudelaire, Rimbaud, Hölderlin*

Pierre Bourdieu, *The Rules of Art: Genesis and Structure of the Literary Field*

Nicolas Abraham, *Rhythms: On the Work, Translation, and Psychoanalysis*

Jacques Derrida, *On the Name*

David Wills, *Prosthesis*

Maurice Blanchot, *The Work of Fire*

Jacques Derrida, *Points . . . : Interviews, 1974–1994*

J. Hillis Miller, *Topographies*

Philippe Lacoue-Labarthe, *Musica Ficta (Figures of Wagner)*

Jacques Derrida, *Aporias*

Emmanuel Levinas, *Outside the Subject*

Jean-François Lyotard, *Lessons on the Analytic of the Sublime*

Peter Fenves, *"Chatter": Language and History in Kierkegaard*

Jean-Luc Nancy, *The Experience of Freedom*

Jean-Joseph Goux, *Oedipus, Philosopher*

Haun Saussy, *The Problem of a Chinese Aesthetic*

Jean-Luc Nancy, *The Birth to Presence*